The Family Business as a Socialisation Context for the Children of Entrepreneurs

Simon Caspary

The Family Business as a Socialisation Context for the Children of Entrepreneurs

Springer

Simon Caspary
Vienna University of Economics
and Business
Vienna, Vienna, Austria

ISBN 978-3-658-43656-8 ISBN 978-3-658-43657-5 (eBook)
https://doi.org/10.1007/978-3-658-43657-5

This Springer imprint is published by the registered company Springer Fachmedien Wiesbaden GmbH, part of Springer Nature.
The registered company address is: Abraham-Lincoln-Str. 46, 65189 Wiesbaden, Germany

Paper in this product is recyclable.

Foreword

Business families must be assigned a key role for the (mis)success and the cross-generational existence of a family business. Business families are, due to the structural coupling with the enterprise, more or less strongly shaped by their enterprise. They must integrate entrepreneurial rules of play into the family system, which can be referred to as the enterpriseness of business families, without giving up their functions as a family.

This largely neglected area of focus is the subject of Mr. Caspary's work. He places the socialization of descendants from business families at the center of his consideration. Because precisely through the structural coupling of the systems, the enterprise as a significant variable for socialization must not be neglected. Especially, against the background of a decrease in family-internal successions, socialization can be attributed a high significance. Since these processes have so far been examined rather fragmentarily, the present work contributes to the broad theoretical perspectives to bring the socialization conditions of (potential) successors into the scientific discourse. The declared goal of the present work is to elucidate the importance of socialization for the dynamics of a family business and the shaping of the identity of the descendants.

The degree of novelty lies on the one hand in the topic itself and on the other hand in the integration and application of various theories. Important findings include the importance of communication and the structural coupling of family and business for socialization, role differentiation, the transfer of structural coupling to an Ecological Systems Model of socialization, and thus the representation of the development from integrated to segmented identities during the multi-generational existence of a family business. Particularly the ongoing examination of enterpriseness throughout the entire work represents the most interesting gain in knowledge from the perspective of research on family businesses and business families.

Vienna, Austria Hermann Frank

Contents

Abbreviations

akt.	updated
Aufl.	Edition
Bd.	Volume
bearb.	edited
bzw.	respectively
cf.	compare
Chap.	chapter
Diss.	Dissertation
durchges.	reviewed
e.g.	for example
e.V.	registered club
Ed.	editor
Eds.	editors
erg.	complemented
erw.	extended
et al.	and others
etc.	et cetera
f.	following
ff.	following and the following ones
Fig.	figure
I.	Interview(s)
i.e.	that is
kompl.	completely
n	sample
neuberarb.	revised
neuüberarb.	newly revised

Nr.	number
o. O.	without place
p.	page
u.	and
u. a.	among others
überarb.	revised
umgearb.	reworked
unver.	unchanged
Vol.	Volume
vollst.	completely

List of Figures

List of Tables

List of Interviews

1 Problem Statement of the Investigation

1.1 Introduction

Family businesses form the backbone of many industrialized societies.[1] According to Gersick et al., they are "the predominant form of enterprise around the world".[2] In Austria, Germany, and Switzerland, family businesses are mostly organized as small and medium-sized enterprises.[3] Estimates suggest that family businesses in Austria account for about 80 percent of the total number of enterprises.[4] However, there is no clear distinction between family and non-family businesses, which can often make precise recording difficult.[5] Many authors therefore speak of a family business when the family and its members have a "significant" influence on the business.[6] For this reason, the following definition is used for a first approximation: "A family business is an enterprise over which the family has a significant influence."[7]

[1] Cf. Krappe and von Schlippe (2010), p. 13; cf. De (2005), p. 236 and cf. Colli (2003), p. 8.

[2] Gersick et al. (1997), p. 2.

[3] Cf. Schneider (1998), p. 71.

[4] Cf. Lueger and Frank (2012), p. 4. In Germany, approximately 80% of businesses are also family owned (Weissman and Schultheiss 2006, 72).

[5] Cf. Felden and Zumholz (2009), p. 5 and cf. Colli (2003), p. 8.

[6] Cf. Stiftung Familienunternehmen (2011b), p. 5; cf. Cravota (2010), p. 3; cf. Rüsen (2009), p. 20; cf. Broer et al. (2008), p. III; cf. Weissman and Schultheiss (2006), p. 72; cf. Klein (2004), p. 17; cf. De (2005), p. 261 and cf. Simon et al. (2005), p. 13.

[7] Klein (2004), p. 18.

S. Caspary, *The Family Business as a Socialisation Context for the Children of Entrepreneurs*, https://doi.org/10.1007/978-3-658-43657-5_1

In addition to the economic significance, the structural peculiarities arising from the family's involvement often justify the special interest in scientific discourse.[8] This is particularly noticeable in the context of ownership, family leadership, and family culture, which can exert their influence on the business.[9] The prevailing focus on cross-generational continuity in family businesses brings the issue of business succession to the next generation to the forefront of scientific consideration.[10] This is crucial for the long-term survival of a family business in addition to economic success.[11] The descendants often fulfill the role of potential successors.[12] However, when choosing a successor,[13] the economic selection criteria often mix with family expectations and emotions, which can negatively influence the succession process or even doom it to failure.[14] The predetermined path can put the children under enormous pressure, and taking over is often seen as a duty.[15] For this reason, descendants can lose sight of how they see their own life path.[16]

It thus becomes clear, what central role must be assigned to the descendants in the successful handover and the long-term survival of the family business. Above all, their own motivation leads them to want to engage in entrepreneurial activities.[17] This is in turn decisively influenced by the transmission of specific values and norms during socialization.[18] Gottschalk et al.[19] speak in this context of the systematic development of successors already in the parental home. Although the socialization of the descendants must be considered central, it is surprising that this sub-area receives little or no attention within the succession literature.

---

[8] Cf. Olson et al. (2003), p. 640; cf. Kersting and Kamper-Jasper (2002), p. 84 and cf. Habbershon and Williams (1999), p. 3.

[9] Cf. Felden and Zumholz (2009), p. 5.

[10] Cf. Simon (2012), p. 95.

[11] Cf. Haubl and Daser (2006), p. 12.

[12] Cf. Haubl and Daser (2006), p. 34.

[13] Relevant for the German edition: For the sake of better readability in this work exclusively masculine terms such as "entrepreneur" or "successor" are used. These always include the feminine form. However, if only the feminine form is meant this is made clear.

[14] Cf. Frank and Hasenzagl (2005), p. 34 and cf. Wimmer et al. (2005), p. 4 f.

[15] Cf. Wimmer et al. (2005), p. 281.

[16] Cf. Simon et al. (2005), p. 61.

[17] Cf. Felden (2012), p. 154.

[18] Cf. Klein (2004), p. 229.

[19] Cf. Gottschalk et al. (2010), p. 45.

To contribute to closing this not insignificant gap, the present work deals with the topic of the family business as a context of socialization. The importance arises primarily from the high failure rates of succession.[20] Due to the dominance of family businesses in the respective economic area, a succession arrangement made has an impact not only on the business and the family, but also on the employees, external stakeholders, and even on the national economy.[21] The present work is therefore intended to raise awareness that the succession and the later success of the family business depend significantly on the respective descendants and their socialization. It therefore seems urgently necessary to introduce the topic of the socialization of entrepreneurial children[22] into the scientific succession discussion.

In general, socialization deals with the question: "How and why does a newborn become an autonomous, societal subject?"[23] In detail, socialization is understood as the process, "*in which an individual learns to adapt to a group by acquiring the social behavior approved by it*" [24]. As a preview of the theory part, the adaptation to a group is realized through expectations that are communicated within a social system. These in turn form the starting point for the formation of roles. Socialization thus takes place through the adoption of roles. The family of origin can be named as the first socialization instance of an individual. There, it learns social interaction with other people, the belief in its own abilities, and a high degree of frustration tolerance.[25] In the child's socialization process not only the personality traits of the parents play a role, but also their experiences at work and their intra-family burdens.[26] In addition, the parents also have a decisive influence on the development of the children through their parenting style. This also contributes to the individual equipment of the children to socialize them.[27] Lukesch understands upbringing as "a form of purposeful action [.], with which

---

[20] Cf. Haubl and Daser (2006), p. 12; cf. Wimmer et al. (2005), p. 4 f. and cf. Domayer and Vater (1994), p. 27.

[21] Cf. Baumgartner (2009), p. 13.

[22] For the distinction "entrepreneur's child" or "enterprise 's child", LeMar speaks of two levels of consideration: "Enterprise 's children" come from an enterprise, which linguistically already declares the children as non-persons. On the other hand, "entrepreneur's children" come from parents who are entrepreneurs by profession (cf. LeMar 2014, 120).

[23] Zimmermann (2000), p. 13.

[24] Prisching (1995), p. 40.

[25] Cf. Löhr-Heinemann (2005), p. 72 and cf. Gerzer-Sass (2003), p. 6.

[26] Cf. Tillmann (2000), p. 16; cf. Zimmermann (2000), p. 73 and cf. Hoff & Grüneisen (1978), p. 65.

[27] Cf. Schneewind (2001), p. 135.

attempts are made to develop certain dispositions perceived as valuable in other people [...]."[28] However, upbringing must not be equated with socialization, as the latter is much more narrowly defined.[29] In upbringing processes the child or adolescent is actively influenced, while this is not the case in socialization processes.[30]

When considering socialization within the sphere of influence of a family business it can be understood as an ongoing process until the end of life, encompassing a range of aspects.[31] People who are socialized in business families exhibit significantly different characteristics than individuals from non-business families. While their character is not determined by this influence, it is significantly shaped by it.[32] Above all, the "attitudes, behaviors, patterns of thought, and action"[33] have an impact on the individual. Descendants whose parents were already entrepreneurs often find it easier to choose the path to entrepreneurship or self-employment.[34] In particular, the interplay of generations, parental expectations, and the family business as a not to be underestimated context of socialization should therefore have effects on the descendants, i.e., their identity and their desire to take over the succession. To adequately depict this assumption and the associated complexity a pluralistic approach is chosen regarding the selected theories. This approach seems particularly suitable for identifying key influencing factors on the socialization of the descendants, and thus, making a significant contribution to theoretical progress.

1.2 Justification of the Research Gap

The following provides an overview of the characteristics of a family business and the dynamics that can occur within it based on selected literature. Two goals are pursued: In addition to presenting the content and results of individual works, the systematic consideration should offer the opportunity to make a statement about, whether the research question has not already been addressed by other authors in this way. Since each family business is usually "rooted" in its regional

[28] Lukesch (1996), p. 154 f.

[29] Cf. Zimmermann (2000), p. 14.

[30] Cf. Schneewind (1982), p. 162.

[31] Cf. Iannarelli (1992), p. 3 f.

[32] Cf. Meyer (2007), p. 29.

[33] Meyer (2007), p. 29.

[34] Cf. De (2005), p. 45.

environment and socialization always takes place in a specific context, i.e., is culturally influenced, only German-language literature is used to justify the research gap. It is assumed that the selected literature considers the cultural peculiarities and dynamics of family businesses better, and thus, allows a clearer location for the family business and the existing influence on socialization. Works focusing on the economic importance or business management topics were not considered as they appear less relevant for the thematic orientation of this work. Another criterion was the selection of works that predominantly reflect the scientific and less the management perspective. In total, 18 contributions (6 articles and 12 books) published between 2001 and 2013 were selected.

1.2.1 Analysis of the Works

At the outset, reference should be made to the literature analysis by Caspary (2014) as his results are also used to verify the research gap. It provides a comprehensive insight into the research performance of German-language succession literature on family businesses. For the gain in knowledge 50 published books were used with the analysis and synthesis of the individual works being in the foreground. The systematization, aimed at in this way, makes it possible to establish cross-connections between the works and to identify subject areas, which are not sufficiently considered in the succession literature in particular. Overall, five main categories were formed based on the evaluation:

1. Nature of the books,
2. types of business transfer,
3. tax and legal aspects,
4. practical relevance, and
5. the family business and succession.

The second, third, and fourth categories are given a high degree of attention in the works examined. However, this reveals the neglect of essential content. Although the cross-generational existence of a family business depends, among other things, on the successors and their will and competence, socialization is hardly considered in the analyzed succession literature, which underlines the statements made in Sect. 1.1.

Regarding the subsequently selected works (see Table 1.1) the concept matrix of Webster and Watson[35] is used for a compact presentation. The focus is "author-centered", which allows a presentation of the content and, above all, the results of the individual works.

1.2.2 Summary of the Analysis

The overview of the selected works provided a comprehensive, albeit not exhaustive, insight into the various topics related to family businesses and business families. In summary, the following main points or overarching terms and findings can be highlighted (see Table 1.2). However, the clear assignment is sometimes difficult as the contents are more broadly based.

As can be seen from Table 1.2 the literature can be divided into different thematic focuses with the greatest emphasis being placed on the topic of succession. This can be justified by the fact that the long-term existence of a family business depends crucially on a successfully executed generational change, which is subject to certain failure rates.[36] The range of content and the different approaches within and across the individual subject areas are also striking. In addition to pure business administration, conflict research, law, sociology, empirical (social) research, and organizational consulting also deal with family businesses. The interdisciplinary interest in family businesses not only highlights the importance of this form of business, but also the difficulty of clearly assigning a family business. The connection of a family to a business creates a "contradictory unity"[37], which requires a pluralistic approach for a complete understanding.

Based on the thematic breakdown, however, it is noticeable that a not to be underestimated topic within the literature is hardly addressed. Although the survival of a family business depends significantly on the descendants, these are rather marginalized. The succession literature almost completely ignores the socialization of the descendants. In addition to parental behavior, the early involvement in the family business also has its influence on the descendants, which reinforces the decision to take over the family business. Therefore, it is not understandable that socialization, as one of the most significant processes in shaping the individual, is hardly addressed.

Thus, it remains open

[35] Cf. Webster and Watson (2002), p. xvi.

[36] Cf. Wimmer et al. (2005), p. 4 f. and cf. Domayer and Vater (1994), p. 27.

[37] Hildenbrand (2005), p. 144.

Table 1.1 Literature analysis using concept matrix

Authors	Characteristics and content	Brief results
Stamm (2013)	–Book with a theoretical-methodological and a qualitative-empirical part; including case descriptions, interview excerpts, and genograms –Presentation of the so-called "BusinessFamilies-FamilyBusinesses Model" (in German: UFFU-Model) of mutual influence –Historical outline of the family –Presentation of the characteristics of business families –Explanation of the life course/guidance of family entrepreneurs –Explanation of the (generational) relationships in business families –Development of a different perspective than the organization-heavy family business research	–Business families can be described as "families of their own kind" with a constant structural core and societal ideal conceptions –The enterprise is part of the everyday reality of descendants. Provides them with a knowledge base about the enterprise as well as the role attributions –Enterprise influences the life guidance and identity of the descendants –Enterprise is very present among the descendants –Influence of partner choice by the enterprise –The question of having children is not necessarily influenced by the enterprise –There is a congruence between the everyday life guidance as an entrepreneur and the way she or he withdraws from the family business
Groth and von Schlippe (2012)	–Article –Comparison of non-business families with business families –Paradoxes in business families –Strategies for dealing with paradoxes –Expansion of the Three-Circle Model through the notation of Decision theory (Spencer Brown[a]) using the example of business families	–Research on business families is very sparse so far –The business families are subject to certain decision constraints –Business families exhibit certain reflection criteria: Value orientation, future security, lawful behavior, and consideration of the needs of family members –The weighting of these criteria then determines the occurrence of paradoxes –Decision theory clarifies the different rationalities and decision structures of business families

(continued)

Table 1.1 (continued)

Authors	Characteristics and content	Brief results
Lueger and Frank (2012)	–Anthology (study) with case descriptions and interview excerpts –Presentation of "Good-Practice" examples –Solution of crises as a transformation process –Innovation management during succession –Succession as a cross-generational process –Planning a handover –Influence of the family business by family and business –Familiness in family business –Dynamics in family business	–Criteria for decision-making should be questioned in critical situations, as these often can be situation-dependent –Establishment of criteria for conflict cases are advantageous –Family-run businesses are very innovative –Three points essential for long-term existence: (1) Integration of family into business; (2) each generation serves the business as a temporal and social bracket; (3) succession as an integral part –Legal design has a significant influence on the design of succession –Familiness includes four significant factors: (1) Communication, (2) trust, (3) fairness, and (4) sustainability
Simon (2012)	–Book –Family and enterprise as social systems –Paradoxes in family business –Characteristics of the family and their various appearances –Characteristics of the enterprise –Presentation of loose and tight coupling –Succession in family business –Conflicts in family business	–Diversity of family business makes clear demarcation difficult –Family and enterprise form a co-evolutionary unit; mutual influence on each other's identity –Each system operates according to different rules, which creates paradoxes and promotes conflicts –The longer a family business exists, the more need for formalism exists within the family due to the increasing number of participating family members –Problem of conflicts: Danger of "passing on" to the next generation and "downfall" of the enterprise
Simon et al. (2012)	–Study with case examples –Examination of the success patterns of multi-generational family businesses based on specific enterprises (including Oetker, Merck, C&A, Haniel) –Management of paradoxes in family businesses (as a success factor) –Separate consideration of family and enterprise –The shareholder value approach versus family business	–Family businesses are neither old-fashioned nor "outdated models" –Competitive disadvantage of publicly listed enterprises. Family serves as a stabilizing element in family businesses –Successful enterprises and family businesses do not rely on the shareholder value approach for their leadership principles –Handling of paradoxes in family businesses under certain conditions better than in publicly listed enterprises. The reason is the cross-generational focus

(continued)

Table 1.1 (continued)

Authors	Characteristics and content	Brief results
Simon (2011)[b]	–Anthology with case descriptions and conversation protocols –Consideration of economic and emotional challenges as well as opportunities and risks from the perspective of the family business –Description of the succession (problems) –Presentation of various consulting methods and concepts	–Family businesses represent a contradictory, inseparable unit due to the structural characteristics of family and business –Frequent need for consultation of business families: In addition to economic problems; emotional problems can also occur –Dynamics within business families should be analyzed using an interdisciplinary approach –Suboptimal handling of conflicts/ problems in business families
Zwack (2011)	–Book with case descriptions and interview excerpts –Characterization of the family business based on values –How values are conveyed in the family business –Presentation and description of cultural values in organizations –Testing of theoretical findings based on an empirical survey	–Family has a significant influence on the cultural values of a family business; relevant for the success of family businesses –Storytelling is a key value transmitter. Values are thereby thematized, communicated, and updated –Establishment of cultural values by founders; starting point for their transgenerational existence –Values can provide identity-forming orientation patterns
Klein (2010)[c]	–Textbook with study and case descriptions –Development of a theory on family business based on the relevant influence areas: Family, ownership, leadership, and enterprise –Explanation of differences between family business and non-family business –Differentiation of business families from "average families" –Clarification of the effects caused by growth in size –Presentation of the life cycles of family businesses	–Study result: At least equal economic importance of family businesses as non-family businesses –Decrease in the societal importance of family due to differentiation of their functions. However, the family in family business still plays a central role for its existence –Each life cycle entails different requirements for the family, the ownership, and the leadership. Therefore, in addition to business economic knowledge, sociological and psychological insights should also be considered

(continued)

Table 1.1 (continued)

Authors	Characteristics and content	Brief results
Rüsen (2009)	–Book with empirical study –Presentation of the specifics of family business –Crises in family business (models, distinction, influencing factors, and behaviors) –Provision of an approach for *crisis management* (CM) in family business –Assistance for the CM	–Suitable models for considering a family business support the adequate dealing with crises –Structural influencing factors (including legal form, shareholder structure, qualification as well as competencies of the family members) significantly influence the CM –Classic contents of a CM: Strategic CM; operational-performance economic CM and operational-financial CM –Additive contents of a CM: Analysis of the family factor, CM in the business family, and restructuring measures in the enterprise
von Schlippe (2009)	–Article with a case example and discussion of intervention possibilities in conflicts –Explanations of paradoxes and conflicts –Familiness in family business –Consideration of the three systems (family, business, and ownership) –Presentation of the different system logics	–Potential of conflicts: Impairment/ destruction of the business and economic performance of a family business –Cause of paradoxes: Different requirements for justice and equality in the three systems –Paradoxes do have the potential for conflict; however, they are not necessarily the trigger of conflict
Meyer and Olden-burg (2008)	–Article with a concrete practical example –Investigation, whether a certain value orientation prevails in family business –Question, whether the orientation based on values can be maintained at all in everyday business	Core theses for a value orientation in family business: –Part of the self-understanding of the enterprise –Components of a value-oriented leadership: Trust, loyalty, appreciation, responsibility, justice, joy, tradition, and commitment –Values that are shared in business family and enterprise are more effective –As many employees as possible should live the commonly lived values –Values serve as a guideline and set the boundaries –Danger of loss of values –Value increase of the enterprise through commonly shared values

(continued)

Table 1.1 (continued)

Authors	Characteristics and content	Brief results
Rossaro (2007)	–Book –Family businesses in the economic science discussion –Presentation and establishment of (a) definition(s) of family businesses –Family business from a sociological perspective –Tension field of ownership and leadership –Effects of personnel policy issues –Decisions about capital structure –The problem of succession	–Deficits in systematic studies; disagreement about prospects of family businesses –Important for the demarcation: The significant influence and the intention of transferring the enterprise –Inconsistent definitions promote unclear statements from theory and empirics about performance –Cross-country comparability of family businesses not as easily possible as often assumed –Research needs: Investigation of the "complexity of the target understanding" in family businesses
Rüsen and von Schlippe (2007)	–Article –Investigation of crisis processes in family businesses –Development of a definition of the crisis concept for business families –Presentation of a description model for crises	–Family and enterprise represent very relevant environments for each other in the context of a family business –A crisis in one system, due to structural coupling, always affects the other system –"Parallel-interdependent crisis processes" characterize crisis situations, which can occur (a)synchronously –Family and enterprise influence the pace of crisis processes –In crisis situations the mutual significance of family and enterprise for each other must be considered
Löhr-Heine-mann (2005)	–Book with case descriptions –Examination of self-employed women through a biographical analysis –Analysis of their genograms –Consideration of their life courses –How do women become successful entrepreneurs?	–Change of the "typical" role model of women. Working mothers are increasingly serving as role models –The identification figure "mother" for daughters should receive greater consideration –Individual socialization as a guarantee of success: This includes the status of the mother and the congruence of the parents' social background –Significant resources of an entrepreneur for successful crisis management: "Self-confidence, frustration tolerance, and creativity" –Formation of three typologies based on the analysis material: (1) The successful, (2) the behaviorally successful, and (3) the unsuccessful entrepreneur

(continued)

Table 1.1 (continued)

Authors	Characteristics and content	Brief results
Wimmer et al. (2005)[d]	–Book with case descriptions and conversation passages –Consideration of family businesses and their structure formation considering the co-evolution between family and business –Presentation of the effects on intra-family communication and the influence of the family through common ownership –Explanation of the life cycles of family and business	–Family businesses tend to have the characteristics of a non-family business from about the third generation onwards. This requires, among other things, a reduction of family influence and a decoupling between the family and business systems –Due to the existing complexity, early planning of succession is essential –Synchronizing the different development logic of family and enterprise is a challenge in family businesses –Value change and dissolution of the family institution make it more difficult in the future to keep a family business in the possession of a business family over several generations
Wimmer et al. (2004)	–Study –Special features of family businesses (family, owner, and business) –Paradoxes in multi-generational family businesses –Dealing with paradoxes during succession in different types of family organizations as well as in tribal organizations	The following success patterns can be found in multi-generational family businesses: –Management of large families as an "organization" –This includes organizing (in)official meetings and promoting the next generation. Creation of a "family relations" feeling –The interests of the business take precedence –Existence of a business constitution; allows protection of the business from the family –Conflict resolution procedures are in place –Family members only reach leading positions if they are as good as any external managers –Investment decisions must not affect the independence of the enterprise –Internationalization is a matter of course

(continued)

Table 1.1 (continued)

Authors	Characteristics and content	Brief results
Müller Tiberini (2001)	–Book with case descriptions –Characterization of family businesses (key features, leadership types and styles as well as strategies) –Consideration of the family and the capital/ownership side –Handling of succession –The role of women in family businesses	–The public discussion increasingly recognizes the importance of family businesses –Just like non-family businesses, a significant societal contribution must be attributed to family businesses –The management of family businesses is subject to very specific requirements for thinking and acting
Steiner (2001)	–Working Paper –Influence of socialization within the family on the propensity of descendants to become entrepreneurs –Examination of upbringing	–Risk-taking is positively linked with the success of the enterprise –The interactions within the family can be seen as a "pathway" for entrepreneurial activity and its success –The parenting style "little strictness and little warmth and support" promotes thoughts of independence –Successful entrepreneurs have fewer hobbies

[a]Spencer Brown, G. (1969): Laws of Form, London: Allen & Unwin.
[b]Adopted from Caspary (2014), p. 164 f.
[c]Adopted from Caspary (2014), p. 166 f.
[d]Adopted from Caspary (2014), p. 164 f.

1. *how* the various influencing factors in business families and especially the context of family businesses affect the descendants and, above all,
2. *how* the identity of the descendants is formed.

This leads to the following problem statement.

1.3 Problem Statement

Based on the summary (see Sect. 1.2.2), the lack of elaboration of the influence of a family business on the socialization of the descendants in the previous scientific discussion becomes clear. For the long-term survival, which depends significantly on the descendants this is not understandable. In the succession literature in particular, the topic is hardly or not at all considered. These mainly try to alleviate the symptoms of the succession problem, often without considering the causes. These are probably already to be found in the childhood of the successors since

Table 1.2 Summary of the literature analysis

Summary of the main points within the analyzed works
–*Methodological*: Case descriptions, interviews, and qualitative as well as quantitative analyses.
–*Paradoxes in family businesses in general, in multi-generational family businesses, during succession, and in conflicts*: Reasons for occurrence; system logics; design of handling.
–*Conflicts*: Causes and handling; possibilities of intervention and their potential dangers.
–*Succession*[a]: Type of handover (sale, purchase, foundation solutions, donation, and gratuitous transfer); tax and legal aspects, checklists, questionnaires, and action recommendations; influencing factors on the succession process; consideration of the entrepreneur and the family; succession as a cross-generational process; importance of early planning.
–*Interaction between family and business*: Tension between family and business; values in family businesses (mediation, description and representation, orientation, benefits for the family business, influence by the entrepreneur); (positive) effect of the family on the business; influence of the business on the participating family(ies).
–*Dynamics in family businesses from a systems theoretical perspective*: Influence of the family business by relevant environmental references; family and business as social systems; effects of the coupling of the systems.
–*Socialization in business families*[b]: Influences on the development of personality; examination of personality traits; consideration of upbringing; influence on the inclination of the descendants to strive for independence.

(continued)

Table 1.2 (continued)

Summary of the findings within the analyzed works
–Family businesses have a not to be underestimated economic importance. –Clear demarcation of family businesses not possible. –Family businesses can be seen as a "contradictory unit" and the business family as a "family of its own kind". –Within the framework of a family business the family and the business form a co-evolutionary unit. –The different, sometimes contradictory system logics cause various forms of paradoxes. –The different, sometimes contradictory system logics make conflicts in family businesses very likely. Through the coupling these can spread to the other systems and lead to strong irritations (weakening of the business and economic performance) up to the dissolution of the family business. –However, the family can also be a stabilizing element representing a competitive advantage over non-family businesses. –Significant influence of the values in family businesses by the family. Values serve as "identity-establishing orientation patterns", and influence everyday life within the family and the business. –Each business cycle poses different demands on leadership and, among other things, on the participating family(ies). –For the development of a family business an interdisciplinary approach is essential. –Family businesses tend to exhibit the characteristics of a non-family business after a certain time/generation. This can lead to a reduction of family influence. –The success and long-term survival of the family business are significantly dependent on early succession planning. It is an "integral component". –Multi-generational family businesses show certain success patterns (see above under Wimmer et al. 2004), which can have a positive effect on long-term survival. –The family business is able to influence the personality and identity of the families and of the descendants in particular.

[a] Adopted among others from Caspary (2014), p. 163. In the context of succession or the transition to the next generation "succession planning" should be mentioned here. This can generally be understood as a process that supports the planning of the transfer of ownership and/or the change of leadership (cf. Ip & Jacobs 2006, 327). For a deeper understanding the following authors are referred to: Ip & Jacobs (2006); Sambrook (2005); Lee et al. (2003); Sharma et al. (2003); Sharma et al. (2000); Hubler (1999); Harveston et al. (1997); Handler (1994)

[b] Adopted among others from Caspary (2014), p. 161.

the potential (non-)successors are possibly already confronted with the so-called "family mission"[38] from birth.

The descendants growing up in business families experience the enterprise's everyday life in most cases actively with all its positive and negative facets and therefore, learn from the beginning to move in the environment shaped by the enterprise.[39] It starts with first experiences in the private as well as in the business area, and extends over the development of career aspirations as well as the transfer of responsibility to the relationship with parents, siblings, and partners.[40] The child develops in many cases emotionally a kind of obligation towards the enterprise and identifies with it.[41] According to statements from interviewed family entrepreneurs the parental enterprise was a "part of the self-evident experience space"[42].

However, the will of the descendants to join the family business does not usually exist from the outset and is determined by many factors. Upbringing, personality, and professional experience have a not insignificant influence on the succession decision.[43] Above all, the descendants learn "intuitively the values and attitudes of the parents towards the enterprise and internalize them"[44]. The family expectations and roles have a lasting influence on the self-concept of the growing up.[45] Also situation-related criteria (e.g., the prospect of a successful enterprise),[46] the perception of the economic environment,[47] and even the emerging value change influence the succession decision.[48]

The fact that the socialization and identity formation of descendants in the context of a family business is insufficiently addressed in science can be seen as a major shortcoming in current research. In detail, the simultaneous influence of an additional frame of reference already during primary socialization. Above all, the focus should be on which social reality or dynamics the descendants within

[38] Wimmer et al. (2005), p. 281.

[39] Cf. Meyer (2007), p. 31 ff.

[40] Cf. Iannarelli (1992), p. 3 f.

[41] Cf. Iannarelli (1992), p. 15.

[42] Stamm et al. (2010), p. 5.

[43] Cf. Gottschalk et al. (2010), p. 45.

[44] Klein (2004), p. 80.

[45] Cf. Gersick et al. (1997), p. 163.

[46] Cf. Gottschalk et al. (2010), p. 45.

[47] Cf. Stiftung Familienunternehmen (2011 a), p. 8.

[48] Cf. LeMar (2014), p. 58; cf. Hennerkes and Hund (2008), p. 260 and cf. Hennerkes (2004), p. 24 f. as well as p. 45 ff.

a family business are exposed to, and how this affects their socialization. The (simultaneous) influence of two contrary frames of reference can have effects on the socialization of the descendants of a business family.

To contribute to closing the research gap, this work examines the socialization context of family businesses with its implications for the descendants and their identity. The guiding *research question* is therefore:

> How is the socialization and especially the identity formation of descendants from family businesses influenced by the family's ties to a business?

For succession it is additionally interesting:

1. Why want some children to take over and their siblings refuse?
2. Are there mechanisms within the respective family that influence this decision (in)directly?
3. How does the influence of the enterprise on the descendants become noticeable?
4. What consequences does the parents' desire for succession have for the descendants and which factors influence the desire for succession positively/negatively?

However, the results obtained must not be considered in isolation. Rather, these can not only serve to support or understand intra-family dynamics during the generational change, but also expand the handover process in advance by another essential dimension and therefore provide important insights in the preparation of the successors.

1.4 Theoretical-Conceptual Approach

For the gain of knowledge a theoretical processing of this selected topic area is provided. This approach seems particularly suitable for identifying major influencing factors on the socialization of the descendants, and thus, making a significant contribution to the advancement of theory. Particular attention must be paid to a careful selection of the existing literature so that a comprehensive and balanced insight can be guaranteed. It should enable the reader to get a comprehensive picture and gain as many insights and suggestions for further research as possible. Of course, not all disciplines can be appreciated to the same extent as in a sole consideration due to the chosen approach. Nevertheless, an attempt is made to represent all subject areas that are considered relevant for the exploration. This ensures the identification and description of the most essential factors.

The following structure is chosen for the present work.

Chapter 2 deals explicitly with the family business by taking an internal as well as external perspective. To present the socialization context of family businesses with all its facets, in addition to theoretical findings, interviews already conducted and empirical surveys by other authors are also referred to. However, the interview excerpts in this Chap. 2 are only for illustration or have only an illustrative character. These are intended to make the argument more vivid and underline the importance of the topic dealt with in this work.

Chapter 3 serves to work up the theories considered relevant. Based on these, the peculiarities of the family business and the identity formation of the descendants can be traced. In detail, the Systems theory, Symbolic Interactionism, and Role theory are used for the argumentation. Luhmannian Systems theory, as a social theory, opens the possibility of presenting and examining different systems with different logics within a common framework. In contrast, the Symbolic Interactionism for explaining the emergence and shaping of identity. As a third theory of greater scope, Role theory is used. In addition to a unified understanding of roles for the present work, the Role theory provides an understanding of why individuals in different social systems act differently and why this can be subject to changes. Finally, Bronfenbrenner's Ecological Systems Model is introduced. This provides an explanatory model about how entering new social systems/life areas can be seen as a starting point for new socialization processes.

Chapter 4 finally links the insights gained in Chap. 2 about family businesses with the theories presented in Chap. 3. By connecting them the characteristics/dynamics within family businesses can be abstracted out. This then allows for making universally valid statements. Especially with regard to the thematic focus of the work, it extensively elaborates on the factors that can influence the adolescents[49]. Based on the gained insights an attempt is made to depict the socialization of the descendants, the formation of identity considering the environment shaped by the family business, and to derive implications from it. Figure 1.1 summarizes the chosen content.

Since existing theories are used for the development of the topic, no new insights are to be expected at this level, but for the pluralistically chosen approach. In addition to the significant clarification of how the influence of the family business on the socialization of the descendants becomes apparent,

[49] In the context of this work, the term "adolescents" is not used in the sense of legal language for persons who have reached the age of 18, but not yet 21. Rather, the lower limit is open.

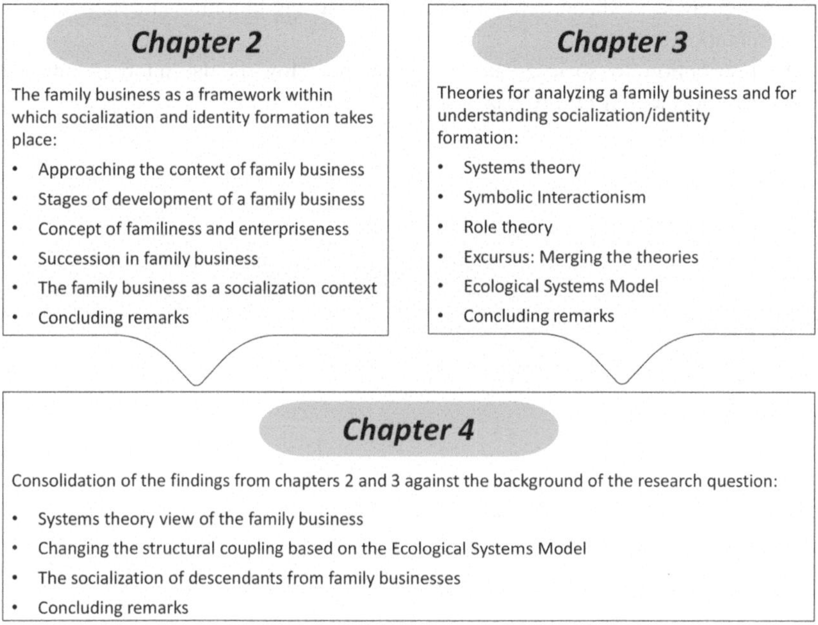

Fig. 1.1 Structure of the work (own work)

valuable insights are provided as to how this influence can change along the multi-generational existence of a family business.

Based on the assumption that the family business has an influence on the descendants, this work can contribute to creating a certain awareness on the part of the entrepreneur parents or the respective consultants for their socialization. Especially for the potential successors and the existing lack in the succession literature the insights can convey a sense of how the family-internal handling of internal and external factors can influence the generational change sustainably positively or negatively. If conflicts arise, these may have already manifested in the childhood of the descendants.

Therefore, this work provides a special contribution to the progress of science through:

1. The depiction of the complex relationships within a family business and their effect on child socialization using a pluralistically chosen approach.

2. A comprehensive theoretical preparation of existing literature and an overview presentation.
3. A contribution to socio-economic research: “How is the intergenerational stabilization within family businesses achieved?”

2 The Family Business

The aim of this chapter is, in addition to creating a basic understanding of the business form of family businesses, to present the influence of the family business on the family members and especially on the descendants. For the development of this framework, the characteristics of a family business are therefore initially discussed. This includes the presentation of the specific value patterns, the possible conflicts as well as the paradoxes that almost inevitably occur in family businesses.

After the first approach to the socialization context of family businesses was provided, the question arises as to what dynamics and changes it is subject to. Therefore, the different development stages of a family business are subsequently presented. This is intended to clarify the diverse frame of reference that the family business represents for the family members acting in it and especially for the descendants.

However, since the demarcation of an enterprise as a family business cannot always be clearly made or is controversially discussed in the literature, the concept of "familiness" serves a better or more founded identification of a family business in the respective development stage. In particular, the concept of "enterpriseness" can be used to illustrate the influence of the enterprise on business families, which is relevant to the focus pursued here.

Subsequently, the frequently discussed topic of succession in the literature is addressed. Here, the assumption is that potential successors are exposed to certain mechanisms that favor or oppose succession. The possibility of potential succession should therefore influence their socialization.

S. Caspary, *The Family Business as a Socialisation Context for the Children of Entrepreneurs*, https://doi.org/10.1007/978-3-658-43657-5_2

Finally, after a general understanding of socialization has been provided, socialization in the context of a family business is highlighted. Influencing factors from the family and the business on the socialization of the descendants are presented. In addition, the influences from the family business on the living environment and identity are explained.

2.1 Characteristics of Family Businesses

2.1.1 Approach to the Business Form

For outsiders, the difference between an enterprise and a family business often only lies in the addition of the word family.[1] However, family businesses embody "two of the most important basic values of our social order"[2]: The *family* and *private ownership.* Although, the exercise of entrepreneurial activity primarily serves family provision, it also contributes to societal well-being.[3] According to Schaller [4], (family) businesses perform important functions within an economy: (Family) Businesses

1. bear the entrepreneurial and capital risk.
2. carry out resource allocation.
3. promote technological progress.
4. are innovative.
5. can influence the development of their environment through radiating effects.
6. can serve as an incentive for others.

However, the family business is also influenced by two factors:

1. The entrepreneur and his/her personality profile(s),[5] and
2. through the environment or the culturally colored context within which it operates.[6]

[1] Cf. Krappe and von Schlippe (2010), p. 6 in reference to Hoffmeister (2001), p. 78.

[2] Klein (2004), p. 1.

[3] Cf. Klein (2004), p. 1.

[4] Cf. Schaller (2001), p. 4.

[5] Cf. Kempert (2008), p. 20.

[6] Cf. Wimmer (2009a), p. 108.

In detail, family businesses therefore differ from each other through the extent of the family's commitment to the business and the number of family members participating in the business.[7] The family business is characterized, according to Meyer [8], primarily by a "person-bound continuity"[9]. Through the presence of the entrepreneur or his family, the employees are given "security, protection, continuity, reliability, and also emotional care" [10], which creates a certain connection to the family business.

For the study of family businesses two levels of consideration can be distinguished:

1. The micro perspective, which deals with the processes within the enterprise, and
2. the macro perspective, which deals with family businesses in the economic context.[11]

According to Wimmer et al.[12], in the study of family businesses an interdisciplinary approach is indispensable, as otherwise the complexity cannot be explained properly. The phenomenon of family businesses can therefore hardly be explained with "purpose-rational categories" [13]. Also, according to Klein [14], the study of a family business from a purely business perspective falls short. Rather, psychological and sociological findings must be considered. Precisely because of the complexity of family businesses, they are also the focus of various scientific disciplines. Thus, among others, psychology, sociology, accounting, and economics deal with this topic.[15] According to Hennerkes and Hund, family businesses therefore belong to the "economically and sociologically most outstanding form of business"[16].

Family businesses cannot be assigned to any specific sector as they exist in many forms. They range from small to multinational enterprises. Due to

---

[7] Cf. Arregle et al. (2007), p. 85.

[8] Cf. Meyer (2007), p. 35.

[9] Meyer (2007), p. 35.

[10] Meyer (2007), p. 35.

[11] Cf. Colli (2003), p. 24.

[12] Cf. Wimmer et al. (2005), p. 19.

[13] Wimmer (2004), p. 268.

[14] Cf. Klein (2004), p. 338.

[15] Cf. Habbershon and Williams (1999), p. 1.

[16] Hennerkes and Hund (2008), p. 255.

this fact, family businesses differ in their mission statements, strategic orientation, and target markets.[17] Thus, many exist not only in commercial, traditional, and labor-intensive sectors, but also appear in scale-intensive or specialized and customer-oriented sectors. On the other hand, they are less located in capital-intensive sectors.[18] Similarly, many family businesses are historically more likely to be "in industries such as trade, textiles, food, or even banks" [19], which are characterized by a lower number of innovative processes. This distribution can primarily be explained by the family's influence on the business. Within a family business it is easier for the family to process more standardized processes so that industries with short product life cycles are predominantly avoided. Another characteristic of family businesses is their location in so-called niches, they havea smaller product range with very innovative products,[20] where the ability to innovate depends largely on the family.[21]

Although family businesses contribute an important part to economic development, there is no universal definition for them. Thus, an exact estimate of the economic relevance is extremely difficult.[22] In addition, official statistics do not have a separate category for this type of enterprise, which further complicates research.[23] Simon describes this situation as follows: "When you deal with the topic of family businesses, you are confronted with a strange phenomenon. It affects many people, there is a lot of talk about it, it is generally considered to be of great psychological and economic importance, and yet there is hardly any systematic knowledge [...] about it."[24] Especially the data material, regarding the frequency of family businesses, must be viewed with some caution, as different results can arise due to the different definitions.[25]

The peculiarity or difficulty with family businesses arises rather from the fact, that it is a so-called "enterprise typology"[26]. This means that different terminologies, such as small and medium-sized enterprises (SME), or the Mittelstand

---

[17] Cf. Lansberg (1983), p. 40.

[18] Cf. Colli (2003), p. 11 f.

[19] Hülsbeck et al. (2011), p. 13.

[20] Cf. Hülsbeck et al. (2011), p. 13.

[21] Cf. Weismeier-Sammer (2014), p. 111.

[22] Cf. Frank and Keßler (2011), p. 1; cf. Wimmer et al. (2005), p. 13; cf. Venter and Kruger (2004), p. 2 and cf. Wimmer (1997), p. 145.

[23] Cf. Frank and Keßler (2011), p. 1 and cf. Freund (2000), p. 15.

[24] Simon (2005), p. 7.

[25] Cf. Colli (2003), p. 16.

[26] Halter and Schröder (2011), p. 21. The first differentiation between family and non-family businesses only took place in the 30s or 40s of the last century. One reason for the still young

(a German expression for the entirety of small and medium-sized enterprises and self-employed persons), are subsumed under it.[27] Family businesses can thus be considered as a subset of all enterprises.[28] In practice, the terms "SMEs, Mittelstand, and family businesses" are therefore often improperly used synonymously.[29] However, for an empirical study, data from small and medium-sized enterprises (SMEs) are often used, as most family businesses are in these size classes.[30] In contrast to SMEs[31] family businesses are predominantly characterized by purely qualitative distinguishing features[32] and are thus not subject to any size restrictions.[33] According to Felden and Zumholz, dealing with SMEs does not automatically consider the family influence "as an integral part of the family business system" [34] although, according to Wallau [35], in family businesses the ownership structure is a characteristic feature. Another synonym often used for family businesses is the term Mittelstand (as already described).[36] In the opinion of Wimmer et al., however, this should be avoided "because this term is particularly popular in the relevant societal and economic debates as an ideological battle term" [37]. On the other hand, the synonymous use of family businesses and Mittelstand, according to Stamm et al.[38], is justified, as in their opinion the

examination of these two forms of business can be found in the fact that before this period practically all enterprises were owned by a family (cf. Felden and Zumholz 2009, p. 6 f.).

[27] Cf. Halter and Schröder (2011), p. 21.

[28] Cf. Klein (2004), p. 2.

[29] Cf. Brost and Faust (2012), p. 6 and cf. Wallau (2010), p. 34.

[30] Cf. Risak and Nagy (1999), p. 43.

[31] Micro and medium-sized enterprises are classified in the Official Journal of the European Commission based on the following quantitative characteristics: (1) *Micro-enterprises:* Less than 10 employees and the annual turnover or the annual balance sheet of EUR 2 million is not exceeded. (2) *Small enterprise:* Less than 50 employees and the annual turnover or the annual balance sheet does not exceed EUR 10 million. (3) *Medium-sized enterprise:* Less than 250 employees. In addition, these either achieve an annual turnover of at most EUR 50 million or their annual balance sheet total amounts to at most EUR 43 million (cf. Commission 2003, L124/39).

[32] It is therefore noticeable that quantitative criteria such as turnover, number of employees, or the balance sheet total are not used as classification features of family businesses (cf. Broer et al. 2008, III).

[33] Cf. Söllner (2011), p. 1088.

[34] Felden and Zumholz (2009), p. 6.

[35] Cf. Wallau (2010), p. 34.

[36] Cf. Hennerkes (2004), p. 16.

[37] Wimmer et al. (2005), p. 16 f.

[38] Cf. Stamm et al. (2010), p. 1.

term Mittelstand primarily includes smaller enterprises. For Gottschalk et al.[39] there is no precise definition for the term Mittelstand in the political and scientific discussion. In their work they assign all enterprises to the Mittelstand that have at least 40 and a maximum of 5.000 employees. However, Wallau[40] sees the Mittelstand as an umbrella term that includes family businesses and SMEs. The argumentation thus reveals the difficulty of classifying an enterprise as a family business.

Nonetheless, a family business is created through the connection of the family with the business.[41] A family business can therefore only be classified as such when the family and the business have a connection to each other. If a separation becomes inevitable, e.g., because the family business must be sold to foreign investors for further survival, the enterprise itself can continue to exist, but loses its specific status as family business. From this point on it is no longer different from the other types of enterprises.[42] However, if an enterprise is founded, it cannot immediately be referred to as a family business. This is only answered by a subsequent analysis. In the pioneering phase, there is usually no family or thought of possible succession. Rather, the pioneer enterprises can be classified as a "special case of a family business"[43] or as a "potential family business" [44]. [45]

However, the extent to which the family can become "entangled" with the business over time can be seen from the possible consequences for the business families associated with the dissolution of the family business:

1. Endangerment of material existence (job loss).
2. Questioning of self-concept (self-esteem is hurt because the business was the center of life).
3. Questioning of the "family concept" as a business family (loss of built-up reputation, social standing, responsibility towards the region).
4. Threat to the transgenerational life's work (the family tradition or the inheritance left behind cannot be continued).

---

39 Cf. Gottschalk et al. (2010), p. 16.

40 Cf. Wallau (2010), p. 34.

41 Cf. Risak and Nagy (1999), p. 49.

42 Cf. Rüsen and von Schlippe (2007), p. 315.

43 Klein (2004), p. 283.

44 Klein (2004), p. 283.

45 Cf. Klein (2004), p. 282 f.

5. Breakdown of family structures (a crisis within the business can lead to severe damage to the family lead).[46]

According to Klein[47], the family is dependent on the respective family business through the following factors:

1. There is an emotional bond.
2. It creates ownership as well as an economic dependency and acts as an employer.
3. It usually carries the family name, which can create a certain reputation for the family.

Especially with family businesses, the existing dependency on the owner family or the future viability of the business must be considered. If the family breaks down, the business usually also breaks down.[48] For this reason, the (continued) existence of a family business is often inseparably linked with the respective family or, in the case of multi-generational families, with the family system.[49] According to Dyer [50], the family either has a direct influence on enterprise performance or indirectly via the choice of industry, enterprise management and characteristics as well as the management of the entrepreneur. He refers to this as the "'family effect'" [51].

In general, there is widespread consensus in the scientific literature that the decisive characteristic of family businesses is the interrelationship between family and business.[52] Therefore, an enterprise only falls into the category of family business if one or more families can exert a determining influence or, as described under Sect. 1.1, have "significant influence" on the enterprise, legitimized by their ownership. However, there are various interpretations of the form this influence should take.[53] These range from the necessary unity of ownership and leadership in family hands to complete external management where the family only acts

---

[46] Cf. Rüsen and von Schlippe (2007), p. 317 ff.

[47] Cf. Klein (2004), p. 89.

[48] Cf. Rossaro (2007), p. 96.

[49] Cf. Wimmer (2007), p. 30.

[50] Cf. Dyer (2006), p. 257.

[51] Dyer (2006), p. 254.

[52] Cf. Stamm et al. (2010), p. 1 f.

[53] Cf. Cravota (2010), p. 3; cf. Keese et al. (2010), p. 202; cf. Broer et al. (2008), p. III and cf. Klein (2004), p. 17.

through control boards.[54] Rossaro defines the family's influence on the business direction in such a way that no "comparable counterpower"[55] may oppose it within the enterprise.[56]

2.1.2 Values in Family Businesses

Characteristic of family businesses is the presence of a specific value system. Values influence the behavior and decision-making processes of the entrepreneur and are passed on to the next generation,[57] whereby these can then have an orientation function specifically for the next generation.[58] In this context, the values prevailing in family businesses do not operate primarily "at the level of moral standards" [59]. Rather, they are based on the views and attitudes of the entrepreneur and can be referred to as corporate culture or philosophy in current usage within corporate identity. Regardless of their origin, they support the decision-making process and serve as a benchmark, even if the entrepreneur is not necessarily aware of them. For the following generations, however, there is often a need to actively recall these values as their presence can decrease. Above all, the existing values can support a business family in developing a common identity that also influences the enterprise,[60] i.e., through the influence of the business family a certain identity is provided to the enterprise.[61] Authentically conveyed and lived values can — in a "quasi-family atmosphere"[62]— increase

[54] Cf. Wimmer (2007), p. 32.

[55] Rossaro (2007), p. 95.

[56] Cf. Rossaro (2007), p. 95. Depending on the size of the enterprise and the possible associated dispersion of shares the demand for a 50 percent unification of shares in family hands can be seen as too high (cf. Rossaro 2007, p. 95).

[57] Cf. García-Álvarez and López-Sintas (2001), p. 209. According to Zwack, values within organizations can be defined as follows: "*Values are therefore identity-creating orientation patterns of an organization, which are protected by emotionality. They are bound to decision situations and become apparent through non-conformist behavior. They are usually communicated implicitly by allusion and depend on their repetition for their existence*" (Zwack 2011, p. 235).

[58] Cf. Müller Tiberini (2008), p. 184.

[59] Baus (2010), p. 82.

[60] Cf. Baus (2010), p. 82 f.

[61] Cf. Simon et al. (2005), p. 76.

[62] Meyer and Oldenburg (2008), p. 22.

the willingness and ability to perform.[63] The well-being of individual employees, regional ties, or coexistence within the enterprise is often a lived reality for the entrepreneur.[64] For Erdem and Baser[65], one of the most significant characteristics of family businesses is therefore to be seen in the (direct) impact of family values on corporate values, which in their view makes family businesses a special type of enterprise.

The importance of the prevailing values in a family business should therefore not be underestimated. In addition to influencing the family business, these can serve as support in decision-making and can serve as a guiding principle, which in turn can be meaningful for the business family. They also act as a "stabilizer". Examples of lived values can be thriftiness, down-to-earthness, freedom, simplicity, trust, etc.[66] Others can be: "Performance- and risk-taking, loyalty to employees, public engagement, family spirit, and sense of responsibility." [67] The mentioned values can then be passed on to the descendants during socialization.[68] According to Müller Tiberini, values are ideally "identification points, guard rails, or directional signs" [69]. Against this background, values can be seen as a significant resource that can contribute to overcoming crises. Especially in times that are characterized by uncertainties, values provide a certain continuity for the decision-making process. However, values can also inhibit strategic changes or entrepreneurial behavior. For this reason, it seems relevant what characteristics the culture and values in family businesses take on.[70] In addition, the values are also determined by the enterprise size, sector-specific characteristics as well as characteristics of the socio-cultural environment.[71]

As has already become apparent, a family business is very much shaped by the entrepreneurial personality(ies). At the beginning, there is usually an idea or a vision that is shaped by the individual values, and thus creates its own culture. Therefore, the beginning and the establishment of such an enterprise cannot be compared with others. Rather, the personality of the (founding) entrepreneur shapes the way services are offered, the position in the market, the willingness to

---

[63] Cf. Meyer and Oldenburg (2008), p. 22.

[64] Cf. Weissman and Schultheiss (2006), p. 76.

[65] Cf. Erdem and Baser (2010), p. 48.

[66] Cf. Baus (2010), p. 83 ff.

[67] Stamm (2013), p. 270.

[68] Cf. Stamm (2013), p. 270.

[69] Müller Tiberini (2008), p. 182.

[70] Cf. Fletcher et al. (2012), p. 127.

[71] Cf. Erdem and Baser (2010), p. 48.

allow innovations, or how the internal organization is carried out.[72] Loos[73] therefore refers to many entrepreneurs as "»alpha people«" [74]. These have a strong pronounced personality, pursue their vision with conviction, and contribute to the shaping of the enterprise's identity. Thus, the cultural values of a family business are initially shaped by the founder's personality and subsequently by other family members or other groups within the family business.[75]

Specifically, adhering to certain values within family businesses is an important characteristic of this form of enterprise. These increase, among other things, the existing employee loyalty and a certain continuity of leadership promotes stability in the face of fluctuations in economic life.[76] In this regard, Haubl and Daser distinguish between two basic values in a family entrepreneur: The "work ethic"[77] and the "employer ethic" [78]. The smaller the family business, the stronger these basic values are often pronounced. This means that the smaller the family business is, the more access the individual employee can gain to the family sphere.[79] The values lived or pursued in business families have a direct influence on the family business. This is reflected, for example, in the investments made or the products manufactured. If the family business has existed over generations, the values and the tradition associated with them have usually evolved. This focus on certain values is often reflected in the social and cultural commitment of many family businesses[80] and is a part of the corporate identity.[81] This "obligation" can have effects on the socialization of the descendants and especially on the potential successors.

---

72 Cf. Meyer (2007), p. 11.

73 Cf. Loos (2010), p. 61 and cf. Dension et al. (2004), p. 64.

74 Loos (2010), p. 61.

75 Cf. Erdem and Baser (2010), p. 48.

76 Cf. Klatten (2002), p. 61.

77 Haubl and Daser (2006), p. 45.

78 Haubl and Daser (2006), p. 45. Haubl and Daser understand the two terms as follows: "While the work ethic measures the value of a person according to his work force, the employer ethic demands the creation and securing of jobs" (Haubl and Daser 2006, 45).

79 Cf. Haubl and Daser (2006), p. 45.

80 Cf. Müller Tiberini (2001), p. 85.

81 Cf. Baus (2010), p. 82.

2.1.3 Conflicts in Family Businesses

From the perspective of Systems theory, a conflict only ever arises when "communication is contradicted"[82] or, to put it another way, "when a contradiction is communicated" [83]. Therefore, when expectations are communicated and non-acceptance is communicated in response, a conflict arises.[84] With regard to family businesses, Hennerkes and Hund describe disputes as the "greatest value destroyer in family businesses" [85], whereby this includes both tangible and intangible assets. According to Simon et al. [86], non-economic reasons for failure are almost 100 percent attributable to the family, whereby the business can quickly become the venue of disputes.[87]

Specifically, family businesses are exposed to two risk factors: The escalation of conflicts and the avoidance of conflicts.[88] When conflicts arise, they are usually not openly addressed. The fear of "shattering the self-image of a 'perfect family'"[89] often weighs more. This can lead to a build-up of conflicts, which then eventually erupt all at once.[90] The major problem usually lies in the absence of solutions within the enterprise that contribute to effectively addressing an

---

[82] Luhmann (1987b), p. 530.

[83] See footnote 82.

[84] Cf. Luhmann (1987b), p. 530.

[85] Hennerkes and Hund (2008), p. 264.

[86] Cf. Simon et al. (2005), p. 165.

[87] Based on Conflict theory three types of conflict topics can generally be distinguished: "the social or relationship level, the factual or content level, and questions of time or timing" (Simon 2012, 111). Now, if conflict research for family businesses is considered, Frank et al. (2010a, 3) identify three clearly distinguishable focuses based on the literature analysis carried out in their article: (1) business-related conflicts, (2) conflicts between the family and the business, and (3) conflicts between generations, with points one and two standing out. Also compare Suchy et al. (2012, 28 f.). In a later article, Frank et al. (2011, 133) specifically investigate business-related conflicts between family members of a family business. They identify the following three frequently addressed topics: (1) the reasons for conflicts, (2) the effects of conflicts, and (3) the management of conflicts. However, when considering the conflicts/causes that could potentially lead to a conflict at the business level Kormann (2011, 394 ff.) identifies the following: (1) factual conflicts (assessment, evaluation, goal, and distribution conflicts), (2) relationship conflicts, (3) structural inequalities, (4) uncertainty, fears, and mistrust, and (5) communicative discrepancies. It becomes clear, what diverse types of conflicts can occur within a family business.

[88] Cf. Simon (2012), p. 110.

[89] Haubl and Daser (2006), p. 11.

[90] Cf. Haubl and Daser (2006), p. 11.

emerging dispute.[91] Instead, attempts are often made to wait it out. Conflicts are always inevitable when the boundaries between family and business cannot be clearly drawn and a high level of conflict sources influences the survival of the family business or the family itself. This can lead family members to leave the family business, reduce their commitment, or not take over the succession.[92] Especially in the context of family businesses, the resolution of conflicts is very individual, i.e., no universally valid solution strategies can be established, as this depends on the individual character of the business family.[93]

In summary, the business family can be described as a "crisis-triggering element"[94] and as an "element influencing the dynamics of the crisis"[95] for the reasons mentioned. They have the possibility to influence the respective crisis both destructively and constructively.[96] Above all, the "emotional-social component"[97] within family businesses has a significant influence on the course of a crisis. This can then justify a "destructive dynamization of the crisis situation" [98]. While, for example, in publicly traded corporations without family involvement public pressure usually contributes to a quick solution to the problem, this can lead to an existential threat in family businesses or drag on for generations if the conflict is "inherited" to the following generations.[99] Nevertheless, in family businesses there is predominantly a "positive approach to forgiveness" [100]. When considering families alone, a conflict occurring there can lead to a disruption of contact between members. In family businesses, however, this is not so easy or hardly possible. Communication is essential due to the joint work in the family business. Therefore, the members must continually approach each other.[101]

---

91 Cf. Hennerkes and Hund (2008), p. 264.

92 Cf. Danes et al. (2002), p. 34 f. In addition to family disputes, succession problems, insufficient qualifications of the leading owners, or conflicts of interest can also affect the continuity of family businesses (cf. Rüsen 2009, 20).

93 Cf. Meyer (2007), p. 142.

94 Rüsen and von Schlippe (2007), p. 320.

95 See footnote 94.

96 Cf. Rüsen (2009), p. 167 and cf. Rüsen and von Schlippe (2007), p. 320.

97 Rüsen (2009), p. 115.

98 See footnote 97.

99 Cf. Hennerkes and Hund (2008), p. 264.

100 LeMar (2014), p. 36.

101 Cf. LeMar (2014), p. 36.

Thus, the prevailing "close interlocking of family and business"[102] in family businesses not only distinguishes this type of enterprise from others in the economy due to their existing potentials. Due to the linkage, family businesses also have considerable risks that can manifest themselves through conflicts.[103] Precisely because of this close interlocking between family and business, conflicts will also influence the socialization of the descendants. As described above, these can cause a rejection of succession or the conflicts between family members are passed on to the next generation.

2.1.4 Paradoxes in Family Businesses

People generally have memberships in various areas and are confronted with different requirements or logics in each. However, as the different contexts are usually separate, this cannot pose a problem for them. For example, a woman can act as a mother within the context of the family and as a teacher in the professional environment. The different environments alternate between the front door and the school gate.[104] Therefore, for most people, there is a spatial separation of the two contexts of work and family. This allows a clear demarcation of the respective communication patterns.[105] This described fact is referred to as "»context marker«" [106]. Context markers serve the purpose of providing individuals with some guidance as to which frame of reference they are currently in.

---

[102] Frank et al. (2010a), p. 1.

[103] Cf. Frank et al. (2010a), p. 1. The negative effects that the participation of certain family members in the family business can cause are examined by Kidwell et al. (2013, p. 5 ff.). They refer to this phenomenon as the "Fredo effect" (Kidwell et al. 2013, p. 5). In an earlier article, Kidwell et al. understand the Fredo effect as follows: "Problematic behaviors that characterize the Fredo effect include dysfunctional and damaging actions toward the firm on the part of children who are seen as obstacles to the firm. More specifically, a family member impediment is seen as someone less capable and less competent than other employees, and as someone who only has a job in the firm because s/he is a family member" (Kidwell et al. 2012, p. 505).

[104] Cf. von Schlippe (2011b), p. 1 f.

[105] Cf. Simon (2008b), p. 15.

[106] Bateson (1992), p. 374 and cf. von Schlippe et al. (2012), p. 290. Bateson describes it as follows: "At this point, it is advantageous to introduce the term»context marker«. An organism reacts to»the same« stimulus in different contexts differently and therefore we must ask for the source of information for the organism. By which perception does it know that context A differs from context B [...]? Certainly, however, in human life , and probably also in that of many other organisms, signals appear whose main function is to *classify* contexts. [...] Such a source of information we will call»context marker« [...]

These markers can be a school building, an enterprise with its own logo, a front door with a family nameplate, etc.[107]

When the two contexts of family and business are compared, they place very different demands or expectations as well as norms and values on the respective members;[108] they follow different "rules of the game". Thus, the behavior that is appropriate in the family is rather inappropriate in the business and vice versa. For those affected, a differentiation of behaviors is therefore self-evident.[109] To illustrate or clarify why paradoxes[110] are in family businesses very likely, the different logics of family and business are ideal-typical summarized in Table 2.1.

Now, considering a family business against the background of the above Table 2.1, decisions in one area can affect the expectations or instructions in the other area due to the connection between family and business.[111] Especially in family businesses, there is usually a "mixing" of the two contexts. Therefore, it may never be clearly recognizable for the participants in which role the counterpart is currently acting, which can expose the participants to high psychological demands.[112] Figuratively speaking, both areas can be seen as "endpoints of a spectrum"[113]. Therefore, von Schlippe et al.[114] name the existing expectation structures within a family business as partially "contradictory" [115]. As the members of the business family operate in different frames of reference, each with

---

"(Bateson 1992, p. 374 f.). According to Simon and Stierlin, this includes "communication about the frame of reference of behavior valid in an interaction ([.] context). [...] It [the context marker] provides information about how certain behaviors of the involved interaction partners are to be understood" (Simon and Stierlin 1994, p. 200).

[107] Cf. von Schlippe and Frank (2013), p. 393.

[108] Cf. Schuman et al. (2010), p. 21.

[109] Cf. Simon (2005), p. 29 f.

[110] According to Luhmann, paradoxes are "the exact opposite of tautologies. They arise when a self-referential operation does not simply confirm itself, but allows the self-confirmation to run via the implication of the opposite" (Luhmann 1987 a, 22). Schuman et al. understand a paradox as follows: "A paradox [in the original bold] is comprised of two sides, that appear to be opposing, but in fact are mutually supportive" (Schuman et al. 2010, 4).

[111] Cf. Rüsen (2009), p. 37.

[112] Cf. Simon (2005), p. 29 f.

[113] Simon (2009), p. 41.

[114] Cf. von Schlippe et al. (2012), p. 289.

[115] von Schlippe et al. (2012), p. 289 and cf. von Schlippe (2012), p. 43.

Table 2.1 Logic of family and business systems[116]

Family	Business
Person-oriented Non-exchangeability of members ("Inclusion vs. exclusion of individuals"[a])	Function-oriented Exchangeability of members ("Inclusion vs. exclusion of functions"[b])
Continuity is ensured by acquiring additional members (birth, adoption, marriage, etc.)	Solvency determines continuity
There are familial ties that are connected by an emotional structure	Rationality dominates, which is oriented towards competition and the generation of profits
The physical and mental well-being of individual members ensures the family's future viability	The offered products or services must constantly be adapted to changing market requirements to guarantee future viability
Interaction rules are based on individual characters and develop haphazardly	Communication can be adapted or aligned based on factual goals
Communication is mostly verbal and takes place between present individuals	Communication is highly formalized and is predominantly documented in writing so that matters can be conducted between non-present individuals
Due to the predominantly non-written communication, memories can only be retrieved by individual members. This means that if certain events are not discussed, they are erased from the family memory	There are procedures for orientation
Each member is unique and therefore not replaceable or exchangeable	The focus is on fulfilling the (task-related) task. This must be achievable regardless of the person
Mutual interaction is guided by feelings, which in turn are influenced by the respective situation	Emotions play a subordinate role
Services rendered do not always require an immediate counter-service. A temporal discrepancy is possible	Services rendered always require an "immediate" consideration. A time gap is unthinkable. Due to the terminability and interchangeability of the members, the period of performance and consideration must be close together, whereby the consideration for the work input is contractually fixed

(continued)

[116] Weismeier-Sammer et al. (2012), p. 183 and cf. Simon (2009), p. 29.

Table 2.1 (continued)

Family	Business
Membership is either accomplished through birth or through emotional reasons	Both the enterprise and the employee actively decide for a membership
Membership cannot be cancelled or only with considerable effort	The relationship can be dissolved at any time by one or both sides
Since the family ensures the survival of individual members, the common good takes precedence over individual needs	Since the relationships are cancellable, the goals of the individual take precedence over the enterprise's goals
The expectations of or between individual members are not formally defined and change over time	Hierarchies, functions, and communication paths are usually fixed and clearly defined
Communication regulates the performance remuneration	Performance is rewarded with money
The profit is of an idealistic nature	The profit is of a material nature
Exchange arises due to unspoken emotion-related principles that direct an individual's attention to the long-term positive development of the other	Exchange is based on economic principles. The individual people are primarily encouraged to consider the market value and timeframe within which the goods or services are exchanged
Keywords: Emotionality, family peace, justice, and solidarity	Keywords: Competition, performance, rationality, objectivity, efficiency, and effectiveness

[a]Weismeier-Sammer et al. (2012), p. 183 and cf. Simon (2009), p. 29.
[b]*Source* Based on Weismeier-Sammer et al. (2012), p. 183; Baus (2010), p. 24; Simon (2009), p. 22 f. and p. 29; Fink (2008), p. 80; Meyer (2007), p. 18; Simon et al. (2005), p. 35 ff. and p. 164 f.; Simon (2005), p. 25 f.; Wimmer et al. (2004), p. 34; Lansberg (1983), p. 42.

a different behavioral expectation, this can lead to "paradoxical situations"[117] or "paradoxical tasks"[118] for them. Within family businesses "paradoxical organizational phenomena"[119] can occur, as a "conflict between a factual-economic and an emotional-personal orientation of action"[120] can arise due to the insufficient

[117] von Schlippe et al. (2012), p. 289.

[118] Rüsen (2008), p. 46.

[119] Wimmer et al. (2004), p. 21.

[120] Simon (2008b), p. 15; cf. Simon (2012), p. 31; cf. Rüsen (2009), p. 37 and cf. Simon et al. (2005), p. 33.

separation of family and business.[121] In this context, paradoxes are understood as "logically excluding contradictions"[122] that can be seen as an inherent element of family businesses.[123] A resolution of paradoxes is not possible, as they would otherwise be simple conflicts.[124] These can and must rather be actively managed.[125]

Many authors speak of so-called "pragmatic paradoxes"[126] in the context of family businesses, which represent a special form of paradoxes. Von Schlippe formulates this as follows: "They arise when a paradoxical action request is given. [...] This is the core of the pragmatic paradox: two action requests that are simultaneously directed at one person, but which contradict each other."[127] Especially within a family business, there is a peculiarity in this regard, as it is not always clearly recognizable for the individual family members in which context they are currently and whether the business or family communication would be appropriate in the specific case.[128] Von Schlippe et al.[129] mention two possible manifestations, against the background of pragmatic paradoxes, that can occur within family businesses:

1. "»Be both a family member and an entrepreneur at the same time!«"[130]
2. "»Be fair in both systems at the same time!«"[131]

When comparing the family and the business in conclusion, the family is oriented based on the existing relationships among each other where everyone is equal to the other. Within the business context, the orientation clearly takes place based on

---

[121] Cf. Simon (2008b), p. 15.

[122] Simon (2008b), p. 15.

[123] Cf. Plate and von Schlippe (2010), p. 2.

[124] Cf. von Schlippe (2011a), p. 11.

[125] Cf. Schuman et al. (2010), p. 5.

[126] Rüsen (2009), p. 37; cf. Simon (2012), p. 30; cf. von Schlippe (2011a), p. 10; cf. von Schlippe (2011b), p. 2 and cf. von Schlippe (2009), p. 19.

[127] von Schlippe (2011a), p. 10 and cf. von Schlippe (2011 b), p. 2. Simon formulates it as follows: "Pragmatic paradoxes always lead to undecidability, i.e., a situation in which it is not possible to»calculate« with the help of any tools or to be told by any experts what needs to be done" (Simon 2012, 31).

[128] Cf. von Schlippe et al. (2012), p. 290.

[129] Cf. von Schlippe et al. (2008), p. 24 ff. in reference to von Schlippe (2007), p. 116 ff. These are formulated as calls to action. Simon (2012, 44–61) also addresses various paradoxes or paradox management.

[130] von Schlippe et al. (2008), p. 24 and cf. von Schlippe (2011a), p. 10.

[131] von Schlippe et al. (2008), p. 26 and cf. von Schlippe (2011a), p. 10.

the tasks to be completed and the decisions to be made move to the center of consideration. Especially as a family member, it is impossible to satisfy both areas at the same time, which can strain the individual greatly.[132] Looking specifically at the entrepreneur, she or he usually must consider both the family (equal treatment) and the business (competence requirement) expectations when choosing a successor.[133] In general, the more pronounced the family influence within the business, the more difficult it is to deal with the paradoxes that arise.[134] Looking specifically at the descendants, they grow up with this ambiguity and must cope with it. Therefore, it seemed important for a further approach to family businesses to address the emerging paradoxes, as their occurrence is also considered relevant for the socialization of the descendants.

2.2 Development Stages of Family Businesses

As became apparent under Sect. 2.1, family businesses have several similarities. However, a small, regionally operating family business will differ from an internationally oriented family business.[135] It is often the case that the older the family business is or the further away it is from the founding generation, the closer the corporate culture approaches that which can also be found in other enterprises.[136] This divergence is not only reflected in the ownership and family dimension. Rather, the size, age, structures, and financial circumstances must also be considered to fully capture a family business. While "young" and small family businesses see the family more as a resource for "cheap" labor, the perspective in large family businesses is directed towards coordination and strategy development with the family usually only fulfilling its role as owner.[137] Often, however, the traditions from the founding phase are maintained (dealing with customers and employees, feeling of not so easy replaceability of individual employees, etc.). Since each family business has different life cycles, i.e., from the founder to the multi-generational family business, the individual members are constantly faced with new challenges, growth dynamics, and problem constellations in each

---

[132] Cf. von Schlippe (2009), p. 19.

[133] Cf. von Schlippe et al. (2012), p. 289.

[134] Cf. Halter and Schröder (2011), p. 31.

[135] Cf. Gersick et al. (1997), p. 103.

[136] Cf. Simon (2012), p. 93.

[137] Cf. Gersick et al. (1997), p. 103.

phase.[138] This should also affect the socialization of the respective descendants or potential successors. The family and the business set the framework for the dynamics within the family business. The family sometimes through the age of the family members, birth, death, or family socialization and the business, among other things, through market developments, supplier relationships, or financing.[139]

Family businesses that have existed for several generations in particular can have an impact on the family(ies) involved, as their development and growth are usually inextricably linked to the business. Due to the diversity of the contexts, the combination of family and business represents a not to be underestimated challenge for the family. Although a correspondingly strong entrepreneurial personality can convey a certain harmony, however, the "distance" between the two contexts over time becomes larger so that conflicts are often to be expected or inevitable. Without active management, these structural crises, in extreme cases, lead to the dissolution of the family business.[140] Similarly, a family business will probably only be passed on to the next generation if it has a certain size or is profitable enough. This can then also be the reason for deciding how many descendants the family business will be handed over to. Subsequently, the various influences and factors are discussed in detail that contribute to the dynamics within a family business. The separation made afterwards between size growth and the different generations participating in the enterprise serves for better understanding. In practice, this cannot be done so easily. Especially for the socialization of the descendants, the assumption is that each business cycle provides a different socialization context or a different life world for the descendants due to the connection to the family.

2.2.1 The Founding/Pioneer Enterprise

Pioneer enterprises are usually brought to life by an idea or a vision.[141] This often involves an interconnectivity — Wimmer et al. speak of a "merging of the two life spaces"[142]— between entrepreneur and enterprise,[143] where the (mis)success in the pioneer phase usually depends on the entrepreneur and his competence,

---

[138] Cf. Wimmer et al. (2005), p. 17 and cf. Habig and Berninghaus (2004), p. 5.

[139] Cf. Frank et al. (2010b), p. 127.

[140] Cf. Wimmer et al. (2004), p. 9.

[141] Cf. Gersick et al. (1997), p. 108 f.

[142] Wimmer et al. (2005), p. 200.

[143] Cf. Fallgatter (2002), p. 22 and cf. Kersting and Kamper-Jasper (2002), p. 85.

his energy reserves, and his ability to act universally.[144] Since the founder significantly influences the enterprise and all processes are tailored to his ideas and to his person, the sudden loss of this dominant part threatens the enterprise in its existence.[145] That is, if the founder leaves, in most cases the enterprise also ceases to exist.[146] Therefore, especially in the pioneer phase, the enterprise under construction is often given priority over the family's needs.[147] The founder must expend immense energy to establish his enterprise to the satisfaction of his customers, the bank, the staff, the suppliers, etc.[148] This necessary prioritization is clear to every participant (family member), which leads to a particularly pronounced bond and accumulation of capacities.[149]

Since the founders are usually also the owners and managers, the family also gets a direct connection to the business. The enterprise not only serves to secure their existence, but also involves the family members with all their emotions. This emotional involvement tends to decrease with each new generation.[150] However, the family serves the entrepreneur primarily in the start-up phase as an important resource. They support him with their work performance and serve the entrepreneur as emotional support. The family members provide their capacities without immediately demanding a return. In this context, however, there is the danger that the entrepreneur loses sight of the family and sees them more as a factor of production that "only" contributes to the success of the enterprise. Often, the entrepreneur expects the same amount of work from the individual family members as he himself provides to the enterprise.[151] A characteristic of the founding family is therefore usually the disproportionately high private sacrifice for the sake of the enterprise. This sacrifice can change in the next generation, which then leads to the founder's discontent.[152] Above all, the values lived by the founder (see Sect. 2.1.2) influence not only his behavior and the decision-making processes in the enterprise, but are passed on to the next generation

[144] Cf. Gersick et al. (1997), p. 36.
[145] Cf. Wimmer et al. (2005), p. 276.
[146] Cf. Fallgatter (2002), p. 22.
[147] Cf. Wimmer et al. (2005), p. 268.
[148] Cf. Gersick et al. (1997), p. 147.
[149] See footnote 147.
[150] Cf. LeMar (2014), p. 227.
[151] Cf. Wimmer et al. (2005), p. 204.
[152] Cf. Domayer and Vater (1995), p. 151.

during socialization.[153] The following three values represented by founders can be mentioned:

1. The "hard" work, which is why the founder dedicates time and diligence to the enterprise to achieve the set goals.
2. Growth, which says something about the founder's idea regarding the development of the enterprise.
3. Ambition

Despite the strong influence of lived values, the behavior of each founder is predominantly influenced by a specific context and must match a specific market environment.[154]

If, on the other hand, the described involvement in the enterprise — especially of the parents — is considered, this is primarily economically justified as excessive personnel costs cannot yet be borne by the enterprise. There is also no clear boundary between the two contexts (family and business) at this stage.[155] Thus, the enterprise in the start-up phase often benefits from the "overlap" of the two frames of reference. As a result, the informal structures prevailing in the family are also reflected in the enterprise's everyday life and become visible through direct communication channels between the employees and the founder. This creates a special commitment to the entrepreneur's orientation.[156] Pioneer enterprises are often seen as part of the family. There is a "personified connection"[157] to the enterprise. This then explains the enormous importance of the enterprise for the family, which is noticeable in an immense need for investment. Thus, the enterprise needs not only labor, but also time and energy from the parents, which is then missing for the entrepreneur's children. The enterprise can rather be seen as an additional child of the parents to whom the parents must devote the most time. Especially, due to this focus on the enterprise, rivalries among the actual children are very likely when it comes to the parents' attention.[158] The first-generation entrepreneur is often experienced as an absent parent by the children due to the high level of work commitment. This situation can then make

[153] Cf. García-Álvarez and López-Sintas (2001), p. 209.
[154] Cf. García-Álvarez and López-Sintas (2001), p. 223 ff.
[155] Cf. Simon (2012), p. 65 f.
[156] Cf. Lansberg (1983), p. 40.
[157] Müller Tiberini (2001), p. 31.
[158] Cf. Plate (2008), p. 70.

the enterprise appear as a competitor in the eyes of the children and lead to a rejection of the enterprise.[159]

For the children, this can also have two other effects:

1. They learn early on what economic demands are made on them, and
2. they are usually aware of the competitive relationship with the enterprise for the parents' attention.

Likewise, a dilemma can arise for the parents. As they often know how much time the enterprise demands, they may feel guilty. They often feel that they are neglecting their children, which makes them vulnerable on an emotional level and can be expressed through subtle feelings of guilt.[160] In many cases, they therefore try to meet the children's needs through financial contributions. However, this can push education-related achievements into the background, which of course cannot be the goal.[161] They often justify their workload with the argument that they are only doing this for their children, which in turn puts pressure on the children ([I.1]). Since it is usually the fathers who act entrepreneurially, the father-child relationship — especially the father-son relationship — must be given a special role. Daughters, on the other hand, usually have different ideal images. Therefore, they often have it "easier".[162]

Since the founding entrepreneur is usually inseparably linked to his enterprise, there is often an enormously high level of attachment and identification with it. The entrepreneur has built the enterprise, invested all his strength and time in the operation. This is then often reflected in the attempt to impose the corporate career on children,[163] which can stem from a certain pressure or obligation ([I.1]). Due to the strong involvement of parents in their enterprise, they can lose sight of the family or act in the family in a similar way as in the enterprise. The behavior of the parents can then negatively affect the entrepreneurial children and endanger the continuation of the enterprise ([I.2]). See Interviews 2.1.

However the family of a pioneering entrepreneur must first develop into a business family,[164] with the birth of the first child marking a transition from a

---

[159] Cf. Gersick et al. (1997), p. 145.

[160] Cf. Simon (2012), p. 66 and cf. Simon (2005), p. 44.

[161] Cf. Risse (1997), p. 37.

[162] Cf. Simon (2005), p. 43 ff.

[163] Cf. Habig and Berninghaus (2004), p. 63.

[164] Cf. Klett (2002), p. 105.

Interviews 2.1 Characteristics of the founding generation [I.1–2]

[I.1]	Female successor: "[…] Usually it is the case that the transferors give the transferees the feeling, you should be glad that you are allowed to continue it — a life's work, so to speak; the humility and the reverence for this great work — these demands were never made of us."[a]
[I.2]	Consultant: "[…] However, considering that often the parental generation of founders belongs to the type of classic doers who ultimately also believe that they can shape the enterprise, but also the integration of the children with entrepreneurial means, the social system family often falls by the wayside. There is often a great discrepancy in terms of mutual acceptance of what the parents or the previous generation have created, but also in terms of respect and confidence, and self-assurance that the next generation will be able to continue this. […]"[b]

[a]Juritsch et al. (2007), p. 82.
[b]Juritsch et al. (2007), p. 97.

founder to a family business.[165] Above all, the birth of a child changes, influences, and disrupts the prevailing family situation[166] and can affect the situation in the enterprise through the connection of the family with the enterprise. Thus, membership in a family business is predominantly determined by birth[167] into the business family. In a non-family business membership can only be achieved through performance.[168] With the differentiation of (non-)family membership "a clear inside-outside distinction is thus made" [169]. Similarly, family businesses try to ensure the continued existence of the enterprise, whereas in an organization the focus is predominantly on personal careers.[170] Usually, the founding of an enterprise is not done with the intention of keeping it going for several generations. Only the involvement of the family leads in many cases to a change of time horizons. This is then reflected in the decisions or investments made, which are designed to be long-term and sustainable.[171]

Finally, if the focus is again directed towards the enterprise, its growth may require a restructuring already in the founding phase. This means that the entrepreneur is forced to rethink and delegate his own tasks, which can reduce

[165] Cf. Klein (2004), p. 79 f. and cf. Gersick et al. (1997), p. 71.
[166] Cf. Meyer (2007), p. 109.
[167] In addition, adoption or marrying into the family should not be neglected.
[168] Cf. Hildenbrand (2005), p. 119.
[169] Simon (2005), p. 57.
[170] See footnote 168.
[171] Cf. Wimmer (2008a), p. 11.

Interviews 2.2 Effects of size growth [I.3–4]

[I.3]	Entrepreneur: "Over time, we realized that WimTec internally, due to the spatial generosity between employees, had to struggle with large communication deficits. I also realized that beyond a certain size of the enterprise, it was impossible for the founder and pioneer to build all bridges between development, production, and sales himself. This difficulty, which is insurmountable even in a small enterprise, meant an overload and a failure to exploit all possibilities. These considerations forced the decision to integrate my son Peter who was considered a possible successor, more into the enterprise from now on. The further focus was now directed towards the employees to achieve further development of the enterprise. This was my biggest challenge and most difficult task. The personal letting go of things that I was used to have in my own hands, to oversee and direct, was anything, but easy. […]"[a]
[I.4]	Long-time female employee of the founder: "'I simply believe that from a certain size of this enterprise, you just can't continue in the consequence as you might have always wanted or even done. […] Something gets left behind. When you become a corporation or when you get big. […] Also, in terms of leadership. So, if you want a very targeted one, it's just like that, you just don't have everything in your hand anymore, you can no longer regulate everything alone, you can only control it by looking for people, where you believe that they do it the way you want to do it. That you bring the values into your leadership crew. You might still have this control, but you don't have anything else anymore. No'"[b]

[a]Wimberger (2006), p. 142 f.
[b]Zwack (2011), p. 144.

direct contact with his employees ([I.3 and I.4]). In addition, this can cause the successor to be involved in the enterprise earlier ([I.3]). Generally, due to the size growth, the integration of successors into the enterprise and the requirements placed on them can change (see Interviews 2.2).

The further consequences associated with size growth are explained below.

2.2.2 Effects of Size Growth

During the pioneer phase, the entrepreneur and his family release an enormous energy potential, which helps the enterprise to quickly establish itself in the target markets.[172] A characteristic feature is the daily presence of the entrepreneur in the enterprise, whereby the management is actively and directly executed by

[172] Cf. Domayer and Oswald (1994), p. 9.

him. Decisions are more tactically oriented. Employees and customers can contact the entrepreneur at any time in most cases. His performance is visible to everyone and the dependence on the entrepreneur for the success and continuation of the enterprise is understandable to all. In this sense, the entrepreneur also exudes a certain role model effect.[173] The style of leadership often equally reflects the personality of the founder. Thus, the demonstrated commitment can form "a strong sense of belonging and community" [174], which creates a special bond between the entrepreneur and his employees.[175] However, the general rule is: "The smaller a family business is, the more likely the family culture will also become the corporate culture" [176] and the smaller the family business, the higher the concentration of task distribution to certain individuals or family members. Therefore, the respective management must fulfill operational tasks to a much greater extent.[177]

This leadership culture can only be maintained if the organizational structures do not exceed a certain level of complexity. From then on, it becomes increasingly necessary to further develop the leadership based on professional structures.[178] This primarily requires a decentralization of the entrepreneurial monopoly position as otherwise effective control is hardly or no longer possible ([I.3 and I.4]). However, this step of change can only be carried out with considerable effort.[179] Leadership becomes increasingly indirect and the entrepreneur must increasingly demonstrate strategic leadership qualities. A large part of his work is done from the desk, which often results in a decreasing presence within the enterprise.[180] Likewise, growth in size usually leads to a gender-specific spatial division of life areas. These diverge increasingly although the enterprise still provides the common framework.[181] Therefore, when considering the organizational structures, it is essential to distinguish between small and large family businesses as the size requires different requirements.[182]

---

173 Cf. Hamer (2001), p. 184.

174 Kersting and Kamper-Jasper (2002), p. 84.

175 Cf. Kersting and Kamper-Jasper (2002), p. 84.

176 Haubl and Daser (2006), p. 11. and cf. Hamer (2001), p. 221.

177 Cf. Felden (2012), p. 144.

178 Cf. Wimmer (2008a), p. 15.

179 Cf. Wimmer et al. (2005), p. 140.

180 Cf. Hamer (2001), p. 184.

181 Cf. Wimmer et al. (2005), p. 219.

182 Cf. Habig and Berninghaus (2004), p. 37.

The change in the connection between family and enterprise is mainly expressed in the reduced arbitrary influence of the family on business decisions, in the emergence of formalized structures between the two reference frames, and in the growing independence of the enterprise.[183] However, this often results in a conflict between the two contexts and can lead to contradictions between the principles of the family and those of the business.[184] The further a family business progresses within its life cycle, the higher the need becomes to employ external managers in the enterprise due to the overload of the entrepreneur. These bring certain resources such as experiences or competencies that the family members often cannot demonstrate. They can also take on the task of preparing the next generation for their entry into the family business.[185] In addition, external managers are also used as a means of avoiding disputes.[186] According to Pfannenschwarz[187] and Gersick et al. [188], changes in the leadership structures protect the family business. They represent a "buffer" that protects the enterprise from improper or destructive family influences.

In conclusion, the explanations show two things:

1. The requirements for the entrepreneur or the management of the family business change due to the growth in size.
2. The connection between family and family business is also affected.

This subsequently influences the socialization of the descendants or potential successors as different requirements for the management of the family business are placed on them. Due to the growth in size and the often-resulting separation of family and business, the family business no longer serves as a living environment or socialization context to the same extent.

2.2.3 The Second Generation

While the business family of the first generation is usually characterized by a strong founding personality who dictates "where it goes" in the family

[183] Cf. Wimmer et al. (2005), p. 332.

[184] Cf. Lansberg (1983), p. 40.

[185] Cf. Gersick et al. (1997), p. 128.

[186] Cf. Löhr (2001), p. 32.

[187] Cf. Pfannenschwarz (2006a), p. 37.

[188] Cf. Gersick et al. (1997), p. 128.

and business,[189] this often changes from the second generation onwards. The family of origin is dissolved and if there are several siblings, different nuclear families [190]emerge, which are linked by the sibling relationships. In addition, potential spouses now also appear. Whether or to what extent these "external" persons are desired or what role is assigned to them in the family business can initially never be answered unequivocally.[191] The (non-)inclusion or the attitude of the in-laws will also influence the socialization of the descendants. If the family of the first generation can still be described as a family growing into the business, the second and third generation are often characterized by growing out of the family business. This happens due to the fact, that some descendants are paid out and it is initially often not clear to the descendants who will be selected for the succession of the family business.[192] Equally typical of family businesses facing the transition from the first to the second generation is the lack of experience with the process of handover and the strong emotional attachment of the old entrepreneurs to their business, which can lead to disagreements/irritations within the family.[193]

When considering the professional context of a second-generation entrepreneur child, it is often determined by the family business. Past, current, and future events influence the child's decisions. This strong influence on individual orientation continues with children of the third generation. In both generations, the influence on the growing children is no longer only exerted by the family of origin, but also by the possibly already existing family tree, which is usually not the case with non-entrepreneur children.[194] Compared to the founders, the second generation is socialized in the context of an enterprise, which can have effects on their world of life and identity. They may have a different value system than the founding generation, which then causes conflicts (see Interviews 2.3 [I.5]).

As several members of the family are usually already employed in the business from the second generation onwards, there is a need for organization. This includes, among other things, the coordination of tasks and competencies. A separation of tasks usually takes place with the interfaces having to be managed through intensive discussions. There is an increasing need for delegation

---

[189] Cf. Simon (2008b), p. 23.

[190] Stamm (2013, 32) defines a nuclear family as the modern family, i.e., a married couple with minor and unmarried children.

[191] Cf. Wimmer et al. (2004), p. 24 f.

[192] Cf. Klett (2002), p. 106 f.

[193] Cf. Bieker and Hirsch (2007), p. 389.

[194] Cf. Meyer (2007), p. 32.

Interviews 2.3 Socialization of the second generation [I.5]

[I.5]	Univ. Prof. for Business Administration: "[…] Entrepreneurs in the 2nd generation are often socialized differently than their parents. They grow up with or in the family business. They learn the fluid boundaries between work and family early on. Many entrepreneurs in the 2nd generation expand their own value system through the»external learning years« at home and abroad, through a more international education. For this generation, the challenge is to integrate these differences and ideally create a successful synthesis. This generation has it the hardest as the topic of identity must be reinterpreted for the first time. On the one hand, there is the strong adherence to the attitudes from the family of origin, on the other hand, the own claim to create something new through external experiences or education."[a]

[a]Juritsch et al. (2007), p. 96.

and transfer to non-family members otherwise the family business may suffer.[195] Thus, family businesses are also shaped by different stages of development, which are influenced by the family generation involved. While the entrepreneur in the founding phase was still characterized by his individual leadership with informally oriented organizational structures, the next generation usually employs specialists for the respective field in addition to their work. The organization becomes larger and increasingly functionally divided through the various areas (sales, technology, etc.).[196] The entrepreneurs of the second generation are often no longer connected to the family business to the same extent or, in other words, the family business no longer necessarily represents the full meaning of life as was the case with the parents or founders.[197] Nevertheless, regardless of the life cycle stage of the family business and how the ownership or control structures have evolved, there is a commonality: The family or family shareholders often see themselves in a certain entrepreneurial obligation towards the family business. This serves them not only as an investment object that has to deliver a regular return, but rather there is also a desire to actively shape the enterprise's direction.[198]

Specifically, successors from the second generation onwards are handed over an already existing enterprise. The culture and internal structures have grown over the years, which makes desired changes difficult ([I.6]). The tradition lived in the

[195] Cf. LeMar (2014), p. 159.

[196] Cf. Habig and Berninghaus (2004), p. 38.

[197] Cf. Simon (2005), p. 46.

[198] Cf. Wimmer (2008a), p. 10.

Interviews 2.4 Culture and tradition in existing family businesses [I.6–8]

[I.6]	Successor: "As the future boss of an already existing enterprise, you encounter a corporate culture that has developed over the years. Even if some things seem strange and unexpected to you, think carefully before ordering changes that affect this culture. This does not mean that you should not eliminate grievances tolerated by your predecessor. However, the elimination of long-established undesirable developments that are detrimental to the business climate is a demanding task. […]"[a]
[I.7]	Successor: "You are not only taking over the economic enterprise, but also its tradition. You should act sovereignly towards the family stories rooted in the business. Show empathy, but do not let yourself be influenced by»talk«."[b]
[I.8]	Female successor: "'…a time when I really physically felt the previous generation in my back. And here and just also this.., you, you must.. make it, so there is no option.. but I can't crash this ship after over 150 years. Some people are watching, some have put all their life energy, time, money into it and uh so that was [omitted] at the beginning of my decision, so the pronounced decision, the responsibility for the past was the biggest, bigger than the one for the future'"[c]

[a] Schaub (2009), p. 28.
[b] Schaub (2009), p. 41.
[c] Stamm (2013), p. 290 f. The enterprise has existed longer than the second generation, however, the content described seems to fit better at this point.

family business must also not be neglected ([I.7]), while [I.8] illustrates the burden and pressure that successors can be exposed to due to the existing tradition. Above all, these factors, due to the connection between family and business, can influence the socialization of the growing generation (see Interviews 2.4).

Similarly, the decision-making monopoly of the founder is often dissolved from the second generation onwards, which harbors increasing potential for conflict as each successor may have different interests and views. If the family then fails to form a unity from this, it can lead to alienation within the family and therefore also from the family business, which may subsequently jeopardize the continued existence of the family business.[199] At the same time, the founding generation often still regulates the relationships between the members and conveys the values. The second generation can also still live their family life according to the patterns of the first generation. This is reinforced by a possible insufficient role separation between the family and the business, which in turn favors conflicts. Decisions within the family business can be determined by

[199] Cf. Baus (2010), p. 15.

family criteria.[200] However, from the second generation onwards, the question often arises, how much "family" can be expected of the family business at all, i.e., the question arises: *family-first* or *business-first*. Although the business family in the first generation often assumes a priority of the business, the family-first thought is reflected in small things like the fuel card for all family members at the expense of the enterprise, the cleaning staff who also clean the private house, or the caretaker who also takes care of the private garden.[201]

In addition, there is generally a difference between the generations: The further the generations progress, the less they are willing to sacrifice their entire life unconditionally for the family business. Especially in the transition from the first to the second generation, this often leads to conflicts, which is due to their different starting positions: While it is usually indispensable for the founding generation to put all their strength — while neglecting the family — into the enterprise, this is not necessarily the case for the subsequent generations.[202] In contrast to the founding generation the children often have a reduced identification potential with the product idea. At the same time, they have not such a pronounced feeling of dependence on the enterprise as their parents, so they would run it with less effort.[203] This is then reflected in the willingness to hand over the management of the enterprise to non-family members as the family business is no longer necessarily seen as an identity and meaningful medium.[204] This "cutting of the cord" is equally noticeable in the relationship with the descendants (third generation) and their succession. In family businesses of the second generation, at least one parent has already gained experience with succession. Due to the possible emotional distance to the family business, the parents can give their children more time, which makes the children feel less responsible for continuing the business.[205] Finally, if we specifically look at the partners of the second generation, they do not necessarily have to be involved in the family business to the same extent as in the first generation. This can, due to the lesser contact with the enterprise, lead to a delay in the socialization of the next generation.[206] To what extent the partners are integrated into the family business will probably also depend on the size of the enterprise, its profitability, and subject matter.

---

[200] Cf. Simon (2008b), p. 23.

[201] Cf. Baus (2010), p. 98.

[202] Cf. LeMar (2014), p. 12.

[203] Cf. Wimmer and Gebauer (2004), p. 247.

[204] Cf. Simon (2012), p. 69.

[205] Cf. Simon (2012), p. 69 and cf. Simon (2005), p. 46.

[206] Cf. Iannarelli (1992), p. 149.

2.2.4 The Third Generation

Löhr[207] refers to an enterprise as a successor business when it has undergone more than one generational change. In general, the longer the family business remains in the hands of the family, the higher the number of family members participating in it.[208] From the third generation onwards, the owners are usually no longer just siblings. This is accompanied by the members being shaped by different parental homes, an increased number of members, and the difficulty of maintaining contacts between relatives.[209] This creates a completely different starting point for the subsequent generations due to the socialization in different families, the increase in shareholders, and the associated reduction in contact opportunities between the shareholders.[210]

From the third generation onwards, there is often a change in the pursued goals. The preservation of the family business is no longer necessarily the focus, but is replaced by the goal of acting as a business family. The reorientation takes place through a familial change in understanding regarding the enterprise. It is "no longer seen as an unavailable factor, but as a disposable asset among others"[211]. Often there is an increasing division of shares in the enterprise, and thus a progressive reduction of emotional attachment,[212] as the familial and entrepreneurial spheres no longer collide to the extent they did in the first two generations.[213] According to LeMar [214], there is often a need to consolidate in the third generation. He also refers to this as the "integration phase" [215]. As the circle of shareholders generally increases in the third generation, there is an increasing need to focus on family-related issues. One question would be, for example, how to deal with family members who hold shares in the business, but do not participate in its active management.[216] In order to maintain the sense of belonging,

---

[207] Cf. Löhr (2001), p. 18.

[208] Cf. Simon (2012), p. 70.

[209] The term "relatives" serves to determine certain behavioral patterns, that is, whether a person approaches another person with appreciation or aversion (cf. Segalen 1990, 66). In detail, relatives can refer to the extended family association (cf. Kormann 2011, 68).

[210] Cf. Kormann (2011), p. 68.

[211] Baus (2010), p. 90 f.

[212] Cf. Baus (2010), p. 90 f.

[213] Cf. Simon et al. (2005), p. 163.

[214] Cf. LeMar (2014), p. 245.

[215] LeMar (2014), p. 245.

[216] Cf. LeMar (2014), p. 159 f. and cf. Meyer (2007), p. 163.

active work must be done. This inevitably requires a structural organization of the extended family so that the whole family can continue to exist.[217] Thus, there is an increasing need for suitable relationship management.[218] Therefore, at this stage, there is a risk of increasing different interests as the individual shareholders, due to the increasing number, are no longer as closely connected. In this context, Löhr[219] speaks of "alienation" [220], which often leads to an increasing need for "institutionalized conflict resolution mechanisms" [221]. However, in this phase, paradoxes are usually handled better (see Sect. 2.1.4). As the number of family members grows from the third generation onwards, communication with all family members becomes increasingly difficult.[222] According to Gersick et al. [223], there are three factors that make information dissemination difficult:

1. Geographical distribution of individual members.
2. Diverging interests, abilities, income differences, etc.
3. Different attitudes towards the various business branches within the family.

This also presupposes the increasingly necessary establishment of formalizing structures to maintain communication.[224]

Finally, when considering the qualification profile of the descendants, technical or commercial education is usually essential in the first two generations, but this changes with each subsequent generation. Then, more and more social as well as psychological skills become important especially in relation to leadership competence.[225] Since at least one parent from the second generation was able to gain experience with succession, a greater understanding of the children's dilemma regarding a possible succession is to be expected. In many cases, however, the connection is no longer as close as with the founding family and the relationship to the family business is therefore not necessarily tied to the same extent to one's own sense of purpose and identity. Therefore, the descendants

[217] Cf. Simon (2005), p. 47.
[218] Cf. LeMar (2014), p. 159 f.
[219] Cf. Löhr (2001), p. 18.
[220] Löhr (2001), p. 18.
[221] See footnote 220.
[222] Cf. Simon (2005), p. 47.
[223] Cf. Gersick et al. (1997), p. 181.
[224] Cf. Simon (2012), p. 70.
[225] Cf. LeMar (2014), p. 132.

Interviews 2.5 Successor's perspective on the family business [I.9]

[I.9]	Univ. Prof. for Business Administration: "[...] The 2nd and 3rd generation often approach succession with a different and broader focus and only partially adhere to previous principles of success. It often happens, that the business and founder identity are very specifically questioned by the subsequent generation. Is the identity, which is so strongly reminiscent of the founding personality even almost is still viable? Is it contemporary to convey the entire value spectrum of the parents or are there new current values that correspond more to the new generation, which need to be lived and communicated? The new generation of the business family is successful when it critically questions this and compares personal attitudes and values with those of the business and the family of origin."[a]

[a]Juritsch et al. (2007), p. 97.

are often given a larger decision-making scope.[226] There is also often a need to realign the enterprise, which can simultaneously question the currently valid values. For this, it is necessary, among other things, to reconsider the previous principles of success (see Interviews 2.5 [I.9]).

2.2.5 The Multi-generational Family Business

Groth and Slevogt refer to enterprises from the fourth generation as "multi-generational family business"[227], provided they are still in family hands.[228] This designation is adopted for the present work. The multi-generational existence of a family business usually implies a dilution of the specific family influence on the enterprise. In contrast to family businesses up to the third generation, multi-generational family businesses are no longer characterized to a predominant extent by decisions that are oriented towards individual persons, which can entail a significant risk reduction.[229] This occurs due to the generational changes, the associated division of the ownership shares among several persons or family tribes, and the handing over of leadership tasks to external managers.[230]

---

[226] Cf. Simon (2012), p. 69.

[227] Groth and Slevogt (2004), p. 3.

[228] Cf. Groth and Slevogt (2004), p. 3.

[229] Cf. Simon (2008b), p. 21.

[230] Cf. Wimmer et al. (2005), p. 17.

Interviews 2.6 Different coupling in multi-generational family businesses [I.10–11]

[I.10]	Case description: "*An industrial furnace construction enterprise founded over a hundred years ago […], had to look for a new operating location. […] At the same time, the industry was experiencing a technological change. Therefore, it was necessary to find a new location, build new production facilities, and at the same time invest funds.* *The enterprise's shares were distributed among the family that had grown over three generations. No shareholder owned more than 5% of the shares. The shareholders' attachment and identity to the enterprise was either non-existent or only rudimentary. Over the past forty years the enterprise was managed by employed managing directors.* *[…] No member of the owner family wanted to commit to increasing the capital. […] Eventually, all rights […] were bought by a competitor, the staff that had been employed for decades was laid off, […], the traditional enterprise was liquidated.*"[a]
[I.11]	Junior Manager: "'*We are about a large family and a large enterprise. Therefore, there are basic rules:* 1. *Only the best people come into the enterprise, we communicate this internally so that everyone can see it. […]* 2. *There must be no financial weakening for the enterprise when an heir leaves as a partner. It must not be that an heir wants to sell his share with as much profit as possible. Here we have a good regulation thanks to the foundation.* 3. *Identification must be more important than profit-seeking, here we need to ensure that everything is planned for the long term.* 4. *Disputes in the family should be avoided.* 5. *Disputes in the enterprise should be avoided. […]*'"[b]

[a]Schaub (2009), p. 46.
[b]Mätzener and Schwarz (2008), p. 62.

At the same time, the dependence of the enterprise on individual employees decreases.[231] However, the increasing number of owners leads to a further fragmentation of the shares in the enterprise, which can lead to a loss of attachment to the family business that has existed over generations. This can be problematic when necessary investments are needed (see Interviews 2.6 [I.10]).

The following therefore applies: In family businesses whose shares are divided among several family tribes, "the family as an emotionally experienced unit"[232] usually no longer exists. The number of family members is often overwhelmingly large and the individual members would probably not even know each

[231] Cf. Simon (2012), p. 73.

[232] Wimmer et al. (2005), p. 334.

other without the common ownership of the enterprise or through the shares held in the enterprise.[233] Through rituals, statutes, etc. alienation of the family must be counteracted [234] so that the family's decision-making freedom remains (see Interviews 2.6 [I.11]).[235]

As from the fourth generation onwards, due to the family members participating in the enterprise, the management of family members becomes very demanding in most cases, this takes up most of the time. For this reason, there is a need for institutionalization and systematic processing.[236] Simon puts it as follows: "The paradoxical consequence of the quantitative growth of the family is that the extended family must give itself formalized rules in order to be able to communicate informally."[237] In order for communication to be likely and to occur at all, there is a need to plan it appropriately by agreeing on places and times that provide the space for it. Within this framework, person-centered communication can take place and familiarity as well as trust can be established.[238] The difficulty with family businesses often arises due to family growth. The more the kinship relationships diverge, the less interest there is in a common family business [I.10],[239] and the less influence the family business could have on the socialization of the growing up.

Against this background, there is a need for the management of multi-generational family businesses to integrate the family into the enterprise as best as possible. According to LeMar[240], this includes the following tasks:

1. Training of future managers from the family circle.
2. Coordination of family members employed in the enterprise.
3. Determination of the dividend policy.
4. Establishment of a family committee.

233 Cf. Simon (2012), p. 64 f. and cf. Simon et al. (2005), p. 45.
234 Cf. Simon (2003), p. 47.
235 Cf. Simon (2012), p. 73.
236 Cf. LeMar (2014), p. 160.
237 Simon (2012), p. 72.
238 Cf. Simon (2012), p. 72.
239 Cf. Habig and Berninghaus (2004), p. 13.
240 Cf. LeMar (2014), p. 159.

Interviews 2.7 Influence of the family business on the descendants [I.12]

[I.12]	Entrepreneur, 4th generation: "*Of course, I also asked myself whether it was my free decision. I did an education to become a bank clerk and then later joined the enterprise because my father also had a hard time. But I can say with certainty, if I had not been born in this family with this business, I would not have gone into the carpentry trade. I can say that. I wouldn't have chosen that. Although ... I mainly do the commercial activity and that was also my direction.*"[a]

[a]Weber (2005), p. 271.

In conclusion, even in multi-generational family businesses it can be assumed that the descendants will be influenced to take over ([I.12]). What also becomes clear from the quote are the changed requirements for the descendants (see Interviews 2.7).

2.2.6 Overview of Development Stages

The following quote initially illustrates the diverging requirements that are placed on the respective generation participating in a family business: "The founder must be guided by the motto: *Look ahead!* For the second generation of the sibling enterprise the motto is: *Become a team!* And the rule for the cousins of the third generation is: *Keep the family together!*"[241] This results in the requirement for the founder to guarantee a successful handover, for the siblings the challenge of cooperation, and the cousins must counteract alienation.[242] The explanations reveal the existence of different forms of family types depending on the development phase of the family business. Therefore, it seems essential to distinguish between small and large or young and old family businesses when considering the organizational structures as the size and age require different prerequisites from the participating business family ([I.4]).[243] This is also reflected in the necessary qualification profile of the descendants or, prior to that, in their socialization ([I.5 and I.9]). According to Siefer [244], the qualification of the descendants increases compared to the parent generation. In addition, the education in most cases has a relation to the family business. Therefore, it makes a difference, whether the

[241] Baus (2010), p. 46.

[242] Cf. Baus (2010), p. 103 f.

[243] Cf. Habig and Berninghaus (2004), p. 37.

[244] Cf. Siefer (1996), p. 31.

enterprise is led by the pioneer or already by several family members as well as in which industry it is located.[245]

Against this background, if the already mentioned *business-first* and *family-first* focus is considered, Schuman et al. provide the following ideal-typical representation (see Fig. 2.1).

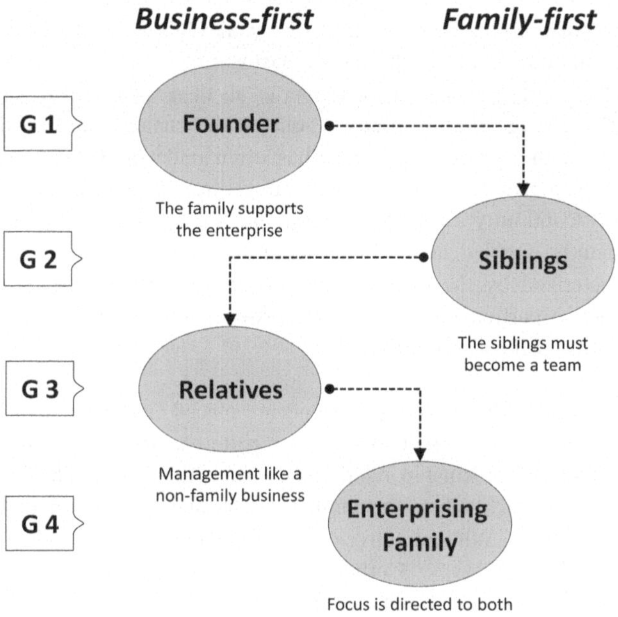

Fig. 2.1 Business and family-first along the generations[246]

1. **Generation 1 (G 1):** In the founding phase, the focus in most cases is directed towards the enterprise (business-first). There is a necessity to ensure the survivability and success of the enterprise. Thus, the children grow up in an environment that gives clear priority to the business.
2. **G 2:** This then results in the second generation having a stronger desire to bring family needs (family-first) more to the forefront to counterbalance

---

[245] Cf. Habig and Berninghaus (2004), p. 37.

[246] Source: According to Schuman et al. (2010), p. 73.

the business-first thinking of the first generation. The family-first thinking of the second generation is often enabled by the good reputation and the good customer base, which originated in the first generation.

3. **G 3:** In the third generation, the weight shifts back towards the enterprise (business-first). However, now in contrast to the first generation, several generations and possibly already non-family members participate in the family business. At this stage, the relatives are often already geographically dispersed and may not know each other very well. Only a small part is often still interested in active work in the family business.[247]
4. **G 4:** In the fourth generation, Schuman et al. then speak of an "enterprising family"[248]. This generation focuses both on the business and on the family. Especially in this phase, the family has often understood how to deal with the different paradoxes as they have managed to maintain a special business and family continuity along the generations. Thus, the enterprising family is predominantly enabled to establish structures and processes ([I.11]), which are characterized by the different involvement of family members — be it through active participation in the enterprise or not — so that all pursue the same "vision of the one family". [249]

It becomes clear, that different requirements are placed on each generation, which should be noticeable in different socialization patterns. However, there is a risk of increasing "dilution" of kinship relationships from the origin. The further these moves away from each other, the more the personal connection to the family business can decrease. Without active countermeasures this can lead to the downfall of the family business.[250] Corbetta refers to this situation as "cooling off" [251]. The loss of the inner emotional connection to the family business can reduce the willingness to reinvest generated profits to secure future viability ([I.11]).[252] Schuman et al. refer to this as the "growth and liquidity paradox" [253]. While the

247 Cf. Schuman et al. (2010), p. 55.

248 Schuman et al. (2010), p. 72. According to Schuman et al., the enterprising family is "one that has lived through successive generations of family business management and ownership, dealing effectively with the in-creasing complexity along the way" (Schuman et al. 2010, 72 in reference to Ward 2003, 78 f.).

249 Cf. Schuman et al. (2010), p. 72 ff.

250 Cf. Wimmer et al. (2004), p. 25.

251 Corbetta (1995), p. 259.

252 Cf. Wimmer (2007), p. 42.

253 Schuman et al. (2010), p. 1.

managers want to provide as much capital as possible to the enterprise, the shareholders are interested in the highest possible dividend.[254] The greatest potential for conflict exists in the second or third generation as it becomes necessary to distribute ownership and management from the pioneer to usually several descendants.[255] Above all, due to the increased number of members, certain structures, communication paths, and coordination mechanisms must be developed. Lone wolf behavior, as the pioneer entrepreneur lived (previously), is no longer in demand and appropriate in this phase. The individual family members must work together as a team to ensure survival.[256] Especially in family businesses that have existed for several generations, the family, and thus also the circle of shareholders have usually grown with each generation. This development also implies a decrease in the necessary technical knowledge and leadership competence of individual members for the family business. This includes, among other things, detailed knowledge of the enterprise's subject matter, market conditions, and leadership.[257]

Even if a separation between the living and working area has usually taken place in larger family businesses, according to Simon, there is still no complete separation between the contexts in most cases. This is particularly noticeable in the mixing of communication. Therefore, the family business can still take up a significant portion of the family's conversations.[258] The following Table 2.2 illustrates the potential consequences of an increasing weakening of the connection between family and business. This was taken from Sundaramurthy and Kreiner[259] and presents two possible identities of family businesses and the resulting consequences for different areas. The illustration can also be interpreted in terms of the direction in which the development of the two frames of reference is taking place due to the growth in size, the more generational stock, and what consequences this may have for the family business.

The two identities can be seen as two endpoints of a spectrum (see Table 2.2). In between, there is a multitude of other possibilities. The form that is in the

[254] Cf. Schuman et al. (2010), p. 1.

[255] Cf. Simon et al. (2005), p. 209.

[256] Cf. Gersick et al. (1997), p. 154.

[257] Cf. LeMar (2014), p. 76.

[258] Cf. Simon (2008a), p. 59.

[259] Cf. Sundaramurthy and Kreiner (2008), p. 419.

Table 2.2 The segmentation-integration continuum of family business[260]

Integrated identities between family and business	**Segmented identities** between family and business
Image	
–Strong association/overlap between names –Acknowledgement of family-owned status in marketing/advertising	–Distinct family and business names –No mention of family-owned status in marketing/advertising
Culture	
–Several artifacts (e.g., pictures of founder) –More informal, "family" atmosphere –Higher commitment to family values –Free cross-realm talk	–No artifacts of founding family in business –More formalized, "corporate" atmosphere –Higher commitment to business values –No cross-realm talk within and about both realms
Personnel	
–Extensive family employment –Family membership critical in hiring –Family employees at high levels –Compensation based on "needs" –Appraisal aimed at identifying high performers	–Limited number of family employees –Family membership not a critical hiring criterion –High managerial positions held by nonfamily –Compensation based on merit and market rates –Appraisal does not discriminate between high [and] low performers
Ownership and governance	
–Substantial family stock ownership –Decision-making controlled by family –Many family board members	–Sizable nonfamily stock ownership –Decision-making not exclusively controlled by family –Many family board members

(continued)

260 Source: Sundaramurthy and Kreiner (2008), p. 419.

Table 2.2 (continued)

Integrated identities between family and business	**Segmented identities** between family and business
Financial and contractual relationships with family	
–Free flow from family to business and vice versa –Web of contractual relations between the business and family	–Limited intermingling of family and business finances –Limited contractual relations between business and business owned by family

middle of the continuum Sundaramurthy and Kreiner call "differential permeability"[261]. This occurs within and between the mentioned areas (image, culture, personnel, etc.) of the family business identity. The extent to which the basic values and beliefs of the business and the family overlap also says something about how pronounced the connection between the family and the business is.[262]

Therefore, when looking at the business family, it should always be considered at which stage of development the family business is as it is characterized by different family types,[263] and thus a different context or life world exists for the socialization of the entrepreneurial children. However, it should be noted that the developments presented in this chapter are to be understood as ideal types. Since every family business is individual and unique, this development takes place somewhat differently in each one. Thus, the participation of several families in a family business is not necessarily required. The family business can be passed on to only one descendant at each generational change. Simon refers to this as the "re-enactment of the nuclear family from generation to

---

[261] Sundaramurthy and Kreiner (2008), p. 420. Regarding "differential permeability", Sundaramurthy and Kreiner write the following: "We define the state of differential permeability as the firm containing some elements of integration and some elements of segmentation. Our assertion of this phenomenon existing at the organizational level is consistent with previous research on identity and boundaries at the individual level, which has demonstrated how multiple identities can be both integrated and segmented within the same person" (Sundaramurthy and Kreiner 2008, 440).

[262] Cf. Sundaramurthy and Kreiner (2008), p. 419 ff. How the "bond" between family and business can be maintained, is described by Kormann (2011) in his work. In detail, he deals with various forms of bonds that the family members and shareholders can have to the business: (1) through the material benefit, (2) through the preservation of assets, (3) through a fair constitution, (4) through offices that relate to the business, (5) through communication, and (6) through the respective history.

[263] Cf. Simon (2012), p. 64 f.

generation" [264]. Thus, the nuclear family appears as a shareholder of a family business either until the second generation from the founding or it is maintained by a strict succession regulation through inheritance to only one descendant.[265] Of course, there is no need for inheritance to several descendants if the family business is not profitable enough. Then, if at all, it is only passed on to one descendant, whereby the structures are probably kept like those of the founding enterprise. Likewise, the family business can be fully handed over to external managers in the first generation and the active participation of subsequent generations may therefore no longer be necessary. If the focus is on the socialization of descendants along each generation, it will take different forms in each generation as the family business has different dynamics and requirements in each generation, and thus places different demands on the family. However, according to Simon[266], it can be assumed that the smaller the number of possible successors, the greater the psychological dilemmas that the descendants may be exposed to.

2.3 The Concept of Familiness and Enterpriseness

As described under Sect. 2.1, the close link between the family and the business can be seen as a characteristic feature of a family business. The family exerts its influence on the enterprise and vice versa so that the occurrence of conflicts and paradoxes is very likely. However, and this also became clear, it is not always clearly recognizable when or whether in a specific case one can speak of a family business.

The second part then presented the different stages of development of a family business or a business family. It became apparent what dynamics the family and the business are exposed to through their connection. Different demands are placed on the family in each generation, which in turn has an impact on the socialization of the descendants. Although the heterogeneity of this type of enterprise has become clear due to the differentiation by generation, i.e., the age and size of the enterprise, a differentiation based on other theory-led criteria appears indispensable.

While family businesses gain their uniqueness through the inclusion of the family in the business or in entrepreneurial matters, the difficulty lies in clearly

---

[264] Simon (2012), p. 75. Simon et al. (2005, 48–62) go into detail on the re-enactment of the nuclear family.

[265] Cf. Rüsen (2009), p. 126.

[266] Cf. Simon (2012), p. 106.

defining them.[267] In the attempts to define family businesses Colli also speaks of the "'concept too many'" [268], i.e., despite the quantitative and qualitative approaches, it is not possible to establish a fitting uniform definition of a family business with a general claim.[269] There are almost as many definitions as there are authors who have dealt with this topic.[270] Therefore, this chapter takes up the concept of familiness. This initially allows the representation of the intensity of the family's influence on the business. In addition, theory-based conclusions can be drawn about the stage of development of the family business or to what extent/if it can be considered a family business at all. This is followed by a discussion of the concept of enterpriseness. This is particularly relevant for the focus chosen in this work as it allows a statement about the influence of the enterprise on the family, and thus on the internal family processes, which in turn influence the socialization of the entrepreneurial children.

2.3.1 Familiness in Family Businesses

The competitive advantages (resources) of a specific family business are declared by Habbershon and Williams[271] with the term "'familiness'" [272]. Therefore, when considering familiness, it enables the exploration of the peculiarities or characteristics of a family business. However, the focus is not on the ownership structure or the leadership of family members in management, nor on the control instances. Familiness rather considers the way in which the family business is influenced by the family involved and what consequences this may have, for example, for the ability to innovate or competitive advantages. Familiness thus considers the influence of the family on the family business and its impact on behavior.[273] According to Frank et al. [274], familiness is one of the most central concepts in the field of family business research, whereby familiness has manifest and latent

[267] Cf. Chua et al. (1999), p. 19.

[268] Colli (2003), p. 19.

[269] Cf. Colli (2003), p. 19.

[270] Cf. Venter and Kruger (2004), p. 2.

[271] Cf. Habbershon and Williams (1999), p. 11. For an overview of the studies conducted on familiness, see: *Irava*, W. J. & *Moores*, K. (2010): Clarifying the strategic advantage of familiness: Unbundling its dimensions and highlighting its paradoxes, in: *Journal of Family Business Strategy*, 1 (3), 131–144.

[272] Habbershon and Williams (1999), p. 11.

[273] Cf. Süss and Weismeier-Sammer (2013), p. 60.

[274] Cf. Frank et al. (2010b), p. 119.

characteristics. The concept attempts to answer the question, to what extent family businesses differ from other types of enterprises. Von Schlippe describes the advantages that arise from the influence of the family in the family business as "positive familiness" [275]. This implies that family businesses can draw on family resources such as knowledge, reputation, long-term business orientation, etc.[276] However, familiness should not only be understood as having a positive influence on the family business. If familiness is not "nurtured and nourished", it quickly develops a destructive force in relation to the family business.[277] For this reason, Habbersohn and Williams also distinguish between "distinctive familiness"[278] and "constrictive familiness" [279] with the former describing the positive influence of family involvement in the family business.[280]

In other words, familiness describes to what extent the structures, norms, and values of the family business are influenced by the structures, norms, and values of the family(ies).[281] In this context, familiness means a non-imitable set of resources of a specific family business, which is determined by the interaction of the family, its members, and the business.[282] For Frank et al.[283] familiness requires, among other things, the following conditions:

1. There must be a connection between the family and business system.
2. The connection must have a certain degree of stability, which results in a perceptible identity as a family business. However, the family business does not have to be aware of all identity-forming qualities.

Subsequently, however, the question arises as to how the "familiness" of a family business can be "measured". One possibility arises through the "F-PEC Scale"[284]

---

[275] von Schlippe (2011b), p. 1.

[276] Cf. von Schlippe (2011b), p. 1.

[277] Cf. Venter and Kruger (2004), p. 6.

[278] Habbershon and Williams (1999), p. 13. See also: *Chrisman*, J. J.; *Chua*, J. H. & *Steier*, L. (2005): Sources and Consequences of Distinctive Familiness: An Introduction, in: *Entrepreneurship Theory and Practice*, 29 (3), 237–247.

[279] Habbershon and Williams (1999), p. 13.

[280] Cf. Pearson et al. (2008), p. 950.

[281] Cf. Weismeier-Sammer (2014), p. 104.

[282] Cf. Habbershon and Williams (1999), p. 11.

[283] Cf. Frank et al. (2010b), p. 128.

[284] In detail, the F-PEC scale includes three clearly delineated dimensions: Power, Experience, and Culture, which measure the family's influence on the business. Each of these

developed by Astrachan et al.[285] According to Zwack, Astrachan et al. thus soften "the dichotomous distinction family business/non-family business" [286]. On the other hand, Pfannenschwarz criticizes the applicability of the F-PEC scale: "A number of questions remain. Even if one does not further problematize the structure and logic of the F-PEC, the feeling remains that one has not necessarily come closer to the *essence* of family businesses."[287] Similarly, Zellweger et al.[288] criticize the objective and standardized possibility of data collection. They see the F-PEC scale more as an empirical scale to depict different types of family involvement. For this reason, they themselves provide a model that differs from the F-PEC scale in two points:

1. They explain how the different dimensions of familiness overlap, and
2. they understand the "family firm identity"[289] as one of the key elements for the creation of familiness.

The approach of Zellweger et al. will be discussed in detail subsequently.

In their contribution[290] Zellweger et al.[291] therefore try to answer the question *how the family contributes to business success* or, in other words, *what different possibilities exist for the family to become involved in the family business.* For this purpose, they expand the existing construct of familiness by a third dimension, the "organizational identity". Specifically, the organizational identity shows

---

dimensions includes further subcategories. As a result, an index of family influence is created, which allows the comparability of different family businesses. This allows the different levels of family involvement in the business and the resulting effects on performance to be measured across businesses. An advantage is therefore also the possibility of objective and standardized collection of family businesses (cf. Astrachan et al. 2002, 47).

[285] *Astrachan*, J. H.; *Klein*, S. B. & *Smyrnios*, K. X. (2002): The F-PEC scale of family influence: A proposal for solving the family business definition problem, in: *Family Business Review*, 15 (1), 45–58.

[286] Zwack (2011), p. 14.

[287] Pfannenschwarz (2006a), p. 28.

[288] Cf. Zellweger et al. (2010), p. 61.

[289] Zellweger et al. (2010), p. 61.

[290] *Zellweger*, T. M.; *Eddleston*, K. A. & *Kellermanns*, F. W. (2010): Exploring the concept of familiness: Introducing family firm identity, in: *Journal of Family Business Strategy*, 1 (1), 54–63.

[291] Cf. Zellweger et al. (2010), p. 54 f.

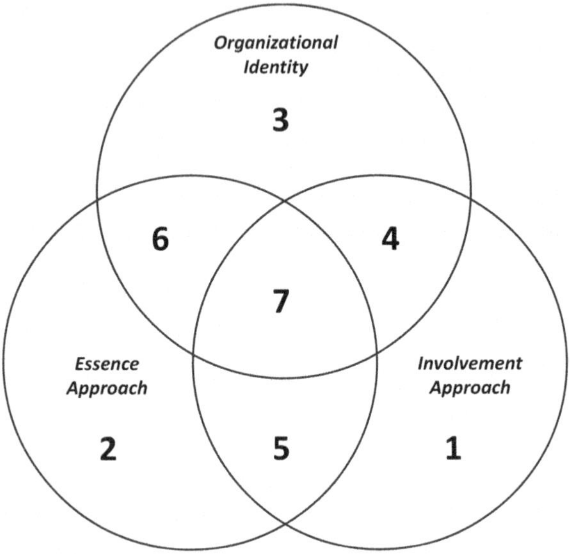

Fig. 2.2 The three-dimensional model[293]

how the family defines or views the family business (from an internal and external perspective). From the combination results the following "Three-Dimensional Model"[292] in Fig. 2.2.

The Three-Dimensional Model (see Fig. 2.2) offers the opportunity to examine the potential of a family business for the manifestations of familiness or to make statements about it.[294] Using the model by Zellweger et al. it is thus possible, to describe seven manifestations of familiness. In the opinion of

[292] Zellweger et al. (2010), p. 60.

[293] Source: Zellweger et al. (2010), p. 59. Zellweger et al. (2010), p. 59 use the term "Components Approach" for sector 1.

[294] Cf. Zellweger et al. (2010), p. 60. Zellweger et al. describe the individual dimensions as follows: "In other words, the components of involvement dimension captures the presence of the family in the firm, the essence approach captures family members behavior in the firm, and the organizational identity dimension reflects how the family defines the firm and how the firm operates as a whole" (Zellweger et al. 2010, 60). However, the essence cannot exist without the involvement. Involvement is therefore an indispensable feature of a family business while essence is not necessarily present in all family businesses (cf. Chrisman et al. 2010, 286).

Frank et al. [295] this results in a significant gain in analysis. The special features of the seven sectors are explained in Table 2.3.

By assigning or locating an enterprise to a sector, a statement can be made about its ability to generate familiness. This multidimensional perspective of the model on the aspect of the family also opens the possibility to represent the diversity of business families. Thus, an explanatory approach is provided why some families become the key resources of their enterprises and others hardly or not at all. In addition, the concept provides insights into how non-family businesses can build a certain degree of familiness. They can imitate some elements that are otherwise considered a unique feature of family businesses.[296] In conclusion: If the family does not appear united and as an identity-forming factor in the business, it will hardly be referred to as a family business.[297] Especially, the knowledge about the different forms (types) of business families as well as the distribution of interests, commitment, and the relationships within the family and the business make it possible to say something about the behavior and performance within the family business.[298] Against the background of the prevailing connection and the ongoing mutual influencing evolution, the extent of familiness should also provide insights into the intensity of enterpriseness within the business family. This in turn allows to depict the influence of the enterprise on the socialization of the descendants. Subsequently, enterpriseness will be discussed in detail.

2.3.2 Enterpriseness in Business Families

After the concept of familiness has been presented, the perspective is changed and the influence of the business on the family is considered. Especially against the background of the focus set in this work (influence of the business context on the socialization of the descendants /successors), this perspective legitimizes or makes it indispensable. The influence of the business on the family sphere is

[295] Cf. Frank et al. (2010b), p. 121.

[296] Cf. Zellweger et al. (2010), p. 60 f.

[297] Cf. Wimmer (2004), p. 268.

[298] Cf. Chrisman et al. (2007), p. 1006.

Table 2.3 Sectors in the three-dimensional model[299]

Sector 1 *Involvement* (family involvement-only firms) focuses on ownership and control. This dimension has its greatest influence on factors such as monetary incentive systems, risk tolerance, and profit distribution. The pure form of participation is especially found in large enterprises, where the typical resources of a family business are limited. As an example, Zellweger et al. mention an investment holding in which a family is involved, but no family member holds a management function. In this case, the family influence is limited and the enterprise is not necessarily seen as a family business. The enterprise rather serves the wealth of the family members. In this case, however, familiness is limited as the influence of the family is restricted to financial capital.
Sector 2 *Essence* (Essence-only firms) focuses on aspects of behavior, resource allocation, and usage. The essence provides information about the family's support for the enterprise and any conflict that arises between work and family. An example of a purely essence-only firm could be a restaurant owner who employs family members (unpaid) for work. In addition, the owner does not perceive the business as a family business, nor do other family members own shares in the enterprise. Even if the wife or children help, the owner (father) sees this as his business. Although the enterprise has some advantages of familiness (contributions of family members in daily business operations), the enterprise does not benefit from the components of familiness such as family-led management or the identity of a family business.
Sector 3 *Identity* (family firm identity-only firms) emphasizes the perception of the enterprise as a family business. Organizational identity has an influence on the interface between family and business that should not be underestimated. An example could be an enterprise founded by an entrepreneur with the aim of passing it on to his child who joins it. Another example could be a business owner who has already taken over the enterprise from his father and in which no other family members work or hold shares. As can be seen, both examples describe enterprises in which neither other family members are employed, nor does anyone else in the family hold shares in the enterprise. Although the entrepreneurs see their enterprise as a family business, the factor of familiness is limited as they forego management and control by the family and therefore these enterprises lack the family's participation.
Sector 4 Families that combine the dimensions of *involvement* and *identity* within their enterprise can consider it a family business. They use family control to influence decision-making, but without a family-oriented strategy, i.e., without the essence of the family, and thus without a cross-generational vision. Therefore, the enterprise will also never be able to take advantage of the full benefits of family influence — be it selfless acts or family support.

(continued)

[299] Source: Based on Zellweger et al. (2010), p. 60 f.

Table 2.3 (continued)

Sector 5 Here the components of *involvement* and *essence* are combined. Examples include IKEA and Wal-Mart. These types of enterprises are supported and controlled by the family, but they do not make a conscious effort to connect the family image with the products offered. Rather, these enterprises try to avoid the image of a family business due to the protection of their privacy. Without the family identity, these enterprises lack the common vision and the benefits of family influence. Especially smaller enterprises that fall into this category, cannot claim external social capital and the goodwill of consumers for themselves. For this reason, a designation as a family business does not seem justified.
Sector 6 Enterprises in this category combine the *essence* and the *identity* and present themselves as family-like. For example, all the employees who work there are seen as one big family. Smaller enterprises announce their family-like culture in advertising messages and explain to consumers what the employees do to satisfy the customers. This category is interesting in terms of how non-family businesses try to use familiness for competitiveness in the market.
Sector 7 Enterprises that combine all three dimensions (*identity, involvement, and essence*) have the best starting point for creating familiness. They can create synergies between the family and the business, which then increases the performance of the family business. Enterprises in this category involve the family, reflect the essence of the family, and perceive themselves as a family business. Thus, the enterprise benefits from the various advantages of family influence and therefore captures the benefits of involving the family in the enterprise. This sector can be found in enterprises that also present themselves externally as a family business.

termed "enterpriseness" by Frank et al.[300] Based on their definition of familiness[301] enterpriseness is defined as follows: *Enterpriseness can be understood as the manifest and latent rule system, which in addition to the quality of the prevailing connection between family and business also takes into account their historical development, which is an expression of problem solving and dealing with crises.* Enterpriseness therefore says something about the extent to which the behavioral rules of the business are integrated into the family and therefore no longer

[300] Frank et al. (2010b), p. 124.

[301] "Familiness can be described and reconstructed as a manifest and latent rule system, which focuses on the quality of the structural coupling of family and enterprise and their specific, historically grown contents, which are the expression of problem solving and handling crises successfully" (Frank et al. 2010b, 129).

perceived as irritations.[302] However, to be able to speak of enterpriseness or to assume that it exists, reference is made again to the conditions for familiness mentioned by Frank et al. These should also apply vice versa.[303]

However, in addition to the size of the enterprise, its life cycle and the generation involved must also be considered when determining the intensity of the influence (see Sect. 2.2). In a figurative sense, the Three-Dimensional Model (see Fig. 2.2) can explain or "measure" the intensity of enterpriseness. The type of enterpriseness says something about the life cycle of the business family and subsequently about the influence of the enterprise on the socialization of the descendants.

2.3.2.1 Definition of Enterpriseness

As already described, business families are connected to their enterprise. Both frames of reference mutually influence each other in their evolution and have a reciprocal dependency, as each context relies on the performance of the other. In this context, one can speak of a co-evolution. This also implies a coordination of actions based on the needs of the other area.[304] Against this background, members of a business family have a "dual role". They are both members of the family and the business,[305] which, as already described, has the potential for conflicts and paradoxes.[306] Especially since the enterprise often represents the life content for the respective entrepreneur, this or business-relevant topics find their way into private/family life.[307] Therefore, the family often feels inseparably connected to their business. Iannarelli[308] also concludes from her own experience as a member of a family business that traditions, emotions, and values are maintained in this context and it is very difficult to separate the family within a family business from the business. The enterprise often sets the priorities. This makes focusing on a pure family life mostly impossible.[309] Unlike employees who can separate work and private life, the family business is the center of life and is therefore usually present in all areas due to the lack of context markers

[302] In their article (Frank et al. 2010b) they describe this only for *familiness*, but this should also apply vice versa for *enterpriseness*.

[303] Cf. Frank et al. (2010b), p. 128, or under Sect. 2.3.1.

[304] Cf. Simon (2012), p. 22 f.

[305] Cf. Memili et al. (2015), p. 143.

[306] Cf. Beehr et al. (1997), p. 298.

[307] Cf. Meyer (2007), p. 11.

[308] Cf. Iannarelli (1992), p. 156.

[309] Cf. Wimmer et al. (2005), p. 192.

(see Sect. 2.1.4).[310] For this reason, in many cases, the family structure adapts to the requirements of the business.[311] The family often puts its expectations back in the interest of the family business.[312] Felden formulates this as follows: "Business families are shaped in their everyday life by the events in the enterprise. The enterprise is opened before breakfast, the employee is visited in the hospital on Sundays, and the competition is watched over the shoulder on vacation."[313] Since the family business usually represents the family's livelihood, individual and private concerns usually take a back seat. This allows the entire family energy to be focused on the development of the family business, which then represents a tremendous competitive advantage.[314] In this context, the owner generation often has a "double bond", i.e., it feels obligated to at least two generations:

1. The children, as they take responsibility for their well-being, and
2. the generation from which they received the enterprise (usually the parents).

Above all, attachment to parents as well as internalization of family tradition can reduce the likelihood of a business sale, even beyond the death of parents.[315]

Usually, the business has the same degree of influence on the family (enterpriseness) as the family has on the business (familiness). Specifically, ensuring the continuation of the business can be meaningful for the family, bring about a disciplining of relationship dynamics, and strengthen the bond between family members.[316] Meanwhile, the influence of the business on the family is influenced, among other things, by the leadership style and the way the boundaries and possibilities of the family business are conveyed to the family. Since the family business is connected with the family, there are many ways the enterprise can influence the dynamics of the business family. However, this does not inevitably lead to stressful situations, but can imply various forms of dilemmas for the family involved in the family business.[317] In business families, there is often an additional connection that promotes the cohesion of the family. This

---

[310] Cf. Meyer (2007), p. 11.

[311] Cf. Frank and Hasenzagl (2005), p. 37.

[312] Cf. Simon (2012), p. 22 f.

[313] Felden (2012), p. 145 and cf. Stamm (2013), p. 190.

[314] Cf. Domayer and Oswald (1994), p. 10 f.

[315] Cf. Froschauer and Lueger (2012), p. 112.

[316] Cf. Wimmer et al. (2005), p. 11 and cf. Wimmer and Gebauer (2004), p. 246.

[317] Cf. Kepner (1983), p. 65.

"bond"[318] is the enterprise; "something third, the common task, the enterprise" [319]. The family business can exert a certain (positive) discipline on the various dynamics of the family.[320] While members of non-business families are usually "only" connected through love for each other, business families therefore have a second connection, the common family business, which requires or enforces the cohesion of the family.[321]

When specifically considering marriage to an entrepreneur, some authors speak of a "marriage in threesome"[322], i.e., the enterprise and husband are often inseparably linked, and thus both shape private life from the start. The usual separation between private and professional spheres is not present. This can lead to a dominance of enterprise-relevant topics in the private sphere at the expense of private life.[323] Similarly, the woman is usually integrated into the "total artwork" [324], where the enterprise contributes to the consolidation of the relationship.[325] According to Simon[326] it makes a difference, whether the parents are employed at one or at separate workplaces as in the second case the family can be seen as a "compensatory counter-world to work" [327]. This compensatory counter-world does not predominantly exist in business families. According to von Schlippe [328], the family business takes on an "omnipresence" in business families, and thus penetrates all areas of family communication. According to Simon, the family business is an "emotionally significant factor that focuses all family members on a common topic and binds them together, [...]" [329]. In relation to the family sphere, the family business or topics from the day-to-day business often take up a disproportionate share of family communication. Thus, personal concerns may be

---

[318] Wimmer et al. (2005), p. 199.

[319] See footnote 318.

[320] Cf. Wimmer et al. (2005), p. 199.

[321] Cf. LeMar (2014), p. 21.

[322] Wimmer et al. (2005), p. 267; cf. Domayer and Vater (1995), p. 151 and cf. Domayer and Vater (1994), p. 10 as well as p. 26.

[323] Cf. Wimmer et al. (2005), p. 267 f.

[324] Domayer and Oswald (1994), p. 10.

[325] Cf. Domayer and Vater (1995), p. 151.

[326] Cf. Simon (2005), p. 9.

[327] Simon (2005), p. 9.

[328] Cf. von Schlippe (2009), p. 17.

[329] Simon (2008a), p. 59 and cf. Wimmer (2008b), p. 110.

neglected.[330] Since the enterprise usually becomes the entrepreneur's life content, family and personal matters often recede into the background or are neglected.[331]

Furthermore, the family business can also serve as a "corrective factor"[332] for a failed family coexistence. This means that if the cohabitation within the family is too close (too loose), an attempt is made in the enterprise to keep more distance (to come closer together).[333] The common task also creates a particularly strong sense of belonging.[334] The family bond within the family business usually implies an unusual motivation, a high degree of loyalty, and trust between family members.[335] Based on an analysis of the existing literature, Eddleston and Morgan[336] identify trust, commitment, and the close relationships as essential factors that contribute to the success and longevity of a family business. However, "personal costs"[337] can arise for each member, which appear in different forms and with which the family will eventually have to deal with.[338] In this context, business families often operate according to the motto "common good before self-interest" [339], i.e., there are certain expectations or self-evident facts for the work commitment, lifestyle, and even the choice of the right partner. A corresponding return is not expected.[340] Often there is a subliminal "promise for the future" [341]. This promises a "reward" for all the sacrifices made.[342]

In addition, business families show certain stability characteristics for the interfamily bond compared to non-business families. These are usually long-term, i.e., multi-generational with a claim to a certain sustainability.[343] Since securing the continuation is of primary importance, individualization tendencies

---

330 Cf. Domayer and Oswald (1994), p. 10.

331 Cf. Baumgartner (2009), p. 14 and cf. Domayer and Oswald (1994), p. 13.

332 Klein (2004), p. 77.

333 Cf. Klein (2004), p. 77.

334 Cf. Domayer and Oswald (1994), p. 10.

335 Cf. Tagiuri and Davis (1996), p. 204.

336 Cf. Eddleston and Morgan (2014), p. 213.

337 Wimmer et al. (2005), p. 11.

338 Cf. Wimmer et al. (2005), p. 11.

339 Domayer and Vater (1994), p. 27.

340 Cf. Domayer and Vater (1994), p. 27.

341 Wimmer et al. (2005), p. 268.

342 Cf. Wimmer et al. (2005), p. 268.

343 Cf. Wimmer et al. (2005), p. 206.

of individual members are rather viewed with aversion.[344] Often, children from business families are therefore given two contradictory messages. Welter-Enderlin describes this as follows: "Acquire education, grow beyond your parents, and expand your professional experience — preferably abroad — but remain loyal to the business and the family at the same time."[345] The parents are, so to speak, in a dilemma between promoting the independence of the descendants and maintaining the bond to the family business. This can also be reflected in the not or only subliminally communicated desire for succession on the part of the parents.[346]

Furthermore, the two reference frames family and business mutually serve as identity-forming contexts. This usually results in a close link between the reputation of the family and that of the business.[347] Due to the connection, the reputation of the family business can also affect the identity of the family members and promote their cohesion.[348] This is usually reinforced by a possible name similarity. These peculiarities promote structural characteristics and act like a catalyst on the willingness to perform.[349] The family feels responsible for the protection and projection of their image of a well-functioning closed family, thereby not allowing the everyday conflicts and tensions to arise.[350] Everyone must be able to rely on everyone and support must not be asked for. The own well-being is placed behind the welfare of the community and the family business. This individual sacrifice is often demanded by all. Any action must be coordinated with the family business and its future. Therefore, acts that serve the personal interest of the members are often seen as unsuitable.[351]

However, due to this interconnection, family members may feel observed both within and outside the family business, which they may perceive as a restriction of their freedom.[352] According to Simon [353], this very connection between the two contexts and the usually associated alignment of the family with the business interests creates an identification platform for the business family. Therefore, "this type of business, for psychological as well as economic reasons, represents a

[344] Cf. Domayer and Vater (1994), p. 27.
[345] Welter-Enderlin (2005), p. 147.
[346] Cf. Schröder et al. (2010), p. 97 f.
[347] Cf. Wimmer (2008a), p. 13 and cf. Wimmer (2008b), p. 111.
[348] Cf. Wimmer (2008b), p. 111.
[349] Cf. Wimmer (2008a), p. 13 and cf. Wimmer (2007), p. 36 f.
[350] Cf. Kepner (1983), p. 65.
[351] Cf. Domayer and Vater (1995), p. 152.
[352] Cf. Tagiuri and Davis (1996), p. 203.
[353] Cf. Simon et al. (2005), p. 49.

model that is hard to beat" [354]. In addition, the strong identification of the family with the business is expressed in the willingness to take certain risks, which is reflected, among other things, in the personal liability.[355] In this context, LeMar speaks of a possible "negative feedback"[356] of actions taken within the family business on the family. For example, if an investment in the enterprise has been made that does not pay off, there may be a need to balance this with private assets.

When difficulties and conflicts are considered, there is generally the problem of expansion from the enterprise to the participating family(ies).[357] Particularly business pressure can contribute to a deterioration of the family climate. This in turn causes tensions, anger, or despair, which can even lead to the downfall of otherwise well-positioned family businesses.[358] Thus, the family depends on a positive development of the business. The success of the family business is not only measured in material terms, but is rather expressed in immaterial amenities.[359] Thus, a well-established enterprise can also have a positive influence on the family by, for example, enhancing the self-esteem of the members and strengthening the cohesion within the family [360] although this can of course also swing in the other direction. How close the relationship or the connection between the two contexts is, is influenced by how much the entrepreneur involves the family in business-relevant matters and how family matters are addressed within the business. It also makes a difference, whether one or both parents work in the enterprise and how far the work and living areas are spatially separated from each other.[361]

---

[354] Simon et al. (2005), p. 49.

[355] Cf. Meyer (2007), p. 11.

[356] LeMar (2014), p. 35.

[357] Cf. LeMar (2014), p. 32 ff.

[358] Cf. Gersick et al. (1997), p. 3.

[359] Cf. Wimmer (2007), p. 34. How corporate success is evaluated in terms of gender is examined by Dej et al. (2010, p. 48 ff.) in their study (n=243 respondents; 57 women and 186 men). There are significant differences in the mean value for the following success criteria in particular: (1) Work relationships (0.89 f(emale)/0.66 m(ale)), (2) Self-realization (0.42 f/0.57 m), (3) Social success (0.26 f/0.13 m), (4) Enterprise performance (0.61 f/0.88 m), and (5) Personal reward (0.18 f/0.06 m).

[360] Cf. Kormann (2011), p. 14.

[361] Cf. Habig and Berninghaus (2004), p. 25.

When the focus is on the children of entrepreneurs, they are usually involved in the daily work.[362] An example of enterpriseness is a family that attaches importance to a certain education for its children. This education then benefits the enterprise during succession. For instance, the children could undergo technical education to drive the technological development of the family business.[363] Specifically, the preparation of succession often represents a challenging time for business families. There is, among other things, a requirement on the part of the entrepreneur to identify a suitable successor. However, this is often preceded by the need to employ the next generation in the family business. The entrepreneur occupies a central position, as he is responsible for assigning work roles to family members.[364] The family's ties to their business in particular make it possible to impart certain views of life to their children at an early age. Of course, this is significantly influenced by how much the young people are involved in various discussions and provided with background information.[365] Similarly, in some business families, the enterprise occupies such a central position that the children can only gain parental attention if they themselves work in the family business (even at a young age).[366]

2.3.2.2 Family Governance as a Form of Enterpriseness

According to Gersick et al.[367], within some business families there are certain assumptions about the family and their business that represent forms of enterpriseness (see also [I.11]):

1. To be considered a true family member, it is essential to work in the family business. This also implies less attention, status, and family identity for those who refuse.
2. There is an obligation to join the family business. This is communicated subtly. If the decision against succession is made, it gives the impression of being disloyal to the parents.
3. If the younger generation does not join the family business, it is doomed to fail. Under this assumption, the children are attributed a potential that they cannot always fulfill.

---

[362] Cf. Wimmer et al. (2005), p. 195.

[363] Cf. Frank et al. (2010b), p. 125.

[364] Cf. Cooper et al. (2013), p. 460.

[365] Cf. Wimmer et al. (2005), p. 205.

[366] Cf. Gersick et al. (1997), p. 77.

[367] Cf. Gersick et al. (1997), p. 164.

Looking again at the cross-generational relationship, this special bond arises due to shared ownership and exerts its influence on the dynamics within the family. The conditions for the family change depending on the life cycle of the enterprise.[368] Froschauer and Lueger[369] identify various cross-generational obligations in their case study that create a bond not to be underestimated. The transfer performance taking place in this context is not only directed at the specific (phase of) handover. Rather, it tries to keep the family and business history present. This can be achieved through the following points:

1. *The obligation of the current generation of owners towards their descendants:* This includes the well-being of the descendants, good educational opportunities, the handover of a sustainable enterprise, and the provision for descendants who do not take over the succession.
2. *The obligation on the part of the successors to continue the tradition of the family business:* This is promoted by the continued support of the parents after the handover by making their experiences available and the often-high degree of intertwining between work and private life. Also, the longer the family business has already existed, the higher is the (expectation) pressure to continue the business successfully. Often, this claim is so internalized that no further external influence is needed.
3. *The obligation to support each other:* This includes all persons who are actively or will in the future play a role within the family business. Although, the decision-making authority lies with the current generation of owners, the older generation can serve as a competent contact.

As can be seen from the introductory argumentation, certain assumptions or obligations can exist in business families (directly or indirectly) that often only arise through the connection with the enterprise and have a significant impact on the family as well as the socialization of the descendants. Subsequently, another way in which the family business influences intra-family dynamics is discussed. The family governance in particular represents an "official" means to legitimize the enterpriseness and increase the solidarity towards the family business.

According to Lueger et al., "family governance efforts can be seen as an expression of an instrumental relationship management"[370]. Family governance

[368] Cf. Simon (2005), p. 35.

[369] Cf. Froschauer and Lueger (2012), p. 110 f.

[370] Lueger et al. (2012a), p. 221.

includes, among other things, the following measures: "Family meetings, family constitutions, (family) advisory boards, emergency plans, and mediation."[371] Depending on how broadly the measures are understood, this also includes a code of conduct for family members. There are also criteria for how family members are selected if they want to take up leadership positions within the family business as well as formal mechanisms for the communication of the business family.[372] Thus, family governance can contribute to controlling the family's influence. For example, it regulates how the family business is protected from the influence of family members who do not work in the enterprise. Family governance promotes the institutionalization and channeling of expectations, particularly when different expectations for the management of the family business exist due to the number of family members. This then becomes valid for all members of the family and provides a guide. This also contributes to a reduction of conflicts.[373] In addition, family governance clarifies what expectations the members of the family are exposed to from the enterprise and what they can expect from the family business in return. According to Aronoff and Ward [374], family governance should, among other things, focus on the following family matters:

1. Establishment of a family strategy or establishment of agreements on how behaviors, actions, or decisions are regulated.
2. Definition of a family mission and vision.
3. Justification of a strategy for family ownership. This then provides the starting point for the corporate culture and objectives, the capital allocation, the rights and obligations of the shareholders.
4. Provision of solutions for conflicts within the family.

In summary, family governance measures contribute to supporting the future-oriented development of a family business by establishing structures.[375] Thus, the introduction of family governance can strengthen not only the cohesion of the business family, but also the harmony within the family. In addition, it contributes, among other things, to securing the family's influence and to strengthening

371 Süss-Reyes (2015a), p. 16. For a more detailed description, see Lueger and Süss-Reyes (2015, p. 217 ff.) as well as Süss-Reyes (2015a, p. 16 ff.).

372 Cf. Süss-Reyes (2015a), p. 23.

373 Cf. Weismeier-Sammer et al. (2012), p. 196 f.

374 Cf. Aronoff and Ward (2011), p. 29 f.

375 Cf. Lueger and Süss-Reyes (2015), p. 199.

the social responsibility for the employees.[376] According to Süss-Reyes, family governance measures are "means to balance and stabilize potentially diverging expectations between the family and the business system" [377]. Especially since different expectations and logics (see Table 2.1) prevail in the two frames of reference, the connection of these contexts has a certain conflict potential (see Sect. 2.1.3). Family governance measures therefore serve to regulate and direct the influence of the family on the business, which can lead to a balance of the ideas and behaviors of the family members. In general, the introduction of family governance measures promotes a formalization of the family and the business.[378] Especially since family governance has effects on the business family, it must also be assumed that it influences the socialization of the descendants. Therefore, it seemed necessary to go into detail on this in relation to the research question.

2.4 Succession in Family Businesses

Another special feature that is typical for family businesses is the parents' desire to pass on the enterprise to their descendants. This desire shapes the socialization of the growing children in a decisive way. Against the background of the chosen research question the topic of succession will therefore be addressed subsequently.

Is there the will of the parents to hand over the family business to the next generation one day, Habig and Berninghaus[379] recommend incorporating the preparation into the upbringing of the children. Through parental upbringing and involvement in the family business the children are introduced to entrepreneurship[380] by entrepreneurial skills being conveyed through upbringing or the subsequent education.[381] In this context, Stamm speaks of the "'pedagogy' of the succession" [382]. By this, she means the preparation of the descendants for a possible succession through upbringing measures.[383] However, parents should

376 Cf. Süss-Reyes (2015b), p. 141.

377 Süss-Reyes (2015b), p. 146.

378 Cf. Süss-Reyes (2015b), p. 146 f.

379 Cf. Habig and Berninghaus (2004), p. 29.

380 Cf. Gottschalk et al. (2010), p. 45.

381 Cf. Simon et al. (2005), p. 59 and cf. Habig and Berninghaus (2004), p. 57.

382 Stamm (2013), p. 315.

383 Cf. Stamm (2013), p. 315.

Interviews 2.8 Upbringing and entrepreneurial habitus [I.13]

[I.13]	Entrepreneur: "[...] in my view, the [woman's sons] are not entrepreneur types [.]. But this is largely due to the upbringing of entrepreneur children, parents should not be too generous. I think it's completely wrong if children have more money available during their school and student years than they need. This has an anti-upbringing effect — that's my opinion. Of course, you can help the children out, but there is a risk that they then lose their bite."[a]

[a]Juritsch et al. (2007), p. 74.

not try to shape their descendants in their own image, but rather act as role models.[384] Thus, an entrepreneur makes the following statement about upbringing (see Interviews 2.8 [I.13]):

How parental upbringing behavior is assessed from the perspective of the descendants is asked by Schmitt-Rodermund and Schröder[385] in their study. The following mean values emerge, with five being the maximum:

1. 4.21 promotion of personal responsibility
2. 4.03 experience of parental warmth
3. 3.78 promotion of independence
4. 3.65 giving space for children's stories[386]
5. 2.97 setting of rules

However, the focus on succession can impair the development of the descendants. In severe cases, the individual potentials of the chosen successors are not considered at all if they do not relate to the orientation of the family business.[387] This is then reflected in the subsequent (unconscious) behavior towards the growing children, which puts the descendants under enormous expectations and at the same time can hinder their individual development.[388]

Since not all descendants are (can be) chosen for a possible succession, an influence on the socialization process is very likely. García-Álvarez et al.[389]

[384] Cf. Habig and Berninghaus (2004), p. 29.

[385] Cf. Schmitt-Rodermund and Schröder (2009), p. 29 f. n=155 business families, of which 255 were teenagers. Average age 16.4 years.

[386] The "space for narratives" can have a positive effect on the parent-child relationship. This can form the basis for a trustful interaction (cf. Schmitt-Rodermund and Schröder 2009, 30).

[387] Cf. LeMar (2014), p. 112.

[388] Cf. Meyer (2007), p. 108 f.

[389] Cf. García-Álvarez et al. (2002), p. 189 ff.

therefore distinguish between the socialization of potential successors and non-successors. Specifically for the successors, they identify, based on their results, two general phases of socialization:

1. The one within the family to which all descendants are exposed. This includes the transmission of values and training.
2. Additionally, a subsequent business socialization, which, however, is only granted to the potential successors.

The family business also influences the socialization of the descendants when it comes to the choice of education (enterpriseness). Be it in the search for a suitable type of school or the "right" course of study. The decision is predominantly influenced by the possible function — be it as a manager or as a shareholder — in the enterprise.[390] Felden and Pfannenschwarz[391] assume both an unconscious as well as a conscious influence of the children by their parents to increase the probability of an internal family transfer of the family business. Thus, effects on the career and life paths of the descendants can become noticeable, which was already evident from the previous explanations (see Sect. 2.3.2). According to Kempert [392], the most intense entrepreneurial imprinting of children takes place between the ages of 10 and 15 years. If the parents manage to arouse or promote interest in the family business during this phase, there is an increased probability of internal family succession. To not hinder this decision, parents should avoid being a bad role model (e.g., as a workaholic or as a despot). In contrast to ownership, the "entrepreneurial habitus" [393], i.e., the ability to lead an enterprise cannot be inherited.[394]

As can be seen from these and the previous explanations, the issue of succession permeates all areas of life of a business family. Due to its importance, it also takes up a significant portion in the literature on family businesses (see Sect. 1.2). As has already been made clear in the previous comments, their influence should not be underestimated. Therefore, the following will focus on succession and its influence on the socialization of the descendants. After introducing the topic of succession, factors that oppose or promote succession will be highlighted.

---

[390] Cf. Kormann (2011), p. 92.

[391] Cf. Felden and Pfannenschwarz (2008), p. 120.

[392] Cf. Kempert (2008), p. 189.

[393] Caspary (2010), p. 231.

[394] Cf. Wimmer et al. (2005), p. 303.

2.4.1 Succession and its Influence on the Descendants

In family businesses is often a desire for continuity so that the enterprise should at least be handed over to a family member.[395] Especially in the succession process, the "systematically built-in potential for danger"[396] for the interaction of family and business is of particular importance.[397] The generational change may therefore be one of the greatest challenges for a business family and may require a huge adjustment of the family structures to cope with it.[398] For this reason, Kailer and Weiß consider the generational change to be one of the "neuralgic points in family businesses" [399]. In general, the question of continuation, and thus the necessity of a change in management arises approximately every 30 years. However, small enterprises in particular are often not continued after this period. The closure rate, however, decreases with increasing size.[400]

To ensure the long-term existence of the family business, there is predominantly a (subliminal) expectation within the family that the business will be taken over by at least one descendant. Therefore, it is not surprising if the wishes, inclinations, or suitability of the descendants are often not or only conditionally considered.[401] Moreover, during the enterprise handover, the family lineage is often prioritized over the qualification of the successor.[402] Likewise, the business environment is often — as far as this is possible at all — adapted to the children. Iannarelli therefore refers to the family business as a "career safety net" [403] as the parents create space for their children within the family business. Thus, they establish new product divisions or new businesses, sometimes regardless of the market economic requirements.[404] In general, according to Pfannenschwarz, the internal family succession is primarily associated with the following advantages and disadvantages for the successor (see Table 2.4).

---

[395] Cf. Wimmer and Gebauer (2004), p. 244.
[396] Wimmer (2004), p. 274.
[397] Cf. Wimmer (2004), p. 274.
[398] Cf. Wimmer et al. (2005), p. 235.
[399] Kailer and Weiß (2005), p. 13.
[400] Cf. Gottschalk et al. (2010), p. 16.
[401] Cf. Wimmer et al. (2005), p. 281.
[402] Cf. Bieler (2012), p. 26.
[403] Iannarelli (1992), p. 98.
[404] Cf. Iannarelli (1992), p. 98.

Table 2.4 (Dis)Advantages of family-internal succession[405]

Advantages	Disadvantages
Long-term preparation for a possible succession. This includes, among other things, personal aspects, education, and qualifications.	Conflict between the family's mandate to take over the family business and one's own interests, strengths, goals, etc.
An enterprise already exists, i.e., there is a resource. Also, this is passed on "cost-effectively" (inheritance or sale at a discount).	Limited view of the future development of the respective market. This can become apparent through the influence of the father/family on the education.
Support from the family (financially and temporally) for specific steps of their education.	Family influence even after the succession, i.e., the handover generation continues to interfere in the family business ("»backseat driving«"[a])

[a]*Source* Based on Pfannenschwarz (2008), p. 166.

However, when considering the preparation of potential successors, von Schlippe[406] distinguishes five phases:

1. Upbringing for succession (0–15 years)
2. Indecision in succession (approx. 15–30 years)
3. Selection of the successor (approx. 20–40 years)
4. Transition of responsibility (approx. 25–55 years)
5. Reorientation in the post-active phase (beyond the 60th year of life of the senior)

---

405 Pfannenschwarz (2008), p. 166.

406 Cf. von Schlippe et al. (2012), p. 293. According to Pfannenschwarz (2006 a, 291), successors go through a kind of successor life cycle consisting of seven phases: (1) Birth/Childhood, (2) Youth, (3) Collaboration, (4) Owner-Entrepreneur, (5) Senior-Owner, (6) Bequeather, and (7) Death. These are illustrated using the Three-Circle Model. Cater and Justis (2009, 14) also provide a model that can be used to trace the development of successors. They divide this into four phases, indicating the role of the descendants as well as the role of the entrepreneur. The role of the entrepreneur and then the successor is given for each phase: (1) Leader/Student and Follower, (2) Ruler/Helper, (3) Supervisor/Manager and (4) Consultant/Leader. According to Gersick et al. (1997, 20 ff.), business families typically go through four phases: (1) Young Business Family, (2) Entering the Business, (3) Working Together, and (4) Passing the Baton; there is a dependency on the age of the members of the respective generation who are actively working in the family business.

Based on the presented phases the influence of the family business on the life world, and thus on the socialization of potential descendants becomes visible. The fact, that a desired succession should not be limited only to the act of handover is also confirmed by Froschauer and Lueger based on their case study. In addition to the family identity, the socialization within the family business or the rules of the handover also have an impact on the succession process.[407] These can, for example, be stipulated in the family governance (see Sect. 2.3.2.2).

However, due to the still prevailing primogeniture,[408] usually only the eldest son is considered for a succession, which attributes competencies to him that he may not be able to or want to fulfill.[409] Therefore, first-born sons have a special role. They usually serve as potential successors from birth. Thus, their future path is often already determined. Therefore, they are often not free in their decisions.[410] On the other hand, the eldest son can pose a direct threat to the so-called patriarch in terms of his replacement. This opens two problem areas that can significantly influence the development of the son:

1. The father can try to outdo the son in all areas (e.g., sports). This rivalry can lead to a diminished self-confidence of the son as his growth is hindered. This makes him appear unsuitable for succession in the long run.
2. Or the father fears a better performance of the son as it could overshadow his own. This unconscious emerging jealousy can hinder the appropriate development of the son, which can endanger the existence of the family business.[411]

Both behaviors of the father or the resulting father-son relationship can have a negative impact on socialization.

In contrast, daughters often have it "easier" in many places. They are often given a larger decision-making scope for their own life planning.[412] However, if daughters are considered as successors, a divergent picture emerges. While some are prepared for business succession from an early age, others first acquire certain professional qualifications and then (rather unplanned) find their way into

407 Cf. Froschauer and Lueger (2012), p. 95.

408 In detail primogeniture means "that the firstborn inherits and all other siblings remain excluded [...]" (Nischak 2008, 89).

409 Cf. Haubl and Daser (2006), p. 34 and p. 42.

410 Cf. Baus (2010), p. 30.

411 Cf. Buchner (2011), p. 86.

412 Cf. Baus (2010), p. 30.

the family business.[413] Nevertheless, daughters usually realize very early whether they meet the gender ideal of their parents. This can trigger depression in them and cause them to withdraw, or they try to replace the desired son and "develop the 'false self' of a son" [414], or compensate for this with a son-in-law who takes over the management without any headwind. Others start a rebellion against their parents. This can then be reflected in their choice of partner by choosing someone who does not appeal to their parents.[415] For a more in-depth discussion, see Caspary (2010). She specifically focuses on female succession and asks why this potential is being wasted.

When looking at the qualification profile of successors, the focus is more on the business management component, while the founders predominantly have a technical background. This change can be related to the life cycle of the family business.[416] If the requirement profile of a business founder is compared with a successor entrepreneur, the founder primarily must overcome the difficulties of starting a business while successors must ensure continuity and development (see Sect. 2.2).[417] However, once the described "hurdles" are overcome, family businesses are often very successful.[418] Therefore, if they make it to the third or fourth generation, family businesses usually have developed certain routines that counteract the typical dangers of this type of enterprise.[419] This can be justified, among other things, by the experiences already gathered by the transferors as successors. For them, there is more of a chance to empathize with the successors and to develop an understanding of their dilemma. Similarly, the growth of the family can lead to a reduced confrontation of the successors with the individual values of the parents. Primarily, the continuation of the family tradition comes into focus.[420] Freund also attributes the most significant influence for a successful transition to the next generation to the "human-psychological component" [421]. Against the background of the topic chosen in this work, it is assumed that succession, i.e., the desire for cross-generational continuity, has a not insignificant influence on the socialization of the descendants. Depending on whether a

[413] Cf. Erdmann (2011), p. 5.

[414] Haubl and Daser (2006), p. 34.

[415] Cf. Haubl and Daser (2006), p. 34.

[416] Cf. Löhr (2001), p. 17.

[417] Cf. Löhr (2001), p. 31.

[418] Cf. Simon et al. (2005), p. 39.

[419] Cf. Wimmer (2004), p. 275.

[420] Cf. Simon (2005), p. 204.

[421] Freund (2000), p. 27.

young person is chosen as a successor or not, he or she is likely to be exposed to different influences and demands, considering the family and business cycle.

Finally, if we look again specifically at the handover process, the demands placed on it increase with the degree of interconnection as "economic-objective and familial-social expectations"[422] merge into each other. Above all, the successors may find themselves exposed to their own and others' expectations. The possible mutual expectations are illustrated below. These were taken directly from Müller[423] (see Table 2.5).

Table 2.5 Expectations in the succession process[424]

Typical *expectations of predecessors* for the role of a successor	Interest in the enterprise; will and readiness to continue the enterprise; committed cooperation; qualification; objective abilities; further development of the family business as a completion of one's own life's work; maintaining traditions; innovation; responsibility; entrepreneurial characteristics; social competence and employee leadership; success; gratitude
Typical *expectations of employees* for the role of a successor	Qualification; objective abilities; continuity; commitment; leadership personality; motivation of employees; authority; understanding of enterprise processes; job security; acceptance and inclusion of employees; knowledge of human nature; interest in the family business; innovation; entrepreneurial characteristics; professional experience in other enterprises
Typical *expectations of successors* for their own role	Qualification; objective abilities; freedom and decision-making authority; legitimization of changes by other role players; gaining an independent position; cohesion in the business family; acceptance by employees; successful handling of the task in connection with recognition by the other role players; willingness of the predecessor to retire; cooperation with the predecessor during the transition phase

[422] Frank and Hasenzagl (2005), p. 37.

[423] Müller (2008), p. 108.

[424] Source: According to Müller (2008), p. 108.

However, the expectations outlined in Table 2.5 will often not only occur during the succession. Rather a large part of the expectations — at least from the predecessor and the employees — are also already conveyed to the successor (directly or indirectly) beforehand, which in turn influences his or her socialization.

2.4.2 Influences on the Succession Decision

The significant reduction of the successor generations' willingness to take over their parents' inheritance, which often takes place within business families, is confirmed by Habig and Berninghaus.[425] According to Simon, children in particular who are to take over the family business in the third generation no longer necessarily feel obliged to continue their parents' life's work. Rather, this is a personal decision.[426] Nevertheless, questioning one's own succession is still one of the "hardest taboos"[427] in business families. There is often an obligation to continue the family tradition. The process of succession can be understood as a "transgenerational transfer of ownership and leadership" [428]. This is precisely what maintains the "reproduction mechanism of corporate influence" [429]. In general, two cases can occur:

1. The entrepreneur wants to pass on his enterprise to one of his children and completely ignores the necessary, but not existing character foundation of his children.
2. The children meet the necessary requirements, but lose interest in the succession because the transferor has often complained about the enterprise.[430]

The attraction and aversion are significantly influenced by the parents' teaching in dealing with independence, i.e., their role model function.[431] Although, a general empirical reduction in the willingness to succeed within the family can

[425] Cf. Habig and Berninghaus (2004), p. 56.
[426] Cf. Simon (2012), p. 69.
[427] Baus (2010), p. 31.
[428] Stamm (2013), p. 7.
[429] See footnote 428.
[430] Cf. Hamer (2001), p. 295.
[431] Cf. Freund (2000), p. 225.

be identified, according to Haubl and Daser[432], a gender differentiation can be made. While sons increasingly seek their own happiness away from the family business, daughters increasingly express their desire to enter management and are increasingly successful in doing so.

The attitude (sympathy or antipathy) towards the parental enterprise begins to manifest itself already in childhood and adolescence.[433] In this context, García-Álvarez et al.[434] also emphasize the importance of the socialization process of the children for ensuring the continuity of the family business. Thus, it appears to be of particular importance to convey to all descendants the feeling or the opportunity to be considered as potential successors. This includes a consistency in the transmission of values or formal education, regardless of gender. This also promotes a harmonious climate among siblings. Although entrepreneurial children are often aware of the difference to their peers, this has no influence on their decision to take over their parents' legacy. Rather, the adolescent phase serves this purpose. During this period concrete ideas about their own future and the (possible) desire for succession emerge.[435] Above all, the challenge for parents is to find "the right balance between imprinting and pressure" [436]. If there are several successors to choose from, (objective) criteria should be established based on which the successor is selected.[437]

Huber and Leitner[438], however, advise against active steering of the children for business succession. Rather, the children should be able to gradually familiarize themselves with the family business to get an overview of the requirements. Also, the children should be given the opportunity to develop as many interests as possible. In particular, the requirements that a family business places on the descendants in the second and third generation are only met if they have decided for themselves to succeed. Above all, mothers can exert a not to be underestimated influence on the children's career decision. They therefore play an important role within the business family.[439] Nevertheless, a successful

---

[432] Cf. Haubl and Daser (2006), p. 13.

[433] Cf. Freund (2000), p. 53 f.

[434] Cf. García-Álvarez et al. (2002), p. 202.

[435] Cf. Felden (2012), p. 159.

[436] Gottschalk et al. (2010), p. 45.

[437] Cf. Gottschalk et al. (2010), p. 45.

[438] Cf. Huber and Leitner (2011), p. 3.

[439] Cf. Iannarelli (1992), p. 134.

entrepreneur needs "visions, talent, implementation power, sense of responsibility, and professional skills"[440] as well as knowledge "in the industry, in market and sales, in personnel management, and more" [441]. According to Risse[442], a successor should have the following five necessary personality traits:

1. Physical and mental health
2. Dynamism, creativity, and flexibility
3. Joy in work and the will to learn new things
4. The ability to assert oneself
5. The right handling of money

In the case of multi-generational family businesses in particular the successors need, apart from the ability to deal responsibly and the interest in the respective business object, the willingness to work closely with other family members under certain circumstances.[443] Finally, if the messages conveyed by the father for a desired succession are considered, Erdmann[444] identifies the following in her survey:

1. Conveying the possibility of one's own choice
2. Fulfillment of the parental dream
3. Succession as an obligation
4. Dissuasion from taking over
5. Incentive for founding one's own enterprise

If the entry into the family business is considered, this took place on average at the age of 25, according to the survey conducted by Pfannenschwarz.[445]

2.4.2.1 Factors Hindering Succession

If we first address the ongoing change in values, it unfolds a certain explosiveness for business families. Like other areas of life these are also influenced or affected by the change in values, which is noticeable in a changing attitude towards family and profession. Therefore, unconditional commitment with

---

[440] Schaub (2009), p. 14.

[441] See footnote 440.

[442] Cf. Risse (1997), p. 36 f.

[443] Cf. Schröder et al. (2011), p. 306.

[444] Cf. Erdmann (2011), p. 16. Survey of 85 men and 49 women (cf. Erdmann 2011, 10).

[445] Cf. Pfannenschwarz (2006b), p. 18. n = 25 respondents.

neglect of personal wishes is no longer expected or exemplified. There is no longer necessarily the compulsion for potential successors to take over the family business. Complete personal devotion has largely given way to self-determination and self-development.[446] The "individualization of societal development processes"[447] in particular leads to an increasing departure from many values represented within the family ([I.5 and I.9]), such as a sense of duty, willingness to perform, and the assumption of responsibility. For this reason, the family can experience destabilization, which can subsequently affect the decision to succeed.[448] Nowadays, traditional virtues such as "service, duty fulfillment, obedience, and recognition of authority"[449] are increasingly receding into the background and are being replaced by newer values ("creativity, joy of life, teamwork, but also a high willingness to change"[450]) of the successor generations. This sometimes leads to a weakening of the strong emotional bond of individual family members to the family business. Increasingly, the benefit of participation is questioned.[451]

While business families are still characterized by adherence to "authority, diligence, thrift, trust, and personal modesty"[452], these characteristics meet a changed environment in a new appearance. Thus, selflessness and willingness to sacrifice for one's own enterprise are increasingly receding into the background.[453] This can be seen, for example, in the primary satisfaction of one's own needs and no longer primarily those of the enterprise. As a result, descendants no longer necessarily feel obliged to succeed.[454] They are more willing to sell their shares. This change in values can lead to a destabilization of the family business.[455] How attractive a potential takeover appears to the potential successor under today's changing societal values is influenced, among other things, by the ability of the parents to convey the joy and the emerging opportunities for self-realization to

---

[446] Cf. Hennerkes (2004), p. 45 ff.

[447] Kempert (2008), p. 177.

[448] Cf. Kempert (2008), p. 177.

[449] Mendel and Piper (2005), p. 139.

[450] See footnote 449.

[451] Cf. Mendel and Piper (2005), p. 139.

[452] Hennerkes (2004), p. 24.

[453] Cf. Hennerkes (2004), p. 24 f.

[454] Cf. Hennerkes and Hund (2008), p. 260.

[455] Cf. LeMar (2014), p. 58.

the next generation.[456] Differences in values and conflicts arising from inadequate delineation of responsibilities have negative effects on a made succession decision.[457]

In addition to the ongoing change in values, Schmitt-Rodermund and Schröder[458] identify in their study the following motives that deter the descendants from succeeding in the parental business:

1. Workload and associated stress (58%)
2. Uncertainty and financial risk (39%)
3. Profession/industry not interesting (27%)
4. Necessary responsibility for the enterprise and employees (11%)

The family business itself can also be cited as a reason for rejecting the succession. Often the central question for the heir is how advantageous a possible takeover is for him/her at all: Does the family business meet the requirements, expectations, and is there the potential to secure a professional and financial existence in the future ([I.17])?[459] In addition, the successors may also lack a future vision, which makes a takeover of the family business appear unattractive ([I.16]). Similarly, a too "high" education level of the descendants can prevent a succession ([I.14 and I.15]). See Interviews 2.9.

Another obstacle to entrepreneurial activity can be the lack of ability to make one's own decisions and to stand up for their consequences. An entrepreneur must accept his self-responsibility for his decisions, represent them externally, and withstand the associated stress. In addition, an entrepreneur should exhibit a kind of generalism even if this becomes increasingly difficult with increasing size (see Sect. 2.2.2 and [I.3 and I.4]). This comprehensive way of thinking can be very useful. The personal maturity level can also be considered. In general, the question arises, whether the successor fits the family business currently (see Interviews 2.10 [I.18]).[460]

Above all, an authoritarian upbringing requires children to obey their parents to a certain extent and to follow their instructions. However, it also undermines

---

[456] Cf. Wimmer et al. (2005), p. 193.

[457] Cf. Felden and Pfannenschwarz (2008), p. 201f.

[458] Cf. Schmitt-Rodermund and Schröder (2009), p. 34. n=155 business families, of which 255 are teenagers. Average age 16.4 years, where there was the possibility of multiple answers.

[459] Cf. Gottschalk et al. (2010), p. 10.

[460] Cf. Wottawa (2006), p. 343 f.

Interviews 2.9 Lack of attractiveness of the family business [I.14–17]

[I.14]	Daughter: "[...] That we could finally all five separate from the task of business takeover has to do with the acquired education and the limited opportunities of the enterprise, not with a fundamental rejection of the family business. Four of us work today in their own, family-like enterprises, where we can use what we have learned better than in anonymous organizations."[a]
[I.15]	Managing Director IfM Bonn: "Very small enterprises, for example, craftsmen, retailers, or restaurants with up to five employees are not gladly taken over by the children for very rational reasons. The descendants see more lucrative opportunities in dependent employment due to their education and personal experience. Sons and daughters have experienced that with a lot of work very little remains. Saturday and Sunday are spent working for the business and the main topic at the family table is the trouble at work."[b]
[I.16]	Son: "'*I simply lacked the idea for a change in the family business, that's why I didn't want to take it over. Everything here was fine; it was well managed, etc.*'"[c]
[I.17]	Business consultant with a focus on family businesses: "*Of course, numerous economic factors are at work in the succession process. For example, the product life cycle has a strong influence on the climate of succession. I am currently experiencing this in my intensive consulting work in the automotive industry. [...] The concern about the future of the car market severely limits the successors in their perspectives.* "[d]

[a]Welter-Enderlin (2005), p. 147 f.
[b]Mendel and Piper (2005), p. 125.
[c]Mätzener and Schwarz (2008), p. 104.
[d]LeMar (2001), p. 17.

Interviews 2.10 Maturity and willingness to success [I.18]

[I.18]	Successor of a construction enterprise: "'*They demand too much from the successors in such a takeover process of this magnitude. Until Matura [high school diploma], all of this would be too much. At 18, 19 years old you should then decide. That's still too much. Then you just study in this field to be on the safe side. The next sticking point is the willingness of the transferor to hand over and the question of the transferee: 'When do I want to be at the top?' I don't care. I enjoy taking over something*'"[a]

[a]Mätzener and Schwarz (2008), p. 84.

their independence, self-motivation, perseverance, and assertiveness, which can be a hindrance in professional life in particular.[461] However, if the adolescents

[461] Cf. Meierhofer (1989), p. 11.

Interviews 2.11 Paradoxical behavior of parents [I.19]

[I.19]	Managing partner of the Munich Institute for Conflict Research and Crisis Consultation: "True, and many [entrepreneurial parents] often behave paradoxically. Many family entrepreneurs have built their business with great energy. The lack of time for the children was compensated with money [...]. The children lacked nothing; difficulties were bought out of the way. [...] If it doesn't work out at school, the next boarding school is tried out [...]. The responsibility for failure is shifted outward. Thus, the parents have created precisely those mental structures in their children that make them incapable of business succession."[a]

[a]Mendel and Piper (2005), p. 159 f.

are spoiled too much and do not learn to deal with failures, this can also stand in the way of a business succession (see Interviews 2.11 [I.19]):

When specifically considering the gender of the descendants, this can serve as a justification for the old owners to exclude a succession. Female descendants in particular are often exposed to the "classic-conservative image of women"[462]. The old entrepreneurs still seem to ask themselves whether the female descendants even have the ability to continue the family business successfully (in the future) ([I.20, I.21, and I.22]). In Iannarelli's study, female descendants justify their departure from succession by the feeling that they were not suitable for continuing the family business.[463] In addition, the strong attachment of the transferor to their enterprise or the entrepreneur's lack of confidence in the skills of their successors can hinder succession. This becomes clear from the interviews [I.23 and I.24]. In both cases, it is precisely because the father is so strongly connected to his enterprise that it is difficult for him to work in the enterprise, which then causes him to turn away from his parents' business (see Interviews 2.12).

In addition to the lack of confidence in the abilities of the successors, the parents' negative view of the enterprise can cause the descendants to dislike the succession or the family business. Thus, the rejection can already arise in childhood when the parents tell at the dinner table what again did not work and how hard they have it.[464] Especially if the entrepreneur always vents his entire frustration about the enterprise or the customers at home and the children only get this one perspective, it should not be surprising if there is no interest in

[462] Stamm (2013), p. 199.

[463] Cf. Iannarelli (1992), p. 95.

[464] Cf. Buchner (2011), p. 78 and cf. Gersick et al. (1997), p. 145 f.

Interviews 2.12 Lack of parental trust [I.20–24]

[I.20]	Daughter: "'There was also the maternal business in the family, which I wanted to take over. When my mother retired it was simply dissolved. My parents did not trust me to take it over. For my father I was never a successor. I was always just a daughter; he always treated me as a child. I only got my father's business because no buyer was found — so he 'disposed' of it to me.'"[a]
[I.21]	Daughter: "'.. because when I'm married later and have children, I could still somehow run a branch. So,.. *that much was trusted in me back then* (ironically).'"[b]
[I.22]	Daughter: "'The boys should ideally join the business. And you [the daughter], he [the father] says, you can of course also join the business, but you would then have to work in the office because women can't do just anything, like real responsibility, but the office is also important. (laughs) like that.'"[c]
[I.23]	Son, 3rd generation: "'I don't understand why my father makes it so hard for himself. He should just hand everything over to me, I will surely build something great out of it. But as long as he wants to make every small decision himself, there is no place for me.'"[d]
[I.24]	Descendant: "[…], I also come from a steel processing enterprise […]. I grew up with the difficulties of our enterprise and I don't see that as a problem. I see another problem, namely that the father is emotionally so strongly connected with the enterprise and the son or daughter can hardly act independently."[e]

[a] Wandl and Habenicht (2011), p. 31.
[b] Stamm (2013), p. 199.
[c] Stamm (2013), p. 299.
[d] Felden and Pfannenschwarz (2008), p. 32.
[e] Mendel and Piper (2005), p. 77 f.

taking over the succession even for profitable family businesses ([I.25–I.29]).[465] The descendants usually experience or witness directly the considerable sacrifices associated with running an enterprise.[466] Although the descendants often cannot remember the content later, however, an unconscious aversion can develop. Thus, the descendants do not want to take over the succession without having a precise explanation for it (see Interviews 2.13).[467]

When considering the father-son relationship, there are various factors that have a certain potential for conflict or even hinder or oppose this relationship.

[465] Cf. Habig and Berninghaus (2004), p. 27.

[466] Cf. Felden (2012), p. 157.

[467] Cf. Buchner (2011), p. 78.

Interviews 2.13 Parents as bad role models [I.25–29]

[I.25]	Entrepreneur: "[…] My son was absolutely capable of taking over the enterprise as an industrial engineer. But I was such a miserable role model as a father to him that he didn't want to be like that. That's why he chose a different path in life."[a]
[I.26]	Case description of two brothers, both exercising corporate leadership: "*[…] The two brothers only interacted with each other for business purposes. […] The strained relationship between the brothers was partly to blame for Heinrich's children not identifying with the enterprise. They developed other interests that had nothing to do with working in the enterprise. […]*"[b]
[I.27]	Entrepreneur: "If you keep telling your children what's wrong, what's going wrong in the enterprise, then as a father you shouldn't be surprised if on the 30th birthday you say:»I have a birthday present for you!«, and the son or daughter replies:»Keep it! It only causes worries, it only causes trouble.« […] We must pass on the joy of entrepreneurship, the joy of shaping, the joy of independence to our next generation. If we didn't enjoy the enterprise, we wouldn't have founded it and led it for 30 years."[c]
[I.28]	Gersick et al.: "Their memories were all the same: 'Every night, she [the mother] would come home and be obsessed with how difficult it was, how miserable her coworkers and customers had been that day, how tough it was working with her brother. Now suddenly, she wants us to see how much fun she was having, and how satisfying the business was all those years. It's too late; I have an idea about what family business is like, and it's not for me.'"[d]
[I.29]	Founder on his role model effect: "*[…] You see, and that's what my children have always experienced because we also talked about it at the breakfast table, […] that we had problems, that we have a bill due at the end of the week and we don't know yet, how we're going to pay for it, and stuff like that. And, and: 'This has to go out today so that we can possibly get the money from him at the weekend!', — or something like that. That's what practically happens. And then the kids could have said: 'I don't want anything to do with this shop!' They never did […].* "[e]

[a]Mendel and Piper (2005), p. 63.
[b]Chaub (2009), p. 95.
[c]Mendel and Piper (2005), p. 73 f.
[d]Gersick et al. (1997), p. 71.
[e]Siefer (1996), p. 122.

If the transferor and successor are too similar, this can hinder future collaboration ([I.30]). Likewise, the entrepreneur may show too little appreciation for the successor after entering the family business ([I.31]), which reduces satisfaction. Different ideas about how the family business should be run in the future also promote a departure from internal family succession ([I.32]). In addition, a direct conflict with the father can lead to leaving the enterprise ([I.33]). However, it becomes clear at [I.34] how the enterprise as a common theme of communication and above all, the mutual appreciation for competence and performance strengthens the relationship between father and son (see Interviews 2.14).

Interviews 2.14 (Conflict-ridden) Father-son relationship [I.30–34]

[I.30]	Son who studies not business administration but theater science: "'*I am very similar to my father and also stubborn. I am used to making my own decisions and so we would — if we worked together in an enterprise — constantly clash. So far, I have only been employed in my father's business in the form of holiday jobs.*'"[a]
[I.31]	Successor: "'*For example, I managed to get us to supply Hofer [discounter]. And my father says in public: 'I got the Hofer'. I endured his actions for three to four years, but it bothered me extremely that he refers everything to himself. For example, my father always called me 'representative' in front of customers and never said that I am his son.*'"[b]
[I.32]	Successor: "'*...at the beginning I had completely different ideas, which I could not enforce against my father. He is an autocratic personality and with him it was like that, it was done and that's it. I was dissatisfied with my situation and developed a concept in my quiet little room [...]. I told him, if we cannot implement this system, then I will apply elsewhere. I then acquired a stake elsewhere. My father saw the success and only then something changed in our business...*'"[c]
[I.33]	Successor, 4th generation: " *[...] I am the youngest, (.) my oldest (.) is, as I said, here in the enterprise and then we have another middle brother [...]. (.) He was actually also planned here for the enterprise, (.) but is very extreme in his way. (.) First of all, // very, very bossy, very difficult! Although very intelligent but for example, he did not get along at all (.) with my father. There was already a lot happened [...]. If anything went wrong, then he immediately complained and grumbled [...]. And then the decision was made that he should leave.*"[d]
[I.34]	Successor: "'So actually a great friendship started between me and my father because he suddenly appreciated what I can do. And I also learned to appreciate what he had built up.'"[e]

[a]Mätzener and Schwarz (2008), p. 25.
[b]Mätzener and Schwarz (2008), p. 25.
[c]Müller (2008), p. 353.
[d]Siefer (1996), p. 129.
[e]Stamm (2013), p. 293.

In addition to conflicts between the old owners/parents and the successors/children, the adolescents can also be exposed to "internal" contradictions regarding the decision for or against a succession. Simon refers to this as an "autonomy-dependency conflict"[468]. Although they are expected to continue the

[468] Simon (2005), p. 52.

Interviews 2.15 (Expected) Pressure on successors [I.35–37]

[I.35]	Young entrepreneur: "'*He kept asking us: 'When are you coming?' The pressure was and is great from his side. But the question is whether you want to accept it. Running my father's business is a topic for me only later. But I also reserve the right to do something else.* '"[a]
[I.36]	Old entrepreneur: "We never really gave our middle son a choice or left him any choice. That was not right. It was clear to us; it was clear to him — at some point he questioned it. He then discovered his artistic side and realized himself there. If we had forced him, it might not have gone so well. For us, of course, it was a shock."[b]
[I.37]	Rudolf Wimmer: "'Many potential successors have grown up since their childhood so naturally with the expectation and the prospect of taking over the enterprise one day. Their education was so naturally aligned with this that they no longer know, whether they really want it in their innermost being or not. Many doubt their own abilities at this stage. The question of whether they are really suitable for enterprise management or whether they have simply slipped into it because they are the son, torments them.'"[c]

[a]Mätzener and Schwarz (2008), p. 73.
[b]Juritsch et al. (2007), p. 81.
[c]Wandl and Habenicht (2011), p. 43. Rudolf Wimmer is a professor of leadership and organization at the Institute for Family Businesses at the University of Witten/Herdecke.

family heritage, they also see the independently made career decisions of their friends.[469] There is usually a great deal of expectation pressure from internal and external stakeholder groups such as the family ([I.35]), the workforce, the customers, or the suppliers (see Table 2.5),[470] which pushes the descendants towards a succession. Above all, the premature determination of the successor carries the risk of rejection if it is questioned at some point and the successor wants to do something else ([I.36 and I.37]). If the successors therefore do not really decide out of their own motivation to take over the family business, but rather under the aspect that they would have to join, this can lead to disappointment and resignation.[471] Then the successor's skills can significantly deviate from the task to be performed (see Interviews 2.15).[472]

Due to the connection between family and business, the family business can also be seen as a "stage of life" for the parents, which is tailored to them. A

[469] Cf. Simon (2005), p. 187.
[470] Cf. Wimmer (2004), p. 274.
[471] Cf. Gersick et al. (1997), p. 163.
[472] Cf. Meyer (2007), p. 32.

Interviews 2.16 The succession as a burden [I.38]

[I.38]	Entrepreneur, 3rd generation: "*Inheritance is therefore experienced as a burden because the successor not only inherits the enterprise, but also the 'stage of life of the parents'. A role is already prescribed for him there. The scenery, the play, the staging, and much more is predetermined by the parents. A change, a rewrite, or even a new staging is difficult. It also presupposes that everyone who has so far played a part in this play understands its redesign. [...]*"[a]

[a]LeMar (2001), p. 235.

Interviews 2.17 Emotional components in family businesses [I.39–41]

[I.39]	Entrepreneur, 3rd generation: "*[...] An open conversation about our relationships in the family would have quickly become emotional. That's why we never addressed it. I believe this is often the case. The participants sense the explosiveness and therefore prefer not to talk about it because they know they would have a hard time handling such a conversation. [...]*"[a]
[I.40]	Transferor: "I would rate the emotional at least as high, if not slightly higher than the»hardware«. Even the best enterprises are unsuccessful if there is strife within the management team — and in this case, that is the family with two generations."[b]
[I.41]	Case description: "He feels like he is in a bind: On the one hand, he is grateful to his parents for enabling him so much; but at the same time, he is also annoyed with his father who has still not fully withdrawn."[c]

[a]LeMar (2001), p. 156.
[b]Juritsch et al. (2007), p. 87.
[c]Bieker and Hirsch (2007), p. 386.

restructuring then requires a tremendous amount of effort, which in turn can hinder a succession (see Interviews 2.16 [I.38]).

In addition, unaddressed conflicts can burden the family and especially the successor ([I.39–I.41]). This can in turn affect the enterprise's performance, which in extreme cases can affect a possible succession decision (see Interviews 2.17).

Also significant for the continued existence of a family business is the relationship of the individual family members to the business. In practice, however, this is not always easy to implement as generational changes promote an increasing distance or alienation of individual family members from the enterprise.[473] A spatial distance from the parental home, the growth of the enterprise, and a different (relaxed) perspective on the indispensability in the enterprise are factors that increase the distance between family and business in the context of the

[473] Cf. Wimmer (2007), p. 42.

succession process.[474] In addition, Pfannenschwarz[475] puts forward the following thesis: If children of entrepreneurs are reluctant to take on tasks that are visible in public, this indicates as "an indirect hint of reservations about their own position in society"[476] and is "at least an ambivalent assessment of their own situation as a successor" [477].

Finally, the children-in-law must also be given an influence on the (non-) success of a generational change or on the long-term existence ([I.42]). Especially if they come from a different family background, this can lead to conflicts if they do not have any understanding for the necessary workload ([I.43]). However, the perspective of the old owners on the in-laws should not be neglected. In [I.44] the parents' aversion to the daughter-in-law becomes clear. This could then subsequently lead to a rejection of the succession. From this and indirectly in [I.43] it becomes clear by which criterion the parents would choose an in-law. This must primarily fit the family business. This is also clear in [I.45]. The youngest daughter was not initially intended to be the successor. It was only when she married someone who also came from a business family that she was considered for succession (see Interviews 2.18).

2.4.2.2 Factors Promoting Succession

Based on successor reports, Felden and Pfannenschwarz[478] list the following factors on how descendants are moved to succession or decide to do so:

1. The senior entrepreneur offers the descendants certain incentives.
2. Already in their youth the descendants encounter the family business, which promotes attachment. Thus, the descendants know the enterprise as well as the requirements and characteristics of the respective industry from an early age.
3. A competitive situation for the possible successor position is artificially and (un)consciously created, for example, by the entrepreneur naming relatives as potential successors in addition to the descendants.

---

[474] Cf. Frank and Hasenzagl (2005), p. 41.

[475] Cf. Pfannenschwarz (2006a), p. 257.

[476] Pfannenschwarz (2006a), p. 257.

[477] Pfannenschwarz (2006a), p. 257.

[478] Cf. Felden and Pfannenschwarz (2008), p. 126.

Interviews 2.18 Influence of the in-laws [I.42–45]

[I.42]	Founder: "I have experienced such things, where the parents have struggled and the son has also struggled and then got married a very nice woman and he then also had health problems [...], then the woman said: 'Yes, but if you continue to struggle like this, you'll have a heart attack, and you're hardly ever at home.' And then he says: 'Yes, then I'll sell the enterprise, we can live well from the rental income of the house.' The father who was then actually too old to take it back: 'I didn't give it to you for this'; that was a real tragedy.'"[a]
[I.43]	Transferor: "'*...well, with the commitment of my son on the weekend there are always tensions, mostly from his family environment because his family comes from the civil service life and they can't understand it at all. I have a 6½ -day week. Apparently, I can't expect that from others...*'"[b]
[I.44]—[I.45]	Senior entrepreneur: "'For a winery, a capable woman is needed who does this job. Other women have other advantages, so (laughs) uh we always said uh.. this daughter-in-law is not really, not born for this business, [...], lovable person.'"[c] [I.44] Senior entrepreneur: "'And the young woman [the daughter] has therefore agreed.. to take on the burden and pleasure, I repeat it again, the burden and pleasure.. of this business,.. thankfully also married a man who fits, who, who comes from a brewery family, but *doesn't matter* (laughing) (laughs), [...].'"[c] [I.45]

[a]Zwack (2011), p. 137.
[b]Müller (2008), p. 351.
[c]Stamm (2013), p. 233.

In addition, Wottawa[479] mentions two psychological aspects that have a positive effect on the decision to succeed: The "'negative-motivation'"[480] and the "'success-saturated boredom'" [481]. The first aspect primarily involves dissatisfaction with the current own work situation. This can be a standstill or the feeling that one's own competence is not sufficiently recognized by higher positions. The second aspect describes the opposite motivation. Due to the success already achieved, the individual now feels competent enough to push for the takeover of

[479] Cf. Wottawa (2006), p. 338 ff.

[480] Wottawa (2006), p. 338. The problem with negative motivation lies in the justification for taking over an enterprise. This is not necessarily based on the possibility of entering an attractive enterprise, but rather on the "escape" from an unsatisfactory situation. Such motivation cannot really be regarded as a "healthy" starting point for succession (cf. Wottawa 2006, p. 338 ff).

[481] Wottawa (2006), p. 339.

the family business. Based on the interview material collected by Stamm [482], four ideal-typical patterns can favor succession if the family business acts as a

1. refuge,
2. mission,
3. starting point of privileges, and
4. emotional home.

However, in most cases personal motivation determines the step towards succession. Especially the classic views on entrepreneurship, such as decision-making freedom or the realization of one's own vision, are seen as central arguments.[483] This is also confirmed by Meyer[484] as well as Felden [485]. In addition to emotional and/or monetary motives, one's own motivation can also be justified by the (un)expressed will of the family. Based on a standardized written survey, Schulte and Wille[486] identify the following takeover motives (1=very important and 5=not important at all):

1. Personal and professional competence (2.1)
2. Decision-making and action freedom (2.2)
3. Family and business tradition (2.2)
4. Contact with people (2.6)
5. Self-realization (2.8)
6. Economic and financial independence (3.2)
7. Job security (3.3)
8. The social position (4.3)

In addition, Schmitt-Rodermund and Schröder[487] determine in their study the following motives that move the descendants to take over the parental business:

---

[482] Cf. Stamm (2013), p. 208–218.

[483] Cf. Gottschalk et al. (2010), p. 48.

[484] Cf. Meyer (2007), p. 32.

[485] Cf. Felden (2012), p. 154.

[486] Cf. Schulte and Wille (2006), p. 401 ff. Survey (n=42) of successors of small and very small enterprises. 77 percent of the enterprises have fewer than 10 employees.

[487] Cf. Schmitt-Rodermund and Schröder (2009), p. 34. n=155 business families, of which 255 were teenagers. Average age 16.4 years, where there was the possibility of multiple answers.

1. Independence (48%)
2. Activity coincides with professional interest (33%)
3. Continuation of tradition (33%)
4. The financial incentives (26%)

A male successor argues in the following order why he took over the family business:

1. "The product: 'Can I identify with it: absolutely yes.'
2. The enterprise: 'Capable of offering an economic future or, for example, regarding the personnel situation: Will everyone retire in five years or where do I get necessary skilled workers from'? [...]
3. The market: Is the business so person-focused that the junior has no chance, 'but everything depends on the senior'?
4. Personal feasibility: From the point of view of commitment still leaving room for a private life with one's own family/children: The father was a deterrent example in this respect.
5. Relief through employees: 'It is important to be able to be dispensable oneself, not so much because of the workload, but rather because of the personal flexibility that may be curtailed. It is therefore important to have high employee motivation'"[488].

Kailer and Weiß[489] consider it sensible for potential successors — as already mentioned above — to first complete a few "'*years of travel*'" [490]. This in their opinion affects the personality by promoting the development of self-confidence and self-esteem. Thus, the distance from the parental enterprise can initially be experienced as something liberating, but in the long term it can increase the desire for succession (see Interviews 2.19 [I.46 and I.47]).

According to Felden and Pfannenschwarz[491], a family-internal succession increases when the entrepreneurs give their children enough freedom and exert as little pressure as possible. This behavior favors the free formation of opinions as well as the idea of one's own career aspirations. It is precisely these behaviors that subsequently encourage the decision to take over the parental business. [I.48]

[488] Freund (2000), p. 75.

[489] Cf. Kailer and Weiß (2005), p. 18.

[490] Kailer and Weiß (2005), p. 18.

[491] Cf. Felden and Pfannenschwarz (2008), p. 127.

Interviews 2.19 Benefits of a distant study location [I.46–47]

[I.46]—[I.47]	Winemaker: "'*If I had stayed at home back then, I would certainly not be working in viticulture today. The study was for me like a second puberty, my political view, etc. has changed.*'"[a] [I.46] The same Winemaker: "'*I studied for several years in the city, I was far away from viticulture and that was a real liberation, I could shake off old connections.*'"[a] [I.47]

[a]Mätzener and Schwarz (2008), p. 103.

also confirms the advantage of being able to go one's own way first, especially if the family background can be disregarded. Even if the descendants are not pushed for succession and initially do something else, the desire for succession can ultimately arise. This allows the necessary development of the descendants ([I.49]). Of course, despite the freedom granted by the parents, it is still possible to choose an apprenticeship that suits the enterprise and then join it ([I.50]) even if the descendant was not intended to be a successor ([I.51]). See Interviews 2.20.

The (in)direct influence of the parents must be considered as a not insignificant factor that moves the descendants to a succession ([I.52, I.53, I.56, and I.57]). A "gentle" introduction to the family business can also strengthen awareness of it and a possible succession ([I.54 and I.55]). However, this carries two dangers: (1) Either a rejection of the succession or (2) the assumption of the succession, but with less motivation on the part of the successor.[492] A clear influence on the professional development of the descendants by the expectations and wishes of the parents is confirmed by Schmitt-Rodermund and Schröder[493] based on the results of their study. Parents influence their children's career choices through their upbringing, their role as professional role models, and their behaviors. The children observe their parents, and thus gain insights into the demands of the family business, which shapes their attitude towards succession (see Interviews 2.21).

Growing up within a family business favors the willingness to succeed. This connection is illustrated by the following quote: "Taste causes one to have what one likes because one likes what one has, namely the characteristics and features that are de facto assigned and de jure assigned by classification."[494] Transferred to the descendants taste can be seen as the family business or entrepreneurship. This taste or interest then arises through early experiences with the family business ([I.61-I.63]). This is liked because it has always been part of the experiential

[492] Cf. Felden and Pfannenschwarz (2008), p. 126.

[493] Cf. Schmitt-Rodermund and Schröder (2009), p. 6. n = 155 business families, of which 255 were teenagers.

[494] Bourdieu (1987), p. 285 f.

Interviews 2.20 Freedom for the descendants [I.48–51]

[I.48]	Female successor: "Having the freedom to do this because we want to do it is very important. I have completed a tourism education and was on the road for ten years. Nobody cared that I came from the Hochschober Hotel. And that was very important to me. I was able to go my own way just like my husband […]."[a]
[I.49]	Entrepreneur: "Ultimately in my opinion, the fact, that I was never pressured to take over was the reason why it worked so well. […] I wanted to do completely different things at the time. […] He [the father] gave me the opportunity to develop myself even in a different direction than him. […] The essential factor was: I had the freedom to develop myself. The timing of the handover was also favorable: for him, to let go and for me, to take on such responsibility."[b]
[I.50]	Successor, 3rd generation: "*[…] No, — They [parents] always left it open to me. […] They said: 'Of course we would like it, if you did that!', but never in the foreground. Instead, the education was more important, having a good education […] and (.), which also corresponded to the inclinations. […] That these inclinations are now what my father did, may be due to a family tradition or whatever then inheritance […] but (.) that has (.) nothing to do with the fact that the parents pushed me to go into the business. 'And if you go into the business, then only the father's job!' [.]*"[c]
[I.51]	Female successor: "Actually not, since my brother was intended for it. My career path went in this direction because I was interested in it and because I always felt very comfortable in this industry. There was no competition in this regard between the siblings. And you can see that in the end everything turned out differently than it was planned."[d]

[a]Juritsch et al. (2007), p. 90.
[b]Mendel and Piper (2005), p. 55.
[c]Siefer (1996), p. 190 f.
[d]Juritsch et al. (2007), p. 81.

space or the lifeworld ([I.59]). The successors usually came into contact with the parental enterprise during their youth: "Holiday jobs, temporary help, special assignments, the installation of PCs, deliveries, etc".[495] ([I.62 and I.63]) can contribute to a strengthening of the connection with the family business ([I.55]). They usually already know what requirements they will have to meet in the respective industry.[496] The motivation of the descendants can be seen in a striving for self-realization, the possibility of free time management, the desire to continue the family tradition, and the business as well as the better opportunity to combine

[495] Felden (2012), p. 155.
[496] Cf. Felden (2012), p. 155.

Interviews 2.21 Direct and indirect influence on succession [I.52–57]

[I.52]	Successor: "'*How my parents managed to get me into the hospitality industry with subtle means I still don't know to this day. They even managed to make sure that I never had other ideas.* '"[a]
[I.53]	Successor: "I have always felt a certain obligation. But the question of whether one really decides to join the enterprise is primarily an emotional one. For me, however, it was an important prerequisite to also have the chance to take a different path."[b]
[I.54]	Entrepreneur explains what in his opinion facilitated his entry into the family business: "*[...] I believe that one must indeed give children a direction. Not to fixate them now: '[...], you look around completely freely, completely uninfluenced!' [...] One has a right, perhaps even a duty, to make certain directions that one knows and considers good clear to the children so that they know what they are deciding for or against [...] in the end.* "[c]
[I.55]	Entrepreneur: "*And one thing is a fact, you can arouse interest in children. You can arouse interest for, even for a cause, even at a young age. (.) You don't have to tell them: 'You have to know how to make a pair of pliers now' [...]. But you can when you walk through here with them, (.) for example, the greatest pleasure for them is to ride on a forklift or something. And these are the little things that, in my opinion, give children an attitude towards the enterprise. And just as you can arouse a lack of interest by, for example, always keeping children away from the enterprise.* "[c]
[I.56]	Influence of the enterprise system on a young entrepreneur: "'*I was at a technical school for textiles and retail for three years. I would have liked to stay there for another year, but my father called me back because he couldn't manage the expansion alone.* '"[d]
[I.57]	Entrepreneur, 4th Generation: "*[...] As my brother has said, I run the business with him, and I have also been in the business for 31 years. The decision to join the business was such that my father already expected me to step in.* "[e]

[a] Mätzener and Schwarz (2008), p. 103.
[b] Juritsch et al. (2007), p. 68.
[c] Siefer (1996), p. 120.
[d] Mätzener and Schwarz (2008), p. 109.
[e] Weber (2005), p. 272.

family and career.[497] In addition, the takeover can be seen as an obligation to maintain certain values even if another career path could not be pursued for this purpose ([I.60]). Early participation is often positively experienced ([I.58]) and reinforces the desire for succession (see Interviews 2.22).

[497] Cf. Huber and Leitner (2011), p. 16.

Interviews 2.22 Family business as an adventure world [I.58–63]

[I.58]	Successor: "'*In my youth I started serving very early and it was great because as a little boy you get a lot of tips. That was very motivating and certainly shaped me a bit, that's when I got a taste for it. Advantage: The parents were always there. Disadvantage: There was almost always work on the weekends, especially for the parents. During the semester breaks we even closed and were able to take regular vacations, which we all enjoyed very much.* '"[a]
[I.59]	Managing Director IfM Bonn: "[…] For children born into a business family there is often no other option than succession. Whether this succeeds then also depends on the extent to which the children can free themselves from their parents. This also includes ensuring that responsibilities in the enterprise are clearly and unambiguously regulated after the transfer."[b]
[I.60]	Son: "'After my father's death I had no choice, but to continue the business. My main motivation was to preserve values and get a business back on track,' he says. 'I do mourn my missed career in Munich a bit, but there was no other family member who could have taken over the enterprise. Even though taking over the family business was not my first choice, it was interesting to further develop the business once the decision was made. […]'"[c]
[I.61]	Successor: "*[…] But I had […] actually more, actually always more of a connection to my father, a line to my father, — yeah. […] And (.) I dealt with things a bit when he let something slip, — yeah. […] And (.) when he took me to the enterprise, — yeah. […] I actually developed more and more interest, than, than was the case with my brother, — yeah.* "[d]
[I.62]	Entrepreneur: "*[…] So we live near the enterprise, (.) or have lived here [clears throat] accustomed in the direct vicinity of the enterprise or on the enterprise premises. As a result, as children or as adolescents, you naturally get quite a lot of insight into the operational process. […] You yourself are also involved, you (.) do a holiday job, and (.) help here and there and go with father, uncle (.) to customers and thus see quite a bit. And this naturally arouses a certain interest (.).* "[e]
[I.63]	Successor: "*So I have neither, (.) no one has either — expressis verbis, expressed the wish to take over here one day — in case of suitability –, (.) nor did anyone have to bluntly (.) point out to me that this also has advantages, but // I grew into it! As a child (.) I walked through the enterprise, actually (.) during the school holidays or even before that, even before my school days I already as a child, (.) I walked around the enterprise for hours. Watched the workers and — I thought that was great!*"[f]

[a] Maetzener and Schwarz (2008), p. 103.
[b] Mendel and Piper (2005), p. 131.
[c] Wandl and Habenicht (2011), p. 46.
[d] Siefer (1996), p. 114.
[e] Siefer (1996), p. 121.
[f] Siefer (1996), p. 122.

Specifically, through the relationship with the family as well as through the interests and the abilities of the young people the opportunity to enter the family business is either perceived as a chance or as a burden.[498] The motivation and joy in a future activity in the family business can manifest through the work in the enterprise ([I.58 and I.64]). In addition, the feeling of being needed ([I.67]) or the transfer of responsibility ([I.66]) positively influences the decision to succeed

[498] Cf. Schröder et al. (2011), p. 306.

the family business. Of course, the attractiveness of the family business ([I.68]) should not be neglected. Also Stamm[499] identifies three motives in her analysis that motivate the descendants to join the family business:

1. Connection with the product/industry
2. Potential for self-determination
3. Assumption of responsibility

Finally, [I.69] illustrates how far-reaching the decision to join the family business is perceived by the descendants. The successor is aware of the associated responsibility and the "finality" if she decides for the family business (see Interviews 2.23).

2.5 The Family Business as Socialization Context

After the various facets of enterpriseness have been extensively discussed in the last chapters, and thus it could be shown how the family business exerts its influence on the participating family(ies), this chapter addresses the influence of enterpriseness on the socialization of entrepreneurial children. However, for the answer to the research question, it is important to first understand socialization in general, i.e., detached from the context of the family business. As the family is largely responsible for primary socialization, its characteristics and influence on the descendants are discussed.

- The family establishes the connection to the family business (familiness) through its members.
- The family business enters the family (enterpriseness) through the family members and can thus also influence the socialization of the descendants.

Finally, it is necessary to limit the horizon of socialization in view of the research question. After this framework has been created, the approach to the socialization context of the family business is made. A distinction is made between the influence of the family and the business on the descendants. A final consideration focuses on the influences of the family business on the life world and the identity of the descendants. To illustrate this, interview excerpts and results of empirical surveys by other authors are used again.

---

499 Cf. Stamm (2013), p. 223 f. Stamm (2013, p. 139 f.) conducted Interviews with a total of 12 business families.

Interviews 2.23 Decision to join the family business [I.64–69]

[I.64]	Successor: "'*My brother and I have always worked in the enterprise. I worked in sales — in manufacturing — in production — in shipping, before later becoming head of sales and moving up to management. My decision to join the enterprise came during my studies. Through working in the enterprise I discovered joy and fascination.*'"[a]
[I.65]	Old entrepreneur: "'*For our son the USA was the promised land and we thought he would stay. When he came back he also said: 'I will not take over!' I said: 'Before you twiddle your thumbs make yourself useful!' [...] He discovered that it is quite interesting and his interest increased suddenly. He said: 'What if I do join after all?*'"[b]
[I.66]	Successor: "*[...] That was, you had asked, whether [clears throat] it had been clear from an early age to join here or not? So, it was not' clear. (.) I initially joined here because I had this commercial education because I was interested in the enterprise in principle. And then came the takeover of the (.) neighboring enterprise and this of course results in certain tasks. [..] And this naturally also resulted in free work areas in the family for a successor. And (.) exactly, and then I, then we decided that I (.) initially (.) join here and see [...] and then (.) one just sticks with this decision [...].*"[c]
[I.67]	Entrepreneur, 3rd generation: "The decision was made quite exactly ten years ago [...]. At that time the enterprise was planning the construction of a new timber market and I told my father that I wanted to take a break from my studies and work on this project. My father was very pleased and immediately gave me responsibility for this project. That was my first step towards joining the enterprise. I was able to approach the matter relatively carefree and without pressure. It was my own free decision and I therefore experienced it as thoroughly positive."[d]
[I.68]	Successor: "*[...] If I may say so casually: I was certainly able to settle into a made nest — although that [...] has always been [emphasized:] attractive, since the enterprise was healthy, even at the time when I joined and still is today — it was certainly (.) a [emphasized:] good made nest.*"[e]
[I.69]	Female successor: "' [...] And it was very clear to me, if I now say 'Yes' and, that I can only say 'Yes' and want to, but that this 'Yes' simply opens a new dimension. Because so far, I was responsible for my life and that of my son.. and.. with the decision the enterprise, to say 'Yes' to the enterprise ultimately then, which was still further away at that time, but to take over the enterprise that is not a, not a couple of years job, that is a 'Yes' for life, so and so I have also felt it about.'"[f]

[a] Maetzener and Schwarz (2008), p. 102.
[b] Maetzener and Schwarz (2008), p. 109.
[c] Siefer (1996), p. 160 f.
[d] Juritsch et al. (2007), p. 67.
[e] Siefer (1996), p. 147.
[f] Stamm (2013), p. 226.

However — and it should be pointed out — the individual statements cannot be adopted universally for every descendant. Particularly in founding enterprises, the enterprise can have a different influence on the socialization of the descendants than in multi-generational family businesses due to the higher degree of connection between the family and the business. This should have become apparent from the explanations under Sects. 2.2 and 2.3. Of course, the contact or influence of the family business is significantly influenced by the parents. The extent to which they give the family business "room or space" or bring the children into contact with the family business will have a different effect on their socialization.

2.5.1 Introduction to Socialization

2.5.1.1 Approach to the Concept of Socialization

All people are united by the commonality of birth into an existing culture. This can be understood as a social context or as a "structure"; a fact that should not be forgotten, especially for the socialization and upbringing of humans. However, human dependence on its social environment begins long before its birth. Thus, traditions and customs already influence the parents' choice of partner and their habits during pregnancy. Above all, the probability of being born healthy is influenced by the current knowledge for pregnancy care. In addition, the family is also surrounded by a whole range of cultural habits. In general, the social circumstances that precede birth not only enable life, but also greatly influence the way of life. However, due to the previous explanations one should not speak of a direct socialization. This begins only with the birth of the child.[500] Erikson describes it as follows: "With birth, the child leaves the chemical exchange of the mother's womb and enters the social exchange of society, in which his gradually growing abilities meet the opportunities and limitations of his culture."[501] Thus, a child is already born into an existing "network of social relationships"[502] and therefore into a specific socio-cultural framework, which is associated with an assignment of precisely defined social positions.[503]

If the focus is now directed towards socialization, socialization processes fulfill the task of socializing[504] the developing individuals and contribute to the formation of a capable individual. Therefore, the earlier the socialization processes take place, the more effective they are. Hurrelmann summarizes socialization in this context as a lifelong "process of processing the inner reality of physical and

[500] Cf. Lukesch (1978), p. 90 and cf. Davis (1966), p. 201.

[501] Erikson (1973), p. 57 f.

[502] Youniss (1980), p. 55.

[503] Cf. Claessens (1968), p. 41.

[504] Under the process of socialization, Popitz understands, "that several people start to orient their behavior towards each other at some point and that this orientation becomes successively more intensive and comprehensive" (Popitz 1980, 1).

psychological impulses and the outer reality of social and physical environmental impulses" [505]. In detail, typical socialization instances can be named as the family, the school, or the education system.[506] The socialization function of the family arises for the growing child "from the anthropologically given dependence of the child on a social support system" [507]. Especially, the research on socialization assumes of the formative effect of the immediate environment on social behavior.[508] For this reason, the idea that human development in terms of social and personal characteristics is linked to societal and social-spatial conditions is predominantly held.[509] The family has a not to be underestimated influence on the respective children as there is a close interaction relationship between the members.[510]

Socialization, therefore, primarily describes the "process of becoming human"[511]. However, this view is not value-free. Rather, the human being is understood as an individual and as a personality, and thus as a living being that acts socially and societally.[512] In this context, Schneewind et al. view the socialization process "as the development of a changing human individual in a changing environment"[513] and Wurzbacher understands socialization as "the integration of the human being into a social group" [514]. Mitscherlich describes it as follows: "The human being comes into the world uneducated and uncultured. It is [...] an *extreme nestling*, that is, his state of maturity at birth is far from the maturity goal."[515] Hurrelmann, on the other hand, refers to socialization as a "permanent coping procedure" [516]. In his view, there is a tension between individualization

[505] Hurrelmann (2002), p. 28. The "inner reality" includes the genetic predisposition, the physical constitution, intelligence, the psychological temperament, and the basic structures of the personality (cf. Hurrelmann 2002, 27). The "outer reality" includes the family, the groups of friends, the upbringing and educational institutions, the social organizations, the mass media, the working conditions, the living conditions, and the physical environment (cf. Hurrelmann 2002, 27).

[506] Cf. Faltermaier (2008), p. 158.

[507] Lenz (2005), p. 13.

[508] Cf. Abels and König (2010), p. 68.

[509] Cf. Dippelhofer-Stiem (2008), p. 117.

[510] Cf. Schneewind (1982), p. 163 f.

[511] Faulstich-Wieland (2000), p. 10.

[512] Cf. Faulstich-Wieland (2000), p. 10.

[513] Schneewind et al. (1983), p. 11.

[514] Wurzbacher (1963b), p. 14.

[515] Mitscherlich (1986), p. 9.

[516] Hurrelmann (2002), p. 38.

and socialization of the human personality that extends over the entire life.[517] Goode, on the other hand, summarizes the process of socialization as follows: "The crucial outcome of the socialization process is that individuals are made to take on the tasks that must be performed if society and its members are to survive."[518]

Sociology often therefore also speaks of a "societal basic process"[519]. This can be understood as a process that contributes to conveying the existing values, norms, and roles as well as the fortunes of life that exist within a society to the individual. To ensure this, (in)direct sanctions or rewards are used to bring about the desired societal behavior.[520] While some information is very widely distributed, such as knowledge about social rules or religious belief systems, other information cannot exist independently of roles.[521] For example in the context of a family business, which tasks are associated with the role of management. The children engage in interaction with others in the reference system of their interests and perspectives. This allows the adolescents to integrate into this reference system by identifying and adopting interaction strategies to develop a sense of order within social events. Thus, children see themselves as part of relationships and perform a description of themselves against the background of these relationships.[522] In detail, a distinction can be made between two categories of people who convey feelings, beliefs, and knowledge about the respective culture to the child:

1. Those who exercise authority[523] over the child as well as
2. those who are equal to the child.

---

[517] Cf. Hurrelmann (2002), p. 38.

[518] Goode (1967), p. 42.

[519] Neidhardt (1977), p. 280.

[520] Cf. Neidhardt (1977), p. 280.

[521] Cf. Baldwin (1974), p. 274.

[522] Cf. Youniss (1980), p. 55.

[523] According to Baumrind, an authority is "a person whose expertness befits him to designate a behavioral alternative for another where the alternatives are perceived by both" (Baumrind 1966, 887). Fromm (2009, 20) distinguishes between rational and irrational authority. While the *rational authority* is based on the recognition of a person's knowledge and competence, the *irrational authority* is based on fear and the exertion of pressure and has its starting point in the emotional subordination of people.

In general, the first category has a higher age and an immediate family relationship with the children, while the second category has approximately the same age, regardless of whether there is a family relationship or not.[524]

Finally, when considering the course of socialization, Parsons and Olds[525] do not see this as a linear process of continuous adaptation leading to a certain maturity. According to their view, it rather proceeds discontinuously, i.e., more in a spiral form. Only when development begins does this lead to greater maturity. Furthermore, socialization can be seen as a lifelong process.[526] This is due to the fact that, in addition to the biological conditions, the sociocultural circumstances or the groups to which the individual belongs are also subject to change.[527]

2.5.1.2 The Upbringing

The way parents educate their children has an impact on the development of the adolescents. As was shown in Sect. 2.4, the entrepreneurial parents can influence their descendant(s) in the sense of the family business and a willingness to take over the enterprise through their educational behavior. Especially how parents interact with their children influences them. While personal detachment, for example, can cause children to withdraw socially, exemplary narcissism may cause children to become self-centered.[528] Habig and Berninghaus formulate it this way: "Upbringing is first and foremost parents' role modeling and secondly a development through word and writing, through praise and blame as well as through reward and punishment."[529] Upbringing primarily fulfills the

[524] Cf. Davis (1966), p. 215 f.

[525] Cf. Parsons and Olds (1966), p. 190.

[526] Cf. Berger and Luckmann (2000), p. 148 and cf. Wurzbacher (1977b), p. 3.

[527] Cf. Wurzbacher (1977b), p. 3.

[528] Cf. Petzold (1999), p. 70 f. For Fromm narcissism is "an orientation in which every interest and passion is directed towards one's own person — towards one's own body, one's own mind, one's own feelings and interests. […] For the narcissistic person, only he and what concerns him is completely real; what is outside, what concerns others appears to him only superficially for his perception as real" (Fromm 2005, 153).

[529] Habig and Berninghaus (2004), p. 26. According to Schmidt and Schneewind, parental upbringing behavior "in a broader sense can refer to all actions and experiences of a certain parent person that directly or indirectly, directed or undirected relate to a specific child" (Schmidt and Schneewind 1978, 165 f.). When specifically considering the parental upbringing style, Witte (2005, 8) distinguishes between four forms: (1) the authoritative, (2) the authoritarian, (3) the laissez-faire, and (4) the indifferent upbringing. However, Leman (2012, 132 f.) and Baumrind (1966, 889 ff.) focus on "only" three upbringing styles: (1) the authoritarian upbringing, (2) the permissive (anti-authoritarian) upbringing, and (3) the authoritative upbringing.

task of knowledge transfer by which no specific knowledge is meant. For class-specific upbringing, Neidhardt[530] identifies three influencing factors that affect the adolescents:

1. *The norm function of parents*: Based on the parental manifest upbringing ideals, the children are educated in a specific way, through reward and punishment.
2. *The demonstration function of parents*: Parents serve the children as a model, which they can orient themselves on.
3. *The steering function of parents*: Parents also have the opportunity to influence their children's socialisation environments outside the family, e.g., in the choice of kindergarten or the choice of their friends.

According to Schmitt-Rodermund and Schröder[531], the following behaviors can provide a framework for upbringing within which the descendants can develop and shape their personality:

1. Parental warmth and appreciation
2. Setting of boundaries and the communication of expectations
3. Allowing independence and the responsibility of the possible consequences arising from it

However, Faulstich-Wieland and Faulstich[532] see upbringing as something finite. The necessity of upbringing is fulfilled when the child is old enough to decide for itself about its life, i.e., when it has reached maturity.

Therefore, if socialization and upbringing are compared, both terms denote a "transfer performance"[533], however, a difference in the way of passing on behavior patterns can be seen. If this is conveyed with intention, it falls into the area

[530] Cf. Neidhardt (1977), p. 282 f.

[531] Cf. Schmitt-Rodermund and Schröder (2009), p. 29 f.

[532] Cf. Faulstich-Wieland and Faulstich (2006), p. 51.

[533] Luhmann (1987a), p. 173.

of upbringing.[534] Although there is a "competence gradient"[535] in favor of the educators, upbringing always requires the process of interaction. Even though the adults are physically and psychologically superior to their children, they adapt their activities to the needs of their children, resulting in mutual influence.[536] However, parents not only pass on their own values, but also those that they received in their childhood through various reference groups (parents, grandparents, relatives, or family friends). They thus give the child (un)consciously to understand, which characteristics are (not) desirable.[537]

2.5.1.3 The Primary Socialization

When considering the industrialized and division-of-labor organized society, many social tasks are performed by specific entities (institutions[538]).[539] The upbringing of children is increasingly being taken over by societal institutions. These include, among others, the kindergarten, the school, or other forms of associations [540], i.e., every social contact.[541] Despite the increasing outsourcing, the family must still be assigned a key function as it influences the children during the formative phase of the socialization process.[542] Hurrelmann therefore refers to the family as the "central coordination point"[543] and according to Frese [544], parental

[534] Cf. Luhmann (1987a), p. 173. Luhmann understands upbringing as follows: "Upbringing, on the other hand, uses the reduction to actions to achieve something, that requires the coordination of a multitude of efforts, and therefore cannot be left to the chances of socializing events" (Luhmann 1994, 281). Luhmann further writes: "[...] Upbringing is, unlike socialization, already a functionally oriented social system, which arises and tends to differentiate precisely because society cannot be satisfied with the results of socialization processes" (Luhmann 1995 a, 91). Zimmermann puts it even more clearly: "Upbringing is not the same as socialization, but socialization is that, which is made possible, among other things, by upbringing, namely the acquisition of societal experiences" (Zimmermann 2000, 14).

[535] Zimmermann (2000), p. 16.

[536] Cf. Zimmermann (2000), p. 16; cf. Petzold (1999), p. 71 and cf. Schneewind (1982), p. 163.

[537] Cf. Meyer (2007), p. 109.

[538] Kormann writes on this: "Institutions steer the actions of the individual in a certain direction, namely in the direction of the goals set by the community" (Kormann 2011, 66) and Mead understands an institution as an "organization of attitudes" (Mead 1973, 255).

[539] Cf. Tillmann (2000), p. 109.

[540] Cf. Klein (2004), p. 67; cf. Simon (2000), p. 142 and cf. Tillmann (2000), p. 108.

[541] Cf. Luhmann (1990), p. 211.

[542] Cf. Hurrelmann (2002), p. 30.

[543] Hurrelmann (2002), p. 30.

[544] Cf. Frese (1983), p. 13.

and school socialization can influence the desire of children to pursue a certain career path.

In this process children do not only move in their "class-homogeneous social milieu"[545]. From an early age they are exposed to contacts, for example, through visits to kindergartens, relatives, playgroups, doctors, etc., which hold higher and lower (social) positions, and thus provide "imitation and identification offers"[546] outside the family's sphere of influence. Not to be neglected are the increasingly occurring mass media. These have an early influence on the children.[547] However, for the individual to accept and live according to these role models, they must be conveyed during the socialization process by the various institutions (family, school, profession, friends, etc.). Compliance is then ensured by various internal (e.g., one's own conscience) or external (e.g., the social environment or societal rules) control mechanisms. However, institutions outside the family are only seen as a supplement.[548] According to Hurrelmann [549], the various institutions can be assigned to three socialization instances.

1. Primary: Family, relatives, and friends
2. Secondary: Kindergarten, school, and educational institutions
3. Tertiary: Leisure organizations, media, and profession

545 Neidhardt (1977), p. 289.

546 See footnote 545.

547 Cf. Neidhardt (1977), p. 289. The special feature of the mass media is that, unlike other organizations, they have an anonymous audience as their addressees. The primary characteristic is the information and entertainment of broad sections of the population. The mass media must therefore be accorded enormous significance for their influence on personality development (cf. Hurrelmann 2002, 34). For further reading: *Postman*, N. (1994): Das Verschwinden der Kindheit, Frankfurt a. M.: Fischer Taschenbuch Verlag GmbH. For a more in-depth discussion of systems theory regarding the mass media, the following work is referred to: *Luhmann*, N. (1996): Die Realität der Massenmedien, 2. erw. Aufl., Opladen: Westdeutscher Verlag.

548 Cf. Busch and Scholz (2000), p. 10 ff.

549 Cf. Hurrelmann (2002), p. 34. For details on *secondary socialization* the following sources are referred to: Ecarius et al. (2008), p. 109; Oswald (2008), p. 321; Hurrelmann (2002), p. 31 and p. 199; Suess (2001), p. 50; Berger and Luckmann (2000), p. 148; Eisenstadt (1966), p. 166 f. and Tillmann (2000), p. 111 ff. For details on *tertiary socialization* the following sources are referred to: Klatetzki (2008), p. 361 and p. 378; Hurrelmann (2002), p. 33; Katz and Kahn (1978), p. 378 and Wurzbacher (1977b), p. 13.

Due to their great importance for the research question we will now go into detail on primary socialization. However, the stereotypical portrayal of the mother and father role should be pointed out right at the beginning. No one can completely escape this. Nevertheless, the role distribution shown is not a natural form. Especially against the background of the pluralization taking place, the increasing emergence of new forms of coexistence as well as social change, it should be possible to comprehend this.

If the focus is now directed towards primary socialization, then in all common societies most people are integrated into a network of familial rights, duties, and role relationships during their lives.[550] Therefore, specifically primary socialization forms a capable subject through the acquisition of a certain basic qualification. It does this in addition to the cognitive also on the motivational level. The importance of primary socialization is particularly seen in its far-reaching impact on the personality structure of the adult.[551] In this context the primary socialization function of the family arises primarily through the early and lasting imprinting of the personality of a member of society.[552] It is precisely the role relationships that the individual becomes aware of through the long phase of socialization during childhood. This enables it to get a sense of what expectations the other family members have of its behavior and the individual understands that this type of behavior is the "only" desirable one.[553] The children are taught certain role expectations by their parents from an early age as they perceive their parents' respective styles, identify with them and imitate them in play. [554] Schneewind and Lukesch describe this as follows: "The family as a social institution and its members as socialization agents have [...] a special role due to the primary character, the duration, and intensity of the relationships".[555] Thus, collected experiences during primary socialization can have a long-term formative impact.[556] Habermas also refers to this as "formation period"[557] and Berger and Luckmann understand primary socialization as "the first

---

[550] Cf. Goode (1967), p. 11.

[551] Cf. Habermas (1968), p. 15.

[552] Cf. Hurrelmann (2002), p. 127.

[553] Cf. Goode (1967), p. 11.

[554] Cf. Kracke and Hofer (2002), p. 97.

[555] Schneewind and Lukesch (1978), p. 11 f.

[556] Cf. Habermas (1968), p. 15.

[557] Habermas (1968), p. 15.

phase, through which the human being in his childhood becomes a member of society" [558].

As the family is regarded as the most important space for socialization, has a significant influence on the personality of the descendants,[559] and also represents the characteristic feature of every family business,[560]an insight into the "construct" of the family is provided below.

2.5.1.3.1 The Family: Convergence and Characterization

In all societies the family usually represents the smallest organizational unit for production and consumption. This tends to a kind of self-sufficiency as long as the daily needs of the members are concerned. To satisfy the needs, there is a division of the work to be done. These complement each other, which is beneficial for each member. Often there is a gender-separated specialization. For this reason, one gender usually only has a vague idea about the activity and the skills required for it of the other.[561] Considering the importance of the family for socialization, the following peculiarities arise: It constitutes the personal as well as the collective and social identity of a person. The family in particular — and this is undisputed in all socialization theories and research — is considered the central place "for the development of basic feelings and of value orientations, cognitive schemas, competencies of social action, achievement motivation, language style, world interpretations, formation of conscience" [562]. Nevertheless, it is not so easy to represent a family clearly.[563]

From a psychological perspective the family is seen "as a group of related people with a common past, present, and future"[564]. This creates a "*predetermined structure of meaning*"[565], which is influenced by the environment and whose social opportunities are predetermined.[566] In contrast, Maihofer et al. describe the family as "central institution of society"[567] and Petzold uses the term "private

---

[558] Berger and Luckmann (2000), p. 141.

[559] Cf. Stamm (2013), p. 33.

[560] Cf. Kempert (2008), p. 176.

[561] Cf. Linton (1965), p. 156.

[562] Zimmermann (2006), p. 84.

[563] Cf. Zimmermann (2006), p. 84.

[564] Kaiser (2005), p. 258.

[565] Häring (1954), p. 62.

[566] Cf. Häring (1954), p. 62.

[567] Maihofer et al. (2001), p. 8.

institution" [568] while Schneewind speaks of the "interaction community family" [569]. On the other hand, Oeter[570] understands the family as a "private entity" [571], which provides special amenities for its members. All other institutions rather connect to the family. Until then, the family has taught the individual the language and the adoption of innumerable social roles.[572] Nevertheless, the family should not only be seen as a relation between wife and husband or between children and parents. The family rather establishes a multitude of connections between the members of the family and the overarching society.[573] Everything that happens in, with, and around the family also has significant effects on the development of society.[574] The family has significant behavioral and endowment characteristics that have an uninterrupted effect on children.[575] However, the family initially consists of two sub-areas: (1) The partnership and (2) the parenthood. This separation is not only for analytical purposes, but is also given by the jurisprudence.

---

[568] Petzold (1999), p. 100.

[569] Schneewind (2008), p. 257.

[570] Cf. Oeter (1960b), p. 14.

[571] Oeter (1960b), p. 14.

[572] Cf. Goode (1967), p. 23. Particularly, language is according to Berger and Luckmann (2000, 144), one of the most important tools of socialization. It unfolds its meaning primarily for the emergence of the motivational as well as the cognitive level. Especially if language is considered a medium within the family, it conveys socialization processes, like the family role structure (cf. Habermas 1968, 25). The importance of language is also evident in Strauss (1974, 13). For him language must be given a central position in the treatment of human identity and action. Especially, identity is predominantly dependent on the possibility of representation through language. Language enables "the discussion of situation interpretations and the dispute about mutual expectations between interaction partners" (Krappmann 1993, 12).

[573] Cf. Goode (1967), p. 65.

[574] Cf. Maihofer et al. (2001), p. 8.

[575] Cf. Claessens (1979), p. 159. When considering individuals, most take on memberships in two different family groups during their lives, which can be explained by two different types of births: (1) when the individual is born and (2) when it begets another individual. In this context, the first family can also be referred to as the orientation family ("family of orientation" (Davis 1966, 399)). In it the ego is socialized and linked with the rest of the social organization. In contrast, the second family is called the procreation family ("family of procreation" (Davis 1966, 399)). In it the ego has children itself. In detail, the ego can be described as a link between these two families. The transition from one family to another can be associated with strains and (change) conflicts for the person concerned (cf. Davis 1966, 399).

Although these two components were always seen as a unit in the past, a more individual consideration is becoming increasingly prevalent in recent views.[576]

For a better distinction from other possible forms of living together, Nave-Herz[577] names three constitutive features of a family:

1. The *biological-social dual nature*: This results from the reproduction as well as the at least existing socialization function.[578]
2. Then the special *cooperation and solidarity relationship*: When groups are considered there are common goals, a limited number of members, and a kind of we-feeling. However, in the family is also a special role structure that only occurs within the family. This includes both the definitions of roles as well as their designations. Above all, the respective culture influences the number of roles as well as the expectations of the respective role.
3. Finally, the *generation differentiation*: Since there are families at different times and in different cultures that are not based on a marriage subsystem, gender differentiation is not used as a criterion. Otherwise, it would not be possible to speak of a family due to death or divorce.

Specifically, the family can be understood as a social structure, which takes care of the needs of its members. This is justified by the emotional connections and the awareness of responsibility as well as a certain loyalty that develops between

---

[576] Cf. Kaufmann (1988), p. 394. *Partnership*: In the Western cultural circle the principle of monogamy prevails. Whether this must be maintained for a lifetime or can only be justified by marriage is increasingly being questioned. This idealization of a lifelong and marriage-based partnership continues to exist, but it is no longer a success factor (cf. Kaufmann 1988, 394 f.). *Parenthood*: In contrast to the partnership a "normative consolidation" (Kaufmann 1988, 395) takes place in the sphere of parenthood. Parents are aware of their responsibility and therefore only consider the birth of a child when a secure future can be guaranteed for it. The low birth rate nowadays is also due to the reduced economic advantages of families with children (cf. Kaufmann 1988, 394). Tazi-Preve (2004, 109) understands parenthood as the care and upbringing of children. Often, a separation of tasks takes place, in such a way, that the mother guarantees the "continuous care" (Tazi-Preve 2004, 109) and the father is ready for the special, i.e., for play and other leisure activities.

[577] Cf. Nave-Herz (2007), p. 15.

[578] Lenz (2005, p. 13 f.) on the other hand, opposes the demand for the "reproductive function" (Lenz 2005, p. 13) to be a prerequisite for the application of the term family. This would imply a covert "biologism" (Lenz 2005, p. 13). He justifies this by referring to stepparents. While they may not become biological parents, they can become legal parents, which can also develop a complete parent-child relationship. Therefore, in his opinion, legal recognition is primarily decisive for the establishment of parenthood.

the members.[579] The family also provides a certain sense of identity. By this, Kormann means that "the group of family members recognizes and understands itself as a group separate from the rest of society" [580]. Metzger refers to the family as a "practice field for human development"[581] or as a "practice ground for human coexistence" [582]. This is ensured by the cohabitation of parents and siblings creating a relationship between the younger and older generation. The parents model their views to the children, and thus convey to them how they should behave, for example, towards their siblings or what rules apply to living together.[583]

In addition, each family has an individual personality. However, this personality profile is more than what is contributed by the personalities of the individual family members. The family is thus more than the sum of its parts. It creates its own culture with a certain dynamic.[584] Compared to an enterprise, the family, according to Rüsen [585], is oriented towards the involved family members. The focus is not on the task to be fulfilled, but on the individual. Therefore, the family has the primary task of maintaining itself as a social structure. It acts less according to economic principles and more according to emotion. Also cohabitation is subject to a certain dynamic. Therefore, the functions of individual members are subject to changes over time, "e.g., from a child who is diapered by its parents to an adult who diapers his (now) elderly and incontinent parents" [586]. Within the family no material compensation is demanded for fulfilled tasks, but rather "'personal debts and merit accounts' are kept" [587]. For a comparison between the characteristics and logics of the family and the business refer to Table 2.1.

In contrast to other groups, the family is also characterized by its relative independence and its "inter-generational continuity"[588]. This makes it particularly interesting in the face of structural changes (economic, cultural, and political

[579] Cf. Kepner (1983), p. 60.
[580] Kormann (2011), p. 74.
[581] Metzger (1960), p. 208.
[582] Metzger (1960), p. 213.
[583] Cf. Metzger (1960), p. 208.
[584] Cf. Klein (2004), p. 56.
[585] Cf. Rüsen (2009), p. 31 f.
[586] Rüsen (2009), p. 32.
[587] See footnote 586.
[588] Wurzbacher (1977b), p. 16.

changes) as the family provides a way of coping with life.[589] According to Neidhardt [590], the family is also characterized by a high degree of structural flexibility. This specifically means: "Authority distribution, position differentiation, and other structural arrangements must be correctable, related role definitions and role interpretations must be arrangeable."[591] In addition to the birth of children and their development into adults, the parents also go through their own life cycle. Thus, the family is subject to constant change to which it must adapt. Another characteristic feature of the family is its pronounced person-orientation. All members who belong to it, know each other or know more about each other than about non-family members.[592] Therefore, Simon refers to the family as an "extreme form of person-orientation" [593] or as the "prototype of the person-oriented system"[594], which puts the well-being of individual persons in the foreground. The relative constancy of the members is seen as a characteristic of this social context, whereby the form of interaction changes due to the physical and mental development of the members. This makes families highly adaptable to external changes in particular.[595]

If the focus is on communication within the family, it is easier to provoke and unsettle psychologically than communication in public.[596] Due to the person-oriented communication, matters of a person are therefore relevant for the entire family.[597] Since the identity of a family is not defined by firmly coupled interaction and communication patterns, it is possible for the family to break up in the event of drastic conflicts.[598] A dissolution of the family in this case resembles a "social bankruptcy"[599] as parents invest time, money, feelings, intimacy, and attention into the family to the same extent. For this reason, there will be a desire to preserve one's own family.[600] For the communication carried out within the

[589] Cf. Wurzbacher (1977b), p. 16.
[590] Cf. Neidhardt (1979), p. 169.
[591] Neidhardt (1979), p. 169.
[592] Cf. Luhmann (1990), p. 196.
[593] Simon (2007a), p. 81.
[594] Simon (2004), p. 85.
[595] Cf. Simon (2004), p. 85.
[596] Cf. Luhmann (1990), p. 202.
[597] Cf. Simon (2003), p. 37.
[598] Cf. Simon (2004), p. 86 and cf. Luhmann (1990), p. 202.
[599] Neidhardt (1979), p. 166.
[600] Cf. Neidhardt (1979), p. 166.

family, von Schlippe et al. suggest the term "bonding communication" [601]. Since family communication has an informal and person-related character, [602] Simon refers to it as a "predominantly individual-related intimate communication" [603]. If less personal relationships are considered first, a justification or the presence of certain criteria is necessary to inquire into other personal areas. For the family the reverse case applies: Personal communication rather implies an obligation to justify for the person who wants to refuse the answer. However, if an organization wants to find out what one of its members did in the evening, it must justify this, for example, because the member was responsible for the night shift. Meanwhile in the family, everything is generally considered relevant so the topic cannot simply be ignored. Accordingly, it can sometimes be difficult to avoid the situation.[604]

Another possibility is to understand the family as a "life and living or household community that includes at least two people and two generations"[605]. This seems particularly useful for two functions that the family fulfills: It serves both the *biological* and the *social reproduction* of society. The family is particularly referred to as the most important institution within our society for social reproduction. It imparts to the new generation "essential key qualifications such as social skills in the familial socialization and upbringing process" [606]. If there were no families, these tasks would have to be performed by other institutions.[607] In general, according to Prisching [608], the following basic societal functions can be assigned to the family institution:

1. Reproduction function
2. Upbringing function
3. Ensuring primary socialization
4. Economic function, i.e., providing basic care
5. Providing a private living space.

---

[601] von Schlippe et al. (2011), p. 526.
[602] Cf. Simon (2004), p. 145.
[603] Simon (2004), p. 145.
[604] Cf. Kieserling (1994), p. 23 f.
[605] Busch and Scholz (2000), p. 31.
[606] Busch and Scholz (2000), p. 9.
[607] Cf. Busch and Scholz (2000), p. 9 f.
[608] Cf. Prisching (1995), p. 165; cf. Burkart (2008), p. 144 and cf. Davis (1966), p. 394 f.

Further characteristics of the family system are (according to Fink[609]):

1. Orientation of values and goals towards the well-being of the members
2. Maintaining relationships between members
3. Person-independent completion of tasks
4. Dominance of emotionally charged behaviors

Similarly, according to Kepner[610], the family fulfills the following two tasks: The satisfaction of social and emotional needs as well as a certain identity formation. Goode[611] extends the societal task of the family to include social placement and social control. Above all, the social position of the parents influences the life situation of the descendants.[612] Within the family there are two levels of interaction: The *vertical* and the *horizontal relationship networks.* The vertical orientation describes the parent-child relationship. Here, the moral obligation of the parents to satisfy the needs of the children exists. The relationship between siblings is referred to as horizontal relationship. Here, the individual's right to receive the same level of resources and attention exists.[613]

2.5.1.3.2 The Function of the Family

As already indicated, the family is the most important transmitter of primary socialization. Due to its specialization, it provides a "psychological stabilization and elementary emotional bonds"[614]. Above all, the face-to-face interaction promotes understanding about the existence of certain expectations between the participants, which connects them with each other.[615] The family is again embedded in further socialization contexts, which influence life within the family, and thus the socialization of the descendants.[616]

Precisely because the family is embedded in a functionally differentiated society and the children are cared for by an institution outside the family from a very early age, i.e., from kindergarten, the socialization function of the family,

[609] Cf. Fink (2008), p. 80.
[610] Cf. Kepner (1983), p. 60.
[611] Cf. Goode (1967), p. 18.
[612] Cf. Hobi-Ragaz (2008), p. 44.
[613] Cf. Lansberg (1983), p. 42.
[614] Burkart (2005), p. 103.
[615] Cf. Abels and König (2010), p. 115.
[616] Cf. Zimmermann (2000), p. 83.

according to Simon[617], is limited to preparing the children in an adequate way for public life, and thus enabling the adolescents to "*communicate inconspicuously in non-family contexts*"[618]. In this context, the family exhibits different types of social relationships and behaviors, which in turn enable the family to provide a socialization function. Against this background, the individual within the family is taught not only different types of behaviors, but also various ways to resolve tensions and frustrations that occur within social life. The individual learns to delay the immediate satisfaction of his needs and to adapt his behavior to the expectations of his role as well as the norms and rules within the family.[619] Psychoanalysis assumes that the child is only capable of developing self-confidence if the parents respond to his behaviors. If the child feels that the parents take little joy in his existence, it does not develop a positive attitude towards itself. Only if the child receives positive reactions from the parents to his behaviors does it develop the feeling of meaning something to the parents. This necessity of emotional transmission is even more important the younger the child is.[620] In addition, parental support of the children contributes to the transmission of a stronger sense of self-worth although excessive support can overwhelm them.[621] According to Davis [622], the family exhibits the following six strategic characteristics, which are significant for socialization:

1. *The child is born into the family-first and initially exhibits a kind of social void ("social blank"*[623]*)*: Therefore, it will not be malleable to a higher degree during its life. Thus, the first steps of socialization begin within the family. All other instances follow only afterwards and build on the foundations set by the family.
2. *The family represents the most enduring factor in a child's life*: The closest contact to the children in their early life is established by the parents. This results in a very intimate and consistent influence of the parents.
3. *The family is a primary group and conveys a "we-feeling"*: The more this is pronounced, the lower are the barriers for the transmission of attitudes and opinions.

---

617 Cf. Simon (2000), p. 144.

618 Simon (2000), p. 144.

619 Cf. Eisenstadt (1966), p. 31.

620 Cf. Diem-Wille (1996), p. 95.

621 Cf. Diem-Wille (1996), p. 144.

622 Cf. Davis (1966), p. 405 f.

623 Davis (1966), p. 405.

4. *The family satisfies the child's needs*: In addition to material needs such as food and drink, the most important mental needs such as security and affection are also satisfied. Although satisfaction decreases from birth with increasing age, there is no other group that can satisfy the child's needs to the same extent.
5. *The family provides two types of relationships in which socialization takes place*: (1) between the parents and the children, which is characterized by authority. (2) between siblings, which is characterized by equality and equal rights. Since the family provides both unique and necessary elements of socialization within a small circle, this allows for a special completeness in the exercise of these functions. This distinguishes the family from playgroups, for example, which operate almost exclusively based on equality.
6. *The family members recognize themselves as a community and integrate the children into their social structure*: The child identifies first and foremost with its family, which is maintained throughout its entire life. Only after the establishment of a family of its own may it be subject to change. However, by then the socialization process is almost completed.

2.5.2 The Family Business as a Context for Socialization

After addressing primary socialization, the family business as a context for socialization will be examined next.

Considering entrepreneur parents first, different initial situations for the upbringing of specific children may arise for them. If the first child is born, for example, during the establishment phase of the enterprise, the enterprise often requires a maximum amount of attention. Therefore, there will probably be less time available for the child. If the next child is born during a phase when the enterprise is already established and business is flourishing, the parents can spend more time with this child.[624] Even if a certain ideal of equality prevails towards children, maintaining it is almost impossible, as children are usually not only born at different times, but above all, parents can find themselves in different life situations (private and professional). Another factor that rather causes inequality is specifically found in the children themselves: They show different abilities and developmental paths.[625]

---

[624] Cf. Simon (2012), p. 52.

[625] Cf. Simon (2003), p. 38.

If descendants are differentiated based on gender, differences in business families become apparent based on this. There are differences, particularly in terms of compensating for the low time budget. The women interviewed reported that their brothers in particular were spoiled by their mothers. As a result, their willingness to perform decreased and they failed. Haubl and Daser suspect "that such mothers unconsciously try to achieve in their sons the emotional responsiveness they have to forego with their husbands"[626]. But the fathers also try to compensate for their absence through material compensations: "They buy their way out of their bad conscience, which the children ultimately always feel, which is why they take their father's money, but despise him for it."[627] The daughters interviewed described the behavior of fathers "in whom high enterprise-related performance expectations went hand in hand with a greatly reduced emotional resonance and pronounced pettiness"[628] quite differently. For them, it was unimaginable to grant the children any kind of amenities, even though, it would have been possible. They presuppose enormous efforts without any compensation. This is a typical image, especially for fathers who spent their childhood during the war.[629]

If gender-specific socialization is examined in detail, girls and boys learn primarily through the observation of women and men what is expected of them when they grow up. Usually, children identify more with adults of the same sex. The desire to be just like them often arises. Thus, role models not only offer children future images of themselves, but also influence their goals and aspirations. Therefore, the role models of adults have a significant influence on the acquisition of gender roles.[630] Especially in the case of entrepreneurial parents, there are often considerable differences in parental expectations regarding the life paths of sons and daughters. While sons are repeatedly expected to acquire technical and business skills at home and abroad to be best prepared for (possible) succession, daughters are rather neglected. From the parents' point of view, it usually seems appropriate for the daughters to acquire their skills through work in the family business.[631] The expectations for the life paths of daughters and sons often differ among fathers. While the daughters are expected to start a family according to the ideal image, the sons are expected to continue the family business.[632] This

---

[626] Haubl and Daser (2006), p. 35.

[627] See footnote 626.

[628] Haubl and Daser (2006), p. 36.

[629] Cf. Haubl and Daser (2006), p. 35 f.

[630] Cf. Weitzman et al. (1972), p. 1139.

[631] Cf. Welter-Enderlin (2005), p. 161.

[632] Cf. Iannarelli (1992), p. 13 f.

was already apparent under the topic of succession (see Sect. 2.4). If the mothers are employed within the enterprise, the daughters are often trained by them as the daughters often perform the same tasks or roles as the mothers. Traditionally, these are jobs in the office or in sales. However, if the mothers are not employed in the enterprise, the daughters can usually choose their employment freely.[633] Nevertheless, Iannarelli[634] concludes from the evaluation of her study that daughters spend less time in the family business, and thus build up fewer competencies. They are also encouraged less often for business-relevant things than their brothers.

Thus, it can often be assumed that the life path of children of entrepreneurs is to some extent "predetermined". Often everything is geared towards taking over the family business from the parents in the future.[635] Thus, children in business families often fulfill the future function of the heir.[636] According to Kersting and Kamper-Jasper [637], this leads in an increasingly individualizing society to inner conflicts of the descendants. They are pressed into a track that they may not want or be able to fulfill and are "unwillingly put in the role of deciding on the meaning and meaninglessness of their parents' lives" [638]. Therefore, the socialization in a business family can be viewed from two sides: In addition to a privileged position through the family business[639] the children often grow up "in the shadow of the business" [640]. LeMar formulates this as follows: "Children of well-known enterprises have, figuratively speaking, a stamp on their forehead and are associated with what the enterprise represents or has represented in the past. In the sense of a 'self-fulfilling prophecy', the children cannot develop according to their own nature. They behave as others consciously and unconsciously expect of them."[641] In addition, descendants generally have connections with their ancestors in addition to their current relationships with family members.[642] Especially in the case of descendants from business families, their personal socialization

---

[633] Cf. Iannarelli (1992), p. 83 and p. 127.

[634] Cf. Iannarelli (1992), p. 179.

[635] Cf. Kersting and Kamper-Jasper (2002), p. 85.

[636] Cf. Klein (2004), p. 79.

[637] Cf. Kersting and Kamper-Jasper (2002), p. 85.

[638] Kersting and Kamper-Jasper (2002), p. 85.

[639] Cf. Meyer (2007), p. 108 f.

[640] Simon et al. (2005), p. 61.

[641] LeMar (2014), p. 122.

[642] Cf. Popitz (1980), p. 80.

history is inextricably linked to the family and, above all, the family business history.[643]

Therefore, when considering descendants from family businesses, they are exposed to an additional socialization context, which owes its existence to the parents or the participating family members and is fundamentally co-determined by them.[644] Due to the often-existing insufficient separation between family and business, the descendants growing up in it learn very early about the emotional significance of the business for their parents or for their family. Simon assumes this for founding families and multi-generational family businesses with the model of the re-staging of the nuclear family. This can put the children under enormous pressure to adapt their life design according to the requirements of the business ([I.1]).[645] Descendants from family businesses are therefore often exposed to a double burden from birth: (1) They must develop their own identity like any other child and (2) additionally come to terms with the idea of being a possible successor to the business.[646]

Above all, entrepreneurial parents must be aware that their children primarily acquire an idea or knowledge about the family business through their conversations.[647] This is referred to as "'shop talk', or the language of the family business" [648]. Especially when entrepreneurs want to pass on their business to the next generation, they should consciously choose their words regarding the business and not constantly complain about difficulties in the family business.[649] Since it makes a difference how parents talk about their own business, i.e., about everyday life in the enterprise, the frequency seems to be particularly interesting. Young people from family businesses were surveyed in the study by Schmitt Rodermund and Schröder[650]: In 41% of the cases, parents spoke about the enterprise on a daily basis. In another 41% of cases, they talked about their workday several times a week. In addition, 27% conveyed positive, 20% negative, and 53% balanced content regarding their professional everyday life. Based on the results an influence on socialization is not ruled out. Thus, the children get to

---

[643] Cf. Berning and Novak (2010), p. 112.

[644] Cf. Kormann (2011), p. 91.

[645] Cf. Simon (2008a), p. 60.

[646] Cf. LeMar (2014), p. 112.

[647] Cf. Cater and Justis (2009), p. 7.

[648] Rashad (2013), p. 146.

[649] Cf. Cater and Justis (2009), p. 7.

[650] Cf. Schmitt-Rodermund and Schröder (2009), p. 23 f. n = 155 business families, of which 255 are teenagers. Average age 16.4 years.

know the enterprise not only through direct growth, but also through stories. They gain insights into the decisions to be made as well as the various expectations placed on the parents. They also see how the parents act within the interplay of family and business. Therefore, they gather knowledge not only about the enterprise itself, but also about the significance of a family business.[651] Iannarelli[652] refers to the children in this context as "participating observers". The knowledge transfer takes place from the older to the younger generation; this can happen anywhere: Be it at the lunch table, at family celebrations, or through practice in the family business. This knowledge collected throughout life, is referred to as "accumulated knowledge", which the children can use as a resource.

Especially when entrepreneurs are at the beginning of their entrepreneurial career, they often have no money to hire caregivers for their children. Therefore, there is often a need to "integrate" these into the daily business routine. Another reason for the inclusion of children in the enterprise is seen in the work of both parents in the enterprise. Often this becomes their "home".[653] Particularly since the enterprise is a constant part of the daily life or daily communication of business families, the children growing up in it are often confronted with economic issues or problems at a very early age. The relevance of the enterprise — be it financial or emotional — for the respective family or families is brought to the children's consciousness every day. For the descendants the enterprise can then either be seen as a competitor for the parents' attention or serve as an object of identification.[654]

When looking specifically at the puberty of entrepreneurial children, there is often no room for this due to the family's involvement in the enterprise. This suppression can have serious consequences for the development of personality. Thus, there is a risk of not developing a sense for one's own opportunities and limitations. In many cases, this lack is then made up for in later stages of life.[655] Many entrepreneurial children find themselves confronted at a young age with the prospect of having to follow in their parents' footsteps, and thus act as entrepreneurs. Therefore, the socialization process within business families, which sees entrepreneurial activity as a matter of course is characteristic.[656] Usually, the influence of the family diminishes during the socialization process

[651] Cf. Stamm (2013), p. 190 f. and cf. Stamm et al. (2010), p. 5.

[652] Cf. Iannarelli (1992), p. 41.

[653] Cf. Iannarelli (1992), p. 74.

[654] Cf. Simon (2012), p. 66; cf. Simon (2008a), p. 59 and cf. Simon (2005), p. 43.

[655] Cf. Wimmer (1997), p. 149.

[656] Cf. Pfannenschwarz (2008), p. 165.

as other stages of socialization increasingly take their place (during secondary and tertiary socialization). However, when looking at business families, the prevailing interaction between family and business does not necessarily result in a loss of significance of the family for the (already in the enterprise employed) successor.[657]

If the siblings in business families are considered in this context, rivalries between them appear to be intensified. In business families these revolve not only around the affection and attention of the parents, but also around the division of wealth, power, and influence. In this context it is often not a question of a purely factual division, but rather of clarifying who is more highly regarded by the parents.[658] However, the rivals do not act on the same eye level if only one descendant is chosen for succession.[659] While there is a principle of equal treatment within the family, this is predominantly not the case in enterprises (see Table 2.1). There are usually clear hierarchies. If two siblings are employed in the family business and they hold different positions, the structures can be threatened by an emotional overlay. It should therefore be considered in advance, whether the successors will even join the enterprise at different hierarchical levels.[660] For many entrepreneurs their children represent a kind of potential reserve. With statements like: "'One of you will take over my business one day. I will decide who that will be when the time comes. Until then, do your best'" [661], a competitive relationship between the siblings can be created at best. Similarly, the uncertainty about which descendant will ultimately be allowed to succeed can lead to the descendants deciding against succession and pursuing a different profession.[662] Particularly in entrepreneurial families, there is often a need to place one's own needs and preferences behind the needs of the enterprise

---

[657] Cf. García-Álvarez et al. (2002), p. 190.

[658] Cf. Simon (2008 a), p. 61. One explanatory approach how the feelings of competition can be invalidated and how additionally the difference between siblings can be explained can be seen in the "process of adaptive radiation" (Sulloway 1999, 102). This allows siblings to create a niche within the family, and thus develop different interests and abilities, which can lead to a reduction of the competition thought (cf. Sulloway 1999, 102 f.). Sohni speaks in this context of the so-called "niche specialization" (Sohni 2011, 59). The starting point is often a required "coexistence of competitors" (Sohni 2011, 59) for the favor of the parents. This can manifest itself through the birth order (cf. Kepner 1983, 66). Siblings therefore occupy adaptable niches in the family system so that they can gain access to parental resources (cf. Sulloway 1999, 205).

[659] Cf. Baus (2010), p. 33.

[660] Cf. Baus (2010), p. 27.

[661] Bieler (2012), p. 29.

[662] Cf. Bieler (2012), p. 29 f.

([I.11]). These are often tabooed. Felden puts it this way: "The sister sees her life's work in the entrepreneurial activity, but does not express this because the brother has been designated as the crown prince for the enterprise from childhood" [663]. These unexpressed wishes can then emerge after the parents' death and lead to conflicts.[664]

In summary, if considering the family business and its influence on the socialization of the descendants, the enterprise cannot exert direct influence, but indirectly through the people involved and, over all, through the entrepreneurial parents. This is illustrated by the following points:

1. If one or both parent(s) are employed in the enterprise, the behaviors from the work environment are likely to find their way into the family as well. This is not only limited to business families, but can be assumed for all professions that demand the personality to the utmost.
2. In the context of the enterprise the descendants often encounter their relatives and co-partners — at least from a certain generation onward. These provide the descendants with additional role models.
3. The employees also serve as further role models. Being in the enterprise or talking to the employees brings the rules and procedures closer to the descendants.[665]

2.5.2.1 Influence of the Descendants by the Entrepreneurial Parents

Looking first at parental behaviors, Freund[666] classifies the following characteristics based on his study, which are positively and negatively received by children of entrepreneurs:

Positive

1. Fair behavior towards employees and business partners.
2. Ability to solve problems regardless of their level of difficulty.
3. Enjoying work.

---

[663] Felden (2012), p. 145.

[664] Cf. Felden (2012), p. 145. Similarly, sibling rivalries in some family businesses may require the enterprise to be split into different divisions as these rivalries are too intense and cooperation appears impossible. Thus, the contact between the siblings can be reduced to a minimum (cf. Davis 1983, 52).

[665] Cf. Kormann (2011), p. 94.

[666] Cf. Freund (2000), p. 94 f.

4. A stable family life, regardless of how much time the father can devote to it, as the mother is attributed a pivotal role; quality is the focus.

Negative

1. Father's lack of time, especially if he does not convey any noticeable joy in his work.
2. Negative exercise of power by the father.
3. Lack of interest in areas of life outside the family business.

In general, the entrepreneur is on his own in everyday business, i.e., in decision-making, setting goals, or monitoring success. Therefore, these individuals are likely to value an independent and self-reliant life.[667] In addition, there may be a desire to serve as a role model ([I.70 and I.71]). Male entrepreneurs are often "more risk-taking, more success and performance-oriented, more innovative, and internally controlled personalities" [668]. When comparing employees with entrepreneurs, entrepreneurs generally show a higher degree of performance motivation ([I.72]).[669] These mentioned character traits can then also affect the family area, thereby influencing the socialization of the growing children ([I.73]). See Interviews 2.24.

Most entrepreneurs have a very intense relationship with their own enterprise. For them the enterprise can be like their own child ([I.75]) to which there is a pronounced emotional relationship ([I.77]). It is precisely the multi-generational existence that strengthens this bond ([I.74]). Therefore, there is often the desire or the wish to pass on the enterprise to their own descendants ([I.76]). This wish is then reflected in the father's upbringing, which in turn has an influence on the socialization of the descendants (see Interviews 2.25).

Nevertheless, it should not be surprising if potential successors suffer from the behavior or personality of the father. Thus, the required willingness to perform within the family and the experienced absence of the father ([I.78 and I.80]) as well as the feeling of not meeting the expectations can significantly affect socialization ([I.79]). Likewise, a lack of attention can be perceived as negative ([I.81]). See Interviews 2.26.

When considering education parents also influence this (in)directly. For the entrepreneur the question may arise, whether the children should do what is best

[667] Cf. Brandstätter (1999), p. 156.

[668] Schmitt-Rodermund and Silbereisen (1999), p. 116.

[669] Cf. Müller (1999), p. 175.

Interviews 2.24 Characteristics of the entrepreneur [I.70–73]

[I.70]—[I.71]	Entrepreneur: "There are around 100 employees who I have known for a long time and who believe in me. As an entrepreneur I have a lifelong obligation to be a role model for my employees."[a] [I.70] The same entrepreneur: "My basic attitude is to be a role model — in everything I do. [...] In short, social status is very important to me. I was born in a small village [...] with 625 inhabitants. There, social status mattered a lot. As a 21-year-old lieutenant, I was taken prisoner of war in Czechoslovakia. Even in this situation it was important to be a role model. My entire career was marked by the obligation to be a role model."[a] [I.71]
[I.72]	Junior of a medium-sized enterprise: "*[...] He is not at all the type who can just do nothing. Enjoying life on a beautiful beach in the South Seas with a drink in his hand, that would not be a pleasure for him, but rather a prison sentence, if he could not constantly keep in touch with his enterprise by phone. [...]*"[b]
[I.73]	Female shareholder: "My father's parenting style was not authoritarian, but clearly permissive. Unlike my mother, he was far removed from the everyday parenting. [...] His wishes were read from his eyes as much as possible. Since he was used to making decisions, he decided with friendly self-assuredness even where he had no expertise. [...] It became very clear that dealing with childish stubbornness was difficult for him when we hit puberty. The teenager's own will had little chance of being enforced if it did not correspond to his will. [...] Discipline and composure were key words in my father's vocabulary. [...] With the help of discipline and composure the rule was to get along with each other: Do not argue, so as not to get entangled. [...]"[c]

[a]Juritsch et al. (2007), p. 77.
[b]LeMar (2001), p. 99.
[c]Haas (2005), p. 91 f.

for them or what they wish for, or whether a course of education is advantageous that brings benefits to the family business.[670] As already addressed under Sect. 2.4.1, this can cause ambivalence among parents. Almost all interview partners of Diem-Wille[671] confirm the influence of parents on the professional biography. Especially if the parents did not have the opportunity to achieve a certain level of education, they can push their children to pursue a specific educational path ([I.82 and I.83]). However, the opposite case can also occur. If the choice of study of the descendants is not compatible with the requirements of the

[670] Cf. Lansberg (1983), p. 43.

[671] Cf. Diem-Wille (1996), p. 18.

Interviews 2.25 Connection between entrepreneur and enterprise [I.73–77]

[I.74]	Entrepreneur: "I grew up on a farm and it was a given that the handover takes place within the family. I also took over the business from my grandfather. But you must prepare for it a bit from the beginning. Of course, you need children who you must upbring accordingly and who bring the prerequisites for a takeover."[a]
[I.75]	Senior entrepreneur: "»[...] And it dissolved the whole connection that I had built up over 25 years — it was my baby — in one fell swoop. [...]«"[b]
[I.76]	Entrepreneur, 2nd generation: "*[...] 'a succession should be somewhere in some form, — yes, it should be there! Because I wouldn't [takes a breath] like to give up or sell the enterprise, so soundlessly. Because for that [takes a breath] two generations have put too much into it! [...]'*"[c]
[I.77]	Entrepreneur: "»I have bought and sold many enterprises and I must say, the more you have built up yourself and the more you have worked on it yourself, the more you sell your lifeblood with it. If you were only (financially) involved, it is easier«."[d]

[a] Juritsch et al. (2007), p. 65.
[b] Loos (2010), p. 12 f.
[c] Siefer (1996), p. 252.
[d] Loos (2010), p. 54.

enterprise, it can be denied by the parents ([I.84]). Thus, the children can either decide for an education in the sense of the enterprise, which does not correspond to their inclinations ([I.82]) or they study out of a certain matter of course exactly what seems beneficial to the family business ([I.85]). The first case in particular can then lead to a break with the family business at a later stage. Through the connection of the family with the business the concerns of the enterprise influence the family sphere, so that a certain pressure is built up by the parents on the successors regarding their education. The extent to which the parents influence the choice of education and the extent to which the enterprise exerts its influence on the decendants becomes clear from the interviews [I.86-I.88]. It gives the impression that the descendants simply submit to their fate without having a choice left. The influence of the family business is particularly evident in [I.88]. The own education is not completed as the father needs an additional workforce (see Interviews 2.27).

After it became clear that parents influence the choice of education, the level of education and its contents are subsequently examined in detail. Looking at the school education of those interviewed by Pfannenschwarz[672], 23 interviewees

[672] Cf. Pfannenschwarz (2006b), p. 14. n = 30 respondents.

Interviews 2.26 Negative influence of paternal behavior [I.78–81]

[I.78]—[I.79]	Eldest son who was intended for succession: "'I didn't want to put all my life energy into the enterprise like my father! Even my grandfather died of overwork. I wanted to implement my own, very different visions of life. I also suffered a lot from the fact that my father was never there for me because he worked so much. I wanted to do it differently with my own family, with my children and my wife.'"[a] [I.78] His second statement also reveals the pronounced family imprint: "'No matter how much I work, it catches up with me. I am in the same stream as my father and my grandfather were: My work comes first for me then the family. Although, I want it differently inside and keep trying, I cannot free myself from this performance claim to self-sacrifice.'"[b] [I.79]
[I.80]	Son who was intended for succession, 3rd generation: "*...I had the feeling from the beginning that you won't make it anyway ... I would probably have been better off if I hadn't had sisters who were so diligent, my two sisters and then a father who stood miles above me.*"[c]
[I.81]	"'...yes, he (predecessor) has always been sparing with praise towards any employees or family members, I never experienced much of that. A little praise would do me good...'"[d]

[a]Wandl and Habenicht (2011), p. 24.
[b]Wandl and Habenicht (2011), p. 25.
[c]Levold et al. (2005), p. 230.
[d]Müller (2008), p. 371.

have a high school diploma, four have a secondary school diploma, and three have a lower secondary school diploma. In the study by Schmitt-Rodermund and Schröder[673], the descendants were asked about their highest desired educational degree. The following distribution resulted:

1. University studies: 52% d(aughters) | 40% s(ons)
2. Vocational training: 31% d | 43% s
3. High school diploma: 15% d | 9 % s
4. Middle school certificate: 2% d | 7% s

[673] Cf. Schmitt-Rodermund and Schröder (2009), p. 15. n=155 business families, of which 255 are teenagers. Average age 16.4 years.

Interviews 2.27 Direct and indirect influence on the choice of education [I.82–88]

[I.82]	Daughter, 3rd generation: "[…] In our situation, mother who also came from a craftsman's business and there as a young woman without much education, had run the office, played a partisan role. Since she herself suffered from a lack of education, she motivated us to attend the Gymnasium *[school form]* and reassured father with the prospect that perhaps one of us would succeed him after the Matura [high school degree]. […] The fact, that this did not happen was difficult for him and for us. Because loyalty to the family was important to us children and is so to this day. For a while our youngest and most loyal sister stayed at home, learned to be a florist against her inclination and ran the business together with our parents until she finally emigrated to New Zealand with her husband. […]"[a]
[I.83]	Daughter: "'Above all, it was immensely important to my father that I complete my studies,' she said. The father himself was not allowed to study because he was supposed to take over his grandfather's business."[b]
[I.84]	Entrepreneur: "'[…] My greatest wish was that what has been built, […] that the children will continue it. […] I asked, what do we want to study?' 'Architecture'. […] Then I said: 'If so, then I'll tear your head off. […] If you follow me, the […] enterprise is like a cow. You must feed it […] properly and then you can milk it properly' […]."[c]
[I.85]	Entrepreneur: "'There was no choice of study in that sense for me. For me it was always clear to study law. […] There was no consciously perceptible family pressure, even though there was certainly a certain expectation in this direction. My father was my 'idol'. And the job suits me well. Above all, you can earn money with it. Of course, my parents were pleased with my decision. I have never questioned it for myself.'"[d]
[I.86]	Successor: "'*…my parents didn't want me to do something else professionally first and there was a big fuss. Then I decided and said, OK, then I will come after my studies directly…*'"[e]
[I.87]	Son: "'*… So basically, I was drilled to study. I always wanted to do … I definitely followed this call, namely the paternal call and started studying…*'"[f]
[I.88]	Successor: "'*We were basically raised towards a handover. It was clear for me. I never questioned this step. I did the HAK [school form in Austria] and then studied business administration for four semesters, but did not complete it because my father needed me in the enterprise. I was only briefly, three months, employed at the Länderbank. Then my father said: 'If you are going to work anyway, you can do it here.' So, I started here in 1979 as an employee and was responsible for cost accounting, IT, accounting.* '"[g]

[a] Welter-Enderlin (2005), p. 147.
[b] Diem-Wille (1996), p. 34 f.
[c] Brückner (2011), p. 178.
[d] Mätzener and Schwarz (2008), p. 82.
[e] Müller (2008), p. 246.
[f] Baumgartner (2009), p. 102.
[g] Mätzener and Schwarz (2008), p. 84.

In the study by Dej et al.[674], 51.4% of the surveyed entrepreneurs have a university degree. The results also show a gender differentiation in addition to the high

[674] Cf. Dej et al. (2010), p. 48. n = 243 respondents.

level of education. When looking at the main areas of study of successors, the survey by Stiftung Familienunternehmen[675] reveals the following distribution:

1. Business Administration (59.0%)
2. Economics (15.4%)
3. Engineering (12.3%)
4. Communication Sciences (10.8%)
5. Law (6.7%)

Above all, an educational degree serves as a starting point for future professional development.[676] The results show the importance of a qualified educational degree within business families. However, this will also be related to the life cycle of the family business. As described under Sect. 2.2.6, the qualification of the descendants usually increases with each new generation.

Nevertheless, pressure induced by parents can also have the opposite effect. Often, the greater the pressure to steer the descendants in a certain direction, the greater their resistance usually is.[677] If the old entrepreneur wants to create a faithful image of himself in his descendants, this will likely fail ([I.89]).[678] In addition, the determination of education by parents can lead to conflicts among siblings, especially when younger siblings are denied the same education because they were not intended for succession ([I.90]). See Interviews 2.28.

In addition to the possibility of influencing school and study choice, the career choice of children can also be influenced by the parents and their role model effect. The children develop an idea of the suitable professions for them and the relevant training paths based on their parents. Specifically, the professional development of daughters or their desire to pursue a non-traditional profession is influenced by the mothers' employment.[679] For mothers who work in family businesses, Iannarelli puts it this way: "When the mothers worked in the business, the daughters shared not only similar roles but also maintained similar goals

[675] Cf. Stiftung Familienunternehmen (2011a), p. 27. n = 202 respondents.

[676] Cf. Schmitt-Rodermund and Schröder (2009), p. 15.

[677] Cf. Felden (2012), p. 153 and cf. Felden and Pfannenschwarz (2008), p. 121.

[678] Cf. Felden and Pfannenschwarz (2008), p. 126.

[679] Cf. Kracke and Hofer (2002), p. 97.

Interviews 2.28 Determination of education [I.89–90]

[I.89]	Statement of a 14-year-old who has been chosen as a future successor: "'*I have a mom and a dad, but they apparently love the enterprise more than me. Whenever I need them, they say: 'Just a moment, sweetheart, I just have to ...' And then they have forgotten what I wanted. This stupid enterprise has already taken my dad away from me. They always complain about how much they must do. And now comes the worst part: They want me to work in this enterprise later in my life. Even though, dad often says: 'I would like to throw the whole thing away!' If only he would do it once. [...] And now comes the absolute worst: they really want to put me in this other school. That would be a better preparation for me to succeed dad, they say. But not with me! I want to become a web designer, at least I would like to do something creative.* '"[a]
[I.90]	Case description: "The father always manages to pit the two brothers against each other, so that they distrust each other and speak little with each other. Anton is jealous of Michael because he is allowed to learn carpentry. Michael did not decide this for himself, but the father decided this for him. Both brothers suffer equally from the lack of conversations in the family and they both would have needed a confrontation in a positive sense with their father."[b]

[a]LeMar (2001), p. 140 f.
[b]Wandl and Habenicht (2011), p. 17.

of supporting the male leaders in the business."[680] Schmitt-Rodermund and Silbereisen[681] conclude from their study that in fact "precursors for entrepreneurial interests seem to lie in the family interaction, which then in turn lead to earlier independent actions and success with it" [682]. They further write: "In summary, it can be stated, [...] that indirectly family characteristics are significant for entrepreneurial success as well as that personality promotes entrepreneurial success."[683] Especially during childhood, the parents and specifically the mothers have the greatest influence on the children.[684] A direct influence on the children must also be attributed to the parental relationship. If there is a certain aggressive tone between the parents, this is likely to be reflected in the interaction with the

[680] Iannarelli (1992), p. 127.

[681] Cf. Schmitt-Rodermund and Silbereisen (1999), p. 124. Survey of entrepreneurs (owners and managers) using 97 written questionnaires.

[682] Schmitt-Rodermund and Silbereisen (1999), p. 136.

[683] Schmitt-Rodermund and Silbereisen (1999), p. 138 f.

[684] Cf. Wilson and Edington (1987), p. 11.

Interviews 2.29 Succession for reasons of obedience [I.91]

[I.91]	Entrepreneur, 3rd generation: "*Usually, it is said that children should be grateful to their parents. [...] For the children of a family business, however, it looks different. They receive more from their parents than 'normal' children, namely an enterprise, which is associated with many material and immaterial values. The acceptance of the inheritance triggers a need for compensation in the children. However, there can be no balance between parents and children on a purely material level. This results in a deep-seated sense of obedience in the children, which is associated with the obligation to successfully continue the family business. In this way, a balance is possible. [...]*"[a]

[a]LeMar (2001), p. 230.

children.[685] In addition, the current life situation of the parents affects the parent-child relationship.[686] According to the study by Higgins et al. [687], the structure of the work performed has a significant influence on family life.

Above all, the children's perspective on the family business is primarily influenced by the parents and their influence on socialization. Depending on how parents convey their relationship with the family business, children approach the enterprise with curiosity or aversion.[688] In combination with the children's personality traits parents can encourage their children to develop traits associated with entrepreneurship. Hobbies or other activities that increase self-confidence are helpful.[689] However, socialization within a family business can also put pressure on the children, leading them to an unwanted succession (see Interviews 2.29 [I.91]).

2.5.2.2 Influence of the Family Business on the Descendants

When looking at business families, an influence of the enterprise (enterpriseness) on the participating family members can be assumed based on the statements already made. This is also evident in the following interview excerpts ([I.92-I.97]). In [I.92-I.94] the enterprise "actively" influences family life, which is perceived as negative in [I.92 and I.94]. [I.93] emphasizes the positive effect

[685] Cf. Petzold (1999), p. 73.

[686] Cf. Suess (2001), p. 49.

[687] Cf. Higgins et al. (1992), p. 71. Although the respondents were not self-employed persons, this can also be assumed for business families since the connection between private and professional life is usually very intensive there.

[688] Cf. Huber and Leitner (2011), p. 3.

[689] Cf. Schmitt-Rodermund and Silbereisen (1999), p. 119.

of the mix; this was the best way to get to know the enterprise. In addition, [I.95 and I.96] show how the enterprise's everyday life enters the family/socialization through (positive/negative) stories, and thus increases the descendants' interest in the family business. Stories about the enterprise can be seen as part of socialization. However, [I.97] again emphasizes the enterprise's priority. See Interviews 2.30.

Interviews 2.30 Enterpriseness in business families [I.92–97]

[I.92]	Daughter: "»Everything has always revolved around the enterprise. In the evenings the folders were scattered in the living room and we had to be quiet because mom was working. She was completely absorbed in the enterprise. […]«"[a]
[I.93]	Successor: "Since my mother was also working in the enterprise and therefore business problems were always an important topic at the family lunch, I knew the enterprise long before I succeeded my father."[b]
[I.94]	Businesswoman, 4th generation: "*[…] We have the situation that we also live at the office, all together, and that is often not easy because of course everything is brought into the apartment and from the apartment everything is transferred back.* […] *Yes, it is very difficult to set boundaries. Here we are as a couple, here we are in business together […].*"[c]
[I.95]	Business owner: "'And they [the children] also take an interest today, so when we're … together, then … I also report from the enterprise and tell them something or they also ask, so that's easy. … So, they don't care at all … what the parents do, … but they do take an interest. …'"[d]
[I.96]	Business owner: "'So, I have thought about it, but this is now really just spoken from the gut… Maybe I'll do it like my parents… I tell her [the daughter] a lot, what happens [in the enterprise], what I do, what_daddy_does, but I won't push her somehow in that direction or steer her or something. That's how I would have tried it now (laughs).'"[e]
[I.97]	Organizational researcher and consultant: "There [in small restaurants] is usually a permanently reserved table at which the family members eat. It forms a private enclave within the otherwise public space. Not the enterprise sits at the table, but the family. However, even this sanctuary is cleared if needed for guests."[f]

[a]Schneider (1998), p. 82.
[b]Hecheltjen (1998), p. 38.
[c]Weber (2005), p. 271.
[d]Stamm (2013), p. 242.
[e]Stamm (2013), p. 247.
[f]Simon (2012), p. 66.

The influence of the family business can already be felt at birth if shares in the enterprise are transferred to the newborns ([I.102]). It is also common to designate the children from birth as successors ([I.99]), although in most cases — as already often mentioned — gender is still seen as a criterion ([I.98, I.100, I.101, I.104, and I.108]). Especially in medium-sized family businesses, the ideal of a family-internal, primarily male, succession often still exists.[690] As a result, the descendants are seen less as family members, but rather instrumentalized as successors in the sense of the family business ([I.103]). See Interviews 2.31.

How much an early determined succession, based on gender, can influence or even determine the family and especially the socialization of the descendants is illustrated by the following conversation excerpts of a business family; they run a craft business (see Interviews 2.32):

Based on the excerpts, the expectation for the son's succession becomes visible first, which was also known to the participants ([I.104 and I.105]). As a result, the son's education was steered in the direction that seemed advantageous for the family business ([I.106 and I.111]). Although the youngest daughter was not averse to the family business, she was advised to take a different path first ([I.107]). For the father it seems quite normal to determine a male successor, especially because of the subject matter of the enterprise ([I.108]). The paternal expectation is also perceived by the daughters ([I.109 and I.111]). Both feel the concentration of paternal attention in favor of the brother ([I.110 and I.111]), with the oldest daughter suffering from it and therefore, trying to draw the father's attention to herself through increased ambition ([I.111]). Finally, the son reports on his conflict ([I.112]). Because of the father the son does not follow his ideas, which is noticeable in a lack of interest in the training and his own dissatisfaction. In summary, this excerpt illustrates how an (too) early determination of the successor affects the individual family members. Especially when this is not made based on the interests and abilities of the children, but only because of the gender.

However, being identified as a successor at an early stage can be just as much of a "reassuring" thing for those involved ([I.68]) as this reduces the pressure for academic success ([I.113]). In addition, the interest can develop already in childhood, whereby the entry is seen as a "natural act" and the education is aligned accordingly as a matter of course ([I.114]). On the other hand, [I.115] shows how the apparent determination of the successor negatively affects the other sibling. This makes it particularly clear how sensitive the question of succession is and what dynamics it can trigger. Particularly regarding the sibling rivalries already mentioned. See Interviews 2.33.

---

690 Cf. Kempert (2008), p. 188.

Interviews 2.31 Determination of the successor [I.98–103]

[I.98]	Female innkeeper: "'*Then my brother took over the business, he was one and a half years older and thus the son. My sister and I have renounced everything, so that the business can be preserved.* '"[a]
[I.99]	Youngest son, successor, 4th generation: "*[...] It was clear from the beginning that I would join the enterprise! // Really from the beginning, from a young age. And it was just as clear that my sister would never get involved here.* "[b]
[I.100]	Daughter: "'*Inheritance was always a very important motive for the handover in our family. The business has been passed on to the oldest son for seven generations (according to my father's version). [...] The women (and daughters) always had shares in the enterprise, but were never actively involved in the business. An important aspect in our family is however: Everyone was always well provided for.* '"[c]
[I.101]	Businesswoman: "'When our eldest was in the stroller and I was walking with him, then.. people investigated the stroller: 'Oh, it's a *boy*' [.] and 'Oh, how nice', and 'He will surely become the boss later!' (laughs) That kind of bothered me. I thought it was so *stupid* (laughing) [.].'"[d]
[I.102]	Successor: "'*My father had to do something for tax reasons and so I was born with enterprise shares. Since I've been working, I've also seen money from it, never before. But maybe I didn't accept it before. I always found the money of my family very burdensome because I wanted to justify my existence myself. [...]*'"[e]
[I.103]	Business owner, 3rd generation: "*My father saw me less as a son, but primarily as a successor. That seemed easier for him. In the interaction on the father-son level he would have had to show feelings. That was very difficult for fathers of this generation. He couldn't give direct fatherly love, but he tried to convey it through the business. As a child, I didn't recognize that. I saw more of his rough shell. Of course, I would have preferred, if he had accepted me as a son on a human level. [...]*"[f]

[a]Mätzener and Schwarz (2008), p. 56.
[b]Siefer (1996), p. 132.
[c]Mätzener and Schwarz (2008), p. 40.
[d]Stamm (2013), p. 240.
[e]Mätzener and Schwarz (2008), p. 40.
[f]LeMar (2001), p. 130.

How the integration into a family business can present itself for the successors is illustrated below in Table 2.6, using some case descriptions carried out by Pfannenschwarz (2006b). These provide an insight into their childhood and youth.

As can be seen from the individual case descriptions, the family business exerts its influence on the descendants, regardless of the number of employees and the duration of its existence. For three of them ([I.116, I.118, and I.120])

Interviews 2.32 Impact of the successor selection on the family [I.104–112]

[I.104]—[I.112]	Mother: "*Maybe I can say something about what I actually think, he [the son] imagined that the father expects him to take over the business someday and maybe it was actually the case that my husband imagined, now you have the 'heir', and he will be the successor. He had taken over and expanded his father's business ... yes, invested a lot ...*"[a] [I.104] Eldest sister: "*...I do think that the thought was always there, the moment a son is there, it is primarily a job for a man, it was never a question for us (daughters). We were never in that direction ...*"[a] [I.105] Mother: "*No, I don't believe that because I know that our son later completed middle school and then said 'I want to do the upper level' ... and that my husband then said to him, 'you know, then better do the higher commercial school, then you already have something in the direction of vocational training and business" ... and then he started quite unlovingly with it and also did not finish ...*"[b] [I.106] Youngest sister: "*...I felt it differently, so I was not like that, that I would not have been interested in it, there was a time, [...] I even worked in the business and eh ... then it was said, yes do something else first, you can always do it later ... and eh, I felt it that way [...]. Interviewer: Stay out of it? [...] Far away, yes.*"[c] [I.107] Father: "*...no one would come up with the idea the daughter can [meaning is the takeover of the craft business] do it.*"[d] [I.108] Eldest sister: "*...so I always had the feeling the business is for my brother. That was always clear to me.*"[e] [I.109] Eldest sister: "*Today I am glad that it turned out this way, I must say. I just think this awareness as a woman, not being recognised as a son somewhere, I think that was difficult for me. So, I always thought somewhere, my goodness, you have the stuff for it, you can do it too. There I developed an incredible ambition to show him that too.*"[f] [I.110] Youngest sister: "*[...] ...actually it was clear to me that my brother should do this and that my father also, what my brother ..., so he left very little to chance. So, he looked at it much more than us, i.e., in terms of education, I think so, he was more interested, ...he couldn't sit there and say, we'll see what the boy brings ...*"[g] [I.111] Son: "*[...] My father of course tried to talk me out of the music, did not support it. ... My father said, first do business school and then you do an apprenticeship ... and I stood then afterwards with the school and did not know then at all, what I should do. Then I did business school, I didn't enjoy it at all because I'm not born to trade. ...I would have been interested in medicine or being an artist.*"[h] [I.112]

[a]Levold et al. (2005), p. 233.
[b]Levold et al. (2005), p. 234.
[c]Levold et al. (2005), p. 235 f.
[d]Levold et al. (2005), p. 236.
[e]Levold et al. (2005), p. 241.
[f]Levold et al. (2005), p. 242.
[g]Levold et al. (2005), p. 243.
[h]Levold et al. (2005), p. 243.

the existence of the enterprise is perceived as something negative. Likewise, all descendants had to work in the parental enterprise between the ages of 12 and 18. This has effects on the socialization of the descendants. Due to the early

Interviews 2.33 Successors and their secondary socialization [I.113–115]

[I.113]	Successor: "*[…] And I was quite glad — if I may interject — that I had my future prospects here, to go into the enterprise, I was quite satisfied with that, even during school. […] So I knew: 'Well, you don't need to overcome a big numerus clausus hurdle! What you want to do later, you're satisfied with that and you think it's good!'*"[a]
[I.114]	Development of the successor from the successor's perspective: "My interest in the enterprise or the industry developed at a very young age. It is important to receive a good education and learn the necessary »hand tools«. I acquired additional knowledge through seminars and courses. […]"[b]
[I.115]	Founder: "'*[…] one day he [the younger son] said to me: 'Dad, if you no longer need the enterprise, will you give it to me?' […] was a childish question for me 'Yes', I say, yes […].' That was a big mistake. […] insofar as the older one also heard it and he was so disappointed at the time, he never talked to me about it, … but he was obviously already from childhood on, he steps into the footsteps, never expressed and he was so deeply hurt that I would give the enterprise to the younger one that these were reasons and he had a performance slump and that was also the reason, why he then massively pushed, he wanted to get away from home, […]. He couldn't stand it anymore, he was so bitterly disappointed, […].*'"[c]

[a]Siefer (1996), p. 132.
[b]Juritsch et al. (2007), p. 68.
[c]Baumgartner (2009), p. 157.

participation in the parental enterprise, a premature tertiary socialization can be assumed.

The family business can take up so much time that there is hardly any time left for the children ([I.89, I.121, and I.122]). Likewise, the priority of the family business experienced in childhood can lead the successors to make a clearer separation between family and business in their own family, so that their own children are not negatively influenced by the enterprise to the same extent ([I.123]). However, this could lead to a weakening or delay in business socialization. In addition, the involvement of children in family businesses is a common sight. In extreme cases, these are seen by the entrepreneur only as labor force (see for example sector (2) in the Three-Dimensional Model), while they view the enterprise as their real child ([I.75]). Thus, the adolescents often must work in the enterprise after school and during their holidays. The family business determines their childhood and youth in many places ([I.116, I.117, I.119, I.120, and I.128]). Compared to non-entrepreneurial children, they often cannot be attributed a carefree youth. They may receive little attention from their parents and especially

Table 2.6 Influence of the family business on the living environment [I.116–120]

Characteristics of the enterprise	Childhood and youth of the respective adolescent
[I.116]: Insurance agency and office for financial services; approx. 12 employees; father is founder; (p. 21)	Father's business always present with oppressive feeling; living area accessible to customers; father is perceived as absent; father justifies this through the possible financial advantages as well the standard of living; good reputation of the father allows the son advantages; he found the prospect of succession unpleasant; at the age of 16, he began to work in the agency; (p. 22 f.)
[I.117]: Service workshop for commercial vehicles; approx. 70 employees; 3rd generation; (p. 31)	Enterprise is part of family communication; at enterprise parties the family is always present; respondent was already walking around in it in diaper; until the age of 13, the enterprise and the house were on the same property; played a lot in the vicinity of the enterprise; at the age of 12, the son was already working regularly in the enterprise; (p. 32 f.)
[I.118]: Confectionery with café; approx. 14 employees; father is the founder; (p. 42 f.)	Succession is not considered because the family burdens caused by the business (working hours) were perceived negatively; parents do not influence his training decision; Sundays he works for pay in the pastry shop; (p. 43)
[I.119]: Car dealership as a car trade; 4th generation; (p. 48)	Succession was inevitable in the sense of family tradition; family, business, and employees were perceived as an unit quite positively; at the age of 9, he switched to a boarding school, which he experienced as positive; explicit involvement with succession at the age of 16; negotiates a business administration degree; studies are completed quickly; works regularly in the enterprise during his studies; performs responsible tasks; feels burned out between 18 and 20 ; by the age of 25, he has overcome this; (p. 49 f.)
[I.120]: Craft business for installations; approx. 5-10 employees; father is the founder; (p. 56)	Memory of the enterprise rather negative as it was a significant burden for the family; work and the operation itself however not perceived negatively; father is perceived as not supportive from the beginning; it is made clear to him that he will once take over the business; perceives this as "strong indoctrination and social pressure" (Pfannenschwarz 2006 b, p. 56 f.); from the age of 14 he has to work in the enterprise, which he finds rather boring; parents influence the son's choice of subjects in the sense of the enterprise; (p. 56 f.)

from their father ([I.78 and I.122]).[691] A "reduction" as a labor force can retrospectively be perceived as exploitation by the descendants, which can affect the parent-child relationship ([I.124]).[692] In [I.125 and I.126] the different perception of the family business becomes clear. While the children suffered from working in the enterprise, the mother tries to put this into perspective by focusing on the enterprise's function of securing her livelihood (see Interviews 2.34).

The priority of the family business can also be expressed through a clear directive or formulation by the father, which can lead to conflicts, but can also provide a clear orientation for the family members ([I.127]). In addition, the entrepreneur can be so absorbed by his enterprise that he loses sight of his family. This can in turn have a negative impact on socialization. However, a related accusation by the descendants can cause them to feel guilty as they participate in the enterprise's profits ([I.128]). Especially since the family business ensures the livelihood, the descendants are often urged to behave accordingly in public, so that no bad light is cast on the enterprise ([I.129]) or the acceptance of the family members in their social environment is ensured ([I.130 and I.131]). See Interviews 2.35.

Finally, considering the possible acquisition of experience through the influence of the enterprise, the respondents show a high degree of human capital, according to the survey by Schulte and Wille[693]. This is particularly evident in the experience for the profession, the respective industry, and leadership. All participants have relevant professional experience (employed or self-employed) before the takeover. Furthermore, Pfannenschwarz expresses the assumption that "this type of early experience [referring to the early contact with the family business] is a crucial factor for aspiring to entrepreneurial or independent life designs" [694]. According to the study by Cater and Justis [695], parents often act as mentors for the successors. They give the following example: "For example, on the day that Mike Johnson, of Finest, Inc., graduated from college, his father, Bill, set up a desk for Mike, next to his own. Bill proceeded to coach Mike for 3 years, ensuring his son's presence at all meetings with clients and coworkers."[696] Similarly, the development of the child often receives attention from the staff.[697]

[691] Cf. Wandl and Habenicht (2011), p. 18.

[692] Cf. Stamm (2013), p. 193.

[693] Cf. Schulte and Wille (2006), p. 404. n=42 respondents.

[694] Pfannenschwarz (2006a), p. 243.

[695] Cf. Cater and Justis (2009), p. 10. n=10 respondents.

[696] Cater and Justis (2009), p. 10.

[697] Cf. Meyer (2007), p. 32.

Interviews 2.34 Negative influence of the family business [I.121–126]

[I.121]	Young entrepreneur: "'*My price of the last years consists not only in the fact that I must take up the money at some point, but also my family suffers from it. I only see my daughter (10 years) a few hours a day, my children can't invite anyone because none of us is at home. Our children must be very independent. [...] My eldest son (12 years) goes to an all-day school (where my daughter will go after primary school) and is on the road from 6 to 18 o'clock. As a result, he has slipped away from me a bit. Until a year ago I went home every day and cooked. Meanwhile, I am almost only in the enterprise. [...]*'"[a]
[I.122]	Daughter: "'We played a lot here as children. As a child I didn't really realize everything. But later I realized that we were left quite alone as children.'"[b]
[I.123]	Entrepreneur: "'*[...] I make sure that we do not discuss my business or my husband's business at home. At our home (family of origin) everything was subordinated to the two enterprises, I don't want that at all. At our home the enterprise was constantly talked about and that always bothered me. Maybe that's why I don't do it. I do not get my life's justification from this enterprise.* '"[c]
[I.124]	Son: "'I hate my parents for ruining my youth and my childhood. So, that … I really have to say it clearly, … for that I just hate them and … it is partly there was also no parental relationship, but it has been more or less a […] community of convenience or it still is today.'"[d]
[I.125]—[I.126]	Daughter: "'*The problem: My mother would never close the business and we suffered a lot in our youth because we often had to help in our free time! [...]*'"[e] [I.125] Mother: "'*The children associate a hard time with the tavern and do not see that it also secured their existence!*'"[f] [I.126]

[a]Mätzener and Schwarz (2008), p. 112 f.
[b]Stamm (2013), p. 196.
[c]Mätzener and Schwarz (2008), p. 120.
[d]Stamm (2013), p. 194.
[e]Mätzener and Schwarz (2008), p. 49.
[f]Mätzener and Schwarz (2008), p. 97.

They can have certain expectations of the growing children (see Table 2.5). The descendants or the successors usually know the long-term employees. These have seen the successors grow up ([I.133]). Especially since the successors grow into

Interviews 2.35 Enterpriseness in business families [I.127–131]

[I.127]	Son reports on the guiding principle of his family: "'My father was shaped by a hard school and clearly said: 'If the enterprise is doing well, the family is doing well.' And that was a dogma that applied to all of us. It was something we lived and worked with for 40 years. First comes the business and then comes the family. This expressed dogma was not always pleasant and there was also rebellion against it within the family. But for me it was helpful because it gave me a clear orientation.'"[a]
[I.128]	Junior of a medium-sized enterprise: "*[…] Basically, I would like to say that he doesn't really have anything other than the company. Other interests and values in his life were always subordinate to the company. That's why I sometimes accuse him of not really knowing us children. Nor his own wife. We always say he is married to his company. But maybe he thinks that we all take advantage of the benefits he has earned with the company. And of course, he is not entirely wrong.*"[b]
[I.129]	Daughter, 3rd generation: "The rule applied, which I know from many other families with small and medium-sized businesses that we children had to greet every adult on the street. It could be a customer, they said."[c]
[I.131]	Entrepreneur, 2nd generation: "'I also believe that each of my children should also hold an honorary office. It doesn't matter, whether he does that at the shooting club, or at the fire department, or wherever. […] And people should see, these are not the ones up there. […] And they can only stabilize this by saying, they have all remained grounded, you can also have a beer with them. This seems to me incredibly important for the social structure, also for the characteristic, to be an entrepreneur. […]'"[d]

[a]Wandl and Habenicht (2011), p. 23.
[b]LeMar (2001), p. 100.
[c]Welter-Enderlin (2005), p. 147.
[d]Zwack (2011), p. 169.

the enterprise culture, they mostly also know to what extent they are respected by the employees ([I.132]).[698] See Interviews 2.36.

---

698 However, when considering vocational training, i.e., tertiary socialization, Wimmer (1997, 149) as well as Felden and Pfannenschwarz (2008, 127) advise against carrying this out within one's own enterprise. In the eyes of the employees the descendants would always be seen as the entrepreneur's children, which means that they are treated differently. This can subsequently lead to personality deficits. Integration into the parental business should only take place once sufficient external experience has been gained (cf. Wimmer 1997, 149). In this way, potential successors not only get to know other enterprises, but also different structures and management styles, which they can then implement in their own enterprise (cf. Felden and Pfannenschwarz 2008, 127).

Interviews 2.36 Early contact with the family business [I.132–133]

[I.132]	Successor: "[...] As a successor from the business family, you know the circumstances and can assess for yourself how you are accepted by the staff. You are familiar with the enterprise culture or a part of it. [...]"[a]
[I.133]	Successor: "When I joined our enterprise, there were employees who had known me since I was in diapers. Of course, it is a challenge to earn the necessary respect. [...] It is also important that decisions made by the successor are not revised by the senior boss. [...]"[b]

[a]Schaub (2009), p. 110.
[b]Juritsch et al. (2007), p. 69.

2.5.2.3 Influences on the Life World of Entrepreneurial Children

If we first consider the daily life world, it represents the reality in which human action and thinking are explained and interpreted. The "human being participates in an inevitable, regular recurrence"[699]. However, one's own ability to act is restricted by the actions of other people, who present the respective person with "obstacles to overcome as well as insurmountable barriers" [700]. An understanding and cooperation of the individual with his fellow human beings is only possible within this area, which then constitutes a "common communicative environment" [701]. The everyday life world is thus referred to as the primary reality of humans.[702] This embodies the reality, which is shaped by experiences. The everyday life world is particularly influenced by the actions taken.[703]

If the focus is on business families, the literature underestimates the family business as a child's life world, according to the assessment of Stamm[704]. In her view, this has a "phenomenal impact"[705] on the growing children. They often experience the family business "as an integral part of the daily way of life"[706] or life world, which is perceived as a unit. The enterprise often serves to gain

[699] Schütz and Luckmann (1994a), p. 25.

[700] See footnote 699.

[701] See footnote 699.

[702] Cf. Schütz and Luckmann (1994a), p. 25.

[703] Cf. Schütz and Luckmann (1994b), p. 11. The everyday life world comprises that area of reality, which is simply taken for granted by a conventional adult. This means that it is accepted because it is experienced as unproblematic (cf. Schütz and Luckmann 1994a, 25).

[704] Cf. Stamm (2013), p. 189 ff.

[705] Stamm (2013), p. 191.

[706] See footnote 705.

the recognition and attention of the parents or the family. Also the contact of the descendants with customers, employees, suppliers, etc. can be seen as a central component of the child's life world. These are perceived as part of the business family and can represent an extended circle of reference persons.

Thus, the world of life is already influenced by the determination of the successor at birth ([I.98-I.102, and I.105]) and does not necessarily have to end with the transfer of responsibility to the successor.[707] A separation between the familial and the entrepreneurial sphere, i.e., between private and work life often cannot be made ([I.92-I.97]); and if it takes place, it often does not happen to the extent that the family and the business can be seen as two independent areas.[708] According to von Schlippe, the enterprise represents the "place of the closest communal life execution" [709] for the family and according to Stamm, the family business grows into an "extended familial space" [710]. However, less for a family than rather as a space of familial action.[711] Especially in family businesses, where the enterprise and the family's living area coincide or are not far apart, the enterprise is an experiential and at the same time a defining world of life for the growing up. The resulting contact with the entrepreneur parents and employees can promote conditions of socialization that increase the likelihood of working in the family business.[712] Often, the parental enterprise is present in the descendants from birth and long-established employees already know them from this point on and have experienced their upbringing ([I.132 and I.133]). For the descendants the challenge then is to deal with the attention they receive. The special position in the enterprise can even lead to a neglect of the development of professional skills.[713] According to statements from interviewed entrepreneurs, the parental business served as a playground and later offered the opportunity to increase pocket money.[714] This is also evident from the following interviews. All report about the presence of the enterprise since their childhood ([I.134-I.138]). For example, it serves as an "'adventure playground'"[715] ([I.135]), homework is done in the mother's office, where customers are also present ([I.136]), or lunch

[707] Cf. von Schlippe et al. (2012), p. 293.

[708] Cf. Hildenbrand (2005), p. 119.

[709] von Schlippe (2009), p. 17.

[710] Stamm (2013), p. 201.

[711] Cf. Stamm (2013), p. 201.

[712] Cf. Siefer (1996), p. 121.

[713] Cf. Meyer (2007), p. 31 f.

[714] Cf. Stamm et al. (2010), p. 5.

[715] Haubl and Daser (2006), p. 35 and cf. Freund (2000), p. 95.

is eaten together with the employees ([I.137]). In addition, the integration of the enterprise into the living environment of the children is carried out, by some of them, through their own work within the family business ([I.116, I.117, I.120, I.125, I.136, and I.137]). See Interviews 2.37.

Interviews 2.37 The family business as a world of life [I.134–138]

[I.134]	Female successor: "*[...] And I've always been here in the enterprise as a kid. When I came from school I went to my grandmother who lived in the office building, and she (.) also took care of me there. I also went to my mother, hammered on the typewriter and such things, — no. I could already — before I even took a typewriter course — type incredibly fast on the typewriter just with two fingers. And so, I pretty much grew into it, the whole time [...]. I was constantly confronted with this.* "[a]
[I.135]	Female successor: "[...] I grew up with the enterprise. I played in our shop window when I was very small. And when I was grown up the connection with the enterprise never got lost. [...] When I returned to Hamburg I continued to work in our enterprise [...] Although we are a quite large enterprise with a turnover in Germany of 630 million euros, it is still»the shop« because it is our family business. I also missed my colleagues back then, my father, my mother. The shop was our living room, our home."[b]
[I.136]	Entrepreneur: "I was born in June 1967, about two years before the enterprise was founded. The Mazda virus [referring to the car brand Mazda] I got, so to speak, with the mother's milk. During my kindergarten time I spent my afternoons in the parental enterprise. In elementary school the homework was done under the strict eyes of my mother, but in the office between the customers. Today one can hardly imagine the situation anymore, the children of today — I count my three among them — grow up quite differently. I can say for myself that it has not harmed me at all. [...] During the secondary school time I was then already assigned simple tasks. My job was to install the radios in the new vehicles, after work in the office and studying for the next test the new vehicles were completed. [...] During the HTL time [school form in Austria] the complete IT organization was taken over by me [...] After completing my Matura [high school graduation] [...] I completed the military service and joined the enterprise in March 1987 (for real). [...]"[c]
[I.137]	Daughter, 3rd generation: "[...] We learned how to deal with responsibility, risk, and ambiguity as children in the one hand closely connected, on the other hand separated spheres family, business, and village. On weekdays there were usually twelve people at the dining table: parents, children, a maid, two apprentices, and two workers. Saturday evening and Sunday was our private time in a room reserved for the family with 'good' dishes, games, and books that only belonged to us. Each of us was unique and unmistakable in the family, but as part of the business we had depending on age and gender our tasks which were subordinate to the whole. Also, the roles of the parents were clearly defined, no one needed a special job title because everyone knew this. [...]"[d]
[I.138]	Female successor: "The company has always been there, [...] since I was born. [...]"[e]

[a] Siefer (1996), p. 199.
[b] Mendel and Piper (2005), p. 56.
[c] Mayer (2006), p. 135 f.
[d] Welter-Enderlin (2005), p. 148.
[e] Mendel and Piper (2005), p. 75.

Even in the interviews conducted by Pfannenschwarz[716] early contact with the family business becomes clear. This occurs predominantly in childhood, but at the latest during school years, often initially characterized by a mix of play and work and then extends to the assumption of staff and performance functions. Excerpts are shown in Table 2.6. In order to obtain an answer as to the "weight" of the enterprise in the lives of young people, they were asked in the study by Schmitt Rodermund and Schröder [717] how often they work in the family business:

- 6% daily
- 16% several times a week
- 15% several times a month
- 53% primarily during holidays and peak times
- 10% never

In the same study they ask, how often the young people "just like that" go into the parental enterprise:

- 31% daily
- 22% several times a week
- 18% several times a month
- 25% rather irregularly
- 4% never

Based on the results it can be assumed that the family business has a significant influence on the world of life of the descendants. Therefore, the enterprise or the area around it is often still very present in the world of life of the descendants in adulthood.[718]

In the phase of youth the entrepreneur's child usually comes actively into contact with the family business. First holiday jobs or temporary jobs are done, and thus money is earned, with the focus often still on the education (school, training, or studies) of the young person. Thus, the children keep switching between the place of education and the parental business.[719] Iannarelli also reported a certain work ethic in many business families, which is mainly represented by the father:

---

[716] Cf. Pfannenschwarz (2006b), p. 14. n=30 respondents.

[717] Cf. Schmitt-Rodermund and Schröder (2009), p. 21 f. n = 255 adolescents. Average age of 16.4 years.

[718] Cf. Stamm (2013), p. 188 f.

[719] Cf. Pfannenschwarz (2006a), p. 292.

"The work ethic involved keeping busy, having a project to work on, limiting amounts of television, being responsible for your share, and completing tasks once started" [720].

Descendants from business families often experience in their childhood and youth phase what position they have compared to the family business. Usually, the enterprise has priority ([I.86, I.88, I.89, I.92, I.121, I.125, I.127, I.128 I.140, and I.141]). Thus, the enterprise impacts on the "subtle level of the family"[721]. Although the children are often "rich" in material things, but "poor" on the emotional level. In particular, the limitation of autonomous, self-determined life planning can possibly be perceived negatively ([I.112, I.118, and I.120]).[722] Looking at self-perception, Iannarelli comes to the following statement based on an interview with two siblings: "These children believed the business was more important than they were. Their father rarely saw them and when he did, he regularly told them to leave him alone".[723]

Von Schlippe describes it as follows: "Whoever owns an enterprise or who grows up as a child in a business family, is strongly limited by the enterprise in their autonomous lifestyle […]."[724] See [I.139 and I.140]. Similarly, the life world of the descendants can be co-determined by the predecessor generation, especially when it comes to succession [I.141]. See Interviews 2.38.

[720] Iannarelli (1992), p. 75.

[721] LeMar (2014), p. 23.

[722] Cf. LeMar (2014), p. 23 f.

[723] Iannarelli (1992), p. 66 f.

[724] von Schlippe et al. (2012), p. 292.

Interviews 2.38 Expectations through the family business [I.139–141]

[I.139]	Founder: "'And my father[725] was imbued with this idea that the enterprise is a task and not a possession that one has to serve it and that everything has to be subordinate to it, [.], the enterprise that of course also … shaped …'"[a]
[I.140]	Son of a Business owner: "'*I grew up with performance, performance and again and again performance. In the last 20 years we have, I think, gone on vacation three times. Somehow, I am an 'uptime' version of my father, which I of course do not like to see […].* '"[b]
[I.141]	Business owner, 3rd generation: "*[…] And my mother attached the greatest importance to the fact that I simply had to go into the enterprise. That was our daily topic [emphasized:] number one! So, if somehow about the // enterprise history of the enterprise Gade, then it means: [emphasized:] 'You will get in there!' [Louder:] And curiously, it was also the case, that my grandfather [emphasized:] after — that was also important, that's a very important argument now […]. Therefore, it was also the reason because it was already determined by my grandfather, that then, his two grandchildren Kurt, Konrad at the age of 21 the enterprise Gade, then as owners, enter the enterprise Gade, […] should. — He had already determined that. That was also the, [takes a breath] the reason always, where one was then pointed out at home: 'Listen, with the 21st year of life' — or possibly later, if it still didn't work out with the training, or if you are still stuck somewhere — [knocks on the table; emphasized:] '… you go into the enterprise!' […] That was, was like a prayer at home—I say now!*"[c]

[a]Zwack (2011), p. 136.
[b]Mätzener and Schwarz (2008), p. 27.
[c]Siefer (1996), p. 188 f.

In general, the family business or its influence on the life world is perceived differently. A differentiation based on gender is also evident at [I.143]. While the daughters perceived the enterprise and the resulting amenities as very positive, the brothers perceived this rather as a burden as they were considered potential successors. Based on [I.142] the effects of different birth ranks are also evident.[726] As the youngest daughter the interviewee was granted more freedoms. Unlike her older siblings she did not have to work in the family business and was able to make her educational decision freely. She also only experienced her father

[725] He was also self-employed.

[726] According to Kasten, birthplace research assumes that "with a certain position in the sibling order typical upbringing and socialization influences are associated, which decisively shape the personality of the child" (Kasten 2003, 46). See also: *Toman*, W. (1996): Familienkonstellationen. Ihr Einfluß auf den Menschen, 6. durchges. Aufl., München: Verlag C. H. Beck.

in a family context. Finally, [I.144] shows the possible negative memory of the enterprise. This is primarily due to the enormous workload (see Interviews 2.39).

Interviews 2.39 Perception of the family business [I.142–144]

[I.142]	Female shareholder: "Unlike my siblings who worked in the enterprise, saw him every day and had to make decisions with him, I did not experience my father in the enterprise's everyday life. As the youngest daughter, I had more freedom in choosing my studies and profession than they did. So, my view is shaped by the fact that every encounter with my father was something special, like the shared holidays and visits on holidays. [...] If he was there, you didn't have to worry and if you did have worries, he knew a solution. [...]"[a]
[I.143]	Daughter, 3rd generation: "What had a horizon-expanding and stimulating effect on me and my sisters [growing up in a family business is meant], the diversity and the roles and the importance that we had as children in the family, school, business, and village, was a burden for the two brothers. They knew as they grew up that one of them should take over the business in the third generation. Hints came indirectly, often from outside. Both showed resistance by playing dumb, not retaining botanical names in their heads, and pretending they couldn't tell a rose from a carnation. [...] Today they say that even as children they found it difficult to identify with the business and especially with our clever, but not very successful in business, father. [...]"[b]
[I.144]	Daughter: "'*She [the mother] is always offended when we complain about our childhood, even though, we really worked hard and we could complain! Everyone always says how great my mother raised it, but no one thanks us, even though, we really contributed a lot. When my father's business was in trouble my mother said: 'What do you think about a Heuriger [a special kind of wine tavern in Austria]? Do you want to?' We were forced to do because we knew there was no money, and we agreed. Initially, we were even enthusiastic because we could help mother. In the first season we were open seven to eight weeks without a day off and I served every day. After a year, all the euphoria was gone. But there was also money and tips and from that I could fulfill many wishes, that was very pleasant. [...]*'"[c]

[a]Haas (2005), p. 75.
[b]Welter-Enderlin (2005), p. 146 f.
[c]Mätzener and Schwarz (2008), p. 97 f.

As can be seen from the argumentation as well as from the interview excerpts, the family business can be seen as a significant component of the life world of the descendants. Stamm[727] also confirms this on the basis of her analysis. This influences their psychological experiences. This results from the perception of the enterprise as a locality, the contact with the different persons who act with

[727] Cf. Stamm (2013), p. 268.

it, the stories about the enterprise, a possible active cooperation, the financial situation of the family as well as by the observation of the parents. In general, the descendants perceive the importance of the family business for the parents. Likewise, the descendants acquire a stock of knowledge about the enterprise and internalize the role attributions. This creates a childlike idea of everyday life within a family business, which can subsequently influence the development and shaping of identity.

2.5.2.4 Influences on the Identity of the Entrepreneurs' Children

The starting point for the development of identity awareness is shared experiences. In addition, the shared identity is promoted by common interests. Especially for members of a family business, the enterprise represents this common interest, and thus supports the shared identity and search for meaning ([I.143 and I.146]).[728] For Stamm[729] the family business has the potential to become an "identity-creating element"[730] for the family. The common task can connect the generations on a vertical and horizontal level. The social identity of the descendants is usually — as already described above — manifested at birth or through birth ([I.99, I.100, I.104, and I.105]).[731] Thus, family businesses often serve the family as a source of identification.[732] In this way, the enterprise can act as a "glue" that holds the family together ([I.145]). This makes the family and the business seen as a unit, which can connect the descendants with the enterprise in a very special way. They not only grow up in the enterprise, but also with it

[728] Cf. Kormann (2011), p. 80. Regarding consciousness, Kormann formulates it as follows: "For a group to develop a common consciousness the group members must spend time together, develop mutual understanding for each other, have common experiences, and be capable of group-specific communication. However, the consciousness of a common history is arguably the most important basis for the communal sense of identity" (Kormann 2011, 80).

[729] Cf. Stamm (2013), p. 91.

[730] Stamm (2013), p. 91.

[731] Cf. Simon (2005), p. 187.

[732] Cf. Habig and Berninghaus (2004), p. 5.

([I.146]). This strengthens the bond, which brings the intangible values and the joy of the activity to the forefront ([I.147]). See Interviews 2.40.

Interviews 2.40 Family business as a supplier of identification [I.145–147]

[I.145]	Youngest son, 3rd generation: "'I believe that if we no longer had the enterprise, it would not be good for the family. I think the family and the business are too closely linked. And if I have the family as far as it is now, I also want to have the enterprise as far as it is now. And therefore, for me, the enterprise is unsellable. I'd rather go bankrupt than sell.'"[a]
[I.146]	Successor, 2nd generation: "*[...] Of course. I mean, our father also understood this very well. [...] Yes, our father understood very well how to motivate us, to guide us, to lead us, to educate us, [...] however you want to say it, that we, we have always seen as ours, not as his, but as our collective // life's work. And, and business or/and family and that, that was one: family, business, operation, that was always one. That was never separated: family — business, [...] that was always one, he understood that very well. [...] the business is, // or he became self-employed in 1955, I was born in that year. That means, I have been there the whole time, // my whole childhood is with the, with the enterprise or with his self-employment, with the growing up, with all the building years, completely connected. [...] Because it is clear, that an entrepreneur does not sit in the office with a white shirt, does a job as a founder, goes home, and says: 'So now we want to have family life!' [...] Yes! My mother, just like my wife, did the payroll, took care of all the wages and I sat there somewhere in the office on the floor and played with the paper clips, which I remember very well. And with the phone and with everything else, that was my nursery: these two rented office rooms,—yes!*"[b]
[I.147]	Successor: "'I live for what I do here and I love it ... with full commitment and for me is ... the joy of an order never connected with the thought of how much money we earn from it because I just like doing it. This is my life, this is my, this gives me pleasure. [omitted] I enjoy the business itself, taking responsibility, developing an enterprise, (takes a deep breath) creating jobs ... or maybe even maintaining them in difficult times'"[c]

[a]Zwack (2011), p. 185.
[b]Siefer (1996), p. 193 ff.
[c]Stamm (2013), p. 253.

Nevertheless, the formation of personal identity within a family business is sometimes difficult since contexts with a different logic (see Table 2.1) relate to each other, which makes it difficult for adolescents to clearly identify their affiliation and contributes to confusion (see Sect. 2.1.4). So, the relationship to family members is different than to employees.[733] For this reason, the problem in business families is the simultaneous socialization in two different frames of reference. The descendants can be exposed to a conflict when it comes to their "»public« and»private« identity"[734] ([I.143]). Often the descendants have an ambivalent relationship to the parents' enterprise. Since the family business receives a maximum amount of attention, descendants usually see this as a competitor. This then either leads to a turning away from the enterprise or strengthens the desire to work in it.[735] Felden formulates this as follows: "Entrepreneurial children must not only decide about their future profession with their career planning. Their decision also always represents a decision for or against the family business and in a broader sense a decision for or against the wishes and traditions of the family."[736] However, the exclusive reduction of the descendants to their future role as successors can provoke early developmental disorders (in terms of their identity). This can then manifest itself in the search for recognition or in insecure behavior.[737]

When considering the family name, it also serves as an identity giver for the family members. The name unfolds a meaning for people within and outside the family. Especially if it coincides with the enterprise name. Relatives who work together also share a sense of identity. In addition, the family relationships create the conditions and rules for the behavior of the relatives. Also positive or negative behavior of a family member can reflect on the whole family. In addition to the family this can also affect the reputation of the enterprise ([I.129]).[738] For the Oetker family, Simon et al. note the following: "Apparently everyone knows that their own actions have an impact on the image of the enterprise, as everyone knows that their own prosperity depends to a large extent on the enterprise."[739] Families, that are connected through a family business, and thus share the same work area reveal a lot of connections. This can create a special interest in each other and sensitize mutual perception.[740] To what extent the descendants identify with the enterprise or see it as their own is influenced by the parents. They can see the family and the business as one unit ([I.146]). Also, the close connection

[733] Cf. Simon (2012), p. 25.

[734] Berger and Luckmann (2000), p. 181.

[735] Cf. Felden (2012), p. 160 f.

[736] Felden (2012), p. 160.

[737] Cf. LeMar (2014), p. 126 f.

[738] Cf. Tagiuri and Davis (1996), p. 202 f.

[739] Simon et al. (2005), p. 78.

[740] Cf. Müller Tiberini (2001), p. 30.

between the families and their businesses is evident from the case studies carried out by Lueger et al.[741] The economy clearly sets the direction, which in turn has an identity-forming effect on the family and subsequently on the descendants. Above all, decision-making processes are adapted to the respective economic conditions or initiated by them. This results in a priority of the enterprise's interests over private interests.

In this context, children of entrepreneurs gradually grow into the corporate culture of their parents' business. If they are born into it without any preconceptions, they become more and more aware over time of the rules by which the enterprise operates ([I.93]). If this contradicts them too much, a turning away usually takes place ([I.78]).[742] However, "independence, work and social responsibility remain relevant practical life orientations. [...] The early life history shaping of an entrepreneurial habitus keeps it awake" [743]. Depending on how the descendants experience the familial and the family-colored entrepreneurial sphere, i.e., their microsocial environment, the development of certain behavioral intentions is also influenced. This includes, for example, a positive basic attitude towards entrepreneurial activity or the acquisition of enterprise-relevant know-how during growing up.[744] According to a study by the Stiftung Familienunternehmen [745], several central value attitudes can be found among its respondents, which can be explained by a high proportion of family business influence. Some of these are listed below:

1. Live and work independently (96%)
2. Have a partner you can trust (95%)
3. Maintenance of a stable economy (95%)
4. Good friends who recognize and accept you (94%)
5. Be diligent and ambitious (92%)
6. Lead a good family life (92%).

The following value attitudes ranked in the last two places:

1. Stick to the old-fashioned (14%)
2. Do what others do (6%)

---

[741] Cf. Lueger et al. (2012b), p. 114.

[742] Cf. Haubl and Daser (2006), p. 45.

[743] Haubl and Daser (2006), p. 45.

[744] Cf. Stiftung Familienunternehmen (2011a), p. 9.

[745] Cf. Stiftung Familienunternehmen (2011a), p. 17. n=202 respondents.

These results primarily illustrate the importance of family and values.

Finally, when considering the identity shaping of the descendants through the family business, this usually takes place through the experiences in childhood. In addition to advantages for one's own succession ([I.148]), this can also evoke a "sense of duty" for the business succession ([I.150]) and even lead to a giving up of one's own business or profession in favor of the parental enterprise ([I.149]). Likewise, promising careers in large corporations are abandoned to take the path into self-employment.[746]See Interviews 2.41.

Interviews 2.41 Connection of identity with the family business [I.148–150]

[I.148]	Successor: "As a successor from the business family, you have huge advantages over one of the external successors. Since your childhood, you learned at the lunch table what was successful in the business and when difficulties arose in the enterprise for whatever reason. Are you well prepared and willing to lead the enterprise into the future? Remember, you will be measured by the achievements of your predecessor. [...]"[a]
[I.149]	Daughter: "'*[...] Back then I said: I'll open my own place, but the parental business will always be my first priority. If it ever gets critical, I'm there — if necessary, I'll then sell my place. Since then, my parents know that nothing can happen with their place.* '"[b]
[I.150]	Successor, 3rd generation: "*[...] As long as I can remember as a kid, I was supposed to join the business. [...] 'Should' or — then you can't say anymore, whether it's a 'must', whether you want it, or whether — it's somehow, // Maybe they also told me that at some point or my parents taught me over the years that a family business remains over the generations. [...] Now they have, that I see myself as, maybe also as obligated, — no, [...] to continue such a business, — no. — That's at least one aspect. I am (.) in my training so far fully committed to the business. [...] And that started in school, [...] where I dealt with 'biology'. // Yes, then you say: at some point [knocks on the table] 'Is that clear!' [...].* "[c]

[a]Schaub (2009), p. 41.
[b]Mätzener and Schwarz (2008), p. 40.
[c]Siefer (1996), p. 185.

2.5.2.5 Horizon of Consideration of Socialization for this Work

After having discussed socialization in detail, it seems appropriate to look at the point in time up to which the socialization of entrepreneurial children should be

[746] Cf. Haubl and Daser (2006), p. 45.

Interviews 2.42 "Second choice" takes over [I.151]

[I.151]	Female successor: "That was in the year 2000. My middle brother [I.118] who was intended for the takeover and had aligned his entire education, accordingly, told my parents at the age of 26, that he would not continue the enterprise. My parents then did not immediately ask me, but at this point it was really up in the air, how it would continue. The initiative then came from my husband and me. We were living in Munich at the time. We posed the question to the room:»We could imagine getting involved, what do you think?« — from this question everything quickly became very concrete and a lot of trust was immediately placed in us."[a]

[a]Juritsch et al. (2007), p. 81.

considered at all. Especially since socialization takes place throughout life and (in the context of a family business additionally) is influenced by various factors, it is essential for answering the research question to limit this period. Based on the preceding argumentation, two points in time seem relevant, which significantly affect the descendants and can therefore be considered as "dividing paths":

1. Up to the beginning of education (apprenticeship or studies)
2. After (non-)takeover of the family business, i.e., the decision for or against the family business

If the beginning of education is first considered as a possible point in time, the choice of education can be seen as a guideline for the extent to which there is interest in wanting to take over the succession. Depending on the focus of the education, it is more or less compatible with the business purpose or beneficial for its long-term existence. With the choice of education the decision for or against the enterprise can therefore be made. This may therefore mark the end of socialization in the context of a family business.

However, the content focus of the education is not necessarily a guarantee for a successful succession as is clear from the interview excerpts [I.36, I.92, and I.112]. All descendants do indeed complete an education that is conforming to the family business, but this is less intrinsically motivated than rather brought about by loyalty to the enterprise and by parental pressure. Thus, those chosen as successors can align their entire education to the requirements of the family business, but then (surprisingly) may not want to take over the succession (see Interviews 2.42 [I.151]).

Similarly, descendants who were not originally intended for succession ([I.151]) can still enter the family business with the intention of taking over. This can again be justified by the individual's connection with the family business. Since the direction of training cannot necessarily be used as a guarantee for the takeover, it therefore seems sensible to consider the socialization up to the (non-)takeover of the family business. Especially from this point on, the reference or connection to the family business changes for descendants, for example, when they are paid out, and thus mutual influence is prevented due to the lack of ownership. When looking at multi-generational family businesses, this applies analogously, although there can be some variations. For example, a descendant can work in the enterprise and have shares in the ownership or they cannot work in the enterprise and still have ownership shares. Even in this case, the (non-)entry into the family business or the decision to work in another enterprise should limit the horizon of socialization. Although the connection to the family business continues in the second case, this can particularly weaken in multi-generational family businesses ([I.10]). Therefore, against the background of the previous argumentation, the socialization is considered up to the point at which the descendants take over or reject the succession in the parental enterprise.

2.6 Final Considerations in this Chapter

The aim of this chapter was to provide an insight into the form of enterprise known as a family business. Above all, an understanding should be conveyed of what characteristics and dynamics the family business has as a context for socialization and in detail, how this affects the descendants. The connection of a family with a business creates a unique framework for the socialization of the descendants, as each of these contexts has different logics. However, the difficulty of classifying an enterprise as a family business was first made apparent by the argumentation. Therefore, a definition was deliberately avoided. A definition always raises the legitimate question of whether all enterprises that do not fall under this definition are really not to be classified as family businesses. For this reason, this chapter provides a meaningful analysis of the socialisation context of family businesses for the focus of this work, so that the characteristics can be understood. This should create an understanding of the framework in which the family members and especially the descendants move.

Nevertheless, it seemed necessary to counteract or invalidate this lack of a "clear" definition by addressing the concept of familiness. Familiness, and in particular the Three-Dimensional Model, offers a theory-guided possibility to represent the influence of the family on the business. Thus, an analysis tool was provided, which, independent of a definition, allows the demarcation of a family business from other forms of business by representing the intensity of the family influence. Due to the connection between the family and the business as well as their co-evolution, the enterpriseness of the business family will be present in addition to the familiness of the enterprise. The extent of the enterpriseness is particularly relevant for the influence of the business on the family (members). The stronger the familiness is, the stronger the enterpriseness will also appear due to the connection, and thus also the influence on socialization or the importance of the family business as a context for socialization will increase.

Against the backdrop of growth in size and the multi-generational existence of a family business, a change in the familiness/enterpriseness is often noticeable. In terms of familiness, the success or survival of the family business may no longer be influenced by just one person — as is often the case in a first-generation family business — but by several families (or family lines). In parallel, the enterpriseness will also undergo a change. Over time, the enterprise will probably not determine the family-internal processes to the same extent as it does, for example, in a first-generation family business. However, especially in multi-generational family businesses, there may be a certain expectation pressure due to tradition for the successors to continue the business successfully. The enterpriseness is reinforced by the establishment of a family governance. Although, the family business is often still seen as an identity-forming context for the family, due to the shared ownership, it no longer necessarily intervenes in the family processes to the same extent as in the first generations. The following factors can influence the extent of familiness/enterpriseness across generations:

1. Industry and the subject of the family business
2. Are both parents employed in the enterprise
3. How far is the living area separated from the working area
4. Intertwining of private and working life
5. Integration of descendants into the family business
6. Size of the family business
7. How many families participate in the enterprise (age of the enterprise)

However, at least at the beginning of the venture, the enterprise is often given priority over the needs of the participating families (or family members). Thus, the family and individual desires, concerns, and issues usually take a back seat to the needs of the enterprise. This can be due to the strong attachment of the entrepreneur to his enterprise as well as the (financial) dependence of the family (or families) on the enterprise. For these reasons, the enterprise can become the focus of the family's life and may lead to a priority of the enterprise over the well-being of the individual. Precisely because the enterprise plays such a dominant role, it often permeates all areas of family life and can completely take over intra-family communication. This leads to the discussion of business-relevant issues within the family sphere and reduces the processing of personal concerns. Business pressure can influence the family climate. For this reason, the family business is often seen as the dominant experience and life world of the descendants, which significantly influences the socialization process. During the growth in size or the multi-generational existence of a family business, the impression of the dissolution of the connection of some family members with the enterprise may arise. Although, the emotional attachment of the members decreases in the process, the members are still involved in the family business, at least through ownership shares. Therefore, it is often still a significant frame of reference for them and thus, also connected with their identity. In contrast to non-business families, business families have the peculiarity that they are connected by ownership or shares in ownership. Even if they no longer work actively in the enterprise, the connection remains. This peculiarity then also supports the maintenance of contact between individual family members, even if the founding family was several generations ago and new families have emerged. Joint ownership of a business helps to maintain this contact, which is largely not the case with non-business families. If a family member sells its shares, this has consequences for both the affected member and the family as well as for the family business. Therefore, in this case, there is no longer a connection to the enterprise causing the member to lose his special status as a member of a business family.

The connection between family and business often manifests itself in the parents' desire to pass on their "life's work" to their children. This is intended to enable or even guarantee the continuation across generations. This initially "harmless" sounding wish influences the life path of the individual children in a decisive way. As it became apparent, this has both positive and negative effects on the dynamics within the family and specifically on the descendants and their socialization. Thus, early determination can put the descendants under pressure. They may feel restricted in their freedom of choice as they cannot or do not want to meet the expectations placed on them. However, the determination also provides a possible guidance for the adolescents. Regardless of how the potential or chosen successors stand against this, the family business or the expectations associated with it will rub off on the socialization. This can happen through the members participating in the enterprise (employees, relatives, parents, etc.)

and their behaviors as well as through the involvement or cooperation in the enterprise or the alignment of the education in the sense of the family business. Especially with several siblings, differences in socialization are very likely. However, the influence of the size and the duration of the family business should not be neglected in the investigation.

As the explanations illustrate, each life cycle of the family business requires a different qualification profile of the successors. However, if successors are initially compared with descendants not intended for succession, there are also differences in the socialization and the identity developing during this. Even if there is a predominantly equal treatment requirement for the members of the family, this is often not possible in the context of a family business. There, a different logic prevails. Due to the connection of the two contexts, this can then become apparent that there are differences in the inclusion in the family business between the (potential) successors and non-successors. It became obvious that the descendants who were not intended for succession were, among other things, freer in their choice of education. They also did not have to work in the family business to the extent as their siblings who were chosen for succession. Their life path is therefore usually not predetermined to the same extent. However, this does not necessarily mean that the influence of the enterprise context is less.

Due to the connection between family and business, the descendants can also have a "dual identity". While they take on the role of children in the family (regardless of age they are always the children of their parents), they are within the business context — at least until the actual handover — rather seen as potential successors. Additionally, as children of entrepreneurs by the employees and the environment, which either grants them a privileged position or "presses" them into a life model, which they cannot or do not want to fulfill. This will also influence socialization. However, among the descendants not selected as successors a feeling of disadvantage may arise, which in turn can have a negative effect on their socialization. This influence of the family business on the life world of the descendants can then be a trigger for rivalries and conflicts between the siblings that have been occurring since/in childhood, which can also have a sustainable influence on the adolescents.

If the focus is therefore directed at the conflicts that often occur in family businesses, these can also influence the socialization of the descendants. Due to the connection of the business with the family, conflicts within the family business quickly have a negative impact on the family and affect the family life possibly significantly. This can cause a dislike of the family business or of issues relevant to the enterprise and therefore prevent the desire for succession. When considering the successors, they will most likely be exposed to an internal conflict if they are expected to take over the succession, but they would rather do something else. Another way in which the prevailing connection in family businesses influences socialization will result from the different logic/expectations/requirements of the reference frames. While this is usually not a problem as the two contexts are separate, these context markers are often missing in family businesses. Thus, due to simultaneous membership in both reference frames, a "mixing" of logics often occurs, which brings about certain contradictions or paradoxes. The descendants thus grow up in an ambiguous environment in which they must find their way.

The connection between family and business often exposes the children of entrepreneurs to business socialization, i.e., tertiary socialization at a much earlier stage than descendants in non-business families. Thus, the family business can initially exert its influence on their world through playful aspects and later through the (un)voluntary work of the children. In addition, the requirements and expectations are conveyed to the adolescents through the parents' conversations. While the playful elements are initially in the foreground, they increasingly grow into the family business and often take on more and more tasks in the enterprise. The enterprise thus influences the family and influences the adolescents in their development. However, this early entrepreneurial socialization can be relativized during multi-generational existence and in view of possible growth, as business families often increasingly resemble the characteristics of non-business families. However, the common task also has the potential to create a strong sense of belonging within the family and to serve as an "identity provider" for each family member. This can in turn lead to a strengthened bond between family members and have a positive effect on the desire for succession. However, this (necessary) preference for the family business can also evoke a feeling of "secondariness" in the children regarding the parents' attention. Thus, certain rivalries towards the family business can arise, which can have a negative effect on the adolescents. Since the enterprise (especially in the start-up phase) may take up an excessive amount of time, this is often lacking for family matters, which can affect socialization.

In summary, there will be various ways in which the family business influences the socialization of the descendants. In addition to the way in which the parents interact with each other in the world shaped by the family business, active participation in everyday business life with its positive and negative aspects and the resulting identification of the descendants with the enterprise can influence the socialization of the descendants. Especially for potential successors, the influence of the enterprise on socialization, on their competence, and subsequently on a possible desire for succession will have an influence. Possible explanatory approaches that influence the willingness to succeed (positively and negatively) were also provided. Of course, and this is emphasized again at this point, for a comprehensive insight or an examination of the influences on the socialization of the descendants, the respective family and business cycle must be considered.

The following Table 2.7 summarizes the influencing factors on socialization that can result from the connection between families and businesses, as explained in this main section.

In conclusion, based on the argumentation carried out in this chapter, it can be assumed that the family business has an influence on the socialization of the entrepreneur's children. Of course, the intensity cannot be generalized. This is due to the family's attachment to the business. Due to the individual appearance of families, it is therefore conceivable that each family business represents a unique structure that forms a non-imitable family and corporate culture. These cultural peculiarities will in turn exert their influence on the socialization of the descendants depending on the size of the enterprise and the respective participating generation.

Table 2.7 Influences of the family business on socialization

Influences on socialization	Brief description
Values and expectations	Parents can impart their attitudes, stance, and behavior towards the enterprise, employees, customers, suppliers, etc. to their children; as well as their expectations for the children's life planning; due to the dynamic aspect these can change over time
Regulations/Sanctions	Active "steering" of descendants; can serve to ensure compliance with expectations such as behavior in public or towards customers
Communication	Business-relevant topics can be brought closer to the children; communication is determined by the common task; children gain knowledge about the enterprise's requirements at a very early age; danger: neglect of personal and individual concerns
Upbringing	Active influence of parents on the adolescents; introduction to the family business; promotion of performance and competition thinking; upbringing towards family business succession

(continued)

Table 2.7 (continued)

Influences on socialization	Brief description
Gender of the children	The gender can influence the selection as successor and thus, the life planning desired by the parents for each child; this also results in a diverging involvement in the family business
Rivalries	Rivalries can occur between siblings for the attention of the parents; also, in view of the role in the family business, e.g., who is allowed to take over the succession
Lack of role separation	Due to the lack of context markers, the enterprise can be a constant part of the communication; the children have a kind of double identity: (1) As a child and (2) as potential successors
Industry and business object	Influences the extent of the connection between family and business as well as the requirements for the next generation (e.g., their education); this can result in a selection of only male successors, i.e., a gender-based selection
Enterprise size	Influences the extent of the connection between family and business; depending on the size of the family business, different requirements are placed on the successors such as their education
Family size	Influences the extent of the connection between family and business; depending on how many members the family comprises not all will be able to actively work in the family business. The majority will "only" be connected to it through ownership shares. This represents a different starting situation/life world for the descendants; the descendants are exposed to an expanded set of expectations as the family members participating in the family business grow. Especially if they are seen as potential successors
Cross-generational continuity	The desire to pass on the family business can "push" potential successors in a certain direction; individual development can be restricted; however, this can provide clear orientation for potential successors

(continued)

Table 2.7 (continued)

Influences on socialization	Brief description
Traditions	These can influence the values of the generation actively participating in the family business, which they then pass on to the next generation; can condition the choice of successor, and thus influence their socialization or life path
Parents' connection to the enterprise	It should make a difference, whether both parents work in the enterprise or only participate through ownership shares; the attitude of the in-laws towards the enterprise must also be considered, as this should have an impact on the entrepreneur's socialization
Enterprise as a life world/experience context	Life world is influenced by the family business; if the enterprise initially represents a "playground", the adolescents get to know it later through holiday jobs or their own work; the family business provides, among other things, the framework conditions for the construction of meaning
Enterpriseness	The enterprise ranks the priorities; the family adapts to the requirements of the business; children must work in the family business; a common task can promote cohesion; the enterprise may be constantly present
Family Governance	Definition of the family mission and vision; selection criteria for future successors; code of conduct for family members participating in the enterprise
Paradoxes	The adolescents can be exposed to different calls to action from their parents, which can trigger internal conflicts in them; they grow up in an ambiguous world, as they are exposed to the demands of the family and the business
Conflicts	The descendants can be exposed to internal conflicts in the course of succession (takeover yes/no); they also actively experience the parents' conflicts, which can diminish their desire to take over the family business one day; conflicts within the enterprise can spread to the family or be carried out within the family or be part of the communication within the family; can color the descendant's view of the family business negatively

3 Systems Theory, Symbolic Interactionism, Role Theory and Ecological Systems Model

Chapter 2 served to introduce the context of family businesses. This was done by pointing out the characteristics of this form of enterprise and identifying as well as presenting the most important influences and dynamics on the socialization of the descendants. However, as was also evident in Chap. 2, there is a wide range of variation in family businesses, which results in differences in the influence on the socialization of the descendants. Nevertheless, there are interdependencies and regularities that occur in every family business or in every business family and to which all descendants are exposed. Therefore, in this chapter, the dynamics and influences presented in Chap. 2 are generalized and theoretically "underpinned" to provide a uniform understanding of terms. This then forms the starting point for the analysis in Chap. 4. In addition, the theoretical presentation is also intended to counteract an erratic impression. This serves in the further course rather the channeling of the interest in knowledge of this work.

First, the *Systems theory*, based on a Luhmannian perspective, will be discussed. This opens the possibility of providing an analytical framework, within which the special features of a family business can be depicted in a generalized manner. Following this, the *Symbolic Interactionism* serves to establish an understanding (of the development) of identity, i.e., the inner perspective of a person. Above all, the research question or the consideration of socialization justifies the processing. Since both theories use the concept of role, additional attention is paid to the *Role theory*. In family businesses in particular, the descendants are simultaneously exposed to different, sometimes contradictory (role) requirements,

S. Caspary, *The Family Business as a Socialisation Context for the Children of Entrepreneurs*, https://doi.org/10.1007/978-3-658-43657-5_3

which can lead to conflicts. It also became clear that the requirements for successors change over the course of generations. Role theory primarily provides insights into how the different expectations influence the behavior of individuals. Against the background of the research question, this also provides an explanatory approach for socialization. Finally, the *Ecological Systems Model* according to Bronfenbrenner is discussed. The model provides insight into how the entry into new systems (life worlds) forms the starting point for socialization processes.

If Systems theory and Symbolic Interactionism are considered, they can be understood as theories of greater reach. Each focuses on a different aspect of reality, which only allows for limited connectivity or compatibility to each other. Thus, Luhmannian Systems theory can be understood as a societal theory, while Symbolic Interactionism is associated with action theory. This different orientation is not a problem when considered separately, but is problematic in the context of this work, as the interest in knowledge is directed at how the external (societal) influences are internalized during socialization and contribute to the formation of identity. To be able to depict or process this accordingly, a combination of these two theories is indispensable. However, since this is primarily a theoretical discussion and does not primarily serve the answer to the research question, this is done as *excursus* under Sect. 3.4.

3.1 The Systems Theory

3.1.1 Social Systems

Every person is a member of various social systems. In general, social systems serve the purpose of reducing complexity by minimizing states/events. That means, they only allow a certain manageable number of states/events and can thus provide some sort of guidance to the members involved.[1] Characteristic of

[1] Cf. Kneer and Nassehi (2000), p. 40 f. According to Willke, complexity denotes "the degree of multilayeredness, interconnection and consequentiality of a decision field [in original bold]" (Willke 1996, 22), where *multilayeredness* refers to the degree of functional differentiation of a social system, *interconnection* the extent of mutual dependency between the parts and between part and whole, and *consequentiality* describes the scope of causal chains initiated by decisions (cf. Willke 1996, 22 f.). In detail consequentiality according to Willke means: "Number and weight of causal chains or consequential processes set in motion by a particular decision within the social system in question" (Willke 1996, 26).

social systems is also that these are "autopoietic, operationally closed, meaning processing, and based on communication"[2]. Additionally, they establish their identity through their differentiation from other social systems. Due to the operative closure, social systems are dependent on their self-organization and can therefore only use their own operations to form structures.[3] Furthermore, social systems cannot perceive due to the ability of their operations. For them, the only possibility is to thematize perception through communication.[4] Due to the importance of communication for social systems, it will be discussed first.

3.1.1.1 Communication in Systems Theory

Specifically, communication[5] can be seen as the starting point for the continuous existence of a social system, with each subsystem defining for itself what it understands by communication and what not.[6] In addition, communication can coordinate actors and actions, and thus makes it possible to form members of social systems from individual acting individuals.[7] According to Gensicke,[8] communication represents the smallest possible unit, respectively is the element of a social system that cannot be further resolved.

When organizations and interactions are compared, the organization as a social system can deal with different topics that are brought up by communication. Interactions, on the other hand, are limited to one topic. It is possible to replace this with a new one, but this can only be done subsequently, i.e., subsequently opened and must be done at the same time for all members involved.[9] For Luhmann[10] social systems consist solely of communication. Thus, communication can be

---

[2] Jahraus et al. (2012), p. 94.

[3] Cf. Jahraus et al. (2012), p. 85. According to Jahraus et al., an operation is "a singular, momentary act, and thus an *event*. Events have no duration, they are point-like, and thus not temporally stretchable and dissolve quasi in their execution. Eventfulness is now the mode, in which the elements of sense-processing autopoietic (i.e., social and psychic) systems take place" (Jahraus et al. 2012, 107).

[4] Cf. Kieserling (1999), p. 112.

[5] Luhmann discusses the concept of communication in Luhmann (1988, 10–18) and Luhmann (1987b, 191–241).

[6] Cf. Simon (2007a), p. 22 and cf. Mingers (2003), p. 107.

[7] Cf. Simon (2007a), p. 36.

[8] Cf. Gensicke (2008), p. 41.

[9] Cf. Kieserling (1999), p. 24.

[10] Cf. Luhmann (2000), p. 62.

understood as an operation that can only arise through communication. A system can therefore only appear as a unit as long as communication connects to communication and the previous determines the subsequent communication.[11]

In this context, all communication is structurally coupled to consciousness, i.e., communication relies on the support of consciousness.[12] Without consciousness, communication could neither appear as an utterance nor as understanding.[13] Therefore, for social systems there is a necessity to be perceived by consciousness. Otherwise, asking for a light for a cigarette, for example, would be difficult if it was not possible to perceive what the other person was doing.[14] According to Luhmann's[15] understanding, consciousness controls, so to speak, the influence of the outside world on communication. Thus, consciousness acts as a kind of filter that prevents the "total reality of the world"[16] from affecting communication. Against the backdrop of this protective mechanism there is the possibility of developing systems.[17] This connection is also referred to as structural coupling. A key feature of structural coupling is its almost unnoticed execution for the involved systems.[18] In this context, consciousness enables a "simultaneous processing of utterance and understanding"[19]. This allows, for example, to interrupt an utterance when the sender perceives a possible disinterest of the receiver.[20]

3.1.1.2 Interactions

Interaction systems arise through physical presence, i.e., through mutual perception of communication partners.[21] This characteristic also marks the criterion of selection and boundary drawing, regardless of whether a closer relationship exists between those present or not.[22] Thus, interaction can also be defined as "communication among those present"[23]. Due to the demarcation by presence, perception

[11] Cf. Jahraus et al. (2012), p. 70.
[12] Cf. Luhmann (1998a), p. 103.
[13] Cf. Luhmann (1990), p. 218 f.
[14] Cf. Kieserling (1999), p. 113.
[15] Cf. Luhmann (1998a), p. 114.
[16] Luhmann (1998a), p. 114.
[17] Cf. Luhmann (1998a), p. 114.
[18] Cf. Luhmann (1990), p. 218 f.
[19] Luhmann (1998a), p. 103.
[20] Cf. Luhmann (1998a), p. 103.
[21] Cf. Baraldi et al. (1997), p. 82.
[22] Cf. Luhmann (1986), p. 10.
[23] Kieserling (1999), p. 24.

processes in particular gain importance, which are responsible for the construction of interaction systems.[24] In this case, perception enforces communication. Therefore, even the rejection of communication is to be classified as communication.[25] If communication in the interaction system is to be avoided, this is only possible through absence.[26] Otherwise, the rule is: If communication ends, so does the interaction. Even if the same participants meet again, this marks a new interaction.[27] In general, interaction systems are subject to a structural constraint that prevents them from acquiring an excessive level of complexity. However, if the interaction system is stable, the mutual expectations of the participants serve as the point of orientation.[28]

3.1.1.3 Organizations

Organizations can be named as another type of social system. They support societal development in many ways. In addition to reducing complexity[29], they perform a functional specialization and serve as a point of orientation for dealing with special problem situations. Organizations provide society with the opportunity to solve very complex tasks[30] by enforcing a regulation of coexistence and providing security for expectations.[31] However, for each organization, there is initially the need to meet two requirements:

1. It must have a relatively stable demarcation from its environment, which then allows the organization to be distinguished from the outside and the inside.
2. It also needs to develop, which is not really compatible with the first requirement.

Nevertheless, organizations are not simply there, but arise within an environment that in turn produces varying conditions through the establishment of an organization. Fulfilling both requirements guarantees the organization to develop its own identity in contrast to others and to successfully maintain its activities.[32]

By focusing specifically on the inner life, a social system is organized when

---

[24] Cf. Luhmann (1987b), p. 560.

[25] Cf. Baraldi et al. (1997), p. 82

[26] Cf. Luhmann (1987b), p. 562.

[27] Cf. Kieserling (1999), p. 15

[28] Cf. Parsons (1976), p. 179.

[29] Above all, the internal life of an organization is controlled via the "*reduction of complexity*" (Königswieser and Hillebrand 2009, 32).

[30] Cf. Froschauer (2012), p. 17.

[31] Cf. Froschauer (2012), p. 45.

[32] Cf. Lueger (2012), p. 99.

1. expectations exert a determining influence on it.[33]
2. membership requires the fulfillment of certain criteria, i.e., entry and exit are associated with conditions.[34]
3. it can be characterized by "personnel recruitment and role specifications"[35].

The formality results, among other things, from the purposeful orientation towards a common purpose, the hierarchical and division of labor-oriented alignment, through written regulations, and the planned assignment of services.[36] The formalized organization is becoming increasingly prevalent in complex social systems and can be located between the social system and the individual interaction systems.[37] An organization is classified as a system that creates itself as an organization.[38]

If the admission to a formal organization is considered first, it neutralizes the different motives for entry through a homogeneous confession of membership. Consequently, the individual motives lose their importance.[39] The organization thus primarily distinguishes itself from its respective environment by granting membership.[40] This results in the conception of different combinations and separation possibilities of roles, which have a structure-determining effect on the formal organization. Therefore, special importance is given to the role of membership. This is the prerequisite for joining or leaving and represents the starting point from which all other formal and informal roles within the organization can be accessed. In addition, the role of membership distinguishes between personal and official matters of the members.[41] As the members commit to the organization, the expectations and behavioral requirements that can be traced back to the organization's decisions for role determination are accepted.[42] For this reason, the role of membership guarantees the system the fulfillment of the set

[33] Cf. Luhmann (1995b), p. 27.

[34] Cf. Luhmann (1986), p. 12.

[35] Baraldi et al. (1997), p. 129.

[36] Cf. Luhmann (1995b), p. 30 f. Luhmann understands "formality as the belonging to a certain system structure [...], which is formal because it secures the identity of the system against changing persons and orientation contents" (Luhmann 1995c, 29 as well as Luhmann 1976b, 29).

[37] Cf. Luhmann (1986), p. 12.

[38] Cf. Luhmann (2006b), p. 46 and cf. Luhmann (2000), p. 45.

[39] Cf. Luhmann (1976b), p. 42.

[40] Cf. Luhmann (1987b), p. 268 f.

[41] Cf. Luhmann (1976b), p. 39–46.

[42] Cf. Wimmer (2012), p. 43 f.

expectations from the members within certain limits. These do not have to be re-established in every situation.[43] However, the membership demands far more than the functional role (e.g., as a gatekeeper). The membership role or the system role requires not only the fulfillment and recognition of specific individually addressed expectations, but also the recognition and support of any other expectations communicated on behalf of the system, regardless of who the recipient is.[44]

In addition, communication in organizations acts as a kind of demarcation mechanism to distinguish the organization as a system from its respective environment.[45] However, the organization must constantly perform connecting actions to distinguish itself permanently from its respective environment and continue to exist. The necessity arises primarily because organizations are not composed of objects, but of communicative actions.[46] In this context, the organization can be seen as a special form of communication. This arises and reproduces itself through decisions,[47] where the basis of any decision is the information about which alternatives are available.[48] In addition to the founding of an organization, the admission of members can also be classified as a decision. Every decision of the system builds on decisions of the system and thus, also offers the possibility of tracing back.[49] In other words, everything is oriented towards the premise of whether a decision is made or not.[50] Decision premises serve as uncertainty absorbers for the organization. While these reduce the cost of decision making, they do not require fully specified decisions to be made.[51]

Since every decision is made or produced against the backdrop of previous decisions, organizations are autopoietic (literally: self-creation) systems to the same extent as all social systems and are specifically classified as operationally closed systems in this sense.[52] Von Schlippe et al. refer to the prevailing communication as "decision communication" [53]. In detail, organizations make decisions by hiring and firing their members, and by filling various positions with these

---

[43] Cf. Luhmann (1976b), p. 42.

[44] Cf. Jahraus et al. (2012), p. 130.

[45] Cf. Simon (2007a), p. 27.

[46] Cf. Froschauer (2012), p. 11.

[47] Cf. Luhmann (2000), p. 63.

[48] Cf. Seidl (2006), p. 41.

[49] Cf. Luhmann (2000), p. 63.

[50] Cf. Kneer (2001), p. 414.

[51] Cf. Luhmann (2000), p. 223.

[52] Cf. Luhmann (1998b), p. 830.

[53] von Schlippe et al. (2012), p. 289.

same members.[54] The structural coupling between the organization and its members leads to the members being able to affect the structure of the organization and the organization being able to influence the psyche of their members.[55] Since members within an organization cannot usually always communicate with all others, communication is subject to certain restrictions. An example would be a hierarchical structure.[56]

However, the operational closure of organizations does not deny the possibility of members assuming other roles in their environment, such as the role of a mother. However, this is not seen as a natural act, but rather results from a decision.[57] Luhmann[58] speaks of an institutional separation of the formal role from the other roles of the system members, which they assume both within and outside the system. This separation of roles means that the other roles are not transferable to the formal system so that no special rights arise in the formal system. Similarly, the separation of roles opens the possibility of being able to reject unreasonable demands made during working hours, e.g., by a relative, but not having to reject them.

For an organization there is also a presumption that its growth will require increasing definition of working and communication relationships. This can, among other things, lead to an increase in the formalization of decisions, the reduction of the ability to penetrate, and the solidification of communication paths.[59] If the overall system, i.e., the organization, is divided into several subsystems, the boundaries, which appear as internal barriers, become a problem for the overall system if a minimum level of common orientation is not established. As a result, there is a particular need for more highly differentiated systems to define formal structures that all members must follow.[60]

The formality allows the system to maintain its identity, even when the individuals and the frame of reference are subject to change.[61]

---

[54] Cf. Seidl (2006), p. 43.

[55] Cf. Simon (2007a), p. 40 and cf. Luhmann (2000), p. 111.

[56] Cf. Seidl (2006), p. 43.

[57] Cf. Luhmann (2006b), p. 63.

[58] Cf. Luhmann (1976b), p. 65.

[59] Cf. Luhmann (1981), p. 351.

[60] Cf. Luhmann (1976b), p. 79.

[61] Cf. Luhmann (1976b), p. 29.

3.1.2 Psychic Systems

Luhmann's theory clearly distinguishes between social and psychic phenomena. Both entities are considered as two clearly delineated systems that do not overlap.[62] Therefore, psychic systems cannot be classified as part of a social system. Nevertheless, both types of systems represent the necessary environment for each other.[63] The existence of one necessitates the existence of the other system as an environment, although both systems are constructed from different starting points.[64] While the social system is caused by a "unified (self-referential) communication context" [65], the psychic system arises from a "unified (self-referential) consciousness context" [66]. Psychic systems therefore do not consist of communication like social systems, but of thoughts.[67] They have no contact with the environment and reproduce themselves or their meaning (in German, *Sinn*) in a closed system[68] based on consciousness.[69] Meanwhile, consciousness has the possibility to influence communication through stimuli and irritations. In addition, consciousness represents a constant reservoir for the course of communicative events. It can inspire communication, and thus influence the choice of topics.[70] Due to the evolution of both systems, it is therefore not possible for an individual to exist without one of the two systems.[71] Just as communication can be cited as the basic condition for the emergence of social systems,[72] communication also

---

[62] Cf. Seidl and Becker (2006b), p. 9.

[63] Cf. Kieserling (1999), p. 404.

[64] Cf. Luhmann (1994), p. 92.

[65] Luhmann (1987b), p. 92.

[66] Luhmann (1987b), p. 92.

[67] Cf. Luhmann (1987a), p. 174.

[68] Cf. Baraldi et al. (1997), p. 142.

[69] Cf. Seidl (2006), p. 32. According to Luhmann, consciousness "should not be understood as something substantially present (to which language constantly tempts us), but merely as the specific mode of operation of psychic systems" (Luhmann 1987b, 355).

[70] Cf. Luhmann (1995a), p. 45.

[71] Cf. Luhmann (1994), p. 92. According to Kneer and Nassehi, "evolution refers to the structural change of a system through self-referential handling of selection and variation" (Kneer and Nassehi 2000, 122).

[72] Cf. Luhmann (1981), p. 27.

relies on the participation of consciousness. Only consciousness enables communication to form as an utterance or as understanding.[73] The convergence of social and psychic systems then forms the starting point for socialization.[74]

3.1.3 Structural Coupling

Simon et al.[75] understand structural coupling to be the ability of the involved systems to interact with each other and to mutually benefit without clearly determining the development of the respective other system. However, for the concept of structural coupling to be applied, some system specifications are required. The systems must have their own operations and they must be autopoietic systems.[76] Structural coupling enables a system to participate in very complex environmental conditions without having to appropriate the respective existing complexity.[77] Although, the environment does not influence the system in the sense of a structural determination, the structures created by the system are influenced by the environment.[78] In other words, the environment provides concrete prerequisites for the system that the system cannot create or even maintain on its own.[79] Baraldi et al. speak in this context of the necessity of a "»materiality continuum«" [80], which ensures the continued existence of the system. Kneer formulates this as follows: "A structural coupling exists, when a system permanently presupposes certain properties of its operationally unreachable environment."[81] The term structural coupling attempts to answer the question, according to Luhmann, "how autopoietic systems, despite their own autonomy and operational closure, can still be thought of as connected with the environment" [82]. [83]

Furthermore, structural coupling can be understood as a "connection" between systems, without however affecting the autonomy of the individual structurally

[73] Cf. Luhmann (1990), p. 218 f.

[74] Cf. Gilgenmann (1986), p. 149 f.

[75] Cf. Simon et al. (2005), p. 21.

[76] Cf. Jahraus et al. (2012), p. 121 f.

[77] Cf. Luhmann (1998a), p. 107.

[78] Cf. Luhmann (2000), p. 397.

[79] Cf. Baraldi et al. (1997), p. 186.

[80] Baraldi et al. (1997), p. 186.

[81] Kneer (2001), p. 417.

[82] Luhmann (1995a), p. 31.

[83] Cf. Baraldi et al. (1997), p. 186.

coupled systems.[84] Structurally coupled systems are dependent on each other, yet they also simultaneously form the environment of the respective system.[85] On the other hand, when considering the structural coupling of functional systems, this is primarily limited to performance relationships. For example, the economic system financially supports all other systems.[86] In considering the structural coupling of social and psychic systems, the thesis is put forward that social systems can only be coupled to the consciousness of psychic systems. Communication operates completely detached from this. Not communication, but only consciousness possesses the ability of perception. Only consciousness enables the perceived external world to be transformed into consciousness.[87] Without the consciousness of the psychic system, it would thus also be impossible for the social system to communicate.[88]

3.2 The Symbolic Interactionism

This chapter provides an understanding of socialization and specifically for the identity formation of the individual. To ensure this, the focus is on how external circumstances are received and processed by the respective individual and what mechanisms these trigger within the individual. The focus is thus on the individual's "internal perspective".

3.2.1 Communication in Symbolic Interactionism

Symbolic Interactionism primarily refers to the theory of action, which in turn builds on social interaction. In detail, according to Reiger, social interaction can be understood as "the mutual relationships and exchange processes between individuals or groups"[89], whereby communication, for example, being facilitated by

[84] Cf. Jünemann and Schuster (2004), p. 10.

[85] Cf. Kneer and Nassehi (2000), p. 62 f.

[86] Cf. Runkel and Burkart (2005 b), p. 7.

[87] Cf. Baecker (2004), p. 270 f.

[88] Cf. Baraldi et al. (1997), p. 187.

[89] Reiger (2007), p. 141.

the medium of language.[90] However, for communication to occur, there is initially a requirement to generate the same meaning in the consciousness of the communication partners involved. Therefore, for successful execution of human communication, each communication partner must have a stock of signs that symbolize the same objects for the participants.[91] Or to put it another way, the used symbol must have the ability to trigger the same reaction in the involved persons.[92] These can be, for example, objects, states, views, visions, etc.[93] Mead uses the term "significant symbols"[94] in this context. Communication arises in this sense only when the gesture emanating from the individual triggers the same reaction in others as it does in him. Only then does the gesture become a significant symbol.[95]

From the perspective of Symbolic Interactionism, the mutual orientation of the communication participants towards each other is therefore an implicit part of the communication process. By using symbols there is the possibility for oneself to not only update meanings within consciousness. Rather, the symbolically mediated interaction enables the attitude(s) of the other(s) to be taken towards oneself.[96] It is precisely the communication process that enables the individual to learn his social roles. Against this background, a social role can be understood as a constellation of learned meanings that enable individuals to perform stable and generally accepted forms of interaction with others. Above all, the communication system thus enables the acquisition of culturally mediated roles. These are brought closer to the individual specifically through the family,

---

[90] Cf. Reiger (2007), p. 141. According to Mead (1973, 203), language consists primarily of "vocal gestures" (Mead 1973, 203) and can be referred to as the most significant "sign system of human society" (Berger and Luckmann 2000, 39) as it enables cooperative activities within a society to be carried out. Mead defines gestures as follows: "By the term »gesture« I mean that part of the action or attitude of a socially acting individual that serves as a stimulus for another individual to perform his part of the overall action" (Mead 1969, 93).

[91] Cf. Burkart (2002), p. 56.

[92] Cf. Mead (1973), p. 189.

[93] Cf. Burkart (2002), p. 56.

[94] Mead (1973), p. 86. When significant symbols are compared with natural signs, natural signs provoke in the observer "instinctively the same bodily reactions and emotional states as in the trigger" (Rose 1973, 269). Thus, communication by means of natural signs differs from communication with significant symbols by the possibility of (un)conscious behavior control of the communication partner and the triggering of a specific reaction to the stimulation of his sensory organs. On the other hand, communication of significant symbols cannot control the recipient, but only influence him (cf. Rose 1973, 269).

[95] Cf. Joas (1987b), p. 217.

[96] Cf. Burkart (2002), p. 433.

the peer group, school, and work.[97] Thus, according to Mead's view, human communication can be seen as a kind of role-taking (in the original: "taking the role of the other"[98]) as well as a "spontaneous self-expression" [99]. This leads to a congruence of emotional state and a physical reaction in the recipient. In addition to the area of communicative skills, developments for general cognitive, motivational, and moral abilities are also included,[100] where the exclusively cognitive ability can also be referred to as empathy.[101]

3.2.2 The Shaping of Identity

Identity (Latin *idem ens* = being the same)[102] is not given at birth, but develops "within the societal experience and activity process" [103]. Thus, identity is subject to a gradual and ongoing development. This becomes increasingly complex

[97] Cf. Bernstein (1973), p. 243. The special feature of the social role is that it arises partly during and partly after the acquisition of the cultural role, whereby a cultural role can be understood as behaviors that are oriented towards concrete expectations and arise through membership in a specific culture. The culture provides the framework for the respective behavior. For example, an individual first assumes the cultural role of an Austrian or a German. Only then does he or she become a member of a specific class, group, or subculture. In contrast to the social role, a change of cultural role is hardly possible or can only be accomplished with enormous damage to the person concerned. In contrast, it is "easier" to change the social role, as this is carried out within the respective orientation system (cf. Claessens 1968, 41 ff.).

[98] Mead (1936), p. 375.

[99] Rose (1973), p. 269.

[100] Cf. Joas (1991), p. 139.

[101] Cf. Krappmann (1993), p. 142.

[102] Cf. Abels and König (2010), p. 20.

[103] Mead (1973), p. 177 and see p. 207. Mead uses the term "self" in his original work. This is translated in the German edition with the term "identity": "Mead's expression »the self« is consistently translated here as »identity«, in the sense of personal or I-identity" (Mead 1973, 39). Mead also developed the concept of I-identity. This uses the assumption that the adolescent constitutes himself as an individual only through participation in social interaction (cf. Döbert et al. 1980, 12). Dreitzel describes this as follows: The I-identity "is formed on the basis of the reciprocity of perspectives in the course of the socialization process in the constant confrontation between the psycho-physical drive claims on the one hand, and the real failures and the internalized norms on the other hand, as the instance in which the autonomy of the individual is revealed" (Dreitzel 1980, 55). The I-identity arises through the ability of people to strike a balance between personal and social identity. The personal identity includes one's own biographical experiences and the social identity group contexts and expectation contexts (cf. Zimmermann 2006, 54 f.).

when the child encounters a wide variety of people who are perceived as relevant situations for the identity.[104] If the individual wants to relate to other people, according to Krappmann, it is first necessary to present his identity. This makes it clear to others who she or he is. In this context, however, identity should not be confused with a rigid self-image. This is rather developed by everyone himself. In contrast, identity constantly links the individual's past interactions with the expectations and needs that exist in the current situation.[105]

In detail, identity is composed not only of "objective identity markers (gender, nationality)"[106], but also of "self-descriptive attributes (personality or competence characteristics)" [107]. Only the combination of this internal and external perspective creates identity,[108] which can also be described as a "the linchpin of healthy personality development" [109]. For Hurrelmann[110] there are certain factors, which are conducive to the formation of identity, and thus represent the starting point for independent and autonomous action. These include: Decision-making ability and action certainty of the individual, coping strategies for social and psychological difficulties, inclusion in secure social relationship structures, and recognition in significant societal role contexts. In relation to this, the more these factors are pronounced, the more effective they are. In addition, Symbolic Interactionism explains the emergence of identity primarily through the appropriation of role-playing with the help of role-taking[111] or through the role-taking of the generalized other.[112] Identity is thus fundamentally, but not only socially mediated.[113] Specifically, the identity development can be seen as a step-by-step process in which the child is integrated "into the symbolic universe of its environment" [114]. [115] According to Strauss [116], however, the examination of interaction

[104] Cf. Stryker (1970), p. 57.

[105] Cf. Krappmann (1993), p. 8 f.

[106] Leipold and Greve (2008), p. 401.

[107] Leipold and Greve (2008), p. 401.

[108] Cf. Leipold and Greve (2008), p. 401.

[109] Hurrelmann (2002), p. 39.

[110] Cf. Hurrelmann (2002), p. 39.

[111] Cf. Reiger (2007), p. 148.

[112] Cf. Abels and König (2010), p. 88 f.

[113] Cf. Reiger (2007), p. 148.

[114] Döbert et al. (1980), p. 10.

[115] Cf. Döbert et al. (1980), p. 10.

[116] Cf. Strauss (1974), p. 45. Strauss focuses on the interaction that "takes place between people in their role as group members" (Strauss 1974, 45).

must not be neglected when investigating identity, as it is only on the basis of interaction that an assessment of oneself and others can be made.

Central to the individual development of the child's identity Mead sees the game. He divides this into two phases, which are each temporally subsequent.[117] If these phases are considered in connection with role-taking, they can be seen in a figurative sense as two phases of socialization,[118] i.e., "as a process of integration into existing role systems" [119]. By putting oneself in the positions of others, the role taker is thus allowed to understand relationships between people and gains an understanding of the factors that enable these relationships or contribute to their breakdown. Any conflicts between people are recognized and there is knowledge about their resolution. Also needs, desires , and social expectations of other people are noticed as a reference to one's own expectations is established. The role-taking in particular is seen as a basic prerequisite for initiating thought processes about friendship, justice, authority, and society.[120]

Thus, the individual can develop an organized personality. By the child adopting the attitudes of others and taking on the moral viewpoints as well as aligning its activities towards the achievement of the common goal, it becomes an "organic limb"[121] of society. Its own immediate expression is therefore determined by the adopted attitudes.[122] As the child over time participates in ever more expansive "symbolic worlds"[123] and internalizes their rules, it understands that in other areas, such as in the family, in organizations, or in society, general ideas for actions exist.[124] The completion of both above mentioned phases is seen as the prerequisite for the complete development of identity.

---

[117] Cf. Garz (2006), p. 45 and cf. Mead (1969), p. 90 f. In detail, it is about the "individual game" (Garz 2006, 45) (play) and the "competition" (Garz 2006, 45) (game).

[118] Cf. Abels and König (2010), p. 81.

[119] Habermas (1968), p. 2.

[120] Cf. Damon (1990), p. 270. Damon (1990, p. 271) originally uses the term "perspective taking". However, as this term is associated with the term "role taking" in the psychological literature (cf. Damon 1990, p. 261), the term "role taking" is used for consistent argumentation.

[121] Mead (1973), p. 202.

[122] Cf. Mead (1973), p. 202 f.

[123] Abels and König (2010), p. 84.

[124] Cf. Abels and König (2010), p. 84.

3.3 The Role Theory

Since the theories mentioned in this chapter (Systems theory and Symbolic Interactionism) repeatedly use the term "role", it is indispensable to provide a basic insight into the Role theory. Above all, the Role theory provides an explanation of how the values, norms, and expectations present in the different systems are internalized by the respective person and why they follow them. Through an understanding of this, the dynamic aspect during socialization becomes clear.

3.3.1 Characteristics of (Social) Roles

According to Claessens [125], the concept of role is particularly suitable for the "social psychological treatment of situations and behavioral constellations" [126]. However, the focus is less on the role itself, but rather on how the respective individual "masters" the requirements of the role. The role is then understood as the "ordering element of action" [127], which is additionally seen as a basic unit for social interaction.[128] In contrast, Popitz[129] refers to roles as "conglomerates of individual actions" [130], whereby in everyday life these are generally conceived as a unit of meaning (e.g., the father role). Thus, the view that the role consists of a multitude of individual actions recedes into the background so that the bearer of the father role is not expected to perform action B in situation A. By using the concept of role, it is therefore possible to identify patterns of how individuals behave or act towards others. Especially, the expectations united in a role exert a certain obligation. Thus, the individual cannot exit this role without damage.[131] Mitscherlich formulates this as follows: "The *role* is a functional form of behavior towards others. Every *role* is a piece of mask, a preformed, which the individual (actively) assimilates or to which it (passively) adapts." [132]

---

[125] Cf. Claessens (1968), p. 9.

[126] Claessens (1968), p. 9.

[127] Zimmermann (2006), p. 51.

[128] Cf. Zimmermann (2006), p. 51. Ischi understands social interaction as the "mutual relationship between two or more individuals" (Ischi 1978, p. 44).

[129] Cf. Popitz (1967), p. 18.

[130] Popitz (1967), p. 18.

[131] Cf. Zimmermann (2006), p. 51.

[132] Mitscherlich (1986), p. 72. However, to initially gain a general sense of the concept of role, Dahrendorf's comparison can be used. He compares the social role with the role of

Specifically, the subject is viewed from the perspective of the social role as the sum of different individual roles.[133] By internalizing its role, the individual participates in the societal environment that is subjectively significant for it.[134] The roles existing within a society are learned during socialization. This applies equally to gender roles, which define the characteristic role behavior of women and men.[135] Since the gender role is acquired very early and is deeply rooted, it is located within the "personality-specific dimensions" [136]. Role learning in particular is predominantly accomplished during the socialization process through imitation and adaptation.[137] However, a role only provides a "meaning offer" [138]. The individual must therefore decide for himself, whether to accept this offer or not. In addition, it should be considered to what extent a role is "meaningful in

---

an actor and identifies five points of intersection: (1) First, the role can be seen as something predetermined, i.e., as something "existing outside of him" (Dahrendorf 1977, 22). (2) Then there is the possibility to characterize the predetermined as a "complex of behaviors" (Dahrendorf 1977, 22). (3) This complex of behaviors can then be combined with other behaviors into a whole. (4) In addition, there is the necessity of learning so that the role can be played. (5) Finally, it is possible for both the individual and the actor to learn and play a variety of roles (cf. Dahrendorf 1977, 20 ff). Furthermore, Dahrendorf describes it in the preface to Goffman's work as follows: "The social world is a stage, a complicated stage even, with audience, performers and outsiders, with auditorium and scenery, and with some peculiarities that the play does not know" (Goffman 2007, VII).

[133] Cf. AG Soziologie (1999), p. 29. Hurrelmann understands the term subject to mean a human being "when he confronts the material, social, and cultural »objects« of his environment as an experiencing, thinking, and acting individual" (Hurrelmann 2002, 7).

[134] Cf. Berger and Luckmann (2000), p. 78.

[135] Cf. Prisching (1995), p. 143. According to Prisching, gender roles are "normative expectations about the division of labor between the genders and about gender-related rules for social interactions within a certain cultural and historical context" (Prisching 1995, 143). Gender roles contribute to how women and men perceive their tasks and responsibilities towards family life. While women tend to align their tasks with the needs of the family, men do this for their work (cf. Gillis-Donovan and Moynihan-Bradt 1990, 156). Above all, the gender role determines moral consciousness. This can be referred to as a "global variable" (Döbert and Nummer-Winkler 1980, 269). It comes into effect directly through a substantive role definition or through the image of a role institutionalized within a (sub)culture. Indirectly, it comes into effect through the action qualifications acquired differently within gender-specific socialization (cf. Döbert and Nummer-Winkler 1980, 269).

[136] Döbert and Nummer-Winkler (1980), p. 271.

[137] Cf. Prisching (1995), p. 61 and cf. Wiswede (1977), p. 34. See also the explanations of Symbolic Interactionism in this work (see Sect. 3.2).

[138] Tugendhat (1979), p. 270.

cooperative activities" [139]. For example, a person may hold the role of a teacher, but not identify with it and therefore perceive their own life as unfulfilled.[140]

Similarly, a role does not exist completely detached and isolated. Rather, every role requires a kind of counter-role, i.e., a "counterpart" with which it is in a relationship.[141] Turner refers to the corresponding counter-role as "alter-roles" [142]. Thus, the mother-role only makes sense when it is opposed by the alter-role of the child. The behavioral pattern of the mother-role is therefore only defined for the behavioral pattern of a child.[143] Such general role dispositions are primarily conveyed during the socialization process and through the interaction of the child with its "socializing agents" [144]. [145] A special feature is the number of roles that a person combines within themselves. This number usually corresponds to the number of different social systems in which the person is involved. Since this is usually several — apart from society as an (all) encompassing system — they also combine several roles within themselves.[146] In addition, each role within a social system can be divided into so-called "'subroles'" [147]. These are roles of subsystems that can be derived from the overarching system and the role assigned within it. Thus, the role of a girl within the context of "family" can be divided into the sub-roles of the feminine sub-context and the non-same-sex sub-context.[148]

When considering the reach of a role, Neuberger speaks of the "extent or degree of penetration of a role"[149]. This varies from roles that can penetrate all areas of life, such as the gender role, to roles that only apply to certain segments, such as the assistant to the executive director. Especially, the switch between a person's roles can cause misinterpretations and uncertainties among role partners. For them, it is not clearly recognizable who is facing them, which can then lead to role conflicts. To counteract this, the ritual of role separation has been established. This allows for the localization of the role through clearly recognizable cues

---

[139] Tugendhat (1979), p. 270.

[140] Cf. Tugendhat (1979), p. 270.

[141] Cf. Wiswede (1977), p. 27; cf. Goldthorpe (1969), p. 8 and cf. Bates (1956), p. 317 f.

[142] Turner (1977), p. 118.

[143] Cf. Turner (1977), p. 118 and cf. Stryker (1970), p. 55.

[144] Eisenstadt (1966), p. 21.

[145] Cf. Eisenstadt (1966), p. 21.

[146] Cf. Parsons (1966a), p. 112.

[147] Parsons (1966a), p. 112.

[148] Cf. Parsons (1966a), p. 112. Prisching uses the term "role diversity" in this context (Prisching 1995, 64).

[149] Neuberger (1976), p. 76.

(clothing, posture, gestures, etc.) or context markers (see Sect. 2.1.4),[150] although this is not always possible.

3.3.2 Emergence and Influence of Roles

After the characteristics of roles have been explained, the following chapter provides an understanding of how roles are created in the first place and how they are influenced. Particularly in family businesses, family members must perform different roles, which can be contradictory. However, roles should not be seen as something static. They are subject to certain dynamics, meaning that they are also subject to change over time. This dynamic is evident, for example, in the different generations. The role of the entrepreneur is always the same, but the expectations placed on him are subject to change. To be able to present this comprehensibly, values, norms, expectations, and roles will be discussed in detail. During socialization in particular, the growing individuals are exposed to these "factors", which additionally influence their development.

3.3.2.1 Values and Norms

Since the individual is born into an existing society, the various forms of action existing in it also influence the individual. This leads to a gradual adoption of the respective forms of action. At the same time, the individual also subconsciously internalizes the prevailing values, which provide significant "orientation facilities"[151] for the actions taken.[152] Above all, values represent the starting point for normative demands. However, for a value to develop into a norm, and thus be enforceable at all, the value must have an explicit formulation with a specific reference to an identifiable behavior of a relevant characteristic.[153] Thus, Wingen defines norms as "action-relevant standards (values) with a sanctioning character" [154].

Norms, on the other hand, are seen as part of human existence. For this reason, they are also attributed a high degree of internalization. However, for the

[150] Cf. Neuberger (1976), p. 76

[151] Claessens (1979), p. 35.

[152] Cf. Abels and König (2010), p. 113. Internalization describes the process of internalizing societal values and norms so that they become the starting point for the actions and thoughts of an individual (cf. Abels and König 2010, 10).

[153] Cf. Katz and Kahn (1978), p. 385.

[154] Wingen (1985), p. 393. Where norms include social, cultural as well as motivational influencing factors (cf. Wingen 1985, 393).

individual growing up within a society, norms do not necessarily take on the rank of external rules that it either follows or not. Rather, they often represent a part of the individual that cannot be objectified. (Social) Norms are more likely to be expressed in the automatic behavior of the individual.[155] Norms permeate, so to speak, the everyday life of human coexistence, i.e., human existence. They have a structuring effect on the socialization of people as well as on institutions and associations. However, not all standardizations of behavior carry normative weight, but only those that have a significance for living together.[156]

The internalized norms in particular cause a control and determination in the sense of an unconscious judgment of oneself and the other fellow human beings because they are more deeply anchored than the consciousness. Above all, the conception of a norm already implies a kind of sense of duty.[157] According to Popitz, they permeate "the everyday existence of humans" [158]. They refer to the expected behavior, which is sanctioned by the respective system and therefore unfold a "should" or "must" function. Regarding this they resemble roles.[159] Thus, according to Davis [160], any culturally transmitted behavior patterns can evoke a sense of obligation, and thus be interpreted as a norm in the long run. If an individual learns a language, for example, there is an obligation to speak it correctly. Therefore, norms are also classified as "obligated expectations"[161] that form the starting point for the construction of roles.[162] When specifically considering system norms, they generally serve the function of binding people to the system. These people thus remain loyal to the system and perform their assigned role. In detail, norms within a system fulfill two tasks:

1. They create a "cognitive map" for the members, which facilitates the work within the system and allows possible adjustments.
2. In addition, norms provide the starting point for the moral and social justification for the system, whether it is for the members or for people who are formally located outside of the system.[163]

---

[155] Cf. Davis (1966), p. 55.
[156] Cf. Popitz (1980), p. 16.
[157] Cf. Davis (1966), p. 55 f.
[158] Popitz (1980), p. 16.
[159] Cf. Katz and Kahn (1978), p. 385.
[160] Cf. Davis (1966), p. 56.
[161] AG Soziologie (1999), p. 31.
[162] Cf. Prisching (1995), p. 59.
[163] Cf. Katz and Kahn (1978), p. 386.

When considering the influence of norms on the role, Popitz[164] refers to behaviors that are obligatorily expected as role norms. Accordingly, social roles can be understood as a "bundle of role norms" [165]. Thus, roles consist of a set of norms that the actor must follow, with the norms specifying how individuals should behave under certain circumstances. In addition, norms or the roles resulting from them are reciprocal. This means that they enable a functional interaction, as a kind of coordination for the actions takes place. Furthermore, they are intersubjective, so the actor knows not only the norms relevant to him, but also the norms applicable to his role partner and consequently expects appropriate behavior.[166] Role action is more successful, the greater the overlap with role norms and the resulting interpretation of these norms by the role holder.[167]

Finally, when comparing roles, norms, and values, the various social systems always have a "binding, collectively shared pattern of norms and values"[168]. According to Ackerman and Parsons, the following distinction is initially made: "Norms are evaluated statements about behavior. Values are evaluated statements about states. Norms regulate 'doing', values regulate 'being'. Norms and values determine sequences and states of roles and collectives." [169] Thus, the difference is primarily due to the degree of abstraction. Norms have many similarities with role expectations. They also define rules that, for example, all members of an organization must fulfill. If such a rule is not followed by a member, the role senders will urge this person to behave correctly. For this reason, norms also play an important part in the social environment of an individual.[170]

3.3.2.2 Expectations

According to Wiswede, the concept of expectations is central to the concretization of social roles.[171] Expectations have a kind of dual character:

---

[164] Cf. Popitz (1967), p. 11.

[165] Popitz (1967), p. 11.

[166] Cf. Geulen (1982b), p. 40.

[167] Cf. Krappmann (1993), p. 100 and cf. Krappmann (1977), p. 309. Role-playing can be understood as communicative action that takes place between interaction partners and is oriented towards norms that also exist beyond the interaction process that is currently taking place (cf. Krappmann 1993, 98).

[168] Kneer and Nassehi (2000), p. 38.

[169] Ackerman and Parsons (1976), p. 80.

[170] Cf. Kahn et al. (1964), p. 163.

[171] Cf. Wiswede (1977), p. 39. In reference to Dahrendorf (1977, p. 37 ff.), three manifestations of expectations can be distinguished, which entail different sanctions: Most social roles include so-called "*Must-expectations*" (Dahrendorf 1977, p. 37). These form the hard core of

1. An "*anticipatory* (A will act like this)"[172], and
2. a "*normative* (A should act like this)"[173].

Since individuals, as already described above, combine different social roles (e.g., entrepreneur and father), they also tend to align their behavior with structurally conditioned expectations represented by the roles.[174] The role concept, according to Gross et al., usually follows the following three basic assumptions: Individuals "(1) in *social locations* (2) *behave* (3) with reference to *expectations*" [175]. Therefore, roles also serve the purpose of making the behavior of individuals predictable. Thus, in every society, there exist so-called "institutional definitions of *roles*" [176]. These reflect behaviors that are expected from certain people in certain situations and relationships.[177] Goldthorpe formulates this as follows: "A role, indeed, can be regarded as a bundle of expectations" [178] or according to Uphoff, as "shared and mutual expectations about what any person in a certain role should and will do under various conditions" [179]. However, a role should not simply be understood as a unit of specific actions. Rather, the same behavior can occur in different roles under different circumstances.[180]

When looking at role expectations again, they are mainly composed of ideas about behaviors that a person should do or avoid. In addition, role expectations include notions about personal characteristics or statements about lifestyle,

---

social roles. They are clearly formulated and the sanctions are invariably of a negative nature. In addition, there are the so-called "*Should-expectations*" (Dahrendorf 1977, p. 38). Their sanctioning is predominantly of a negative nature. The person who always fulfills these, will be shown goodwill (sympathy) by his fellow human beings. Lastly, there are the so-called "*Can-expectations*" (Dahrendorf 1977, p. 39). In contrast to the first two expectations, it is more difficult to identify the exact content and sanction of the Can-expectations. Compliance leads to appreciation and increases the reputation with the reference persons or groups. In short, these can be understood as "Must-(Law), Should-(Custom), and Can-(Habit) Expectations" (Haug 1994, p. 34), which hold different manifestations of sanctions. For example, parents can "steer" the behavior of their children through positive or negative sanctioning. This influence decreases during the growing up of children (cf. Schneewind 1982, 163).

[172] Wiswede (1977), p. 39 and cf. AG Soziologie (1999), p. 25 as well as p. 42.

[173] Wiswede (1977), p. 39 and cf. AG Soziologie (1999), p. 25 as well as p. 43.

[174] Cf. Merton (1995), p. 112.

[175] Gross et al. (1966), p. 17.

[176] Parsons (1968), p. 141.

[177] Cf. Parsons (1968), p. 141.

[178] Goldthorpe (1969), p. 7 and cf. Dahrendorf (1977), p. 33.

[179] Uphoff (2000), p. 228.

[180] Cf. Turner (1977), p. 124.

i.e., what the person should think or believe.[181] In general, general experiences, values, perceptions, and experiences with certain individuals contribute to a conditioning of expectations. These can then be seen as "standards" that allow an assessment of the appropriateness of behavior.[182] Orienting oneself to the behaviors of others not only means orienting oneself to already completed facts and immediately obvious things. It also includes orienting oneself to expectations or assumptions, whereby most actions are based on the expectation of actions taken by others in the future.[183] In this sense, the future actions or behaviors we expect from others are part of our current social reality. However, to rely on the behavior of others trust is necessary — without trust, there is no functioning socialization. Trust thus also enables a kind of credit towards others.[184]

3.3.2.3 Roles as Dynamic Entities

According to Neuberger [185], most of the sociological and social psychological literature for the concept of role follows the view that it is a construct that can be used to explain observed regularities of behaviors. This assumes that the same person exhibits different behavior in different situations and that different people in the same situation exhibit similar behaviors and can empathize with the role of the other.

If roles, norms, and values are initially compared again, these three represent mutual reference sizes for integration into social systems.[186] However, successful role action requires, among other things, orientation to only one role in a particular situation and a match of the mutual expectations of the role partners to ensure joint action.[187] Since roles mutually refer to each other, this can serve as

---

[181] Cf. Katz and Kahn (1978), p. 190.

[182] Cf. Rizzo et al. (1970), p. 155.

[183] Cf. Popitz (1980), p. 2.

[184] Cf. Popitz (1980), p. 2 f. According to Luhmann, trust is "the expectation of a future satisfaction, which becomes the motive for one's own committing behavior. Trust thus serves as an elementary social process of bridging time differences in performance relationships" (Luhmann 1995c, 72). For Luhmann, trust represents a social relationship (cf. Luhmann 1989, 4) and enables a tremendous increase in the potential for action. Uncertain conditions are made certain by the application of trust as it is not easy to mislead existing trust (cf. Luhmann 1994, 180). Especially when the participants do not immediately receive a counter-performance for their performance, i.e., this is temporally divergent, trust must exist between the involved persons so that the exchange or cooperation can take place at all (cf. Luhmann 1995c, 72).

[185] Cf. Neuberger (1976), p. 72 f.

[186] Cf. Katz and Kahn (1978), p. 46 and cf. Ackerman and Parsons (1976), p. 80.

[187] Cf. Krappmann (1993), p. 100.

a general explanation for why behaviors are subject to change. If a change in one's own role takes place, this happens against the background of a change in the assessment or perception of the role of the other. The interaction is subject to constant control of the ideas about the role of the other. The subsequent reaction of the other fulfills the task of confirming or refuting one's own idea. The result of the control serves to maintain one's own role or to make an adjustment.[188] Therefore, the maintenance of a system of norms can only be guaranteed if there is the possibility to also subject a sanction action to standardization in the event of non-compliance with a norm.[189]

The following should be noted: A person can present his individuality only if his partners in action and conversation allow it. This is because they also develop ideas that the person concerned must consider. For example, a scientist is expected to have a rational argument or an artist is expected to be creative. If the affected person repeatedly fails to meet these generally held expectations for his group of people, this can lead to a rejection of his individuality. Therefore, to create an understanding of one's own individuality, the expectations of others must be considered as a starting point.[190] When the interaction between a child and its parents is taken as an example, this can only function if the participants are able to put themselves in the place of the other.[191] For the child, there are two consequences for the execution of a role takeover: (1) The subject gains knowledge about social reality and (2) it develops expectations for possible obligations, responsibilities, and rights. Thus, it acquires a system of moral rules and

---

[188] Cf. Turner (1977), p. 118 and cf. Popitz (1980), p. 11. In formal organizations in particular, the "tentative character of interactions" (Turner 1977, 123) is limited. They do this by replacing the role of "relevant others" (Turner 1977, 123) from the perceptions of the counterpart and replacing them with role prescriptions that limit the design process. Despite these guidelines, however, they are relativized by the mostly informal structures within an organization (cf. Turner 1977, 123).

[189] Cf. Popitz (1980), p. 64.

[190] Cf. Krappmann (1993), p. 7 f. Expectations, however, only develop social relevance if they can be expected at the same time. Only in this way is it possible to subject situations with double contingency to an order (cf. Luhmann 1987b, 411 f.). Luhmann refers to this context with the term "expectation expectations" (Luhmann 1987b, 413). He describes these as follows: "Expectation expectations cause all participants to mutually assume time-spanning and in this sense structural orientations" (Luhmann 1987b, 414). Or in other words: "A person forms expectations about what expectations others have of them" (von Schlippe and Schweitzer 2009, 12). In this sense, if a behavior of a counterpart is accepted even though it disappoints one's own expectations, the counterpart can assume that he will no longer expect the disappointment in the future (cf. Luhmann 1987b, 412).

[191] Cf. Garz (2006), p. 45 f.

principles by which it can subject its own and foreign behavior to a review.[192] Above all, the role takeover in children is designed to the extent that they adopt the roles assigned to them by their parents and any siblings. In addition to the role holder, the rest of the family members also have an interest in maintaining this.[193] Only when the child succeeds in taking on the roles of others and shaping these roles into general attitudes, it becomes a member of the family, the school, or its group.[194]

In summary, the conformity of role behavior with existing expectations is ensured by two "adjusting screws": (1) The internal control, which is internalized during the socialization phase, and (2) an external control, which is maintained by various sanction mechanisms.[195] In this regard, social roles are "bundles of normative behavioral expectations [...], which are equipped with certain internal and external sanction threats to guarantee role-conforming behavior to a certain extent" [196]. However, for the role expectations to be internalized, the individual must internalize the social system as a superior object and its own role as an organization of stimulating components. This primarily includes the levels of its own internalized object system, which is not contained in the superior social system.[197] In contrast to adults, the child has not yet internalized the roles of society. Therefore, according to Mitscherlich[198], the child is more individual than the adults surrounding it. Nevertheless, through participation in the family role system the child increasingly internalizes the expectations complementary to the roles of the other members, which are associated with its person.[199]

3.4 Excursus: Merging of Systems Theory and Symbolic Interactionism

The following attempts to connect Luhmannian Systems theory and Mead's Symbolic Interactionism. As already pointed out at the beginning of this chapter, the two theories are only partially compatible. Therefore, special attention must be

[192] Cf. Keller (1980), p. 165.
[193] Cf. Toman (1996), p. 117.
[194] Cf. Joas (1987b), p. 107.
[195] Cf. Dreitzel (1980), p. 46.
[196] Dreitzel (1980), p. 46.
[197] Cf. Parsons (1966b), p. 162.
[198] Cf. Mitscherlich (1986), p. 67.
[199] Cf. Krappmann (1977), p. 312.

paid to possible theoretical incompatibilities. Nevertheless, both theories have their justification for the chosen topic of this work:

1. Systems theory to depict the structural peculiarities of a family business, and
2. Symbolic Interactionism as a socialization-theoretical approach so that the development of descendants from family businesses can be traced. See Chap. 4 for this.

3.4.1 Approaching Symbolic Interactionism to Systems Theory

The argumentation depicted in this chapter is based on Nassehi[200]. For a detailed elaboration of content, reference is made to his contribution.

Although, Luhmann can be assigned to Systems theory and Mead to Action theory, Nassehi sees a "subtle commonality"[201] in the two theory concepts, which can be accessed via Mead's problem definition.[202] As a common starting point for Luhmann and Mead, Nassehi mentions the event philosophy of Alfred North Whitehead[203]. In addition to Luhmann [204], Mead[205] also refers to Whitehead. Thus, both tie into the "event-philosophical thought-construction of the concept of structure" [206]. Nassehi writes: "The groundbreaking aspect of Mead, however, seems to me to lie precisely in the fact that actions cannot be explained biologically or psychologically on the basis of his event-theoretical starting point, because this would have to presuppose that the drives for action come from the organism itself. This is precisely what Mead rejects – and thus, formulates the initial condition for switching from action to communication. [...] Mead can therefore be read in such a way that his theoretical system virtually

---

[200] *Nassehi*, A. (2012): George Herbert Mead (1863–1931), in: Jahraus, O.; Nassehi, A.; Grizelj, M.; Saake, I.; Kirchmeier, C. & Müller, J. (Eds.): Luhmann-Handbuch: Leben-Werk-Wirkung, Stuttgart und Weimar: Verlag J. B. Metzler, 269–271.

[201] Nassehi (2012), p. 269.

[202] Cf. Nassehi (2012), p. 269.

[203] (1) *Whitehead*, A. N. (1987): Prozeß und Realität. Entwurf einer Kosmologie, Frankfurt a. M.: Suhrkamp. (2) *Whitehead*, A. N. (1984): Wissenschaft und moderne Welt, Frankfurt a. M.: Suhrkamp.

[204] Cf. Luhmann (1987b), p. 393 and p. 600.

[205] Cf. Mead (1969), p. 229.

[206] Nassehi (2012), p. 270.

forces us to leave the path of action theory and take the event-based nature of self-referential order genesis seriously in terms of communication or systems theory."[207] According to Nassehi[208], Mead does not explicitly address this; however, this could be inferred from the reference to Whitehead and thus, from the Event theory as a starting point.

As the argumentation shows, a connection of the two concepts seems possible. Therefore, the following two steps will be taken:

1. Formation of a unified understanding of communication
2. Linking the concept of *person* with the *me* of identity.

3.4.2 Formation of a Unified Understanding of Communication

The most important points of the two theories for communication will be presented below. Subsequently, the perspective of Symbolic Interactionism will be integrated into Systems theory. As a supplement, refer again to Sect. 3.1.1.1 (communication in Systems theory) and Sect. 3.2.1 (communication in Symbolic Interactionism).

According to Luhmann, the emergence of social systems is tied to the existence of communication.[209] These are created through communication and produce their own structures, communicative processes, and environment.[210] Kneer and Nassehi therefore also refer to social systems as "communication systems"[211], which reproduce themselves through the continuous connection of communication to communication.[212] From a systems theoretical perspective, communication cannot be equated with actions. Rather, communication focuses on selective matters, while actions emphasize the act of utterance.[213] Luhmann therefore does not consider communication as a type of action.[214]

---

[207] Nassehi (2012), p. 271.

[208] Cf. Nassehi (2012), p. 271.

[209] Cf. Luhmann (1994), p. 218.

[210] Cf. Akerstrom Andersen (2003), p. 242.

[211] Kneer and Nassehi (2000), p. 65.

[212] Cf. Kneer and Nassehi (2000), p. 65.

[213] Cf. Luhmann (1994), p. 225 and p. 240.

[214] Cf. Seidl (2006), p. 34.

Communication serves the social system as a mode of autopoietic reproduction.[215] Communication systems can therefore be understood as autopoietic systems, as they can independently generate as well as replicate their components and structures as a completely embedded, closed system within their environment. Consequently, only communication influences communication. In addition, communication has the possibility to control and renew itself.[216] Above all, the peculiarity of communication arises from its reference to the present, i.e., a social system lasts only as long as the communication continues.[217] If communication ends, so does autopoiesis.[218]

However, the process of communication utilizes various events through selection, which have a certain informational value.[219] For communication to be spoken of at all, according to Kneer and Nassehi, "the three selection points of information, utterance, and understanding must be synthesized into a unit" [220]. Luhmann speaks in this context of the "synthesis of three selections" [221]. Above all, communication arises through the connection or combination of the three different selections:

1. Determination of information
2. Selection of the utterance of the information
3. Selective (mis)understanding of the utterance or the information included therein

Therefore, all three elements must exist for communication to occur at all.[222] According to Luhmann, communication takes place in every situation "in which one makes his sense-related experiences accessible to others, intentionally or

[215] Cf. Luhmann (2006a), p. 66.

[216] Cf. Luhmann (1995a), p. 118.

[217] Cf. Simon (2007a), p. 22.

[218] Cf. Mingers (2003), p. 107.

[219] Cf. Luhmann (1981), p. 314.

[220] Kneer and Nassehi (2000), p. 91; cf. Luhmann (2000), p. 92 and cf. Kieserling (1999), p. 154.

[221] Luhmann (1987b), p. 203.

[222] Cf. Luhmann (1995a), p. 115. Information is from the perspective of a recipient something "new" or what eliminates his "‘ignorance‘ about something. […] Information thus brings about a certain balance of knowledge between sender and receiver" (Ulrich 1970, 129).

unintentionally" [223]. However, the emergence of communication is tied to the existence of communication media. These can be seen as the starting point for the development of social systems. Language can be cited as an example of such a communication medium,[224] although language should not be used as a criterion for communication. Rather, communication uses language as a medium,[225] which "opens access to the mental processes of other people, which would otherwise be inscrutable from the outside" [226]. Thus, body movements can also contain all three selection points.[227] Nevertheless, language fulfills the function of increasing the probability of understanding communication.[228] It contributes to distinguishing communication from other actions and results in an unlimited increase in the number of behaviors with which others can be informed.[229] Language thus establishes the structural coupling between consciousness and communication systems.[230] Luhmann therefore refers to language as the "fundamental medium of communication that guarantees the regular, continuation-expecting autopoiesis of society" [231].

For communication to occur, the difference between utterance and information must first be understood.[232] This must be identified during the communication process, which is accomplished by understanding and consequently considered as the starting point of communication.[233] Thus, the utterance from the perspective of the communication system is irrelevant if it is not attached to information and this in turn flows back into communication as another utterance through understanding.[234] However, communication can capture both sides and choose, whether to respond to the information or to the expressive behavior. Above all,

---

223 Luhmann (1976a), p. 43.

224 Cf. Simon (2007a), p. 82 f.

225 Cf. Simon (2007b), p. 71. Luhmann defines media as follows: "Those evolutionary achievements that start at those breakpoints of communication and serve precisely to transform improbabilities into probabilities, we want to call *media*" (Luhmann 1987b, 220).

226 Simon (2007b), p. 71.

227 Cf. Kneer and Nassehi (2000), p. 91.

228 Cf. Baraldi et al. (1997), p. 180.

229 Cf. Luhmann (1976a), p. 43.

230 Cf. Luhmann (1998a), p. 108.

231 Luhmann (1998a), p. 205.

232 Cf. Luhmann (1995a), p. 115.

233 Cf. Gensicke (2008), p. 43.

234 Cf. Gensicke (2008), p. 55 and cf. Luhmann (1995a), p. 115.

understanding as a selection subsequently forms the prerequisite for further communication.[235] Any further communication then either refers to the utterance or to the information in the form of a subsequent communication. This in turn reproduces the difference between utterance and information.[236] In addition to the three elements of communication, there is a fourth selection component. If the communication is not interrupted, the fourth selection includes either the acceptance or rejection of the meaning content of the communication. This fourth selection step — Luhmann speaks of the "acceptance or rejection of the communicated reduction of meaning"[237]— is already part of the next communication. The significance arises primarily from the fact that understanding does not include acceptance.[238] Specifically, meaning serves communication as a kind of resource, since without it, communication cannot generate information.[239]

In Mead's view, communication creates order[240] and is considered as "the basic principle of human social organization"[241]. Communication is made possible by the common language existing in a society.[242] For an analysis from the perspective of Symbolic Interactionism, however, social action must first be considered. The starting point of a social action involves at least two individuals who consider each other for the satisfaction of impulses. Over time, gestures emerge from these actions, which in turn are seen as an indicator for subsequent stages of action.[243] The reaction of the recipient of this gesture is then determined by the meaning attributed to this gesture. Thus, the gesture develops a meaning not only for the sender, but also for the receiver. If there is a common intersection for the meaning, both participants understand each other.[244] In this regard, gestures only become significant symbols when they unfold the same meaning for the sender

---

[235] Cf. Luhmann (1995a), p. 115 f.

[236] Cf. Luhmann (1998a), p. 97.

[237] Luhmann (1987b), p. 203.

[238] Cf. Seidl (2006), p. 30.

[239] Cf. Gensicke (2008), p. 57 f. In detail, there is the possibility to divide meaning into three levels (subject, social, and time dimension) that are involved in the communication process in parallel. The *subject dimension* targets the object of communication, while the *social dimension* focuses on the reciprocity of communication between individuals. On the other hand, the *time dimension* locates communication in the present time. This arises from a difference between past and future (cf. Gensicke 2008, p. 57 ff.).

[240] Cf. Abels and König (2010), p. 13.

[241] Mead (1973), p. 299.

[242] Cf. Abels and König (2010), p. 13.

[243] Cf. Stryker (1970), p. 54.

[244] Cf. Blumer (2013), p. 73.

and the recipient. For example, language is seen against the background of a social aspect as a system of significant symbols and subsequently as a system of shared meanings. Therefore, language is also understood as a system of shared behavior.[245]

As can be seen from the respective explanations, both schools of thought use the concept of communication, but this is subject to different assumptions. Luhmann[246] also addresses the different perspectives of both theories in his work "Social Systems" [247,248]. According to Nassehi, however, Luhmann overlooks the "event-theoretical character of Mead's action theory"[249] in this context. In his opinion, Luhmann restricts Mead too much to Action theory.[250] For this, he refers to the contribution "Zeit, Handlung und Sozialität bei G. H. Mead" by Bergman.[251] As already described above, Nassehi[252] sees a way to transition from action to communication. The question now arises as to how the different conceptions of communication can be reconciled. In detail, since Luhmann presupposes double contingency, how specifically Symbolic Interactionism can "dock" with Systems theory so that double contingency is maintained. Thus, what is sought is a kind of smallest common multiple.

---

[245] Cf. Mead (1973), p. 180 f. and cf. Stryker (1970), p. 54.

[246] Cf. Luhmann (1987b), p. 154.

[247] *Luhmann*, N. (2005): Social Systems, Stanford University Press.

[248] Luhmann formulates it as follows: "Just as little, although for very different reasons, the »Symbolic Interactionism« satisfies. This line of theory builds an alter ego into the ego as acting contingently and sees, quite rightly, the mediation process in the use of symbols. But it treats the problem only on one side of the interaction, assuming that it is the same on the other side. It treats, so to speak, only the halved double contingency, and thus remains a theory of action. Social systems, however, arise through (and only through) the fact that both partners experience *double* contingency and that the indeterminacy of such a situation for *both* partners give structure-forming meaning to *every* activity that then takes place. This cannot be grasped with the basic concept of action." (Luhmann 1987b, 154).

[249] Nassehi (2012), p. 270.

[250] Cf. Nassehi (2012), p. 270 f.

[251] *Bergman*, W. (1981): Zeit, Handlung und Sozialität bei G. H. Mead, in: *Zeitschrift für Soziologie*, 10 (4), 351–363. Nassehi notes: "Even if Mead is actually mostly read as Luhmann does here, it should have become clear that with Mead's concept of action, there is already an event-theoretical theory form, on which the basic theoretical problem of Sociological Systems theory can be studied" (Nassehi 2012, 271).

[252] Cf. Nassehi (2012), p. 271.

A suitable starting point is provided by Burkart.[253] In his opinion, there is the possibility of also understanding Mead's concept of significant symbols from Luhmann's perspective. Luhmann understands communication more as a "joint actualization of meaning, which informs at least one of the participants"[254] and less than a pure "»transmission« of meaning or information" [255]. The assumption of a transmission is unrealistic in his opinion, as this "presupposes the identity of what is to be transmitted, and thus the task of possession in passing on [...]" [256]. According to Luhmann, the identical in communication is not embodied by a transmission of the meaning structure, but by a commonly presupposed meaning structure.[257] Simon[258] also refers to meaning as a medium that contributes to the shaping of social and psychic systems. Meaning can be seen as a form of order for human experiences and as a prerequisite for the reception of information as well as for the conscious processing of experiences. Meaning enables conscious handling of complexity for the capture and the reduction.[259] This is compatible with the concept of significant symbols, as these also provide a common basis of experience. Significant symbols allow the communication partners to update almost the same meanings within their consciousness,[260] which can also be seen as a common meaning structure. Now, when meaning is processed, understanding arises. Merely grasping the meaning does not yet imply understanding.[261] Specifically for meaning, there is the possibility of either appearing as consciousness by integrating into a sequence that is oriented towards the "bodily feeling of life" [262] or it is included in a sequence that conditions the understanding of others, and thus appears as communication.[263] The medium of meaning must therefore be seen more as a starting point for the emergence of social and psychic

[253] Cf. Burkart (2002), p. 57. The idea or the starting point for the following argumentation is provided by Burkart. Therefore, this is partly based on his explanations.

[254] Luhmann (1976a), p. 42.

[255] Luhmann (1976a), p. 42.

[256] Luhmann (1976a), p. 43.

[257] Cf. Luhmann (1976a), p. 42 f.

[258] Cf. Simon (2007b), p. 97.

[259] Cf. Luhmann (1976a), p. 61.

[260] Cf. Burkart (2002), p. 434.

[261] Cf. Luhmann (1987b), p. 110.

[262] Luhmann (1987b), p. 142.

[263] Cf. Luhmann (1987b), p. 142.

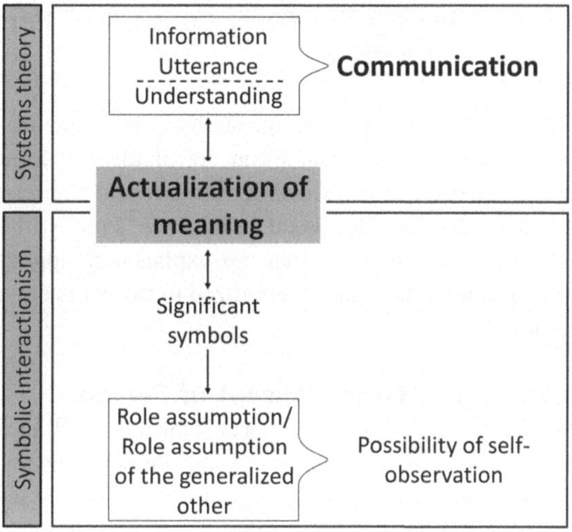

Fig. 3.1 Connection of the significant symbols to the communication (own work)

systems.[264] In conclusion, however, it should be pointed out again that communication depends on consciousness so that it can also form as an utterance or as understanding.[265]

The following Fig. 3.1 illustrates the connection just worked out once again.

As can be seen in Fig. 3.1, it is possible to integrate Mead's concept of communication into Systems theory. The significant symbols can be understood as an actualization of meaning so that they in turn contribute to understanding. This subsequently opens the possibility of viewing the significant symbols as a component of the three selection points of communication required by Luhmann. Due to the integration into Systems theory, the condition of double contingency can also be maintained or the concept of communication within Symbolic Interactionism can be expanded. Since from the perspective of Symbolic Interactionism all communication using significant symbols also includes role-taking, it is additionally made possible to integrate role-taking and specifically the role-taking of the generalized other into Systems theory. The role-taking of the generalized other in particular contributes to the emergence of identity through its internalization and the possibility of self-observation. This can then, due to the structural coupling of communication and consciousness, unfold its influence on consciousness.

264 Cf. Sutter (1997), p. 308.

265 Cf. Luhmann (1990), p. 218 f.

3.4.3 Linking the Form Concept of Person with the Me of Identity

This chapter answers the question of how the psychic and the social system can be linked with Mead's concept of identity formation. For this purpose, the system-theoretical *form concept person* and the term *identity* used in Symbolic Interactionism are discussed in advance. Finally, these two theories are brought together. Thus, there is then an explanatory approach as to "how the external (societal) influences are internalized in the course of socialization, and this shapes identity".

3.4.3.1 The Form Concept of Person

The *form concept of person* was established by Luhmann. In his view, social systems consist only of communication and not of people. These are assigned by him to the environment of social systems.[266] If people were seen as parts or elements of social systems, any perception or cell function would have to represent a social event.[267] For this reason, Luhmann refers to people as "non-communicative systems" [268]. The *form concept* thus does not include the complete human being, nor the entire psychic, or the entire organic system. The *person* focuses only on the expressions and therefore only on participation in communication.[269] For this reason, the human being is not regarded as an autopoietic system. Rather, it contains different autopoietic systems, which show a structural coupling.[270] Similarly to the human being, the individual cannot be conceived as a unit or as a system. Accordingly, a group of individuals is not classified as a system either. This view would neglect that the individual indeed feels internal processes.[271] The concept of the individual rather encompasses the single human being,[272] whereby the individual simultaneously influences the environmental conditions of other individuals, and thus his previous experiences rub off on other individuals who are involved in the same context.[273]

---

[266] Cf. Kneer and Nassehi (2000), p. 65 f.

[267] Cf. Luhmann (1995a), p. 29.

[268] Luhmann (2000), p. 62.

[269] Cf. Simon (2009), p. 22 and cf. Kneer and Nassehi (2000), p. 66.

[270] Cf. Kneer and Nassehi (2000), p. 155.

[271] Cf. Luhmann (1994), p. 68.

[272] Cf. Luhmann (1995a), p. 125.

[273] Cf. Dippelhofer-Stiem (2008), p. 122.

On the other hand, according to Luhmann, people are created "through participation of people in communication. [...] They do not live, they do not think, they are constructions of communication for the purposes of communication"[274]. Persons are created by the observation of a psychic system by other psychic or social systems.[275] However, under the term *form*, neither the consciousness, nor the body of individuals should be understood.[276] The construct or the addressee person rather represents a social structure, and thus does not represent a property of a psychic system.[277] It only arises within the communication.[278] The term *person* is derived from "»Persona« (mask, role, legal status)"[279] and contributes to a "differentiation of person and role" [280]. [281] However, a prerequisite is also the ability of the person to assume different roles and to perform a different role in each situation.[282] In this context, Luhmann uses the term "circle of roles"[283] and refers to the different roles of the same person.[284]

Therefore, the term *form* is also used by Luhmann for "the designation of the social identification of a complex of expectations [...], which are directed at an individual"[285]. In this respect, persons are classified as "action systems of their own kind"[286] or as "collages of expectations" [287]. This always implies a

---

[274] Luhmann (2000), p. 90 f.

[275] Cf. Luhmann (1987b), p. 155.

[276] Cf. Baraldi et al. (1997), p. 78.

[277] Cf. Jahraus et al. (2012), p. 102.

[278] Cf. Simon (2007a), p. 41.

[279] Luhmann (1987b), p. 430.

[280] Luhmann (1987b), p. 430.

[281] Cf. Luhmann (1987b), p. 430.

[282] Cf. Luhmann (2000), p. 91.

[283] Luhmann (1976b), p. 65. Wiswede speaks of a "*role household*" (Wiswede 1977, 81). This role household can include, among others, the father, the entrepreneur, the party member, or the chairman of the board (cf. Wiswede 1977, 81). On the other hand, the term "role set" (Goldthorpe 1969, 8 and cf. Merton 1973, 322) is often used for the different roles that are realized within a position. If the position of the medical student is used as an example, not only the role of a student can be identified there, but also a multitude of other roles that establish a connection with other students, doctors, nurses, social workers, etc. (cf. Merton 1973, 322). On the other hand, the role set of the entrepreneur's position could include, among others, the following roles: shareholder, manager, supervisor, father, and husband.

[284] Cf. Luhmann (1976b), p. 65.

[285] Luhmann (1987b), p. 286.

[286] Luhmann (1995b), p. 25.

[287] Nassehi (1997), p. 159.

confrontation with the expectations placed on them, which, in addition to various demands, also implies numerous opportunities for irritation and ambiguity.[288] The special thing about the concept of person, according to Kieserling [289], is that the person when switching from one social system to another, maintains a certain constancy in fundamental aspects through their "symbolically generalized identity" [290]. This allows the unit person to transcend the boundaries of all social systems existing in society. However, persons primarily fulfill the task of maintaining the structural coupling between psychic and social systems.[291] Thus, persons, due to the lack of an operational mode, are not systems, but are referred to as "identification points of communication" [292]. Or to put it another way, the involved persons in this context act as recipients of communication.[293] They fulfill the function of enabling the structural coupling of psychic and social systems.[294] However, the *concept of form* should not be equated with the psychic system. Rather, it is a role that is played.[295] Thus, a person can combine various roles within themselves and therefore, must fulfill different expectations.[296] In particular, the perception of a person as a "bundle" of roles creates the necessary connection point to Symbolic Interactionism and specifically the connection to identity.

3.4.3.2 The Formation of Identity

If we now consider the nature or composition of identity, it is understood in Symbolic Interactionism as a two-part process — consisting of the "*I*" and the "*me*".[297] The *I* and the *me* are classified as two "spheres" of identity,[298] which should not be seen as two separate areas. The *I* is "presocial and unconscious"

---

[288] Cf. von Schlippe (2011a), p. 9 f.

[289] Cf. Kieserling (1994), p. 20.

[290] Kieserling (1994), p. 20.

[291] Cf. Luhmann (1995c), p. 153.

[292] Kneer and Nassehi (2000), p. 87; cf. Luhmann (1995a), p. 146 f. and cf. Luhmann (1990), p. 202.

[293] Cf. Gensicke (2008), p. 42 and Luhmann (2000), p. 89.

[294] Cf. Luhmann (1995a), p. 153.

[295] Cf. Simon (2007a), p. 41.

[296] Cf. Luhmann (2000), p. 91.

[297] Cf. Roberts (1977), p. 100. For the term "me" used by Mead, there is no real German translation. This "refers to the self-experiencing itself as an object" (Mead 1973, 216).

[298] Cf. Stryker (1977), p. 260.

[299]. Zimmermann describes it as a "kind of psychological component of a person [...] (spontaneity, creativity, drive equipment)" [300] and Abels and König refer to this as the "impulsive *I*" [301], as the *I* is characterized by unplanned sensory and physical desires. A complete socialization of the *I* is not possible. Rather, it tries to dissolve the social self-discipline of the individual, which is achieved by aligning with the generalized other.[302] Thus, the *I* reflects the unorganized and spontaneous part of the individual and is considered the aimless as well as impulsive aspect of human experience.[303] Moreover, the *I* serves a person in a certain way as a point of identification, as it reflects the "reaction of the organism to the attitudes of others" [304]. The *I* is not only the starting point of the *me*, but it also reacts to it.[305]

Meanwhile, the *me* represents the "organized group of attitudes of others"[306] that the persons themselves adopt. Through the attitudes of others, the organized *me* is subsequently formed, with individuals responding to it through the *I*.[307] Abels and König refer to the *me* as a "reflected *I*" [308], i.e., as "the identification of the individual by others"[309] and consequently as the controlled as well as guided part of the individual. The *me* thus reflects the social aspect — the "social self"[310] or a "social component"[311]— of a person. This includes the representation of society through the organization of attitudes, expectations, and meanings that can be derived from the group. The result of this internal interaction is action.[312] In other words, the *me* represents the idea of what people think about a person, i.e., the image they have of the person.[313] Above all, the *me* arises from the experiences of the *I*, which it makes accessible to the *me* through its actions.

---

[299] Abels and König (2010), p. 89.

[300] Zimmermann (2000), p. 50.

[301] Abels and König (2010), p. 89.

[302] Cf. Abels and König (2010), p. 89.

[303] Cf. Roberts (1977), p. 100.

[304] Mead (1973), p. 218.

[305] Cf. Mead (1973), p. 221.

[306] Mead (1973), p. 218.

[307] Cf. Mead (1973), p. 218.

[308] Abels and König (2010), p. 90.

[309] Abels and König (2010), p. 90.

[310] AG Soziologie (1999), p. 59.

[311] Zimmermann (2000), p. 50.

[312] Cf. Roberts (1977), p. 100.

[313] Cf. Zimmermann (2000), p. 50.

When the *I* speaks, the *me* listens. When the *I* hits someone, the *me* feels the blow.[314] Abels and König therefore understand the *me* as follows: "The»me« is the sum of the social images of us, which we have internalized over the course of many relationships with others and under the gentle pressure of socialization, and with which we find ourselves confronted with in concrete interactions."[315] For this reason, the *me* is considered as a "social identity"[316]. It serves as a starting point for the emotional reaction to the values represented by a member within a society so that the experiences of others can be appropriated.[317] In addition, the *me* also represents the "equivalent to social roles"[318], and thus includes the internalized and organized attitudes of others. In contrast, the *I* reflects the response to these attitudes.[319]

The required "calibration" between the *I* and the *me* takes place during the socialization process.[320] Based on this, the *me* structures unplanned impulses. It acts as an instance for evaluation and represents a component for the developing self-image. Thus, contact with different reference persons also results in different *me's*. For the individual, for their behavior to be consistent, there is a need to synthesize a homogeneous self-image. As a result, identity develops subsequently,[321] which is created through communication, according to Mead's view.[322] However, identity becomes a problem in modernity, as individuals are simultaneously exposed to a greater number of roles that they must perform. Likewise, they must prioritize them, although there is uncertainty as to which roles are preferable and how they should be performed.[323]

In particular, the *me* can be used for the connection to the *concept of person*. Like the person, the *me* also combines different roles. Thus, Reck[324] equates the term *me* used by Mead with the role and according to Stryker, the *me* represents "the equivalent to social roles, the internalized organized attitudes of others" [325].

---

[314] Cf. Joas (1987a), p. 242. Joas uses the terms "I" and "me" in his work.

[315] Abels and König (2010), p. 90.

[316] Abels and König (2010), p. 90.

[317] Cf. Mead (1973), p. 243.

[318] Stryker (1977), p. 260 and cf. Stryker (1970), p. 53.

[319] Cf. Stryker (1977), p. 260.

[320] Cf. Zimmermann (2006), p. 54.

[321] Cf. Joas (1991), p. 139.

[322] Cf. Abels and König (2010), p. 21.

[323] Cf. Abels and König (2010), p. 121.

[324] Cf. Reck (1981), p. 103.

[325] Stryker (1970), p. 53.

3.4.3.3 The Emergence of Identity in Social Systems

Since Systems theory and Symbolic Interactionism occupy a central position within this work, the aim of this chapter is to bring together these differently located theoretical strands in the literature. The aim is therefore to provide an explanation of how social systems can exert their influence on an individual's identity, i.e., for the focus of this work: How a family business shapes the identity of the successors. The combination of the theories can be realized in two ways:

1. The first point of contact was the actualization of meaning (cf. Sect. 3.4.1). This "bridge" allows the significant symbols to be integrated into the understanding process, and thus continues to ensure that the three selection points of communication are maintained. In addition, there is a possibility of explanation as to how the role-taking or the role-taking of the generalized other is accomplished through communication. Communication in particular enables the child to gradually acquire more and more significant symbols. Above all, there are interrelationships between the significant symbols and the *I* of identity.
2. The second point of connection arises through the concept of the role. The role represents the "link" between the *form concept person* and the *me* of identity. Since the person establishes the structural coupling between the social and the psychic system, the *me* can assert its influence on these two systems. Likewise, the person is influenced by the two systems, which in turn has effects on the design of the role(s) and in further consequence also affects the *me* and unfolds its influence on the identity.

Finally, there is now the need to connect the two points of connection. This is first illustrated using the Fig. 3.2.

The illustration (see Fig. 3.2) initially distinguishes between an inner world (of the individual) and an outer world (family, enterprise, society). If the external perspective is considered, the roles united in a person are influenced by values, norms, expectations, and sanctions and vice versa. There is a reciprocity within the inner world and to the outer world or between the different roles. In relation to the inner world, the *form concept person* serves as a point of connection to Symbolic Interactionism from the perspective of Systems theory. The person establishes a connection with the social and the psychic system due to the structural coupling. In addition, the person combines different roles and can also be seen as an author as well as an addressee of communication. Thus, the person initially opens the connection to the *me* via the role since the *me* also combines

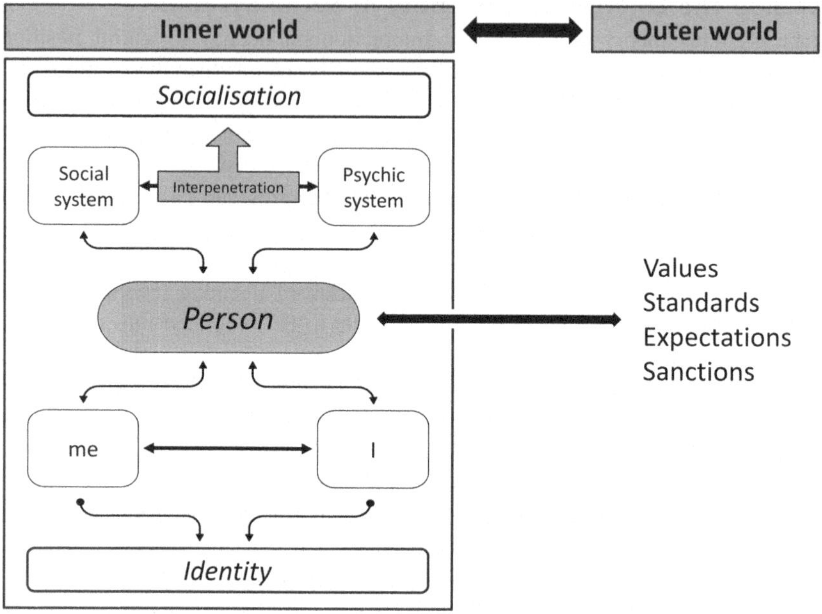

Fig. 3.2 Socialization and emergence of identity (own work)

different roles in itself. In addition, a "bridge" to the significant symbols is established via communication and especially via understanding, as these contribute to understanding through the actualization of meaning, which in turn is a part of communication (see Fig. 3.1). The significant symbols fulfill a dual function: (1) They enable the *I* as a subject to communicate and (2) through the possibility of self-observation, to observe itself as an object, and thus from the perspective of the *me*. Identity arises when communication becomes a part of behavior. The Role theory also made it clear that the roles must not be understood as something static (see Sect. 3.3.2.3). These are subject to certain reciprocal dynamics and adjustment mechanisms. Above all, however, the expectations of one's own role(s) are conveyed during socialization. This takes place through the existing interpenetration between social and psychic system, which in turn has an influence on the identity formation.

According to Sutter[326], socialization can be understood against the background of the systems theoretical view as a relationship between different systems. However, for socialization to occur, systems must mutually provide inherent complexity for each other through interpenetration.[327] This subsequently enables the creation and maintenance of system boundaries, which in turn condition each other. As a result, psychic systems emerge within a social environment, a process referred to as socialization. In the same way, this process serves the reproduction of social systems, which in addition to consciousness also require organic life. Thus, against the backdrop of Systems theory, interpenetration is seen as a central concept for Luhmann's theory of socialization. In detail, for Luhmann, socialization always takes place through social interpenetration[328] and through participation in communication, i.e., the behavior of others must be understood not only in its factual meaning, but also as an informative aspect.[329]

Based on Mead's understanding, socialization is seen as a "continuous interaction between concrete individuals with certain expectations and, more generally, communication between the individual and the generalized other"[330]. Abels and König formulate this as follows: "The individual is in a continuous reciprocal relationship with other people and a symbolically ordered world and in this reciprocal relationship, it develops as a social being and into a social being." [331] However, the individual only becomes aware of its identity when it views itself from the perspective of its counterpart, as identity development depends on others.[332] The relevance of communication for the development of identity and (self-)consciousness can therefore be seen in the generation of behaviors that allow the organism or individual to understand itself as an object.[333] Through communication using significant symbols, the individual is enabled not only to act as an *I* (communicatively), but also from the perspective of the other. Thus,

---

[326] Cf. Sutter (1997), p. 320.

[327] Based on the interpenetration, assumptions can be linked to Role theory and Socialization theory. Luhmann formulates this as follows: Interpenetration "thus replaces the doctrines of natural law, but also sociological attempts that had worked conceptually with role theory, with concepts of need, with theories of socialization. This relationship can be understood more fundamentally as interpenetration than with the aforementioned sociological concepts" (Luhmann 1987b, 290 f.).

[328] Cf. Faulstich-Wieland (2000), p. 132.

[329] Cf. Luhmann (1994), p. 280 and cf. Luhmann (1987b), p. 330.

[330] Abels and König (2010), p. 84.

[331] Abels and König (2010), p. 80 f.

[332] Cf. Abels and König (2010), p. 21.

[333] Cf. Mead (1973), p. 180 f.

the individual can view itself as a subject and as an object (as the *me*) to be able to assume the role of the counterpart.[334]

As can be seen, communication in particular plays a crucial role in socialization. Through interpenetration communication can influence consciousness. It is precisely through communication that certain expectations are conveyed to the individual. Above all, symbolic communication enables the acquisition of meanings, with Mead[335] arguing that an individual's identity can only emerge through communication with others. By identifying points of connection, it is now possible to examine systems and trace the influence of the interplay of systems on socialization and subsequently on identity formation.

3.5 The Ecological Systems Model

After relevant theories for an understanding of social systems, the emergence of identity during socialization, and the shaping of roles have been provided in this main chapter, it will finally be shown, how the systems relevant to the development of the individual are "nested" within each other and can influence socialization. Although, other systems operate according to a different logic, the insights from Systems theory help to analyze these within a unified framework. Expectations are also communicated therein, which serve to shape roles and can contribute to the shaping of identity by the growing individuals through role assumption. For further knowledge gain, the Ecological Systems Model according to Bronfenbrenner is subsequently presented, as this provides an understanding of the interrelationships of various systems and their influence on socialization. This rounds off the consideration, so to speak. That is, from the macro perspective to the micro perspective and vice versa.

The starting point of the Ecological Systems Model is the idea of how the relationship between person and environment is shaped. In detail, Bronfenbrenner's model enables a step-by-step exploration of living spaces, i.e., from immediate to distant areas of life.[336] In detail, the Ecological Systems Model can be assigned to the socio-economic research approach. This pursues the view of the existence of complex interrelationships between people and their environment, which in turn initiate socialization processes. Thus, the human being is influenced by the experiences from the environment by these influencing it. In addition, the environment is influenced by

[334] Cf. Burkart (2002), p. 165.

[335] Cf. Mead (1973), p. 280.

[336] Cf. Hurrelmann (2002), p. 77 ff.

actions taken. The focus of the interest in knowledge is therefore primarily the question of what influence the concrete conditions of the human environment have on the development of personality. The development of personality can only be understood if it is considered in its respective environmental contexts. For example, an infant will see his environment more as a "single here and now living area" [337]. Only with increasing age does his living area expand increasingly. As a result, the child can acquire new action structures and learn new requirements for social roles and relationships. For the representation of the various relevant structures for socialization, Bronfenbrenner developed the so-called Ecological Systems Model.[338] In this regard, Bronfenbrenner summarizes human development as "*a lasting change in the way the person perceives the environment and deals with it*" [339]. According to Bronfenbrenner, socialization can be understood as follows: "Human development is the process by which the developing person acquires expanded, more sophisticated, and more reliable ideas about his or her environment. In the process, they are motivated and empowered to engage in activities and activities that enable them to recognize and maintain the characteristics of their environment or to transform them to a similarly complex or more complex level in terms of form and content." [340]

Thus, based on the ecological perspective, there is the possibility of viewing the environment as a "nested arrangement of concentric structures, each enclosed by the next"[341]. Based on Bronfenbrenner, the structures are called micro-, meso-, exo-, and macrosystems (see Fig. 3.3).[342] The benefit of the Ecological Systems Model, according to Petzold,[343] lies in considering the substantial life dimensions of an individual by breaking them down into different subsystems. This means that in addition to considering the micro- and macrosystems, variables for individual development and psychological personality are also included. Against this background, the different systems are seen as areas of life that promote development.[344] These enables the developing person to participate in "progressively more complex activities, interpersonal relationships, and social role structures" [345], which in turn represent the elements of the microsystem. Thus, the area of

[337] Zimmermann (2006), p. 45 and cf. Zimmermann (2000), p. 43.

[338] Cf. Zimmermann (2006), p. 45 and cf. Zimmermann (2000), p. 43.

[339] Bronfenbrenner (1989), p. 19.

[340] Bronfenbrenner (1989), p. 44.

[341] Bronfenbrenner (1989), p. 38.

[342] Cf. Bronfenbrenner (1989), p. 38.

[343] Cf. Petzold (1999), p. 81.

[344] Cf. Bronfenbrenner (1989), p. 21.

[345] Hurrelmann (2002), p. 78.

life can be classified as a place, where people are enabled to exchange direct interactions with other people.[346] The area of life includes, among other things, the parental home, school, or workplace. The entry into a new area of life and the associated change of role is referred to as an "ecological transition" [347]. This can be understood as the entry into school, a transfer, marriage, or retirement. However, ecological transitions occur continuously, extend over the entire life of an individual, and represent the starting point for a development process.[348]

[346] Cf. Bronfenbrenner (1989), p. 38.

[347] Bronfenbrenner (1989), p. 43. According to Bronfenbrenner, an ecological transition occurs "when a person changes their position in the ecologically understood environment through a change of their role, their life area, or both" (Bronfenbrenner 1989, 43).

[348] Cf. Bronfenbrenner (1989), p. 43.

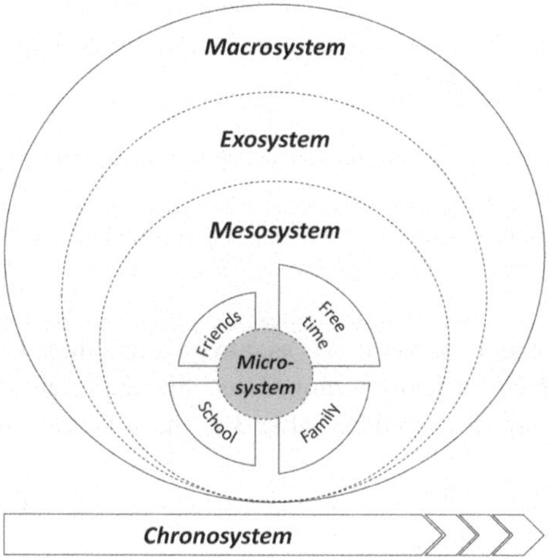

Fig. 3.3 The ecological systems model[349]

Bronfenbrenner's model appears advantageous because it attempts to depict the entire environment of a developing child and at the same time record the structural nature of this environment. In this context, this model emphasizes the importance of various environmental conditions during socialization,[350] where Bronfenbrenner, as already mentioned, understands the environment "as a set of nested structures"[351]. Within these structures several levels can be identified. Above all, the microsystem represents the immediate living area and is represented, among other things, by the family.[352] The family is embedded in other systems that are superordinate or subordinate to it, whereby the family at the same time distinguishes itself from these (sub)systems. If the aspect of embedding is considered, this can be illustrated using the taxonomy presented below.[353] From Bronfenbrenner's perspective, family socialization must be considered in relation to the structural conditions of the overall system,

[349] Source: After Zimmermann (2006), p. 46 and Zimmermann (2000), p. 44.

[350] Cf. Kreppner (1991), p. 322.

[351] Bronfenbrenner (1989), p. 19.

[352] Cf. Bronfenbrenner (1989), p. 19.

[353] Cf. Hofer (2002), p. 13.

where the micro-, meso-, exo-, and macrosystem represent the context for an individual's development.[354] If the child is focused, this can be influenced in two ways by the parents' social contacts:

1. Through the *direct* confrontation with a certain number of people included in the parental network as well as
2. *indirectly* through the contacts that influence parental behavior, which also affects the children.[355]

Bronfenbrenner's model is based — as already mentioned above — on the "differentiation of concentrically arranged socialization contexts"[356]. Before the individual systems are discussed in Table 3.1, the following Fig. 3.3 illustrates their interaction.

The following Table 3.1 provides a description of the individual systems of the Ecological Systems Model:

Table 3.1 The systems in the ecological systems model

The Microsystem The most immediate system of a person is represented by the microsystem.[a] This represents the starting point of socialization and can be classified as the "lowest" system. In detail, it includes the individual's immediate relationships such as friends, leisure time, and school.[b] Above all, however, the microsystem includes the modern nuclear/small family, which is predominantly characterized by dyadic or triadic structures.[c] First, the microsystem includes the interaction relationships between father, mother, siblings, and relatives and is therefore limited to the people, with whom the child can come into contact at home. At this stage of life in particular, the child's development depends on the stimuli provided within the family. This can thus lead to an enhancement or a limitation of the role repertoire.[d] From the perspective of ecopsychology, in addition to the relationships between people, physical, and material conditions are also included. These include, for example, housing conditions.[e] According to Bronfenbrenner[f], if the child's construction of reality is to be reconstructed, only the activity patterns that find expression in "activities, roles, and relationships"[g] are suitable for this purpose; only these are called elements of the microsystem

(continued)

[354] Cf. Schneewind et al. (1983), p. 17.

[355] Cf. Schneewind et al. (1983), p. 76.

[356] Zimmermann (2000), p. 83.

Table 3.1 (continued)

The Mesosystem

When considering the mesosystem, it is composed of various microsystems. The mesosystem thus emerges or unfolds through the entry of the developing person into new areas of life.[h] Hobi-Ragaz puts it as follows: "The microsystem thus encompasses direct interpersonal interactions in a context. The relationships between these contexts form a mesosystem, which is therefore a system of microsystems."[i]

As already illustrated, the mesosystem enables the establishment of relationships between microsystems, with the emerging interrelationships being of primary importance. For the family, for example, the relationship between the nuclear family and the parents' family or between the nuclear family and the school can be understood as a mesosystem.[j] If the parents, for example, watch a sporting event of the child, two areas of life also come into contact there. As a result, a development taking place in the mesosystem implies a continuous enlargement of different spheres of life. Supportive accompaniment can promote development in this context.[k] According to Bronfenbrenner[l], the mesosystem therefore encompasses at least two areas of life in which the developing person is involved. The following variations are possible:

The basic form represents the connection between two areas of life. This appears when the same person performs activities in more than one area of life. For example, a child can spend time in kindergarten as well as at home. The mesosystem, however, only begins to exist when the person concerned first enters a new area of life. (see above ecological transition). Since the person concerned cannot participate in both areas of life at the same time, this is also referred to as a *first-order social network.*

In the second form of manifestation, there is an indirect connection. This means that the two areas of life are not connected by the active participation of a person. Rather, a third party establishes a connection so that the participants of both areas of life do not meet personally. This can also be classified as a *second-order network.*

Another possibility arises through communication between two areas of life. This includes messages that are transmitted between the areas of life to exchange certain information. In addition to personal conversations, communication can be carried out through phone calls, written messages, or announcements.

Finally, there may only be knowledge about the other area of life. This means the existence of certain information from one area of life about the other and can be accomplished during communication or against the background of other sources outside the affected area of life.

(continued)

Table 3.1 (continued)

The Exosystem The characteristic of the exosystem is to be seen in the fact that the individual in question does not belong to it as an acting person. Nevertheless, indirect interactions arise for this person.[m] From the perspective of a child the exosystem could be, for example, the parents' workplace, the school classes of older siblings, or the parents' circle of friends,[n] as there is no interaction with them.[o] Thus, areas of life with which the child does not directly interact are located in the exosystem. Nevertheless, the events occurring in them have their effects on the family. In this respect, the child's socialization can also be influenced by areas with which the child is not directly connected.[p] Particularly important for the family, is the dynamic aspect between the relationships within the Ecological Systems Model. While the parents' professional world can initially be seen as a mesosystem for the respective parent, it represents an exosystem from the children's perspective. After the children enter a profession, the professional world becomes a mesosystem for them as well. If the parents retire from the professional world, it becomes an exosystem for them. For this circular process, the family provides a common setting within which the interaction is subject to constant change, as the relationships within the subsystems change.[q]
The Macrosystem Despite the differences that characterize the micro-, meso-, and exosystem, various similarities can still be identified. All systems are defined by a cultural framework, which is specifically determined by the macrosystem of a society. The macrosystem includes (sub)cultural norms and values, which do not directly affect the child. For example, interactions with adults not belonging to the household can allow children to encounter the macrosystem and positively influence their development.[r] Rather, the macrosystem includes the interrelationships that take place at the level of society as a whole. These include, for example, non-family forms of childcare or certain role expectations for mothers and fathers.[s] Therefore, the macrosystem also has the possibility to control all systems included in it. In addition, it holds societal relationships together.[t] Social measures that are carried out at the level of the macrosystem also affect the specific characteristics of the exo-, meso-, and microsystems, which in turn control behavior and development at their respective levels.[u]

(continued)

Table 3.1 (continued)

The Chronosystem As a fifth system, Bronfenbrenner subsequently introduced the chronosystem. This specifically considers the influence of a temporal dimension and includes "significant biographical transitions"[v]. Examples would be graduation from school or the completion of vocational training. These events always have an impact on future development.[w]

[a]Cf. Petzold (1999), p. 80.
[b]Cf. Zimmermann (2006), p. 46.
[c]Cf. Petzold (1999), p. 80.
[d]Cf. Zimmermann (2006), p. 46.
[e]Cf. Petzold (1999), p. 80.
[f]Cf. Bronfenbrenner (1989), p. 27.
[g]Bronfenbrenner (1989), p. 27.
[h]Cf. Bronfenbrenner (1989), p. 41.
[i]Hobi-Ragaz (2008), p. 45.
[j]Cf. Petzold (1999), p. 80.
[k]Cf. Zimmermann (2006), p. 47.
[l]Cf. Bronfenbrenner (1989), p. 199 f.
[m]Cf. Petzold (1999), p. 80.
[n]Cf. Bronfenbrenner (1989), p. 42.
[o]Cf. Kracke and Hofer (2002), p. 95.
[p]Cf. Zimmermann (2006), p. 47.
[q]Cf. Petzold (1999), p. 82.
[r]Cf. Zimmermann (2006), p. 48.
[s]Cf. Petzold (1999), p. 80 f.
[t]Cf. Zimmermann (2006), p. 46.
[u]Cf. Bronfenbrenner (1989), p. 25.
[v]Zimmermann (2006), p. 48.
[w]Cf. Zimmermann (2006), p. 48.

3.6 Final Considerations of this Chapter

The goal of this chapter was to provide theories by which a meaningful analysis and explanation of social systems can be accomplished. Due to the topic of socialization within a family business, it was necessary to provide suitable theoretical approaches. As can be seen from Chap. 2, family businesses are very heterogeneous. This complicates analysis. In addition, a suitable theory had to be found that can explain socialization and specifically the formation of identity. This must be able to consider the different variations of the context so that generalizable statements can be made. This could only be achieved through a pluralistic approach to the chosen theories:

1. The Luhmannian Systems theory was considered for the investigation of a family business.
2. For the explanation of how identity is formed during socialization in a certain context, Mead's Symbolic Interactionism proved to be suitable.
3. As a third theoretical concept, Role theory was used. Its justification during this chapter or within this work arises because the concept of role is used both in Systems theory and in Symbolic Interactionism.

The processing serves for a uniform understanding of terms. In addition, Role theory in particular serves to represent the dynamics to which the descendants within a family business are exposed. The construct of the role enables the connection of Symbolic Interactionism to Systems theory.

While Systems theory rather asks the "how", i.e., how societal units (systems) can be described and how they interact or influence each other, Symbolic Interactionism focuses on the question of "through what". It thus attempts to provide explanations for the processes/dynamics through which, among other things, the identity formation takes place. Above all, Symbolic Interactionism can be seen as a meaningful complement to Systems theory, as was evident in the merging of these only partially compatible theories. This becomes particularly clear in communication: According to Luhmann, all social systems consist of communication and only of communication. Everything else is to be assigned to the environment of the social system. According to Mead's view, communication is only possible when the symbols used mean the same to all participants. They become significant symbols. Significant symbols require or arise in a societal process of experience and behavior. Thus, understanding is always dependent on the environment or the surroundings. Through the process of understanding, meaning is subsequently produced. Communication and language in particular, as one of the most important communication media, enables the acquisition of roles and the formation of identity during socialization. The final presentation of the Ecological Systems Model also provided an explanatory model, of how the different social systems interact or are connected, and how entering a new system marks the starting point for socialization processes.

4 The Family Business as Socialization Context

Looking back at Chaps. 1–3, each part provided a different perspective on the area of investigation:

1. Chapter 1 provided a comprehensive insight into the relevant literature about family business to serve an understanding of the topic.
2. Chapter 2 then served to illuminate the family business. In addition to the peculiarities, dynamics, and characteristics of a family business, the succession, and the effects of the family business as a significant context of socialization were extensively discussed. These first two chapters primarily took an external perspective.
3. Chapter 3 adopted a kind of internal perspective. Since every family business is individual, it was necessary to select theories by which the field of study can be generalized and an explanation provided as to how this affects the socialization and identity formation of the descendants.

The individual findings are now finally linked in this chapter to answer the research question. The family business or its peculiarities as a context of socialization are illuminated using the theories presented. This opens the possibility of making a statement about how or by which peculiarities the family business exerts its influence on the descendants. In detail, the question arises: *How are outside influences on adolescents internalized during socialization to form identity?*

To finally answer the research question, it is therefore first necessary to describe the family business based on the systems theoretical findings from Chap. 3. This allows for a generalization of family businesses and facilitates the examination of the dynamics taking place within them. Since the family as the

S. Caspary, *The Family Business as a Socialisation Context for the Children of Entrepreneurs*, https://doi.org/10.1007/978-3-658-43657-5_4

primary instance of socialization plays a particularly important role, it is essential to examine it from a systems theory perspective as well. Like family businesses, the family has a wide range of possible manifestations. The systems' theoretical view opens the possibility of generalization. This has already been done for the enterprise or the formal organization in Chap. 3. Once the research framework is "staked out" the focus is on the descendants.

The Ecological Systems Model is first used to illustrate the diverse socialization context of the family business. During this, the "evolution" in enterpriseness is also discussed. Afterwards, the possible influence of the business system on identity development is presented. Finally, the most essential findings of this work are summarized once again, to shed light on the influence of the business system on the descendants.

4.1 The Family Business from a Systems Theoretical Perspective

4.1.1 Benefits of Systems Theory

Systems theories understand "social entities of all kinds — families, production companies, social clubs, states, market economies, churches, societies — as very complex systems of action that have to solve a multitude of problems if they want to survive in their environment"[1]. The benefit of Systems theory therefore arises particularly from its ability to understand, and thus analyze the different social systems, despite their different logics within a unified framework.[2] For example, the family follows a different logic than an organization (see Table 2.1). Since Luhmannian Systems theory in his Social theory examines systems of all kinds, it can subsequently be applied to both the family and the business.[3]

For family businesses in particular, from a systems theoretical perspective, there is the assumption of the "connectedness" of the two systems (family and business). The family provides the enterprise with a special identity as a family business (familiness) or the enterprise provides the family with a special entrepreneurial identity (enterpriseness).[4] The family is for the business and the

[1] Luhmann (1970), p. 70.

[2] Cf. Kühl (2011), p. 2.

[3] Cf. Simon (2012), p. 10.

[4] Cf. Frank et al. (2010b), p. 125 f.

business is for the family respectively the meaningful environment.[5] By using Systems theory as an analytical framework, different reference points can then be identified:

1. How are expectations ranked to ensure the stability of the family business?
2. What rules exist regarding membership, especially if family members work in the enterprise?
3. How is the boundary between family and business drawn?
4. What solutions exist for the business and the family to resolve mutual irritations?

In general, the question arises, *how the emerging complexity can be solved and a specific horizon of meaning for the family business can be established?*[6]

The suitability of Sociological Systems theory for the analysis of dynamics within family businesses is justified by Groth and Slevogt[7] by the possibility of being able to focus on the specific logic of each individual system. Based on this, the co-evolution can then be analyzed with the best possible understanding. Stierlin describes the co-evolution with the following terms: "Interplay, interdependence, and mutual conditioning" [8]. In addition, Simon[9] as well as Weismeier-Sammer et al.[10] point out the advantages of Luhmannian new Systems theory for understanding and analyzing family businesses. Weismeier-Sammer et al. formulate it as follows: "Moreover, adopting a system-theoretical perspective helps to view family businesses as a construct of two distinct systems (family and business) that are structurally coupled and derive their unique characteristics from the individual design of this coupling." [11] Apart from its suitability, which

[5] Cf. Weismeier-Sammer et al. (2012), p. 183.

[6] Cf. Frank et al. (2010b), p. 128. Wimmer understands complexity as follows: "The term complexity is often used here to address relationships in systems that are shaped by a multitude of influencing factors, which interact with each other in an ultimately incomprehensible and causally uncontrollable interaction, whereby the dynamics of this mutual influence can change in an unpredictable way over time, i.e., surprising breaks can occur, exponential trends can start, self-organizing order patterns can emerge, stabilize and also dissolve, etc." (Wimmer 2012, 9 f.).

[7] Cf. Groth and Slevogt (2004), p. 4.

[8] Stierlin (1987), p. 127.

[9] Cf. Simon (2008b), p. 13.

[10] Cf. Weismeier-Sammer et al. (2012), p. 184.

[11] Weismeier-Sammer et al. (2012), p. 184.

has already been scientifically and practically proven in the literature,[12] Frank et al.[13] provide three reasons why Luhmannian Systems theory should be used to analyze a family business:

1. The focus on communication, which forms the basis of every social system as well as the relative mutual stabilization with the respective environment. This allows an answer to the question of how the development of structures within the family and the business, which arise from behavioral expectations, is carried out.
2. The consideration of the connection between the system and the respective environment. This results in two significant relationships for the family business:
   (a) Between the family and the business, with the interplay between the respective behavioral and decision-making premises of both systems being particularly important.
   (b) The relationship between the individuals, i.e., the psychic systems and the family business, i.e., the social system. Although both systems are different, they interact with each other and are dependent on each other.
3. Since the Systems theory focused here is understood as a Constructivist theory, each system's environment is created by the system itself. The perception of family businesses can therefore differ depending on the system (family or business) from which they are viewed.

As the argumentation shows, Systems theory provides a suitable starting point or a comprehensive theoretical foundation to analyze the dynamics within the family business to a sufficient extent. This makes it possible to provide generalized statements despite the individual manifestations of each family business. This is particularly relevant for the implications of the family business as a context of socialization.

However, it is first necessary to look at the family and specifically the business family from a system-theoretical perspective. Due to the uniform theoretical starting point or the same understanding of the term, the family business can be analyzed and specifically its influence on identity formation can be shown.

---

[12] They refer exemplarily to: *Simon*, F. B.; *Wimmer*, R. and *Groth*, T. (2005): Mehr-Generationen Familienunternehmen, Heidelberg: Carl Auer.

[13] Cf. Frank et al. (2010b), p. 123.

4.1.2 Systems Theory View of the Family

4.1.2.1 The Changing Family

When considering the family its inherent logic has changed in recent years (see Sect. 2.5.1.3). Here, various individualization tendencies of the individual participants have been evident for a long time, resulting in a weakening of the stabilizing effect of the family. Due to the possibility of independently shaping one's life today, there is no longer necessarily the need to seek support within a large family. This trend away from large families towards small families or alternative lifestyles can endanger the continuation of a family business, as the lack of cohesion can lead to insurmountable conflicts that make it impossible to work together within the business. Without active management, these processes cannot be stopped.[14]

In addition to the pluralization of life plans,[15] one reason for the (continuous) change of the family can be found in the following: A change of values, the legal framework, the social structure, or the role of women.[16] Apart from patchwork families,[17] single parents, unmarried partnerships with children, or homosexual partnerships with biological or adopted children are increasingly appearing.[18] Similarly, there is a tendency to have fewer and fewer siblings, but the types of siblings are increasing.[19] Among others, the following types of siblings can be subsumed:

1. Biological siblings (same mother and father)
2. Half-siblings (same mother or father)
3. Stepsiblings (no blood relation)

---

[14] Cf. Wimmer et al. (2004), p. 10 ff.

[15] Cf. Busch and Scholz (2000), p. 10.

[16] Cf. Matthias-Bleck (2005), p. 53. A comprehensive overview of the change in the modern nuclear family is provided by Stamm (2013, 39 ff.). She also typifies the peculiarities of three family forms: whole house, nuclear family, and multilocal multi-generational family (cf. Stamm 2013, 45 f.). Pluralism can be understood in detail as follows: "Term for the structure of modern industrial societies in which a multitude of economic, religious, ethnic, and other groups compete with each other and fight for societal influence" (Reinhold et al. 2000, 495). However, pluralization should not only be understood as the coexisting existence of different family or life forms within a society, but rather the sequence of different family or life forms within a life course of an individual (cf. Zimmermann 2000, 89). Also compare Beck (1986, 163 f.).

[17] Cf. Busch and Scholz (2005), p. 156.

[18] Cf. Maihofer et al. (2001), p. 39.

[19] Cf. Kasten (2003), p. 15.

4. Adoptive siblings
5. Foster siblings[20]

Peuckert refers to this as the "*erosion of the bio-social dual nature of the family*"[21]. Especially today, more and more minors are hardly related to their social parents.[22] In this context, Peuckert[23] uses the term established by Gross and Honer[24] of "multiple parenthoods", which can also include patchwork-families. Particularly due to the new forms of family, such as the patchwork-families, people who have a direct influence on the upbringing of the children are now counted as family. This can include immediate family members as well as life partners, stepsiblings, or relatives.[25] "Extramarital relationships, divorce, remarriage, threesomes, same-sex partnerships, and other forms of cohabitation"[26] are becoming increasingly common in modern society. Due to the many variations, it must be assumed today that there is a multitude of different family models.[27]

As can be seen from the explanations in addition to Sect. 2.5.1.3, the family is also subject to continuous change so that the term family can no longer be clearly defined in language use. Therefore, it seems appropriate to establish a "new version" of the term (business) family according to the focus set in this work, which also includes the new forms of life, and thus fulfills a more universal claim. Especially since a family business cannot exist without the family as such, it is necessary for the analysis to make a uniform understanding accessible, which includes the various dynamics and manifestations. To meet this, the (business) family will be examined from a systems theoretical perspective.

---

[20] Cf. Sohni (2011), p. 36.

[21] Peuckert (2008), p. 25.

[22] Cf. Peuckert (2008), p. 25.

[23] See footnote 22.

[24] *Gross*, P. and *Honer*, A. (1990): Multiple Elternschaften: Neue Reproduktionstechnologien, Individualisierungsprozesse und die Veränderung von Familienkons-tellationen, in: *Soziale Welt*, 41 (1), 97–116.

[25] Cf. Busch and Scholz (2005), p. 156.

[26] Kormann (2011), p. 81.

[27] Cf. Simon (2012), p. 62 f.

4.1.2.2 The Family as a Social System

From the perspective of sociology, the family can be seen as an independent system consisting of individuals, which moves within societal norms.[28] In detail, the family can be understood as a "unit composed of individual elements (=system)" [29]. In this context, Burkart refers to the family as a "special societal subsystem" [30], which maintains complex relationships with other systems within society due to its functional assignment.[31] Hofer sees the individual members of a family as a "dynamic unit" [32] that interacts with the other members, and thus continuously influences and shapes its environment. In addition, the environment exerts its influence on the members, resulting in a continuous process of mutual influence.[33]

Simon[34] perceives families as "organic systems (bodies) and psychic systems in the form of individuals"[35] with both systems structurally coupled to each other. This connection also largely determines the selection of communication participants (parents and children). During communication, no distinction is made between the two systems, but the construct of the person is used. The person includes "not the whole human being, not the whole psychic and not the whole organic system, but only their expressions, i.e., their contribution to communication" [36].

When the family is viewed against the background of a social system, there is initially the difficulty that a system is more of an "impersonal arrangement"[37] and therefore stands in contrast to the characteristics of a family. Particularly problematic is the view of the family as a system consisting of people. This view significantly complicates a more detailed investigation, as not only the members, but also the level of molecules must be declared as sub-processes of the family system.[38] Luhmann solves the difficulty as follows: "We take this problem into account by strictly distinguishing between a biological, a psychic, and a

[28] Cf. Baldwin (1974), p. 261.

[29] Simon (2012), p. 10 f.

[30] Burkart (2008), p. 139.

[31] Cf. Burkart (2008), p. 139.

[32] Hofer (2002), p. 13.

[33] Cf. Hofer (2002), p. 13.

[34] Cf. Simon (2009), p. 22.

[35] Simon (2009), p. 22.

[36] See footnote 35.

[37] Luhmann (1990), p. 196.

[38] Cf. Luhmann (1990), p. 196.

communicative reality and assuming different, mutually closed autopoietic systems at all these levels." [39] The family can then be understood as an autopoietic system, "which consists of self-produced elements, but not from other autopoietic systems" [40]. According to Simon [41], against the background of the theory of autopoietic systems, the family fulfills the function of a boundary that can be located "between society and an organized environment" [42]. First and foremost, however, the family realizes a production function, i.e., "the production of potential participants in communication" [43].

Similarly, Neidhardt[44] classifies the family as a social system, as its "social units"[45] are interdependent.[46] They have a relationship and differentiate themselves from their environment. These two characteristics are constitutive for the family. However, from the perspective of a social system, there is a necessity for the family to understand or reconstruct the societal unit as a difference between system and societal environment so that the family can differentiate itself. Specifically, the difference between system and societal environment is organized within the family by the orientation towards the individuals of the respective members. The communication does not exclude personal matters, nor does it exclude the "total area of their external behavior in other functional systems" [47]. This is particularly ensured by their own involvement. Therefore, in families "the unity of the person is the organizing principle of communication" [48]. While in other systems the type and extent of communication in the sense of personalization is

[39] Luhmann (1990), p. 196. However, Luhmann separates himself from the theoretical considerations of Humberto Maturanas for the term "autopoiesis" (cf. Luhmann 1990, 196).

[40] Luhmann (1990), p. 197.

[41] Cf. Simon (2000), p. 140.

[42] Simon (2000), p. 140.

[43] Simon (2000), p. 143. Luhmann characterizes a family as follows: "In the following, a family system should only be spoken of at the level of communicative events. The social system family therefore consists of communications and only of communications, not of people and not of 'relationships' between people" (Luhmann 1990, 196 f.).

[44] Cf. Neidhardt (1979), p. 164.

[45] Neidhardt (1979), p. 164.

[46] The interdependence suggests a kind of dependency relationship between the family or system members. If changes in the behavior of one member occur, this inevitably causes a change in the behavior of the other members. This is particularly due to the size of the group or the number of members and the resulting high number of social contacts between the members (cf. Neidhardt 1979, p. 164).

[47] Kieserling (1994), p. 23.

[48] See footnote 47.

considered a variable that occurs in different forms and levels, communication within the family is to be understood as a given structure. In other words, there is no restriction within the family as to what the members experience or perceive as a person, and thus is considered a topic of communication.[49]

After discussing the prerequisites for when a family can be understood as a social system, a useful system-theoretical understanding of the (business) family will be provided in the following.

4.1.2.2.1 Working Definition of the Family

For Simon [50], the concept of family is rather colloquial and not clearly defined. Therefore, the question arises, whether, for example, a couple's relationship can be classified as a family. Adamaszek formulates the difficulty of defining/ delimiting the concept of family as follows: "A definition of the social construct family is made in different disciplines from very different perspectives and with different concepts. Thus, there is no uniform concept for family as an intimate relationship system, family as a socialization institution, or as a legal institution and therefore there are very different ideas of how family is organized, which variables contribute to its constitution and how families differ from other forms of life." [51] Due to this wide range of possible perceptions of the family, it will be defined for the purposes of this work based on the role of membership. The elaboration of this concept has already been done for the formal organization (see Sect. 3.1.1.3). Thus, the family fulfills the general task of preserving the interests of its members against non-members.[52]

However, the family cannot per se be understood as a formal organization. A system is, among other things, formal when it maintains its identity independently of the respective persons and orientation contents[53] and there is the possibility to acquire and lose membership through decisions.[54] The family cannot fully meet this claim. According to Domayer and Vater[55], membership in a family is only possible through marriage or birth. However, due to new forms of living, the criterion of marriage for this argument is increasingly moving into the background. Birth and adoption, on the other hand, represent a significant characteristic for

[49] Cf. Kieserling (1994), p. 22 f.

[50] Cf. Simon (2000), p. 140.

[51] Adamaszek (2005), p. 296.

[52] Cf. Linton (1965), p. 157.

[53] Cf. Luhmann (1995b), p. 29.

[54] Cf. Luhmann (1995b), p. 41.

[55] Cf. Domayer and Vater (1995), p. 151.

the membership of children in the family. This "production" of new members allows the family to be understood as an autopoietic system. However, the members must not be understood as humans, as this would include further autopoietic systems.[56] Another constitutive characteristic is the prevailing "»forced membership«"[57] of all members. Thus, the family can be characterized as an organization with special qualifications. This also results in a difficult "termination" of membership. While parents can be divorced or separate, the connection through the children usually remains.[58] Therefore, unlike many organizations, the role and function of membership is not subject to any temporal and content limitations. The individual member is thus "lifelong and throughout the day in a wide range of functions"[59] called upon to respond to the concerns of the other members.[60]

Membership is clearly established by the possible common family name and the exclusive assignment of positions (step)mother, (step)father, (step)daughter, (step)brother, etc.[61] In organizations behavior is determined by the various position holders through norms, expectations, rights, and duties.[62] These characteristics can be transferred to the family. In addition, each member has an individual personality profile, which creates a unique family culture.[63] If there is also a congruence with the household community, a clear spatial demarcation from the environment is evident.[64] In addition, families and organizations obviously differ "in possible size, internal order, function, and aspects of the appropriateness of behavior (not to say rationality)" [65]. In addition, the family fulfills the significant task of social reproduction, i.e., it provides for the socialization and upbringing of children[66] and assigns them a position — Winch speaks of a "position-assignment function"[67]— within society.[68] Another central feature is the prevailing generation differentiation within families between at least one

[56] Cf. Luhmann (1990), p. 197.
[57] Claessens and Menne (1973), p. 328.
[58] Cf. Claessens and Menne (1973), p. 328.
[59] Wurzbacher (1977b), p. 14.
[60] Cf. Wurzbacher (1977b), p. 14.
[61] Cf. Neidhardt (1979), p. 164.
[62] Cf. Heuring and Petzold (2005), p. 8.
[63] Cf. Klein (2004), p. 56.
[64] Cf. Neidhardt (1979), p. 164.
[65] Luhmann (2006b), p. 436.
[66] Cf. Busch and Scholz (2000), p. 9 f.
[67] Winch (1970), p. 24.
[68] Cf. Winch (1970), p. 24.

Table 4.1 Working definition family

The family can be classified as an autopoietic system, which is characterized by compulsory membership that opens access to further (in)formal roles and rules for individuals based on their membership role and from which various expectations, rights, and duties arise for the role holders. There must be at least a generation differentiation between two members and the socialization function must be fulfilled.

(step)parent and the respective (step)child(ren).[69] The generation differentiation results from the "replacement function"[70] of the family, and thus assigns it a production function for the creation of potential communication participants.[71] In contrast to an organization, however, specific types of communication prevail within the family.[72] There are no membership rules that dictate communicative behavior, which generally classifies everything as relevant.[73] Against this background and considering the newly emerged forms of life, Nave-Herz replaces the term family, which is in everyday use, with the term "'familial system'" [74].

As can be seen from the argumentation, the family encompasses a series of specifics that distinguish it from organizations or groups. Nevertheless, it is precisely the concept of the membership role with the special features mentioned above that is suitable for establishing a definition of family. In detail, regardless of the form of life and the number of people participating in it; this seems functional for the further course of the work. Considering the previously depicted argumentation the following definition of a family is introduced (see Table 4.1).

By using the membership role, it is now possible to subsume other living communities/forms under the family concept. Subsequently, the business family and its peculiarities will be discussed.

4.1.2.2.2 Working Definition of the Business Family

The often-enormous energy potential present in family businesses is usually due to the respective business family involved in the business. This family shapes the business day-to-day through their personal commitment and motivation.[75]

[69] Cf. Nave-Herz (2007), p. 15; cf. Lenz (2005), p. 13 and cf. Busch and Scholz (2000), p. 9.

[70] Winch (1970), p. 24.

[71] Cf. Simon (2000), p. 143.

[72] Cf. von Schlippe et al. (2011), p. 526; cf. Simon (2004), p. 145 and cf. Luhmann (1990), p. 204.

[73] Cf. Kieserling (1994), p. 24.

[74] Nave-Herz (2003), p. 47.

[75] Cf. Wimmer (1997), p. 145.

The business family also includes family members who are not actively working in the enterprise, i.e., those who are "only" involved through ownership of the family business. These individuals then serve more as a "solidarity and network resource" [76]. Groth and von Schlippe, however, describe the business family in today's prevailing societal environment as an "(explanation-needing) deviation" [77]. Klein[78] understands a business family as a family, which includes the direct descendants of an original marriage as well as their spouses and which strives for family continuity through joint entrepreneurial activity. This connection can subsequently limit individual decision-making freedom in favor of family stability. For Stamm[79] a business family exists when (a) family(ies) own(s) and manage(s) (a) business(es). Von Schlippe believes that "owning an enterprise makes a significant difference for a family (and vice versa) compared to the experiences and dynamics in other families or enterprises" [80]. Above all, values are lived and conveyed to the younger generation by the parents (see Sect. 2.5). The peculiarity in business families then lies in the connection of these values with the enterprise. Therefore, the following questions often arise:

1. What is important for the family business,
2. for its continuity,
3. for the employees and
4. for the image?

This prioritization can then lead to a downgrading of family needs (see Chap. 2).[81] Stamm's[82] analysis also shows that all social relationships within the business family are shaped by the enterprise. According to Kempert [83], a family business and in detail the business family must cope with the following four challenges in addition to succession planning:

---

[76] Stamm (2013), p. 49.

[77] Groth and von Schlippe (2012), p. 3.

[78] Cf. Klein (2004), p. 11.

[79] Cf. Stamm (2013), p. 44. In detail, Stamm defines business families as follows: "The term business family refers to those families who own business assets and/or generate income through their activity in the enterprise whose family everyday life is therefore not oriented towards gainful employment, but is influenced by one (or several) enterprise(s)" (Stamm 2013, 7 and cf. 109).

[80] von Schlippe (2011a), p. 8.

[81] Cf. Kempert (2008), p. 204.

[82] Cf. Stamm (2013), p. 276.

[83] Cf. Kempert (2008), p. 31 f.

Table 4.2 Working definition business family

The starting point for the emergence of a business family is the union of ownership of a business by a family. Ownership creates the structural coupling between the two autopoietic systems of family and business, which then stand in a co-evolutionary relationship to each other. Membership in the family system is characterized by compulsory membership, which opens access to further (in)formal roles and rules in both systems due to their membership role and from which various expectations, rights, and duties arise for the role holders. At least one generational differentiation must exist between two members and the socialization function must be fulfilled.

1. Globalization
2. Dealing with information technology
3. Change in values
4. Changes in society and the social environment

Descendants from business families in particular often experience everyday life with the enterprise as something very natural (see Sect. 2.5.2.3).

When looking at the descendants, they often strive for their own independence (as successors, as founders, or as freelancers) out of a complete matter of course, even though they are familiar with both the positive and negative sides.[84] Two opposing forces usually affect the descendants of a business family: (1) The desire or the feeling of obligation to follow in their parents' footsteps and (2) the need to lead their own lives.[85] Another ambivalence arises for the children of entrepreneurs in relation to the enterprise: It often attracts the complete or predominant attention (of the parents) and at the same time serves the family's existence.[86] Even if the entrepreneurial parents leave the descendants free choice for their future, the framework conditions, i.e., the enterprise and its impact on the descendants are often forgotten. They are often denied a truly free choice.[87] A characteristic of business families is also the promotion of performance and competition through the upbringing of the children.[88] Against this background and the already established definition of family and the explanations on the organization, the business family is therefore defined as follows (see Table 4.2).

[84] Cf. Felden (2012), p. 154 and cf. Felden and Pfannenschwarz (2008), p. 122.
[85] Cf. Felden (2012), p. 154 and cf. Simon (2012), p. 108.
[86] Cf. Plate (2008), p. 71.
[87] Cf. LeMar (2014), p. 125.
[88] Cf. Klein (2004), p. 88.

As can be seen from the argumentation or the established definition, the special feature of the connection to an enterprise comes to the fore in business families compared to families. As was evident under Sects. 2.4 and 2.5, the enterprise influences the individual members, which is particularly relevant for the chosen focus of this work. The nature of the connection, i.e., the concept of structural coupling, its special feature and the associated consequences will be discussed subsequently.

4.1.3 Systems Theoretical Access to Family Businesses

After the (business) family and the enterprise have been "processed" systems theoretically, generalizing statements about the systems can be made, despite the respective individual appearances and logics. This "detachment" now also makes it possible to view the family business systems theoretically. Although, every family business is individual and unique, there are still many overlaps between them. The systems' theoretical view allows these to be identified to work out dynamics valid for every family business that influence the socialization of the descendants.

4.1.3.1 The Family Business as Two Structurally Coupled Systems

In Chaps. 1 and 2 a "connection" between family and business was discussed. The systems theoretical insights now serve to analyze this connection in more detail, to illustrate the implications for the two systems family and business. For further consideration, the connection is now understood as structural coupling.

Simon[89] as well as Frank et al.[90] also see the special features of the family business because of the predominant coupling. For further argumentation, the family business is therefore understood as two structurally coupled social systems (the system family and the system business). This view should be understandable for the enterprise with reference to the explanations under Sect. 3.1.1.3 and for the family through the explanations under Sect. 4.1.2. Both systems represent significant environments for each other, which mutually influence each other, as they interpenetrate each other and "a close interlocking of two very different types of social systems can be observed" [91]. To exist in a changing environment,

---

[89] Cf. Simon (2005), p. 8.

[90] Cf. Frank et al. (2010b), p. 124.

[91] Hilse and Wimmer (2002), p. 344.

the systems need to have "structural variation possibilities" [92]. Schulze-Böing and Unverferth[93] speak of a relative invariance of the system structures towards the environment. In reference to Luhmann[94], Frank et al.[95] understand the family and the business as structures consisting of communication and not of people or relationships. Likewise, the family and the business are seen as social systems that generate themselves, define themselves structurally, and are operationally closed. The simultaneous membership in both systems can cause the transfer of mutual requirements and irritations (e.g., role conflicts) to the respective other system, and thus creates easily overcome boundaries, as the people can appear as family or as business members.[96] Therefore, as already described, there are two ways for the systems to adapt to their environment: (1) They can transform themselves and (2) can actively shape their environment.[97]

To illustrate the implications that structural coupling can have for the members of an business family, it is first contrasted with "loose coupling"[98]: As an example of a (relatively) loose coupling, Simon[99] mentions the existing employment relationship between an organization and its members. If members leave the organization, this has no consequences for the identity of the members or their families, nor for the identity of the organization. For this reason, the respective autonomy of the social systems family and business is preserved by a clear demarcation. However, when the two social systems are considered against the background of a family business, it can no longer be spoken of a loose coupling between family and business. The difference arises primarily from the coupling of family members to the ownership of the business. The enterprise thus represents a

---

[92] Schulze-Böing and Unverferth (1986), p. 17.

[93] Cf. Schulze-Böing and Unverferth (1986), p. 17.

[94] *Luhmann*, N. (2000): Organisation und Entscheidung. Opladen: Westdeutscher Verlag; *Luhmann*, N. (1995): Social systems, Stanford: Stanford University Press; *Luhmann*, N. (1990): Sozialsystem Familie, in: Luhmann, N. (Ed.): Soziologische Aufklärung 5: Konstruktivistische Perspektiven, Opladen: Westdeutscher Verlag, 196–217.

[95] Cf. Frank et al. (2010b), p. 123 ff.

[96] Cf. Groth (2008), p. 33.

[97] Cf. Luhmann (1995b), p. 123.

[98] According to Weick, a loose coupling exists "when two separate systems either have only a few variables in common with each other or their common variables are weak in comparison with the other variables influencing the system" (Weick 1995, 163). Thus, loose coupling grants the greatest possible flexibility at the level of actions. Seen from the outside, the impression is that everyone does whatever comes to mind. Accordingly, the predictability of certain behavioral expectations is very low (cf. Simon 2004, 82 ff.).

[99] Cf. Simon (2008a), p. 56.

significant environment for the family(ies) or their members, which can influence the family (enterpriseness).[100] The family also serves the business (familiness), due to the structural coupling, as a unique environment. This arises from the characteristics of the family in particular. It creates its own structures and its own identity and consequently its own history, which allows a distinction between families. Since the family represents a specific environment for the business and vice versa, changes within one system have direct effects on the other.[101] As a result, both systems develop co-evolutionarily.

However, there is no possibility for the structurally coupled systems to intervene "structure-determining"[102] into the respective other system. Therefore, this is also not congruent with autopoiesis, although the structural coupling influences the structures produced in the system itself over a longer period.[103] The structural coupling, so to speak, breaks through the logic of the system, i.e., "that the involved systems mutually use each other for their own structure building, without being determined in their own development by the respective others" [104]. The following Fig. 4.1 illustrates this relationship. The systems family and business are considered as two autopoietic systems that are structurally coupled to each other (symbolized by circles and arrows). They can thus go through a common, co-evolutionary interaction history and therefore relate the development of their respective structures to each other without being determined by the respective other system.

Against the background of structural coupling, Zwack defines a family business as follows: "*An enterprise is always a family business when it expects that a structural variation in one (or more) families could coincide with a structural variation in the business and therefore observes this family (or families) as a relevant environment.*"[105] When considering factors that can influence the intensity of the structural coupling between the family and the business, Froschauer and Lueger[106] mention the following based on the results of their case study:

---

[100] Cf. Rüsen (2009), p. 32; cf. Simon et al. (2005), p. 19 and cf. Wimmer et al. (2004), p. 5.

[101] Cf. Frank et al. (2010b), p. 124.

[102] Luhmann (2006c), p. 397.

[103] Cf. Wimmer et al. (2004), p. 5.

[104] Wimmer et al. (2004), p. 5 and cf. Rüsen (2009), p. 32.

[105] Zwack (2011), p. 30 f. According to Simon et al. (2005, 133 f.), a family business can count on the family when reserves are created for the expected inheritance tax. This counteracts a potential "existential crisis" (Simon et al. 2005, 134) of the enterprise in the event of an inheritance.

[106] Cf. Froschauer and Lueger (2012), p. 102 ff.

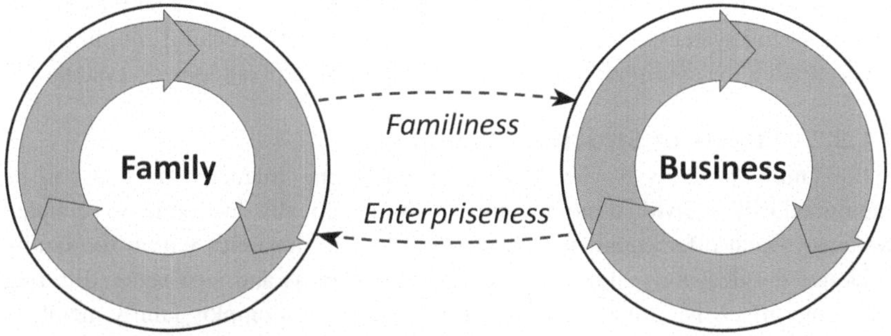

Fig. 4.1 The family business as two structurally coupled systems[107]

1. Proximity of the living area to the business
2. Integration of the descendants into the daily work routine
3. Intertwining of leisure and work life
4. Portrayal of the family as a business family (external impact)
5. Enterprise's ability to secure the long-term existence of the family

In this context and against the background of system-theoretical considerations, the structural coupling between the family and the business — like the psychic and social system — only takes place via persons and not via humans.[108] A person combines different roles in themselves. These are in turn "bundled and addressable behavioral expectations; they have their unity in the extent of what an individual can perform" [109]. The membership role guarantees the systems the fulfillment of the set expectations from the side of the members within certain limits. Thus, these do not have to be set up again in every situation.[110] In family businesses in particular, the structural coupling between the family system and the business system takes place based on expectations of any kind,[111] which are conveyed through communication and primarily through language. The assumption of structural coupling neither presupposes an overlapping of the systems,

[107] Source: Based on Simon (2012), p. 14.

[108] Cf. Zwack (2011), p. 32 and cf. Luhmann (1970), p. 45.

[109] Luhmann (1986), p. 41.

[110] Cf. Luhmann (1976b), p. 42.

[111] Cf. Weismeier-Sammer et al. (2012), p. 198.

nor that they have one and the same overall system — except society as an all-encompassing system — as environment. In this respect, structural coupling does not contradict the assumption of the operational closure of autopoietic systems.[112]

4.1.3.2 Effects of Structural Coupling

If the family business is viewed as a "whole", one characteristic that can be mentioned is its individual momentum. This is specifically due to the two coupled systems, which offer countless possibilities.[113] The dynamics within the family influence the decisions and actions within the business and vice versa, differing from enterprises that are neither owned by a family, nor employ family members in management.[114] As already explained, a family business consists of at least two different contexts or two fundamentally different social systems: The family and the business.[115] Kersting and Kamper-Jasper[116] refer to family businesses in this context as two social systems that have completely different modes of operation, but are connected in "vital dependency"[117] or are inseparably intertwined with each other.[118] Wimmer et al.[119] speak of a clash of different rationalities (see Table 2.1). However, as each system depends on the performance of the other, a mutual dependency relationship arises. Therefore, subsequent actions must be coordinated with the concerns of the other system.[120]

Since a family business combines familial and entrepreneurial structural features, this can be seen as a unit characterized by contradictions due to the difference and close linkage, making the family business appear as a "*family*

---

[112] Cf. Kneer (2001), p. 419. "Operative (self-referential, recursive) closure means that the own operations of the system can only be produced and reproduced in the network of the system's own operations, i.e., only by referring back to other own operations of this system" (Luhmann 1990, 198). Therefore, the term operative closure refers to "the network of interactions that creates the boundaries of the system and thereby brings forth the system as a delimited unit" (Simon 2007b, 34).

[113] Cf. Frank et al. (2012b), p. 15.

[114] Cf. Chua et al. (1999), p. 22.

[115] Cf. Wimmer et al. (2005), p. 7. Hering and Olbrich describe an enterprise "as a system of production factors, which is characterized by the principles of economy, autonomy, self-determination, commercial economy, and financial balance" (Hering and Olbrich 2003, 9). Simon (2005, 61) refers to enterprises as "task-oriented systems" (Simon 2005, 61) whose task is to offer products or services on the market, and thus generate profit.

[116] Cf. Kersting and Kamper-Jasper (2002), p. 84.

[117] Kersting and Kamper-Jasper (2002), p. 84.

[118] .Cf. Domayer and Oswald (1994), p. 7.

[119] Cf. Wimmer et al. (2004), p. 21.

[120] Cf. Simon (2012), p. 22 f.

of its own kind"[121]. [122] While there appears to be independence of both systems, each system develops its own sphere of influence considering the other.[123] In the enterprise, this is evident, for example, through the familial leadership behavior (familiness).[124] Fritz et al. therefore also refer to family businesses as "systems with a strong emotional imprint" [125]. In particular, the emotions that arise influence ways of thinking, motivations, and behaviors and can play a significant role in a family business's strategy and decision-making.[126] On the other hand, the day-to-day business with all its daily challenges often encroaches on the family sphere, which can lead to a reduction in family communication time.[127] Simon et al. refer to this as "providing resources" [128].

However, if the interrelationships do not balance and the boundaries between the family and business system blur too much, "you see families that function like a business or businesses that function like a family"[129]. The first case often results in enormous psychological stress for family members and the second case makes it difficult to effectively manage the business.[130] Therefore, when considering the existing interactions, they differ due to the influence of the family on the business ("'familiness' of the enterprise"[131]) as well as the influence of the business on the family ("'enterpriseness' of the family"[132]). For interpenetration, these influences always occur together, i.e., the receiving system also always has its effects on the structure formation of the penetrated system.[133] Through the interaction of both systems, which follow different basic patterns, one is influenced by the other. This increases the adoption of characteristics of the respective other system[134] and

[121] Hildenbrand (2005), p. 144 and cf. Stamm (2013), p. 7 ff. as well as 31 f.

[122] Cf. Hildenbrand (2005), p. 144.

[123] Cf. Kepner (1983), p. 59.

[124] Cf. Wimmer (2007), p. 33.

[125] Fritz et al. (2001), p. 42.

[126] Cf. Bee and Neubaum (2014), p. 323.

[127] Cf. Wimmer (2004), p. 270 f.

[128] Simon et al. (2005), p. 157.

[129] Simon et al. (2005), p. 157 and cf. Wimmer et al. (2004), p. 21.

[130] Cf. Simon et al. (2005), p. 157.

[131] Frank et al. (2010b), p. 124.

[132] Frank et al. (2010b), p. 124.

[133] Cf. Frank et al. (2010b), p. 124.

[134] Cf. Wimmer (2007), p. 33.

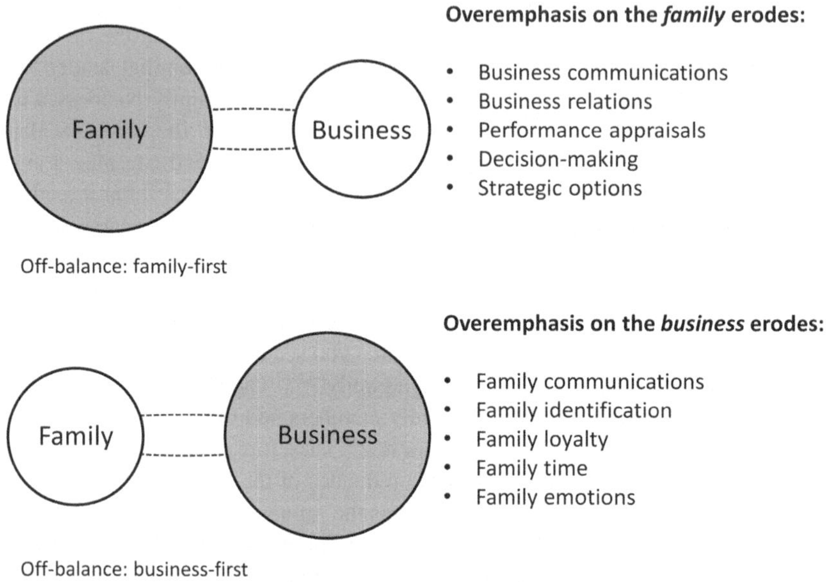

Fig. 4.2 Off-balance: family-first or business-first[136]

can cause internal contradictions.[135] Figure 4.2 illustrates the potential impact of overemphasizing one system on the other.

According to von Schlippe [137], if the social systems of family and work are initially considered separately, they follow different functional logics:

- The family is characterized by a "person-centeredness". In this, the individual with his strengths and weaknesses is the focus of consideration. Membership is non-cancelable and long-term. The "wage" is not compensated by money, but by intangible values, such as recognition or mutual belonging. The communication structures are hardly formalized and predominantly oral. The principle of equal treatment prevails for the position of the members.

[135] Cf. Stamm (2013), p. 75.

[136] Source: Based on Carlock and Ward (2001), p. 6 f. according to Hubler and Ayres (1996).

[137] Cf. von Schlippe (2011b), p. 2.

- In contrast, the business is characterized by a factual functional logic. Communication is predominantly formalized and written, which is to be seen as an ideal-typical view.

Just as communication in enterprises is carried out orally in certain situations, certain things are also put in writing in families. For intra-family communication Simon et al. formulate this as follows: "The family is one of the few places, where the full spectrum of emotions can legitimately be shown and allowed."[138] In contrast, emotion-related communication within an enterprise is not desired: "Here there are factual tasks that ensure focused and emotion-free communication [...]." [139] As can be seen, the two systems differ by "different selection criteria of communication" [140]. Another significant difference also lies in socialization. While the family represents the primary socialization instance, the enterprise usually acts as a tertiary instance for socialization (see Sect. 2.5.1.3). In the context of a family business, adolescents are in most cases already exposed to entrepreneurial socialization during primary socialization due to the structural coupling and the prevailing enterpriseness. For the descendants, there can therefore be the peculiarity of being exposed to a "double socialization" at the same time.

Family communication is often characterized by the common task and the relationships within the family.[141] The family communication is in many cases crucially shaped by the events in the business.[142] The communication is therefore rather purpose bound. This can then lead to a lack of processing of emotional conflicts.[143] Rüsen speaks in this regard of a "functionalization of family members to the enterprise" [144]. For this reason, family communication is often relegated in favor of the family business so that individual concerns are not or hardly addressed.[145] Typical for family businesses is also the transfer of family communication patterns to the level of the business, and thus to the way decisions are made.[146] Since communication within the family can quickly become emotional,

---

[138] Simon et al. (2005), p. 161.

[139] Simon et al. (2005), p. 161.

[140] Simon (2012), p. 15.

[141] Cf. Domayer and Vater (1995), p. 151.

[142] Cf. Wimmer et al. (2005), p. 10.

[143] Cf. Wimmer and Gebauer (2004), p. 247.

[144] Rüsen (2009), p. 33.

[145] Cf. Rüsen (2009), p. 33.

[146] Cf. von Schlippe (2009), p. 19 and cf. Wimmer et al. (2005), p. 110.

coupling to a business increases the likelihood of the "breaking through" of the required factual level within the family business.[147] Generally speaking, conflicts in family businesses run the risk of spreading from one system to the other.[148]

It becomes apparent that the family and the business each adhere to their own values, demands, and process logics. This can lead to the same situation being deemed appropriate in one system, but not in the other.[149] Bieker and Hirsch phrase it as follows: "When two social systems with different functional logics meet, irritations and conflicts are inevitable because the differences are rarely consciously perceived and reflected upon by the participants." [150] However, the extent to which the family exerts its influence on the business or its internal structure is influenced by many factors. This could include, among other things, the size and multi-generational existence of the family business.

In addition, the family system is characterized by "an unbreakable relationship spanning at least two generations"[151]. This means that the (biological) parents remain the parents. This component cannot be changed. However, certain patterns or intra-family processes can change over time.[152] This is different in organized system types. They have clear views on who is classified as a member and who is not and they realize the clear recognition of behavioral expectations for at least a critical part of their members.[153] Another divergence between family and business lies in the acceptance of different individuals. While a family member is accepted as a "whole person"[154] with all their strengths and weaknesses and the focus is on the relationship between individuals, the opposite is true in an enterprise. In this context, it is not the individual person with their subjective emotional state that is the focus of attention, but solely the performance, i.e., the fulfillment of the requirement profile for the position to be filled. Mistakes or weaknesses are predominantly not accepted there, unlike in the family environment.[155]

---

[147] Cf. Wimmer et al. (2004), p. 67.

[148] Cf. Frank and Hasenzagl (2005), p. 37.

[149] Cf. Plate and von Schlippe (2010), p. 4.

[150] Bieker and Hirsch (2007), p. 390.

[151] Domayer and Vater (1995), p. 150.

[152] Cf. Domayer and Vater (1995), p. 150.

[153] Cf. Jahraus et al. (2012), p. 130.

[154] Wimmer et al. (2004), p. 52.

[155] Cf. Wimmer et al. (2004), p. 52 f.

Due to the familial proximity to the business, i.e., the coupling of the family's private life with the business, Lueger and Suchy[156] suggest the following advantages and disadvantages for individual family members and their social relationships:

Advantages

1. The common task can be meaningful for the family. This is favored by the responsibility borne by all and the joint implementation and usually also influences intra-family cohesion. This is particularly pronounced in small and medium-sized enterprises, where spatial proximity is also found to a greater extent. This proximity specifically supports direct communication in the event of ambiguities or problems.
2. Decision-making paths are often short. Since the family is connected with the ownership, the decision-making power is often in family hands. This additionally promotes an increase in trust.

Disadvantages

1. The family business usually takes a very dominant part in all aspects of the family members' lives. In addition to discussing enterprise-relevant topics at the breakfast table, it is often not possible to completely distance oneself from it, even on vacation. This dominance becomes particularly noticeable when the family business is going through a crisis.
2. The sacrifice for the family business can necessitate the renunciation of alternative life plans, as the success of the enterprise often requires the postponement of one's own interests.

The mentioned factors have the potential to influence the complete life planning of the individual family members (positively and negatively) and can thus also affect the socialization of the descendants.

The structural coupling between the family and the business system usually results in a "community of fate"[157]. In particular, the structural coupling implies a

---

[156] Cf. Lueger and Suchy (2012), p. 53 f.

[157] Simon et al. (2005), p. 154; cf. Simon (2012), p. 40; cf. Groth (2008), p. 32; cf. Wimmer (2008b), p. 110; cf. Meyer (2007), p. 105; cf. Wimmer et al. (2004), p. 7 and cf. Hamer (2001), p. 232 f.

co-evolution of systems and environments.[158] Against the background of a family business, co-evolution can then be understood as the joint development of the family and the business.[159] They coordinate with each other and respond to changes in the other system.[160] According to Wimmer et al., it is precisely in the co-evolution of systems that "the extraordinary opportunity potential of this type of enterprise lies, which fundamentally distinguishes it from listed public enterprises" [161]. However, as each system follows a different logic and changes are very likely over time, conflicts cannot ruled out due to mutual influence within and between the systems. If so-called development crises occur in one system, they can often only be overcome by conscious counter-steering. This usually also implies a structural change in the other systems, otherwise their continued existence is endangered.[162] Above all, the decision-making process in the family follows a different logic than in the business. Decisions that are considered correct at the business level can be completely inappropriate in the family area and vice versa.[163] Therefore, if an understanding of family businesses is to be generated, they must be seen as the result of the co-evolution of two fundamentally different social systems that influence each other. In addition to being a rich resource, the problems of one system can spill over to the other system and vice versa.[164] Although the two social systems are perceived as "oppositely structured types" [165], the prevailing co-evolution has a "structure-shaping effect"[166] for both systems. Thus, properties of the other system are adapted. For this reason, many processes within the family business take on familial characteristics over time. This can then be noticeable in the leadership style, the way conflicts are handled, in personnel management, or in dealing with external stakeholders.[167]

Risks mainly exist in the case of family conflicts. These are often continued in the family business due to the co-evolution. Likewise, problems that occur in the enterprise's daily business can be "dragged" into the private sphere, which the

---

[158] Cf. Luhmann (1995a), p. 17.

[159] Cf. Simon et al. (2005), p. 38.

[160] Cf. Simon (2012), p. 22 f.

[161] Wimmer et al. (2004), p. 8.

[162] Cf. Simon et al. (2005), p. 19 f. and cf. Simon (2005), p. 54.

[163] Cf. Simon (2005), p. 56.

[164] Cf. Wimmer et al. (2005), p. 7 f.

[165] Wimmer (2009b), p. 8.

[166] Wimmer (2009b), p. 8.

[167] Cf. Wimmer (2004), p. 270 f.

children actively experience. If the family falls apart, the continuation of the family business is also at risk in most cases. This happens because the enterprise's success often depends almost exclusively on the family members and not, as in the case of publicly traded enterprises, on people who can be easily replaced.[168] There is therefore a fine line between success and susceptibility to crisis in family businesses. Because of this, structural characteristics develop that clearly distinguish this form of enterprise from others.[169] Thus, the coupling and co-evolution of these two social systems confront individuals with specific social and psychological demands.[170] However, in family businesses, the increasing number of family members can sometimes hinder their direct, personal communication. While there is still an emotional relationship to each other in the small family, this often decreases with an increasing number of members. Since in large families the gathering of members has to be organized more and more, the co-evolution between family and business can rather take place as "co-evolution of two formal organizations" [171], i.e., the familial and person-oriented influence within the business fades and the family business increasingly adapts to the characteristics of a corporation.[172] This development has an impact on the business family due to the structural coupling. The consequences associated with this will be thoroughly examined in the following chapters.

4.1.3.3 Effects of Context Mixing

If the focus is placed on the members of a business family against the background of the insights of systems-theoretical role theory, it is not always possible to speak of a complete separation of roles there. For the members of the business family, the structural coupling provides the opportunity to actively influence the other system as a system participant[173] and to act simultaneously in the different systems. Thus, the entrepreneur can appear as owner, managing director, and father. This can increase the likelihood of pragmatic paradoxes. Actions that are considered appropriate in one system are rather hindering in the other. Since it is not always clear to the family members in which context (family or business) they are currently speaking, the paradox is based on the uncertainty from which

168 Cf. Wimmer et al. (2004), p. 8.

169 Cf. Wimmer (1997), p. 146.

170 Cf. Simon (2005), p. 36.

171 Simon (2005), p. 71.

172 Cf. Simon (2005), p. 70 f.

173 Cf. Meyer (2007), p. 105.

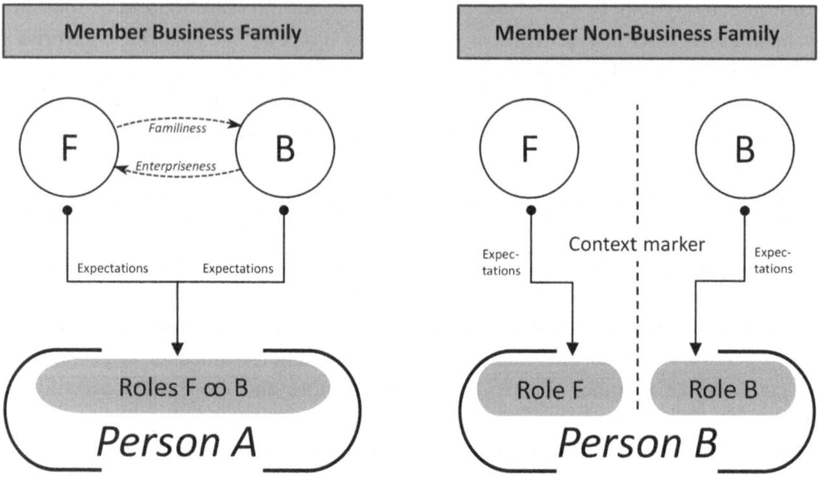

Fig. 4.3 Role separation and mixing in (non-)business families (own work)

role they are currently communicating.[174] Before we now turn to the further consequences resulting from the structural coupling, Fig. 4.3 illustrates the difference between the members of a (non-)business family.

First, Role theory provides a framework for analysis and understanding to make statements about, *why people act differently in different contexts and situations*? Precisely because a person is embedded in a multitude of systems and these usually differ in their values, norms, expectations, and the way they sanction, a person also combines different individual roles in themselves. Which role the person then has to "use" is made clear to them by different clues. In this context, the already explained term "context markers" (see Sect. 2.1.4) is relevant. This enables a separation of roles and is illustrated in Fig. 4.3 by the right representation. Person B can simultaneously be a member of a family (F) and a business (B). However, both systems are separated from each other by context markers. Thus, person B can separately or independently perform role F and role B without the different values, norms, or expectations prevailing in the respective systems affecting each other. There is at most a loose coupling (see Sect. 4.1.3.1). The two system contexts alternate over the course of a day. In the morning, the family system with its specific "rules of the game" is left and entered the business

[174] Cf. von Schlippe (2009), p. 18 f.

system, which is then left again in the evening to re-enter the family system. The context markers provide the affected persons with a certain orientation aid as to what expectations are placed on them and how these are sanctioned in case of non-compliance. The scope or degree of penetration is limited to the respective system. Of course, this does not exclude that the business or work can be a topic within family communication and vice versa.

If a member of a business family is now considered, they often lack context markers due to the structural coupling. Since the business usually represents the family's livelihood, all possible energy is dedicated to the business. The family and business contexts "blur" together. Thus, they can no longer be clearly distinguished, which also makes it difficult to separate the individual roles and the resulting expectations. For this reason, the business can be a permanent part of any interaction.[175] This is illustrated by the left-hand representation in Fig. 4.3. For Person A, a separation of roles is not possible, so they are simultaneously exposed to the expectations of the two contexts or systems (Roles F ∞ B). The two roles "merge".

Precisely because there is predominantly no separation between private and professional life in family businesses, the members of a business family face the challenge of managing the different, sometimes contradictory requirements at the same time. Thus, the members, as already described at the beginning, take on the roles of owner, managing director, and employee in addition to the role of mother, father, daughter, or son.[176] As family members their primary focus is on the prosperity and unity of the family, while owners are interested in the profitability or return of the enterprise. Managers, on the other hand, try to increase the effectiveness and efficiency of an enterprise.[177] While Simon refers to this as a "(potential) multiple identity" [178], von Schlippe and Kellermanns speak of a "role confusion"[179] and Baus titles this as "multiple role structure" [180]. Meyer speaks in this context of "role dilemmas"[181] and Holleis of a "permanent role overlap"[182] between family and business. The family members are confronted with different identities in each context, so different expectations are placed on

[175] Cf. Domayer and Vater (1995), p. 151.
[176] Cf. Lueger and Suchy (2012), p. 52.
[177] Cf. Kormann (2011), p. 312 and cf. Tagiuri and Davis (1996), p. 201.
[178] Simon (2003), p. 35.
[179] von Schlippe and Kellermanns (2009), p. 182.
[180] Baus (2010), p. 93.
[181] Meyer (2007), p. 106.
[182] Holleis (1998), p. 54.

them.[183] Due to the differences between the individual systems, this can lead to enormous potential for conflict, which can be further intensified by external environmental influences.[184]

For the members of the business family this results in the necessity to be able to access their "double identity" in every situation simultaneously, i.e., the member must instantly decide in which role or function they are currently speaking.[185] For the family members who are employed together in a family business, the challenge lies in a "balancing act" in terms of in which context or in which role (family or business) they act and in which context the other members are moving.[186] It is precisely through coupling that the family can see its "collective existence"[187] as linked to that of the business. There is also a problem for the head of a family business who performs the role of management. This person usually serves as the interface between the family and the business system. Due to their central, irreplaceable position, there are often no structures that could compensate for the loss of this person.[188]

If we specifically consider the possible role conflicts of a business family, these differ from members of a non-business family. This is due, among other things, to the existing role duality and the influence of the members on the business-specific socio-psychological factors of their enterprise.[189] Particularly in entrepreneurial families, the members are committed not only to work during the day and only to the family in the evenings or on weekends. Rather, there is a constant interplay.[190] The difficulties within family businesses arise precisely because the same people must fulfill obligations in both systems. The parents are not only parents, but at the same time also the entrepreneurs.[191] Likewise, the descendants are not just descendants, but also serve the continuation of the family business, i.e., they are always "traded" as potential successors. As can be seen in Table 2.5, they are repeatedly exposed to different, sometimes contradictory expectations, which confronts them with role conflicts. The conflicts occurring in family businesses in

---

[183] Cf. Simon (2012), p. 15.

[184] Cf. Meyer (2007), p. 140 and cf. Simon et al. (2005), p. 21.

[185] Cf. Simon (2009), p. 45.

[186] Cf. Weismeier-Sammer et al. (2012), p. 183.

[187] Klett (2002), p. 109.

[188] Cf. Simon et al. (2005), p. 60.

[189] Cf. Memili et al. (2015), p. 147.

[190] Cf. Simon et al. (2005), p. 32 f.

[191] Cf. Gersick et al. (1997), p. 5.

particular can primarily be understood as role conflicts.[192] According to the opinion of Beehr et al. [193], members of a business family are often primarily exposed to inter-role conflicts. In the context of a family business, inter-role conflicts arise because contradictory expectations are placed on the business and family roles. The overlap of the systems necessitates a special challenge for the management of the different roles and their balance.[194]

Against the background of the focus chosen in this work, it can be assumed that this role mixing or the simultaneous experience of different expectations has an influence on the identity formation. Precisely because the identity is composed of different roles, the lack of context markers allows for an early "confrontation" with the different role requirements. As already described, this can thus lead to an early tertiary socialization, as the family business represents a defining world of life for the entrepreneur's children.

4.2 Change of the Structural Coupling Based on the Ecological Systems Model

After the dynamics of a family business have been theoretically worked out or a solid theoretical framework has been provided, the bridge to the descendants is built, i.e., *how the enterpriseness specifically affects the growing up.* As explained in detail in Sect. 2.2, it makes a difference, whether we are talking about a first, second, or multi-generational family business. Due to the prevailing co-evolution, each phase requires different demands on the respective participating generation and provides a different socialization context for the descendants. In this context, a change in the structural coupling between the family and business system must be discussed, which also affects the context mixing. This dynamic of structural coupling and its effect on the descendants is then described in detail using Bronfenbrenner's Ecological Systems Model (see Sect. 3.5).

As already explained, Bronfenbrenner's Ecological Systems Model allows a representation of the different areas of life of the developing individual. The family is embedded in other systems that exert their influence on it. Thus, family socialization takes place depending on the structural conditions of the overall system. Specifically, Bronfenbrenner's model allows the importance of different environmental conditions on socialization to be worked out. In addition, the

[192] Cf. Korunka and Nosé (2012), p. 151.

[193] Cf. Beehr et al. (1997), p. 298.

[194] Cf. Cooper et al. (2013), p. 460.

model provides an analytical gain for the localization of family members and especially the descendants during size growth as well as the multi-generational existence of a family business. This allows a better understanding of the influences on the socialization of the descendants.

4.2.1 Representation of Structural Coupling Using the Ecological Systems Model

As already explained, the social systems family and business in the context of a family business can also be understood as two structurally coupled systems.[195] It is precisely the structural coupling that allows the explanation of how autopoietic systems, although operationally closed, can still influence each other.[196] The concept of structural coupling can thus be used, among other things, to theoretically substantiate the "system-to-system relationships"[197] in an appropriate framework.[198] Since both systems are subject to temporal change, the structural coupling will also show different gradations.

Against the background of the explanations on the Ecological Systems Model under Sect. 3.5 there is a possibility to provide additional understanding of how the structural coupling between the two systems influences the socialization of the descendants. It should be pointed out at the outset that this is an ideal-typical representation. To what extent and at what point the business system "decouples" from the family system is largely influenced by the family. Due to the focus laid in this work, the possible development of the structural coupling is explained from the perspective of the descendants. Figure 4.4 and the content under Sect. 2.2 provide a better understanding.

The *first generation* (see Fig. 4.4) of a business family is usually characterized by a (very) close connection to the business. There is a kind of simultaneity of the two systems. Usually, both parents work in the enterprise (for economic reasons). They must meet the demands of two systems (family and business). The boundary between the two systems is very permeable in this phase. Against the background of the Three-Dimensional Model, these family businesses can be located in sectors (2), (3), (4), or (7). Due to the usually missing context markers, role mix-ups between the two systems are very likely. In relation to Table 2.2, we

[195] Cf. Frank et al. (2010b), p. 125.

[196] Cf. Jahraus et al. (2012), p. 121.

[197] Lieckweg (2001), p. 268.

[198] Cf. Lieckweg (2001), p. 268.

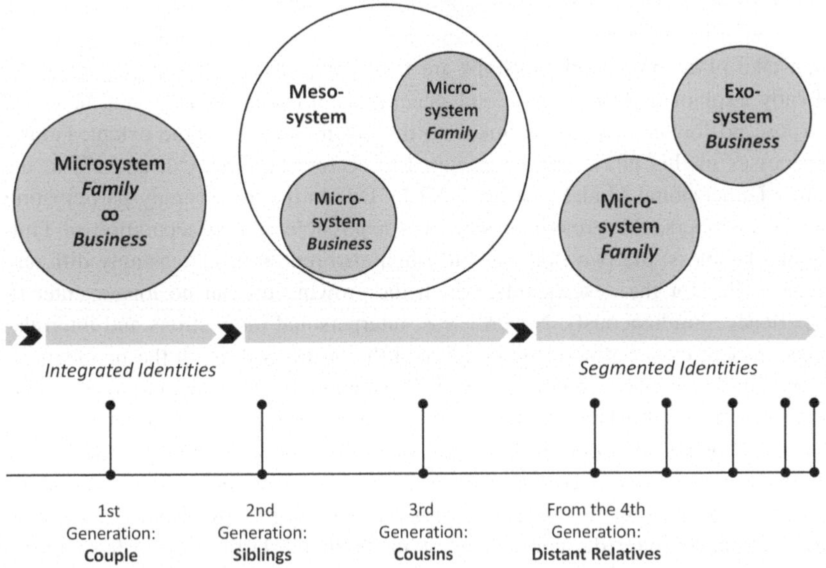

Fig. 4.4 Development phases of structural coupling in family businesses[199]

can speak of *integrated identities*, with the business-first idea being in the foreground. This is reinforced when the family's place of residence coincides with the enterprise's location. For enterprises in the start-up phase in particular, this is not unlikely. These provide the basis of life for the family and require their full strength, which also promotes a high degree of enterpriseness. For the descendants, both systems therefore represent the most immediate area for socialization. They are usually in direct interaction relationships with the parent entrepreneurs. Due to the "simultaneity", from the perspective of the family members and the descendants in particular, the family and the business can be seen as a structurally coupled microsystem, especially in the first and at the beginning of the second generation. Since this represents the most immediate living environment for the growing up, both systems influence the socialization of the descendants. The child is also exposed to their interaction relationships as entrepreneurs, in addition to the interaction relationships between the parents, whereby it receives additional stimuli and can acquire an extended role repertoire. Above all, primary and tertiary socialization will take place simultaneously.

---

[199] Source: Based on Simon et al. (2005), p. 48 as well as Tables 2.2 and 3.1.

Over the course of the *second generation* and during the *third generation* (see Fig. 4.4), a growing division of the one microsystem into two microsystems can then take place whose relationships are then connected by the mesosystem. As already explained, from the second generation onwards, identity and sense of purpose no longer need to be linked to the business to the same extent. Family businesses in this phase can be assigned to sectors (1), (4), (5), and (7) in the Three-Dimensional Model (see Sect. 2.3.1). Due to the increasingly participating family members, the growth in size, and a possible spatial separation of family and business, the two systems will often also represent increasingly different areas of life for the descendants, which the growing up can no longer enter or experience simultaneously. Nevertheless, interpersonal interactions and interrelationships can exist between the family and the business through the membership of the family members in both systems. Thus, an indirect connection to the enterprise can be established by the parents, which corresponds to a second-order network. For the growing up there may initially be no opportunity to personally enter the microsystem business. However, this can grow into a first-order social system or be present in this form from the very beginning, from the moment the adolescents enter the corporate system. Although both microsystems represent immediate systems for the descendants, simultaneous participation in both microsystems and life worlds is no longer possible.

If the focus is on the *fourth and further generations* (see Fig. 4.4), these multi-generational business families can consist of several hundred distant relatives. Without the common ownership of the family business or shares held in the enterprise, the individual members would probably not know each other anymore.[200] These family businesses can be found in sectors (1), (4), (5), and (7) of the Three-Dimensional Model. With respect to Fig. 4.3, the contextual mix will have progressively weakened and approached the role division of the non-business family, but with the key difference of structural coupling to the enterprise. Referring to Table 2.2, the family and the business are experienced as *segmented identities.* At this stage and especially due to the possibly large number of family members participating in the enterprise, the descendants will no longer belong to the enterprise as an acting person, which also means that there is no interaction with the business system. This represents an exosystem for the growing children. However, indirect relationships can still arise through the parents. Also, events in the enterprise can still have effects on the socialization of the descendants, for example, if the enterprise must be dissolved and the family loses its status as a business family. If the children then enter the family business

[200] Cf. Simon (2005), p. 42.

during succession and/or the shares are transferred to them, the enterprise grows into a mesosystem for the descendants. In this phase, one can no longer speak of simultaneous experience of primary and tertiary socialization. Rather, the tertiary will only take place during or after secondary socialization.

In summary, the use of the Ecological Systems Model opens the possibility of understanding the extent of structural coupling and changing enterpriseness. In addition, it becomes apparent how the intensity of the family business as a (determining) life world for the entrepreneurial children presents itself and can change and what consequences are associated with this. This subsequently provides insights into the extent of the imprinting (of the identity) of the descendants. To what extent socialization should be considered was explained under Sect. 2.5.2.5. However, this ideal-typical representation is dependent on a multitude of factors. Nevertheless, the family must be granted the greatest influence, as it acts as a socialization agent and primarily influences the descendants through the business system. Depending on how much space they allow the business within the family system, this has an influence on the socialization of the descendants.

4.2.2 Change of Enterpriseness

As can be seen from the previous explanations or Fig. 4.4, the structural coupling is subject to a temporal change, resulting in a different context for socialization and identity formation each time. Parallel to the structural coupling being subject to change along the generations, the enterpriseness must also undergo a change. It should be emphasized again that it is a structural coupling as long as the family participates in the ownership of the enterprise. If the family no longer has a stake in the family business, the structural coupling no longer exists. The family or individual members can then only be loosely coupled to the enterprise if they are (still) employed in it. The structural coupling undergoes a change or a kind of evolution through the division of ownership shares among several family members. If the ownership in the founding business is united in the hands of the entrepreneur(s), this is increasingly fragmented by the increasing number of family members participating in the family business in each subsequent generation. Of course, under the premise of no re-enactment of the nuclear family from generation to generation (see Sect. 2.2.6). Although the family business evolves due to the existing co-evolution, at a certain point, there will no longer be the possibility to employ all members in the family business. The multi-generational existence, favored by the changing participation of members in the business management and the division of shares, promotes an increasing "distance" from the family business, which can also endanger the enterprise's continued existence. At the same time, context markers solidify, which in turn can favor an increasing role separation. An alignment with the characteristics of a non-business family is very likely.

For the enterpriseness and the influence on the socialization of the descendants by the family business, there can be a (significant) difference whether both parents work in the enterprise or whether only one parent is involved in the business. In the second case, the quality may also depend on whether the mother or the father is in charge of the enterprise. Particularly if only one parent works in the enterprise, the question arises as to how the person who is not employed in the company relates to the enterprise. Does she or he also come from an entrepreneurial environment and does she or he have a positive or rather a negative attitude towards the enterprise? As already described, with increasing growth in size or multi-generational existence, both parents are likely no longer working in the enterprise. They may also only participate in it through shares. These factors also influence the impact of the business system on the identity formation of the growing children. Above all, the views of the main reference person toward the enterprise influence the descendants.

Since primarily the parents are the "link" between family and business, their involvement in the family business has effects on the extent of structural coupling, and thus on the identity formation of the descendants. As already mentioned, the involvement of the parents can change during multi-generational existence. Using the Segmentation-Integration Continuum (see Table 2.2), we speak of integrated identities in the first generation. There are no context markers, which makes role separation (almost) impossible. The enterpriseness necessitates a simultaneous experience of primary and tertiary socialization. During long-term existence, segmented identities will increasingly crystallize. The starting point, in addition to the changed ownership conditions, is the parents' work in the enterprise. This may no longer be necessary. At this stage, the enterpriseness will undergo a change, reducing the influence of the business system as a living environment for the descendants. As a result, the simultaneity of primary and tertiary socialization may no longer necessarily be given. As shown in Fig. 4.4, the business can develop from a micro to an exosystem from the perspective of the descendants.

The change in enterpriseness due to multi-generational existence, can often lead to a further decrease in the emotional attachment of individual family members to the common family business. This development finds its justification in the usually only indirect connection with the family business, as not all members are employed in the family business or only participate in the enterprise through shares. This development is reinforced by a frequently encountered spatial distance to the family business.[201] The developing extended family must then actively organize and introduce structures. Thus, the members connected only through ownership can safeguard their interests. This necessary reorganization is often in strong contradiction with the nature of the nuclear family.[202] In contrast to nuclear families, families with increasing growth increasingly need formalized rules for communication. The people meet, e.g., only at shareholder meetings.[203] This necessary structural change also influences the enterpriseness. This then comes less from the enterprise, but is rather induced by the family system itself. Thus, formalized practices by the family, such as recurring family meetings, a family strategy,[204] or the resulting family charter[205] are further forms of enterpriseness to strengthen the structural coupling to the family business. This can subsequently influence the identity of the family and the children in particular. Likewise, many large business families implement so-called family statutes. These can regulate the internal family succession or the employment of family members in the business.[206]

In general, due to the possibly increasing number of shareholders, a change from a material to an immaterial attachment to the family business can take place. In this case, participation is predominantly limited to the ownership function and the bond to the family business arises due to the developing tradition. Along the multi-generational existence, the family business will in most cases evolve into an enterprise led by external managers. Klein[207] suspects the existence of three factors that favor this transformation:

1. Increasing size growth generally requires more professional management.

---

[201] Cf. Meyer (2007), p. 163.

[202] Cf. Wimmer et al. (2005), p. 335.

[203] Cf. Simon (2012), p. 70.

[204] Felden and Pfannenschwarz (2008, 52) understand a family strategy as "a summary of the values and structures" (Felden and Pfannenschwarz 2008, 52) of the business family, whereby it can be used as an instrument to prevent arising intra-family disputes in advance.

[205] According to Baus (2006, 56), a family charter represents the "keystone" (Baus 2006, 56) of a family strategy. A family charter includes "the sum of shared beliefs and the results of the family governance discussion" (Baus 2006, 56). Above all, a family charter should clarify essential issues for the management, participation, and cooperation of the business families in/at the enterprise. This involves not only the shareholders, but also the entire family and should serve as the basis for the shareholders' agreement.

[206] Cf. Kempert (2008), p. 35.

[207] Cf. Klein (2004), p. 218.

2. Increasing sales development enhances the attractiveness of the family business for non-family managers. The family then also has the opportunity to compensate them adequately.
3. Requirement to adjust the number of people employed in management with increasing sales. Since the replacement of family-internal members is usually limited, the need for external staffing arises.

Therefore, it is particularly important that individual family members can get in touch. For this, rituals, such as regular family meetings, need to be established.[208] This then also makes it possible to maintain the bond to the family business along the generations.

In summary, it becomes clear that the enterpriseness is subject to certain dynamics along the multi-generational existence of a family business or a business family. Whereas the enterprise tended to have a direct influence on the family in the first generations, the family itself must increasingly "regulate" the bond with the enterprise. To what extent this happens or in what form this is designed, depends on the family participating in the business.

4.2.3 Excursus: Evolution of the Business Family

In the course of this work, the importance of the business system as an additional socialization context is emphasized. With the help of the Ecological Systems Model in particular, the dynamics of the structural coupling, and thus also the development of the enterpriseness as a relevant influencing factor on the socialization of the descendants, can be represented. Even though this work primarily considers the influence of the business system on socialization, the "evolution" of the business family should not be ignored. After all, business families are also subject to development dynamics that can also be understood using the multi-level model.

In general, a system has the possibility to carry out a "system differentiation"[209] or differentiation within its system by repeating the system formation

[208] Cf. Simon (2012), p. 81 f.

[209] Luhmann (1970), p. 148; cf. Luhmann (1994), p. 22, 37 as well as 261 and cf. Luhmann (1981), p. 158. Jahraus et al. understand differentiation as "the formation of further system/environment differences within a system" (Jahraus et al. 2012, 74), whereby this is referred to as system differentiation. The term "differentiation" must be distinguished from the term "difference" (cf. Jahraus et al. 2012, 74).

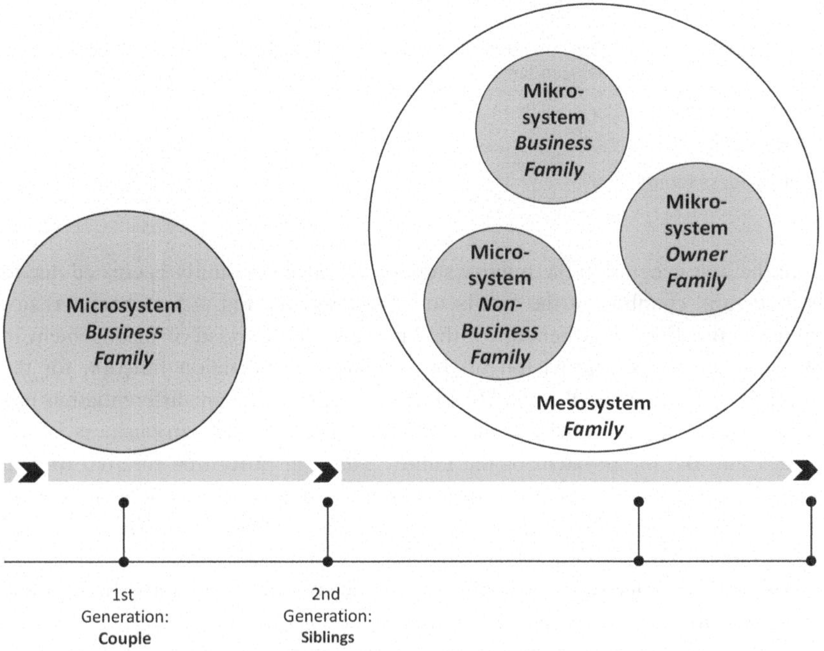

Fig. 4.5 Evolution of the business family (own work)

internally.[210] The overall system uses itself as an environment in order to form subsystems. Consequently, system differentiation is "nothing more than the repetition of the difference between system and environment within systems"[211] and, in other words, creates "system-internal environments" [212], whereby a completed differentiation contributes to an increase in the complexity of the overall system.[213] Since each subsystem also represents the environment for other subsystems, the change of one subsystem also influences other subsystems.[214] If this fact is transferred to a business family, including the Ecological Systems Model, the picture in Fig. 4.5 emerges.

[210] Cf. Luhmann (1995b), p. 76 and cf. Luhmann (1976b), p. 76.

[211] Luhmann (1994), p. 22 and 37 and cf. Luhmann (1990), p. 67.

[212] Luhmann (1998b), p. 597.

[213] Cf. Luhmann (1994), p. 261.

[214] Cf. Luhmann (1998b), p. 599.

Table 4.3 Functions of the differentiated microsystems

Microsystem	Socialization of the descendants	Ownership of the enterprise	Management in the enterprise
Business family	✓	✓	✓
Owner family	✓	✓	
Non-business family	✓		

In the first generation the microsystem of the business family is created due to the structural coupling of the family to a business (see Fig. 4.5). Characteristics are the unification of ownership of the business, the exercise of management in the business, and the provision of the (primary) socialization function for the descendants. Assuming the growth of both systems, system differentiation can already take place from the second generation. The microsystem business family merges into the mesosystem of the family. This can in turn be referred to as a "meta-system" in which (1) the business family, (2) the owner family, and (3) the non-business family differentiate as microsystems or subsystems. The individual microsystems have the following characteristics (see Table 4.3).

Although all microsystems fulfill the socialization function, only the business family and the owner family are structurally coupled to the enterprise, whereby only these co-evolve with the enterprise (see Table 4.3). This results from the ownership of the enterprise. Nevertheless, the business system can also influence the non-business family, for example, if a person from this microsystem is chosen and ownership is transferred to them. Since the mesosystem family establishes the connection between the individual microsystems, there is of course also the possibility for the individual members to come into contact with or enter the other areas of life. This in turn represents the starting point for socialization processes. Since these are different systems, they will also be characterized by different communication patterns and forms.

In summary, this development of the business family results in different starting points for the descendants. Due to the already existing complexity and the focus set by this work, however, this will not be further discussed. For the sake of completeness and as an idea for further research, this had to be mentioned. As shown in Table 4.2 and Fig. 4.1, no distinction is made between the business family and the owner family. These are used "synonymously", since both subsystems have ownership of the family business and this represents the starting point for the structural coupling in this work. Only in this way the business system can emerge as an additional socialization context.

4.3 The Socialization of Descendants from Family Businesses

This chapter completes the circle of the line of argument pursued in this work. Based on the knowledge gained, an attempt is made to cite the most essential factors that can influence the socialization of descendants in the context of a family business and specifically their identity. At this point, it should be noted that the presentation is ideal-typical and not exhaustive. For the gain in knowledge or the final consideration, the identity and its shaping are first considered again. Finally, the family business is viewed as a dynamic socialization context to answer the research question based on this.

4.3.1 The Identity Formation of Entrepreneurial Children

As was repeatedly evident from the explanations in this chapter as well as in Chaps. 1 and 2, the succession or the desire for the multi-generational existence of the family business is often an integral part of a business family. This is reflected, for example, in possible family governance measures. Only through successful transfer within the family can an enterprise continue as a family business and the family maintain its status as a business family. However, as became apparent, the transfer is also subject to a certain range of variation. If the succession in the second generation is (still) associated with a management handover in addition to ownership, family growth often makes a change necessary. As more and more people usually have membership in the business family, not all of them can actively work in the family business, meaning that they are predominantly "only" connected through shares. There is a tendency for dilution or the emotional decrease of the binding force to the family business. However, there are certain mechanisms within business families that promote succession or loyalty to the enterprise, but can also counteract it. In particular, the parents' desire for long-term existence can then manifest itself in the (communicated) expectations towards the descendants, which in turn have their influence on identity formation (see Fig. 4.6). Therefore, the parents' desire for succession or parental behavior must be attributed a significant influence on the shaping of the identity of the descendants.

As detailed under Sect. 3.2, the development of identity requires a societal process of experience and activity. This means that identity is not given at birth, but must first develop during socialization. As further evident under Sect. 3.3, a role is composed of different expectations, the observance of which is ensured by sanctions. The norms occurring within a society also have an influence on the roles. These represent rules that must be followed. However, the dynamics to which the roles are subject were also evident. Thus, the "specifications" are subject to temporal change. However, for a change to be made, another essential component is required: Communication. It is the starting point for the emergence of social systems and enables the mutual orientation of the participants. Through this, the role takeover takes place. This therefore makes it possible to convey expectations. The thematization is ensured by language. Especially, identity depends on language and its possibilities of representation. This enables the appropriation and definition of roles during socialization, which in turn are components of identity.

Language "transports" the different expectations that are directed at the respective individual, whereby communication in each social system differs from each other. If the focus is now on descendants from family businesses, there are some special features for them. Through structural coupling, the communication of the business system, and thus the therein prevailing (role) expectations enter the family system. Therefore, the business system inevitably becomes an identity-forming system for the descendants. The most significant influences on the identity of entrepreneurial children are shown in the following Figure 4.6. Individual factors are explained in Table 2.7.

Ideally, the identity of entrepreneurial children is shaped during socialization by three different systems (see Fig. 4.6). *Society* represents the most comprehensive system. In the sense of Bronfenbrenner, this can be described as the macrosystem (see Table 3.1). This system provides the cultural framework for the other systems. In it, values, norms, and expectations are established, which then exert a certain binding force on the other systems. In relation to the Fig. 4.6, these are the *family* and *business* systems. For example, in the family, which expectations are placed on the role of the mother and father. Within the business, which role expectations the entrepreneurs must consider. There are reciprocal relationships between the systems, i.e., certain dynamics with feedback effects. Each system represents the environment of the other systems. Changes in one system therefore also influence the other systems.

However, the primary reference system for the growing children is the family system. This is where primary socialization takes place. All other socialization instances tie into this or are subordinate to it. The family can be assigned to the microsystem in the sense of Bronfenbrenner. This is, as can be seen in Fig. 4.6, influenced by the society system. This means that society represents a relevant environment for the family. Depending on which macrosystem the family operates in, the communicated norms, expectations, and sanctions differ. This subsequently

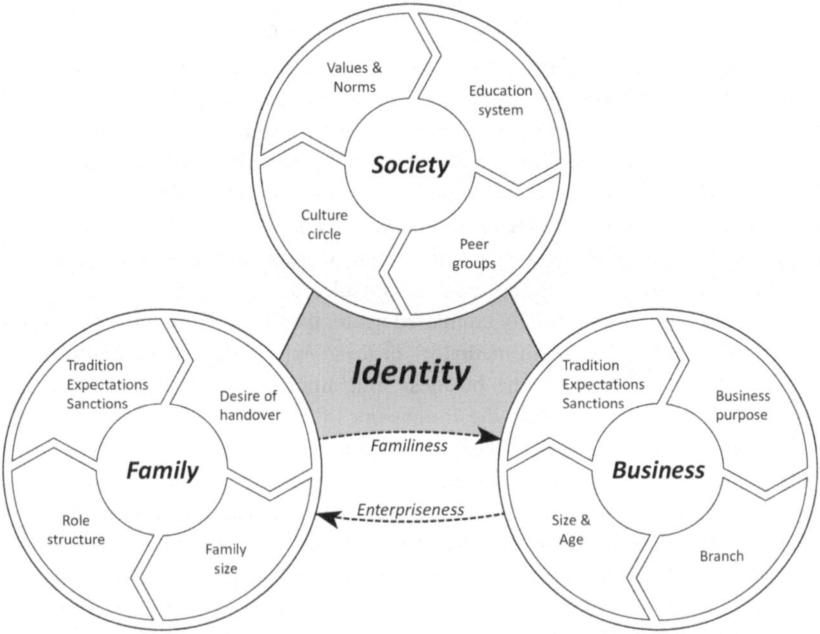

Fig. 4.6 Influences on the identity of the descendants in business families (own work)

defines, which function is assigned to the family, which expectations are placed on its members and which expectations are conveyed to the descendants during their socialization. In the context of a family business, the peculiarity is that there is an additional system influencing the socialization, and thus the identity formation of the growing children. This results from the structural coupling of the two systems family and business. Since the family members usually have memberships in both systems, the contexts often cannot be clearly separated from each other. The business system or the prevailing expectations therein thus enter the family system, which is referred to as enterpriseness. A clear role separation is therefore not so easily possible in many cases. As has become apparent, the family business grows into an additional or a shaping world for the growing children. Therefore, the descendants are exposed not only to the expectations from the family, but also those from the business, which becomes particularly clear in the succession process. It also became clear that the structural coupling is subject to certain dynamics. If the business initially represents a microsystem for the growing children, this can develop along the generations into an exosystem. This results in differences in enterpriseness and therefore different influences on identity. Finally, the peculiarity of the structural coupling should be pointed out. If members from non-business families are considered, an enterprise can also shape their identity, but this usually only happens during tertiary socialization. Due to the lack of structural coupling, i.e., the lack of ownership of the enterprise, the business will not enter the family to the same extent. For descendants from family businesses, this is different. There, the family business influences the family due to the structural coupling and shapes their family communication. Of course, the gradations of structural coupling must be considered.

If all three systems are finally compared again, then pose different expectations on the adolescents. The "main mediator" of these expectations is the family. The expectations of society and the business are, among other things, (in)directly conveyed by the family. Within the framework of a family business, the parents' desire to pass on the business to their descendants has a decisive influence on their socialization, and thus on their identity. Other influencing factors are the size of the family and the prevailing role structure within it. The business system, on the other hand, is shaped by the subject of the enterprise, the industry, the size, and the age. These factors characterize the family business, and thus also the structural coupling with the family system. As it became clear, the nature of the family business, for example, affects the parents' upbringing behavior and the choice of education and often leads to gender differentiation. Both systems are embedded in society or this represents the environment for both systems. Here too, the social system can only exert its influence on the descendants via members or communication. It sets, among other things, the cultural framework within which the other two systems operate. Therefore, the role of communication and language in particular should be emphasized again. Without it, no identity can be formed. The identity of children from family businesses thus develops in the "field of tension" between society, family, and business.

4.3.2 The Family Business as a Context of Socialization

After the last chapter identified three essential systems (society, family, and business) that influence the development of identity, this chapter is dedicated to the socialization context of family businesses. Although Fig. 4.6 represents the influences on identity, it is too static or incapable of adequately representing the dynamics. The business system has many stages of development. As became apparent under Sect. 2.5, the family business must be attributed an effect on the descendant's living environment due to the structural coupling. The structural coupling can be seen as a "regulatory mechanism". Through it, the two systems develop co-evolutionarily. Since the family business requires different competencies at each stage, this also affects the family and the education of the successors in particular. The theoretical foundation was developed in Chap. 3. In addition, reference is made to the merging of the three theories carried out under Sect. 3.4. This provides an analytical framework and enables a basic understanding of how social systems work, their dynamics, and how these affect the identity of the members acting within them. Since family businesses are individual and differ along the multi-generational continuum, the theoretical basis opens the possibility of uncovering commonalities, irrespective of the respective form of appearance. The findings then in turn represent the starting point for generalizable statements.

To be able to comprehensively represent the influence of the business system and its possible evolution, the following form of presentation (see Fig. 4.7) is chosen. In it, the factors identified in this work are taken up to provide an answer to the research question, i.e., "*how the socialization and the identity formation of descendants from family businesses in particular is influenced by the structural coupling of the family to a business*".

First, Fig. 4.7 makes a distinction based on the different generations. This considers the special feature that family businesses place different demands on the (family) members in each generation (see Sect. 2.2). Along the multi-generational existence, an ideal-typical growth in size of the family and the business is assumed. For each generation, the theoretical insights gained are then used to identify factors that can have a (in)direct impact on the identity formation of the demands during their socialization. The upper half depicts the possible dynamic aspects. These factors provide an understanding of why the family business is a unique socialization context for the descendants in every life cycle (see Sect. 4.2). In the lower part, it is then discussed how the family business, through its structural coupling to the family, can influence the formation of the identity of the descendants. This differentiation allows to gain an understanding of the life world encountered in each generation for the descendants.

If we first look at the individual generations in Fig. 4.7, the following picture emerges:

1. In the *first generation* only one family usually participates in the business. This typically consists of the parents and the children. The ownership of the enterprise is bundled in the hands of one family.

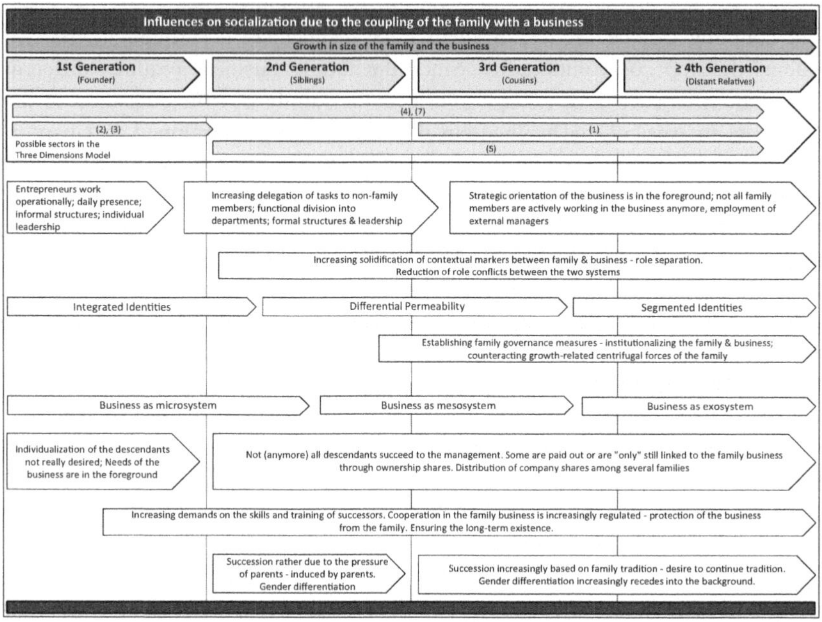

Fig. 4.7 Influences on the socialization of entrepreneurial children (own work)

2. Assuming that in the *second generation* several descendants succeed to the business and they establish their own families, the ownership of the business is divided among several families. Due to the larger number of family members, there may be an increase in complexity, although this does not necessarily have to be the case.
3. In the *third generation* the circle of shareholders continues to grow. The kinship relationships may become looser as the family members may not necessarily know each other anymore. The complexity continues to increase.
4. From the *fourth generation* onwards, we speak of multi-generational family businesses. The participating family members are distant relatives. Non-family members may also already participate in the family business. Due to the increased number of members involved, it is very likely that the individual's share of the family business's assets is small.

In addition to this, the possible sectors of the Three-Dimensional Model (see Sect. 2.3.1) are depicted. It becomes apparent how the family business changes along the generations. Thus, sectors (2) and (3) are more likely to occur in the first generation. Family businesses that fall into sector (3) can also be inherited, but only to a descendant. In Fig. 4.7, however, a family growth is assumed, i.e., the re-enactment of the nuclear family from generation to generation is excluded. On the other hand, a family business will fall into sector (1) when the family and the business have a certain size. This is only assumed from the third generation onwards. On the other hand, a family business can already be located in sector (5) from the second generation onwards, as the bond to the family business can already decrease. This can be particularly due to the strong involvement of the first generation, which also puts the family members in the public focus. Finally, if the two sectors (4) and (7) are considered, their occurrence is assumed for all generations. Sector (7) combines all three dimensions and therefore has the greatest potential to generate familiness. Although, the maintenance of all dimensions along the generations will increasingly be more difficult, it is not impossible. Due to the structural coupling and the resulting co-evolution, conclusions can thus be drawn about the extent of enterpriseness. This will in turn influence the life world, and thus the socialization of the descendants.

After the family constellation of each generation and the possible location in the Three-Dimensional Model has been explained, this section deals with the resulting structural changes for the family and the business (see Fig. 4.7). If the first generation is initially considered, the participation of both parents in the enterprise is usually necessary due to their financial burdens. As a result, they are present in the enterprise every day, which can lead to a reduction in family time. The enterprise grows into a relevant life world for the entrepreneur's children, as they may spend a lot of time in it. Due to the size of the enterprise, the structures are informal and the leadership is individual, i.e., shaped by the personality of the entrepreneur(s). Due to the growth in size, these structures are increasingly overloaded. There is a need to delegate management tasks to non-family members as well. To reduce complexity, the family business is usually divided into functional departments, such as sales, purchasing, etc. In particular, the handover to several descendants may require or favor this division so that each descendant receives his "fair" share of the family business. Likewise, the entrepreneurs will no longer be involved in operational activities to the same extent. As communication becomes increasingly complex, there is a growing need for formal structures and formal or indirect leadership. From the third generation onwards, the strategic orientation of the family business will increasingly come to the fore. Due to family growth, an ever-increasing number of family members participate in the family business. Also, not all management tasks are necessarily performed by family members. The family business is approaching the characteristics of a non-family business. Due to this development, context markers between the two systems are very likely, as individual family members are no longer involved in the business to the extent required in the first generation. This leads to a reduction of conflicts between the family and the business role. The family business will no longer determine communication within the family to the same extent. A separation of roles becomes possible. In this context, a development from integrated to segmented identities (see Table 2.2) can take place, with many variations possible against the background of the Three-Dimensional Model. As the "distance" of family members to the business increases, the emotional attachment to it can decrease and family governance measures can counteract these centrifugal forces. These must be actively established by the family to "regulate" their influence on the business or, above all, to ensure the long-term survival of the family business. This will also change the form of enterpriseness. If this initially emanates from the business, the influence of the business on the members is more likely to be induced or determined by the family itself through the justification of family governance measures.

Now, if we specifically consider the descendants who are socialized in the context of a family business, or in the "tension field" between the family and business system, the factors or dynamics already presented, contribute to the effect of the business system on the growing up. The development of the two systems from integrated to segmented identities also has an influence on the descendants. In the first and partly during the second generation, the family business often represents a microsystem. This has the consequence that the family business acts as an additional immediate living environment. The boundaries between the two systems — family and business — are fluid. Since context markers do not yet exist, business-related communication can have an unimpeded effect on the descendants. Along the multi-generational existence, the family business will increasingly develop into an exosystem from the perspective of the descendants. This is primarily driven by the growth of the family and the business. Due to the developing context markers, the descendants are no longer exposed to the business-specific communication to the same extent. Also, the parents' work roles are no longer as tangible for the children as they often are in the first generation. Rather, contact with the family business no longer necessarily takes place in childhood and no longer represents an immediate living environment for the growing up. Socialization will rather take place as in non-business families. However, the influence of the family business can be "replaced" by possible family governance measures or transition into these.

The (co-)evolution of the two systems often results in a changed perspective on the descendants. The first generation will give the growing up and the potential successors in particular less opportunity for individual development. There, the needs of the enterprise are predominantly in the foreground. This can be explained by the fact that there is only a limited number of successors and the desire to pass on the "life's work" to the next generation. As the family grows, the second generation has a larger pool of potential successors available. In addition, the growth of the family business can promote the employment of non-family managers. Thus, not all descendants have to take over the management succession or this is not even possible due to the limited positions in the family business. The enterprise is increasingly divided among several family members, which can lead to a decrease in emotional attachment. Some members are paid out, which results in a decoupling of the structural coupling. Others limit themselves to the role of owner. Due to the increasing complexity within the family business, potential successors are also confronted with increasing demands on their education and competencies. Due to the number of family members participating in the business, access to the family business is increasingly controlled, for example, by family governance measures. This serves to maintain the family business in the long term and to protect it from the family. Since at least one parent from the second generation has experience with succession and the associated requirements, future generations are often given more freedom. Succession is no longer necessarily considered due to parental pressure, but rather because of a certain obligation to family tradition or the desire to be a member of the business family. In addition, along the multi-generational existence, there can be a dissolution of gender differentiation during succession. Also, since potential successors are given more freedom, male descendants no longer feel obliged to follow in their parents' footsteps, which increases the chances for female successors.

If the research question is brought to the foreground again, i.e., *how the socialization and the identity formation of descendants from family businesses in particular is influenced by the structural coupling of the family to a business*, the question of "how" cannot be answered unequivocally in the sense of a cause-effect view. The diversity of possible influencing factors complicates this possibility. What can be assumed, however, is an influence of the family size and the business size as well as the respective age of the family business or the participating generation. The subject of the family business and the industry will also influence socialization and identity formation, for example, through a corresponding choice of education or work in the enterprise. These were not explicitly shown in Fig. 4.7, as they are considered dispositional factors along the generations. As was evident from the inclusion of the Three-Dimensional Model, the extent of the family's influence on the business is significantly influenced by the family participating in the enterprise. Due to the structural coupling, this in turn affects the influence of the family business (enterpriseness) on the socialization and identity formation of the descendants. Although a "drifting apart" of the two systems can be assumed along the multi-generational existence, the extent is determined by the family itself. This also includes the extent to which the family business grows into an exosystem or a segmented identity. Since the family and the business are social systems, communication serves as a transmitter that conveys the (role) expectations directed at the descendants or potential successors. As the structural coupling changes, the patterns of communication will also change. The developing context markers increasingly prevent the "appropriation" of family communication by business communication and vice versa. However, the family then often creates a bond with the business out of itself. Even if multi-generational family businesses (must) approach the characteristics of non-family businesses or the business family participating in the family business no longer actively works in the business over time, there is still an essential difference to non-business families: Through ownership of the enterprise, every family member is structurally coupled to the family business, whereby the business enters the family system. The extent to which this occurs is determined by the business family participating in the family business. In contrast to non-business families, mechanisms exist that counteract the centrifugal forces of family alienation and open the possibility for the family business to have a formative influence on the family and subsequently on the socialization and identity formation of the descendants in each generation.

4.4 Final Considerations in this Chapter

4.4.1 Summary of Results

Before the findings are summarized in relation to the research context, the following sections serve to present the most important points of the theories used. Since different perspectives were considered in this work, i.e., *how external societal influences are internalized by an individual during socialization,* this also had to be considered when selecting the theories used. To meet this requirement, Luhmannian Systems theory and Symbolic Interactionism were initially used. Both approaches can be described as theories of greater reach, although they differ in their respective perspectives. While Systems theory takes a more analytical focus and tries to provide (abstracting) explanation and representation of societal contexts, Symbolic Interactionism looks at the inner perspective of an individual.

The starting point is the view that development always takes place in relation to a societal context of experience and events.

For both theories communication plays a central role. Systems theory serves as the starting point for the emergence of social systems. Communication represents the irreducible element of a social system and works as an operation that serves the social system for autopoietic reproduction. Thus, communication is the basic prerequisite for the continuation of a system. If it ends, so does the autopoiesis. Furthermore, communication is structurally coupled to consciousness, whereby consciousness can support and irritate communication. In comparison, communication in Symbolic Interactionism enables a mutual orientation of the participants. For this to succeed, the same meaning must first be generated in the consciousness of the participants, which is done through a stock of signs that have the same meaning for everyone. Communication therefore only occurs when the gesture made by an individual triggers the same reaction in the other person as it does in itself. This then becomes a significant symbol. Subsequently, communication enables role-taking and creates identity. In both theories, language in particular must be attributed a significant role. This is seen in both theories as an important medium of communication. While language from the system-theoretical perspective enables an understanding of psychological processes of other people, and thus favors an increase in the number of behaviors with which others can then be informed, language in Symbolic Interactionism serves as the most meaningful tool of socialization. Identity in particular is dependent on the possibilities of language representation. Expectations between individuals can be addressed in this way. Language is seen as a system of significant symbols that contributes to an increase in possible diversity of meaning and promotes the definition and appropriation of roles.

In symbolic interactionism, the role in particular is understood as a "constellation of learned meanings". Communication enables the individual to learn his social roles. The family, the peer group, the school, and the profession are seen as significant role mediators. Above all, an individual's identity includes a variety of roles. From the perspective of Systems theory, the person combines different roles. In each situation it can perform a different role, whereby expectations serve as a point of reference. Since both theories use the concept of roles, it was also necessary, in the course of this work, to establish a common understanding of this. For this purpose, Role theory was used as a third theory of greater scope. This allows for a characterization of social systems and human actions as the primary unit of analysis and description. As with the other two theories, the assumption is that a person/individual combines different roles, depending on how many social systems they participate in. Learning takes place during socialization and allows for a connection to the respective social system. Roles of different people refer to each other, which allows for role adaptation. Therefore, roles can be understood as dynamic structures. The expectations placed on a role allow for a kind of "prediction" of behavior or role actions. They can be understood as ideas about what is desired or what should be avoided. Sanctions serve as a control mechanism that require a change in behavior. To finally gain an understanding of how the different social systems (areas of life) can be connected and how entering a new area of life enables socialization processes, Bronfenbrenner's Ecological Systems Model was used. In each area of life, different expectations prevail, which are communicated to the person, and thus contribute to their shaping. Areas of life to which the individual does not belong as an active person can also have an indirect influence on them.

If we now focus on the context of the investigation, considering the theoretical findings, the family business can be seen as an entity that is composed of at least two social systems; each operates according to different logics. When analyzing systems and family businesses in particular, it therefore makes sense to carry out a system specification as a first step. This could include the following questions:

1. What are the (common) elements in the systems?
2. What relationship do they have to each other?
3. What arrangements are associated with this?
4. What purpose does the system serve?
5. What relationships exist with the environment?

For example, the family members (in the sense of the formal term person) can be understood as elements that serve the business system to maintain communication, whereby the persons also have a family relationship with each other in addition to the entrepreneurial relationship. Thus, they are simultaneously exposed to different (role) expectations. Furthermore, there is a hierarchical structure in it and the purpose is to provide for the family. To achieve these goals, there is an exchange relationship with the environment in the form of products or services for a counter value. Specifically for the analysis of systems, Systems theory offers a common framework to analyze systems with different logics.

However, to gain a well-founded understanding of the family business as a (special) form of enterprise from a systems theory perspective, it must be understood as two structurally coupled social systems. If a family has no ownership interest in the business, it or individual members may be loosely coupled to a business at most. However, then there will be no possibility for the business or the family to have a structure-determining influence on the other system. If there is no structural coupling, the family business is "only" an enterprise and the business family is "only" a family, i.e., both systems lose their special status. The structural coupling is further intensified by the family members' participation in the family business. Through structural coupling each system represents a relevant or significant environment for the other. The family and business systems mutually influence and utilize each other without clearly determining the autonomy of the other system. Changes in one system cause adaptations in the other system. The intensity or extent of the coupling then depends on the variables shared by the two systems. In the case of a family business, the family members have membership in both systems. This allows the respective systems to influence each other. This has been extensively explained with the concepts of familiness and enterpriseness. Through the (family) members the communicated expectations of one system can rub off on the other system and vice versa.

Another peculiarity resulting from the structural coupling is the existing co-evolution between the systems. Specifically, this contributes to the simultaneous or mutual development of both systems. Thus, any growth of the family and/or the business may require a (structural) adjustment in the other system. For example, if the family business is to be handed over to several descendants as part of the succession, this may necessitate the establishment of new areas/divisions in the enterprise, which enables all successor families to make a financial living or avoids disputes. Similarly, the family business may require adjustments (e.g., for the education of the descendants) within the family due to potential growth. This work has shown that children of entrepreneurs, unlike children from non-business families, are exposed to additional influences that affect their socialization and specifically their identity. If the family and the business are therefore viewed against the background of a family business, these two systems each represent important environments for each other. The peculiarity lies in the permeability of the boundaries and in the presence of family members in both systems. In addition, the family can influence the business as a significant environment and vice versa. For the respective system, there is then either the possibility to change itself or to modify the environment. For example, internal family succession may be ruled out if the family business requires a high level of management competence and no one in the family meets this requirement. Similarly, there will be an aversion to internal family takeover if the profitability of the family business is not guaranteed. However, the Ecological Systems Model also showed, to what extent the business system as a socialization context can be subject to change. Therefore, a meaningful analysis always requires a look at the development stage of the family business.

For the systems theoretical view, society — the macrosystem — as a comprehensive social system must also be granted the ability to influence family businesses and the business family linked to them. Depending on the societal framework in which family businesses operate, the starting point for the analysis will be different. The potential influence of other institutions embedded in a certain cultural context should not be neglected. For example, secondary socialization takes place in kindergarten or school. Their task is primarily to provide the growing children with a certain level of education and to introduce them to the demands of the performance society and professional life. In doing so, the first two socialization institutions influence the growing children in their career choice or steer them in a certain direction. However, the family business must also be granted an influence on the secondary socialization of the descendants. Depending on the sector and phase the family business is in as well as the competences it requires from the future entrepreneurs this will affect the choice of school type and the choice of education or studies. It is therefore particularly relevant to narrow down the context or area of investigation when examining socialization.

If communication is considered, it serves the systems to generate meaning to distinguish themselves from the environment through so-called sense boundaries. Since the family and the business represent different social systems, they exhibit different communication patterns. The coupling of the two systems within a family business can lead to misunderstandings, paradoxes, and conflicts, or increase the frequency of their occurrence. Specifically, the structural coupling between the family and the business or between the business and the family members influences the construction or structure of the family business. If language is viewed as a form of communication and the role structures within the family, these have an influence on the socialization that takes place. Expectations of the role are primarily conveyed through language. In the context of a family business, an additional influence on the socialization of adolescents should therefore be attributed due to the existing structural coupling of the "language of the business" and the expectations that prevail or are communicated within it. This will also provide an understanding of the roles prevailing in the family business. Specifically, identity can then be understood as an "ability" to respond to the various role requirements.

According to Symbolic Interactionism, it is precisely the communication that occurs in social systems that enables roles to be assumed. Due to the structural coupling to a business, the family gains the status of a business family, and thus gains access to the (in)formal roles in their business. The family members are subsequently exposed to the expectations, traditions, rights, and duties of the business system. Therefore, when considering the development of identity within a family business, the business system also exerts its influence on it. Above all, the structural coupling can be seen as a starting point for additional influencing factors and role models to which the children of entrepreneurs are exposed in contrast to children from non-business families. In the context of a family business, the meaning and processes of the family business are conveyed to the descendants through the interaction with the involved family members and employees. Since communication is the origin for role-taking, this allows the growing children to take on the role of the entrepreneur or other (family) members employed in the family business at an early stage. The child can, for example, "play" the entrepreneur and during socialization put themselves in the shoes of a variety of people or role models (worker, manager, shareholder, etc.). Through the structural coupling, the growing children therefore gain an understanding of the role as an entrepreneur, manager, or owner, i.e., the expectations attached to it at a very early stage. In addition, role-taking enables the child to gain insights into the social reality within the family business and to estimate the expectations for possible obligations, responsibilities, and rights of a child of an entrepreneur or potential entrepreneur. Thus, role-taking gives the growing children an understanding of how social systems work and promotes the acceptance of social expectations such as rules or laws. Specifically, the role-taking of the generalized other encourages the descendants to act as expected of them. Since different expectations, norms, and traditions apply within the family and within the business in family businesses, the child has the opportunity to acquire these at a very early stage. However, the development of identity within a family business can also be problematic, as adolescents are simultaneously confronted with an increased number of different, sometimes contradictory roles and the resulting paradoxes, which they perceive and whose expectations they (have to) fulfill. This can include the role as a descendant, as a potential successor, as a future heir, etc. The diverging expectations have a certain potential for conflict and their impact on socialization should have become apparent in the course of this work.

When considering the norms and expectations that exist within systems, there are many that are valid for all members within a society. Others, however, differ from family to family, which means that each family has its own individual form of appearance. Due to the structural coupling with the business, each family business also has an individual form of appearance with a specific set of expectations. In addition, the business (due to the industry, the enterprise's subject matter, size, etc.) has its own individual set of expectations, which in turn influences the actions of the family members. This has an impact on the socialization of the descendants. Also, the young people are exposed to a kind of extended sanctioning if they do not meet these expectations. In addition to the family expectations, they often must follow the business expectations as well. However, as has been shown, the possible "simultaneity" of expectations can increasingly disappear during growth in size and the multi-generational existence of the family business. This was clarified by the change in structural coupling using the Ecological Systems Model.

As the family can be seen as a transmitter of values, the values are not only transferred to the adolescents. These values also find their way into the corporate system, which explains the familial character of many family businesses. If values now change within the family or across generations, this will also rub off on the business due to the coupling. Specifically in an increasingly individualized society, the willingness of potential successors to take over the business can be reduced as they prefer to go their own way, which then jeopardizes the continued existence of the family business. Another problem associated with the change in values is the increasing competition between starting a family and other life plans. Regarding this, however, there is a presumption that precisely because of the link to the business there is a desire to pass on the family business or the shares in it to descendants at some point in the future. Due to the importance of the business for the family and for the parents in particular, certain values can therefore be represented or conveyed within the family, which limit the individualization tendencies of the descendants and strengthen their desire for succession or continuation of the tradition.

The pluralization of lifestyles that is taking place should also be mentioned, which also has an influence on business families. Along with the loss of power, this can also lead to an increasing loss of function of the family. Since the family must be seen as a constitutive characteristic of a family business, it was essential to establish a (more universal) definition of (business) family. In addition to a link to Systems theory, this enables new lifestyles (e.g. cohabitation or same-sex couples) to be taken into account and thus leads to an expansion of the concept. If the bond between the individual members and the parents within a family in particular is also considered, it becomes increasingly loose, i.e., the connection between the parents dissolves more and more frequently. However, in the case of business families, the opposite is likely to be the case due to the coupling to the business. The family business has the potential to strengthen the parents' sense of meaning for a shared life. On the other hand, this may also be due to the joint debt burden, as a separation entails serious financial burdens. In addition, the shared reputation as well as the social status or amenities provided by the enterprise can have a strengthening effect on the common bond.

When it comes to business succession and the socialization of descendants (as potential successors), gender often has a differentiated influence on the intensity of the business on young people. Based on the work differences became evident. In the literature on succession and the interview excerpts shown here, the majority of references are to (first-born) male successors. However, due to increasing individualization, the first-born no longer necessarily feel obliged to succession. This then opens the possibility for any siblings to take over the family business. For the influence of the enterprise on the siblings the life cycle of the family business must be considered again. In the start-up phase, parents are likely to spend less time with a child than if it is born at a stage when the company is already established. On the other hand, children are more likely to be confronted with or involved in the enterprise because their parents spend a lot of time there, which may change in later generations. Therefore, it must be considered in which generation the family business is. If one child can be given more attention due to the development of the enterprise, this could provoke sibling rivalries.

If the upbringing, i.e., the "active guidance" of the entrepreneur's children by the parents is considered, then this must be attributed a significant influence. It is precisely through the structural coupling that the business context will find its way into the parents' upbringing behavior. The parents can actively convey certain perspectives, expectations, and abilities to the children that are considered relevant for the enterprise. As has become apparent, differences between the various generations are to be expected. Another special feature in business families is the possibility of the father, in his work role, to serve as a direct role model for the sons. In non-business families with a traditional role distribution, this is usually reserved for the mothers. They mainly look after the children, although their role model function is more limited to the daughters. As the fathers work outside the home, they are not available as role models, especially for the sons, due to the different contexts. The father's working world represents an exosystem for them. The situation is different in business families. Due to the structural coupling, the enterprise often finds its way into private life and the enterprise represents an additional living environment for the adolescents, whereby the children actively experience the working world or the work within the enterprise. However, as can be seen from the findings of the Ecological Systems Model, this influence also undergoes changes along the multi-generational existence.

In summary, the family business must be attributed an influence through the members acting in it (specifically the parents as primary caregivers and other family members) on the socialization and upbringing be granted. Thus, the adolescents will often be exposed to a tertiary socialization at the same time. Due to the usually early contact with the enterprise, be it through communication or work in it, tertiary socialization can take place earlier in the case of entrepreneurial children than in the case of non-entrepreneurial children. This will take place parallel to primary and secondary socialization. However, this can also expose the descendants to role conflicts. For them, the problem may be to recognize in which role the family members are currently speaking to them (mother or entrepreneur). Dealing with the resulting expectations can increase the psychological strain on the descendants, as these can be contradictory. On the other hand, children also have the opportunity to learn how to deal with this "mixing" and the resulting paradoxes at an early age. For them, it can be something completely natural. The descendants thus gain knowledge about the work as well as about the various processes in the family business. If multi-generational family businesses are considered, not only the parents, but also the relatives who actively work in the family business or participate as owners in the family business also exert their influence on the descendants. As the descendants grow up in or with the family business, this is probably perceived by them as a kind of natural living environment.

In families that are only connected to the business through ownership/ownership shares, the socialization of the descendants will increasingly align with that of non-business families, whereby the simultaneous experience of primary and tertiary socialization is no longer given. While the descendants mostly experience the enterprise in the first and second generation as a (single) microsystem, in the case of multi-generational family businesses there will mostly be an increasing division of the system. Therefore, the business is no longer available to the same extent as a socialization context or living environment. The descendants experience the family "only" as a microsystem and the business "only" as an exosystem. As a result, the descendants will no longer be exposed to the paradoxes and (role) conflicts to the same extent, as the simultaneous experience of the roles is no longer given to the same extent. Likewise, there will no longer necessarily be a need for business succession, as the management function can be performed by external managers. The family members can rather focus on their ownership function. However, precisely due to the multi-generational existence and the resulting family history, considerable pressure can be exerted on the descendants to continue the family tradition or the management of the family business successfully. This means that the structural coupling also has a certain effect on members who are only connected to the family business through ownership shares, e.g., on the choice of education or studies. Due to the ownership shares, these belong to the business family, which in turn can shape the identity of the family as a business family and the growing up in particular. Intensity, on the other hand, is influenced by identification with the family business, with the following factors having an impact on this:

1. Distance of the living area to the family business
2. Work both parents in the family business
3. What attitude does the in-law parent have towards the family business
4. Integration of the descendants into the family business
5. Intertwining of private and working life
6. Enterprise's potential to provide for the family (in the long term)
7. Existence of family governance measures
8. Industry, the enterprise's subject matter, the size and age of the family business

Regular meetings of family members or a family constitution intensify this. This can pose a particular challenge for old family businesses, where hundreds of family members may have a stake in the family business. Above all, any family governance measures reinforce the enterpriseness, which in turn affects the behavior of family members, and thus also socialization.

This work makes clear, what range of variation family businesses have. They differ not only from each other, but also along their existence. For an understanding of the influence of the family business on the descendants or an investigation of the living world of the descendants, it is therefore necessary, to take these dynamics into account. In conclusion, however, it must be assumed that the influence of the business system on the socialization and identity formation of the descendants is largely determined by the business family itself. This acts as a "transmitter" of business communication into the family system, i.e., expectations, traditions, etc. This is made possible because the individual family members have memberships in both systems.

4.4.2 Relevance of Results

The primary concern of the present work was to create an awareness for the socialization of descendants from family businesses. Since this topic has not yet been worked up in this form, the focus was primarily on theoretical concepts or explanatory approaches that were considered helpful for the development. Particularly regarding the conflicts that often occur in family businesses (during succession), this work should sensitize people to the fact that the causes may already be found in the childhood of the descendants. Based on the selection and presentation of the contents, it became clear, to what extent socialization or contact with the family business can reduce or increase the willingness to succeed. In particular, if the descendants cannot decide freely and their life path is determined from birth, this can have negative effects on the personality of the successors, put them under stress, and, in extreme cases, endanger the continuity of the family business.

In particular, the succession literature usually comes too late regarding this. When advising business families in the succession process, this should therefore not only include business management or legal components. Likewise, the focus on potential successors should not begin with the actual handover. Rather, holistic consulting must also take into account the childhood of the successors, as events that occurred or were experienced there can have a negative impact on the family dynamics, on the relationship between the descendants, and on the succession. Thus, the findings of the present work should sensitize or provide an understanding of how the life world and subsequently the identity of the descendants is influenced and how this affects a possible willingness to succeed. The secondary interviews in particular made it possible to clarify the perspective of the descendants. Although these served for illustrative purposes, they provided insights into the experience of the descendants, i.e., how they experience growing up in a family business.

Looking at the research on family businesses, it is characterized mainly by its interdisciplinary approach. The use of the systems theory makes it possible to present the characteristics of a family business. Nevertheless, the analysis usually comes too late. If conflicts, the change of generations, or the dynamics in family businesses are considered, they often ignore sociological explanations. Therefore, the presentation of socialization using Systems theory and Symbolic Interactionism carried out in this work can provide new impulses for the existing content. Similarly, Role theory provides additional explanations for the mechanisms by which conflicts arise or how expectations affect the (role) behavior of individual members and especially on the descendants and their socialization. The business family (parents, siblings, and relatives) and employees can serve as role models for the descendants. This and the expectations tied to it can shape the identity of the growing children. Although, this approach provided a basic insight into the socialization, it is essential for further research and in detail for further theory gain to substantiate the gained knowledge using empirical survey methods. This should provide further insights regarding the topic presented here.

In summary, the selection of theories and the comprehensive processing of the literature make it possible to present the complex relationships that occur within a family business and can significantly influence the socialization of the descendants in a comprehensible manner. Above all, the stabilization that takes place across generations within family businesses could be presented.

Finally, further research questions are presented, which arose in the course of this work, but could not be dealt with further due to the necessary limitation.

4.4.3 Further Questions

Based on the topic chosen in the present work, the following additional contents arise, which could be interesting for further research:

1. How does the life path of entrepreneurial children who were socialized in the context of a family business, but did not take over the succession, look like? Is there a lasting influence on the values, attitudes, or a possible entrepreneurial activity to be recognized?
2. To what extent does the industry or the subject of the family business affect the intensity of the structural coupling between family and business, and thus the socialization of the descendants?
3. How does birth order affect the choice of successor and the socialization of the descendants?
4. How can the socialization of entrepreneurial children be explained with the concept of social capital?
5. What effects does the development of the family system into multiple subsystems have on the members residing therein?

Bibliography

Abels, H. & König, A. (2010): Sozialisation. Soziologische Antworten auf die Frage, wie wir werden, was wir sind, wie gesellschaftliche Ordnung möglich ist und wie Theorien der Gesellschaft und der Identität ineinanderspielen, Wiesbaden: VS Verlag für Sozialwissenschaften.

Ackerman, C. & Parsons, T. (1976): Der Begriff „Sozialsystem" als theoretisches Instrument, in: Parsons, T. (Ed.): Zur Theorie sozialer Systeme. Herausgegeben und eingeleitet von Stefan Jensen, Opladen: Westdeutscher Verlag, 69–84.

Adamaszek, M. (2005): Kernkonflikte kindlicher Loyalität. Ein familienbiografischer Zugang, in: Busch, F. W. & Nave-Herz, R. (Eds.): Familie und Gesellschaft: Beiträge zur Familienforschung, Oldenburg: BIS-Verlag, 292–316.

AG Soziologie (1999): Denkweisen und Grundbegriffe der Soziologie. Eine Einführung, 14. Aufl., Frankfurt a. M. und New York: Campus Verlag.

Akerstrom Andersen, N. (2003): The undecidability of decision, in: Bakken, T. & Hernes, T. (Eds.): Autopoietic Organization Theory. Drawing on Niklas Luhmann's Social Systems Perspective, Frederiksberg: Copenhagen Business School Press, 235–258.

Arregle, J.-L.; Hitt, M. A.; Sirmon, D. G. & Very, P. (2007): The Development of Organizational Social Capital: Attributes of Family Firms, in: *Journal of Management Studies*, 44 (1), 73–95. https://doi.org/10.1111/j.1467-6486.2007.00665.x

Aronoff, C. E. & Ward, J. L. (2011): Family Business Governance. Maximizing Family and Business Potential, New York: Palgrave Macmillan.

Astrachan, J. H.; Klein, S. B. & Smyrnios, K. X. (2002): The F-PEC scale of family influence: A proposal for solving the family business definition problem, in: *Family Business Review*, 15 (1), 45–58. https://doi.org/10.1111/j.1741-6248.2002.00045

Auwärter, M.; Kirsch, E. & Schröter, K. (1977) [Eds.]: Seminar: Kommunikation, Interaktion, Identität, 2. Aufl., Frankfurt a. M.: Suhrkamp.

Baecker, D. (2004): Niklas Luhmann: Einführung in die Systemtheorie, 2. Aufl., Heidelberg: Carl-Auer-Systeme Verlag.

Baecker, D. (2002): Wozu Systeme?, Berlin: Kulturverlag Kadmos.

Bakken, T. & Hernes, T. (2003) [Eds.]: Autopoietic Organization Theory. Drawing on Niklas Luhmann's Social Systems Perspective, Frederiksberg: Copenhagen Business School Press.

S. Caspary, *The Family Business as a Socialisation Context for the Children of Entrepreneurs*, https://doi.org/10.1007/978-3-658-43657-5

Baldwin, A. L. (1974): Theorien primärer Sozialisationsprozesse. Aus dem Amerikanischen von Dietrich Eggert, Bd. 2, Weinheim u. a.: Beltz Verlag.

Baraldi, C.; Corsi, G. & Esposito, E. (1997): GLU: Glossar zu Niklas Luhmanns Theorie sozialer Systeme, Frankfurt a. M.: Suhrkamp.

Bates, F. L. (1956): Position, Role, and Status: A Reformulation of Concepts, in: *Social Forces*, 34 (4), 313–321. https://doi.org/10.2307/2573663

Bateson, G. (1992): Ökologie des Geistes. Anthropologische, psychologische, biologische und epistemologische Perspektiven. Übersetzt von Hanz Günter Holl, 4. Aufl., Frankfurt a. M.: Suhrkamp.

Baumgartner, B. (2009): Familienunternehmen und Zukunftsgestaltung. Schlüsselfaktoren zur erfolgreichen Unternehmensnachfolge, Wiesbaden: Gabler.

Baumrind, D. (1966): Effects of authoritative parental control on child behavior, in: *Child Development*, 37 (4), 887–907. https://doi.org/10.2307/1126611

Baus, K. (2010): Die Familienstrategie: Wie Familien ihr Unternehmen über Generationen sichern, 3. Aufl., Wiesbaden: Gabler.

Baus, K. (2006): Die Familienstrategie in der Unternehmernachfolge, in: Brost, H.; Faust, M. & Thedens, C. (Eds.): Unternehmensnachfolge im Mittelstand, 2. Aufl., München: Bankakademie Verlag GmbH, 43-60.

Beck, U. (1986): Risikogesellschaft. Auf dem Weg in eine andere Moderne, Frankfurt a. M.: Suhrkamp.

Beckmann, R.; Brost, H. & Faust, M. (2012) [Eds.]: Unternehmensnachfolge im Mittelstand, 3. kompl. überarb. Aufl., Frankfurt a. M.: Frankfurt School Verlag.

Bee, C. & Neubaum, D. O. (2014): The role of cognitive appraisal and emotions of family members in the family business system, in: *Journal of Family Business Strategy*, 5 (3), 323–333. https://doi.org/10.1016/j.jfbs.2013.12.001

Beehr, T. A.; Drexler, J. A. & Faulkner, S. (1997): Working in small family businesses: empirical comparisons to non-family businesses, in: *Journal of Organizational Behavior*, 18 (3), 297–312. https://doi.org/10.1002/(SICI)1099-1379(199705)18:3<297::AID-JOB805>3.0.CO;2-D

Berger, P. L. & Luckmann, T. (2000): Die gesellschaftliche Konstruktion der Wirklichkeit. Eine Theorie der Wissenssoziologie, 17. Aufl., Frankfurt a. M.: Fischer.

Berning, D. & Novak, A. (2010): Erfolgsfaktoren der Kanzleinachfolge. Jenseits von Recht und Steuern, Wiesbaden: Gabler.

Bernstein, B. (1973): Ein sozio-linguistischer Ansatz zur Sozialisation: Mit einigen Bezügen auf Erziehbarkeit, in: Claessens, D. & Milhoffer, P. (Eds.): Familiensoziologie. Ein Reader als Einführung, Frankfurt a. M.: Athenäum Fischer Taschenbuch Verlag, 241–270.

Berufsverband Deutscher Psychologinnen und Psychologen e. V. (2010) [Ed.]: Psychologische Expertise für erfolgreiches Unternehmertum in Deutschland, Berlin: Deutscher Psychologen Verlag GmbH.

Bieker, U. & Hirsch, H. (2007): Vom Übergeben und Übernehmen: Zwei Beispiele aus Familienunternehmen, in: *Organisationsberatung, Supervision, Coaching* (OSC), 14 (4), 376–391. https://doi.org/10.1007/s11613-007-0048-2

Bieler, S. (2012): Psychologische Hürden der Unternehmensnachfolge aus Sicht des Senior-Unternehmers, in: Beckmann, R.; Brost, H. & Faust, M. (Eds.): Unternehmensnachfolge im Mittelstand, 3. kompl. überarb. Aufl., Frankfurt a. M.: Frankfurt School Verlag, 17–36.

Blum, U. & Leibbrand, F. (2001) [Eds.]: Entrepreneurship und Unternehmertum: Denkstrukturen für eine neue Zeit, Wiesbaden: Gabler.

Blumer, H. (2013): Symbolischer Interaktionismus: Aufsätze zu einer Wissenschaft der Interpretation. Herausgegeben von Heinz Bude und Michael Dellwing. Aus dem Amerikanischen von Michael Dellwing unter Mitarbeit von Viola Abermet, Berlin: Suhrkamp.

Bourdieu, P. (1987): Die feinen Unterschiede. Kritik der gesellschaftlichen Urteilskraft, Frankfurt a. M.: Suhrkamp.

Brandstätter, H. (1999): Unternehmensgründung und Unternehmenserfolg aus persönlichkeitspsychologischer Sicht, in: Moser, K.; Batinic, B. & Zempel, J. (Eds.): Unternehmerisch erfolgreiches Handeln, Göttingen: Verlag für Angewandte Psychologie, 155-172.

Broer, E.; Ernst, C.; Huber, S.; Kirchdörfer, R.; Peters, B.; Rotfuß, W.; Schmidt, S.; Schröder, M. & Westerheide, P. (2008): Kurzfassung: Wirtschaftliche und gesellschaftliche Bedeutung von Familienunternehmen, Abschlussbericht für das Bundesministerium für Wirtschaft und Technologie, in: *Zentrum für Europäische Wirtschaftsforschung GmbH*, Mannheim.

Bronfenbrenner, U. (1989): Die Ökologie der menschlichen Entwicklung. Natürliche und geplante Experimente. Herausgegeben von Kurt Lüscher. Aus dem Amerikanischen von Anges Cranach, Frankfurt a. M.: Fischer Taschenbuch Verlag.

Brost, H. & Faust, M. (2012): Unternehmensnachfolge im Mittelstand – Daten und Fakten in Deutschland, in: Beckmann, R.; Brost, H. & Faust, M. (Eds.): Unternehmensnachfolge im Mittelstand, 3. kompl. überarb. Aufl., Frankfurt a. M.: Frankfurt School Verlag, 3–16.

Brost, H.; Faust, M. & Thedens, C. (2006) [Eds.]: Unternehmensnachfolge im Mittelstand, 2. Aufl., München: Bankakademie Verlag GmbH.

Brückner, C. (2011): Der Nachfolger kommt! Eine Analyse des Generationenwechsels in Familienunternehmen, Diss., Mering: Rainer Hampp.

Buber, R. & Holzmüller, H. H. (2007) [Eds.]: Qualitative Marktforschung: Methoden – Konzepte – Analysen, Wiesbaden: Gabler.

Buchner, R. (2011): Psychologische Hürden bei der Betriebsübergabe, in: Urnik, S. (Ed.): Unternehmensnachfolge: Betriebswirtschaftliche, rechtliche und psychologische Erfolgsfaktoren, Wien: Linde, 75–92.

Burkart, G. (2008): Familiensoziologie, Konstanz: UVK Verlagsgesellschaft mbH.

Burkart, G. (2005): Die Familie in der Systemtheorie, in: Runkel, G. & Burkart, G. (Eds.): Funktionssysteme der Gesellschaft: Beiträge zur Systemtheorie von Niklas Luhmann, Wiesbaden: VS Verlag für Sozialwissenschaften, 101–128.

Burkart, R. (2002): Kommunikationswissenschaft: Grundlagen und Problemfelder. Umrisse einer interdisziplinären Sozialwissenschaft, 4. überarb. u. akt. Aufl., Wien u. a.: Böhlau Verlag.

Busch, F. W. & Nave-Herz, R. (2005) [Eds.]: Familie und Gesellschaft: Beiträge zur Familienforschung, Oldenburg: BIS-Verlag.

Busch, F. W. & Scholz, W.-D. (2005): Zwischen Bewahrung und Veränderung. Ehe-, Familien- und Erziehungsvorstellungen von Jugendlichen, in: Busch, F. W. & Nave-Herz, R. (Eds.): Familie und Gesellschaft: Beiträge zur Familienforschung, Oldenburg: BIS-Verlag, 125–145.

Busch, F. W. & Scholz, W.-D. (2000): Brauchen Familien Leitbilder?, in: *Oldenburger Universitätsreden*, Nr. 128.

Carlock, R. S. & Ward, J. L. (2001): Strategic Planning for the Family Business. Parallel Planning to Unify the Family and Business, New York: Palgrave.

Caspary, C. R. (2010): Töchter in der Nachfolge von mittelständischen Familienunternehmen. Warum werden oft 50 % des Nachfolgepotentials verschenkt? Eine deskriptive Untersuchung auf Basis der Sozialisationstheorien, Diss., Meckenheim, Wershofen: WDV.

Caspary, S. (2014): Forschungsleistung der Nachfolgeliteratur zu Familienunternehmen – eine Analyse deutschsprachiger Bücher, in: *Zeitschrift für KMU und Entrepreneurship*, 62 (2), 153–182. https://doi.org/10.3790/zfke.62.2.153

Cater, J. & Justis, R. (2009): The Development of Successors from Followers to Leaders in Small Family Firms, in: *Family Business Review*, 22 (2), 109–124. https://doi.org/10.1177/0894486508327822

Chrisman, J. J.; Chua, J. H.; Pearson, A. W. & Barnett, T. (2010): Family Involvement, Family Influence, and Family-Centered Non-Economic Goals in Small Firms, in: *Entrepreneurship Theory Practice*, 36 (2), 267–293. https://doi.org/10.1111/j.1540-6520.2010.0040

Chrisman, J. J.; Sharma, P. & Taggar, S. (2007): Family influences on firms: An introduction, in: *Journal of Business Research*, 60 (10), 1005–1011. https://doi.org/10.1016/j.jbusres.2007.02.016

Chua, J. H.; Chrisman, J. J. & Sharma, P. (1999): Defining the Family Business by Behavior, in: *Entrepreneurship Theory and Practice*, 23 (4), 19–39. https://doi.org/10.1177/104225879902300402

Cizek, B. (2004) [Ed.]: Familienforschung in Österreich: Markierungen–Ergebnisse–Perspektiven, in: *Österreichisches Institut für Familienforschung*, Nr. 12.

Claessens, D. (1979): Familie und Wertesystem. Eine Studie zur „zweiten, sozio-kulturellen Geburt" des Menschen und der Belastbarkeit der „Kernfamilie", 3. überarb. u. erw. Aufl., Berlin: Duncker & Humblot.

Claessens, D. (1968): Rolle und Macht. Grundfragen der Soziologie, Bd. 6, München: Juventa-Verlag.

Claessens, D. & Menne, F. W. (1973): Zur Dynamik der bürgerlichen Familie und ihrer möglichen Alternativen, in: Claessens, D. & Milhoffer, P. (Eds.): Familiensoziologie. Ein Reader als Einführung, Frankfurt a. M.: Athenäum Fischer Taschenbuch Verlag, 313–346.

Claessens, D. & Milhoffer, P. (1973) [Eds.]: Familiensoziologie. Ein Reader als Einführung, Frankfurt a. M.: Athenäum Fischer Taschenbuch Verlag.

Colli, A. (2003): The History of Family Business, 1850-2000, Milan: Cambridge University Press.

Cooper, J. T.; Kidwell, R. E. & Eddelston, K. A. (2013): Boss and Parent, Employee and Child: Work-Family Roles and Deviant Behavior in the Family Firm, in: *Family Relations*, 62 (3), 457–471. https://doi.org/10.1111/fare.12012

Corbetta, G. (1995): Patterns of Development of Family Businesses in Italy, in: *Family Business Review*, 8 (4), 255–265. https://doi.org/10.1111/j.1741-6248.1995.00255.x

Cravota, S. (2010): Managementstrukturen in älteren deutschen Familienunternehmen (verarbeitendes Gewerbe). Eine bundesweite Recherche des Wittener Instituts für Familienunternehmen, in: *WIFU Working Paper Series Nr. 6*, Witten/Herdecke.

Dahrendorf, R. (1977): Homo Sociologicus: Ein Versuch zur Geschichte, Bedeutung und Kritik der Kategorie der sozialen Rolle, 15. Aufl., Opladen: Westdeutscher Verlag.

Damon, W. (1990): Die soziale Welt des Kindes. Übersetzt von Uta S. Eckensberger, Frankfurt a. M.: Suhrkamp.

Danes, S. M.; Rueter, M. A.; Kwon, H. K. & Doherty, W. (2002): Family FIRO model: An application to family business, in: *Family Business Review*, 15 (1), 31–43. https://doi.org/10.1111/j.1741-6248.2002.00031.x

Dasgupta, P. & Serageldin, I. (2000) [Eds.]: Social Capital: A Multifaceted Perspective, Washington D. C.: The World Bank.

Davis, P. (1983): Realizing the Potential of the Family Business, in: *Organizational Dynamics*, 12 (1), 47–56. https://doi.org/10.1016/0090-2616(83)90026-8

Davis, K. (1966): Human Society, New York: The Macmillan Company.

De, D. A. (2005): Entrepreneurship: Gründung und Wachstum von kleinen und mittleren Unternehmen, München: Pearson Education Deutschland GmbH.

Dension, D.; Lief, C. & Ward, J. L. (2004): Culture in Family-Owned Enterprises: Recognizing and Leveraging Unique Strengths, in: *Family Business Review*, 17 (1), 61–70. https://doi.org/10.1111/j.1741-6248.2004.00004.x

Dej, D.; Sztuba, J. & Stephan, U. (2010): Geschlechtsspezifische Unterschiede in der Bewertung von Unternehmenserfolg, in: Berufsverband Deutscher Psychologinnen und Psychologen e. V. (Ed.): Psychologische Expertise für erfolgreiches Unternehmertum in Deutschland, Berlin: Deutscher Psychologen Verlag GmbH, 47–56.

Diem-Wille, G. (1996): Karrierefrauen und Karrieremänner. Eine psychoanalytisch orientierte Untersuchung ihrer Lebensgeschichte und Familiendynamik, Opladen: Westdeutscher Verlag.

Dippelhofer-Stiem, B. (2008): Die Gestalt von Sozialisationsumwelten, in: Hurrelmann, K.; Grundmann, M. & Walper, S. (Eds.): Handbuch Sozialisationsforschung, 7. vollst. überarb. Aufl., Weinheim u. a.: Beltz Verlag, 117–128.

Döbert, R. & Nummer-Winkler, G. (1980): Jugendliche „schlagen über die Stränge". Abwehr- und Bewältigungsstrategien in moralisierbaren Handlungssituationen, in: Eckensberger, L. H. & Silbereisen, R. K. (Eds.): Entwicklung sozialer Kognition: Modelle, Theorien, Methoden, Anwendungen, Stuttgart: Klett-Cotta, 267–298.

Döbert, R.; Habermas, J. & Nummer-Winkler, G. (1980): Entwicklung des Ichs, 2. Aufl., Königstein/Ts: Verl.-Gruppe Athenäum, Hain, Scriptor, Hanstein.

Domayer, E. & Oswald, M. (1994): Der Pionier, sein Unternehmen und die Übergabe. Schlüssel-Fragen für Familienunternehmen, in: *OrganisationsEntwicklung*, 3, 6–16.

Domayer, E. & Vater G. (1995): Das Familienunternehmen. Chancen und Risiken, in: Grossmann, F.; Krainz, E. & Oswald, M. (Eds.): Veränderungen in Organisationen: Management und Beratung, Wiesbaden: Gabler, 149–163.

Domayer, E. & Vater, G. (1994): Das Familienunternehmen – Erfolgstyp oder Auslaufmodell, in: *Hernsteiner*, 2, 26–29.

Dreitzel, H. P. (1980): Die gesellschaftlichen Leiden und das Leiden an der Gesellschaft. Eine Pathologie des Alltagslebens, 3. neuberarb. Aufl., Stuttgart: Ferdinand Enke Verlag.

Dyer, W. G. (2006): Examining the "Family Effect" on Firm Performance, in: *Family Business Review*, 19 (4), 253–273. https://doi.org/10.1111/j.1741-6248.2006.00074.x

Ecarius, J.; Fuchs, T. & Wahl, K. (2008): Der historische Wandel von Sozialisationskontexten, in: Hurrelmann, K.; Grundmann, M. & Walper, S. (Eds.): Handbuch Sozialisationsforschung, 7. vollst. überarb. Aufl., Weinheim und Basel: Beltz Verlag, 104–116.

Eckensberger, L. H. & Silbereisen, R. K. (1980) [Eds.]: Entwicklung sozialer Kognition: Modelle, Theorien, Methoden, Anwendungen, Stuttgart: Klett-Cotta.

Eddleston, K. A. & Morgan, R. M. (2014): Trust, commitment and relationships in family business: Challenging conventional wisdom, in: *Journal of Family Business Strategy*, 5 (3), 213–216. https://doi.org/10.1016/j.jfbs.2014.08.003

Eisenstadt, S. N. (1966): Von Generation zu Generation. Altersgruppen und Sozialstruktur, München: Juventa Verlag.

Eisner, M. & Ribeaud, D. (2008) [Eds.]: Forschungsbericht aus der Reihe z-proso. Zürcher Projekt zu sozialen Entwicklung von Kindern, Bericht Nr. 06, Zürich.

Erdem, F. & Baser, G. G. (2010): Family and business values of regional family firms: a qualitative research, in: *International Journal of Islamic and Middle Eastern Finance and Management*, 3 (1), 47–64. https://doi.org/10.1108/17538391011033861

Erdmann, C. (2011): Töchter in der Nachfolge, in: *WIFU Working Paper Series Nr. 10*, Witten/Herdecke.

Erikson, E. H. (1973): Identität und Lebenszyklus, 17. Aufl., Frankfurt a. M.: Suhrkamp.

Fallgatter, M. J. (2002): Theorie des Entrepreneurship. Perspektiven zur Erforschung der Entstehung und Entwicklung junger Unternehmungen, Wiesbaden: Deutscher Universitäts-Verlag GmbH.

Faltermaier, T. (2008): Sozialisation im Lebenslauf, in: Hurrelmann, K.; Grundmann, M. & Walper, S. (Eds.): Handbuch Sozialisationsforschung, 7. vollst. überarb. Aufl., Weinheim und Basel: Beltz Verlag, 151–172.

Faulstich-Wieland, H. (2000): Individuum und Gesellschaft: Sozialisationstheorien und Sozialforschung, München und Wien: Oldenburg Verlag.

Faulstich-Wieland, H. & Faulstich, P. (2006): BA-Studium Erziehungswissenschaft: Ein Lehrbuch, Hamburg: Rowohlt.

Felden, B. (2012): Auswahl eines familieninternen Nachfolgers, in: Beckmann, R.; Brost, H. & Faust, M. (Eds.): Unternehmensnachfolge im Mittelstand, 3. kompl. überarb. Aufl., Frankfurt a. M.: Frankfurt School Verlag, 141–170.

Felden, B. & Pfannenschwarz, A. (2008): Unternehmensnachfolge: Perspektiven und Instrumente für Lehre und Praxis, München: Oldenbourg Verlag.

Felden, B. & Zumholz, H. (2009): Managementlehre für Familienunternehmen – Bestandsaufnahme der Forschungs- und Lehraktivitäten im deutschsprachigen Raum, Working Paper 48, Institute of Management Berlin.

Fink, M. (2008): Nachfolgeregelung in Familienunternehmen, in: Ludwig, C. & Widinski, M. (Eds.): Generationenwechsel: Steuerliche, unternehmensrechtliche und betriebswirtschaftliche Aspekte. Festschrift für Karl Bruckner, Wien: Linde, 77–88.

Fletcher, D.; Melin, L. & Gimeno, A. (2012): Culture and values in family business – A review and suggestions for future research, in: *Journal of Family Business Strategy*, 3 (3), 127–131. https://doi.org/10.1016/j.jfbs.2012.06.001

Frank, H. & Hasenzagl, R. (2005): Die Nachfolge in Familienunternehmen aus systemischer Sicht, in: *Zeitschrift für Organisationsentwicklung*, 24 (4), 34-45.

Frank, H. & Keßler, A. (2011): Strategisches Verhalten und Erfolgsfaktoren von Familienunternehmen. Eine vergleichende Analyse österreichischer Familienunternehmen und Nicht-Familienunternehmen. Kurzzusammenfassung der Studie, Wirtschaftsuniversität Wien.

Frank, H.; Kessler, A.; Nosé, L. & Suchy, D. (2011): Conflicts in family firms: state of the art and perspectives for further research, in: *Journal of Family Business Management*, 1 (2), 130–153. https://doi.org/10.1108/20436231111167219

Frank, H.; Korunka, C. & Lueger, M. (2012a) [Eds.]: Konfliktbewältigung in Familienunternehmen. Eine Studie des Forschungsinstituts für Familienunternehmen an der WU, Wien: facultas.wuv.

Frank, H.; Lueger, M. & Korunka, C. (2012b): Good Practice Fallanalysen als Forschungsstrategie, in: Lueger, M. & Frank, H. (Eds.): Wie erfolgreich Familienunternehmen handeln – Good Practice Fallanalysen. Eine Studie des Forschungsinstituts für Familienunternehmen an der WU, Wien: facultas.wuv, 12–29.

Frank, H.; Korunka, C.; Lueger, M.; Nosé, L. & Suchy, D. (2010a): Erfolgsfaktoren österreichischer Familienunternehmen. Das Zusammenspiel von Familie und Unternehmen in Entscheidungs- und Konsens- bzw. Konfliktprozessen. Kurzzusammenfassung der Studie, Wien.

Frank, H.; Lueger, M.; Nosé, L. & Suchy, D. (2010b): The concept of "Familiness": Literature review and systems theory-based reflections, in: *Journal of Family Business Strategy*, 1 (3), 119–130.

Frasl, E. & Rieger, H. (2007) [Eds.]: Family-Business-Handbuch. Zukunftssicherung von Familienunternehmen über Generationen, Wien: Linde Verlag.

Frese, M. (1983): Der Einfluß der Arbeit auf die Persönlichkeit: Zum Konzept des Handlungsstils in der beruflichen Sozialisation, in: *Zeitschrift für Sozialisationsforschung und Erziehungssoziologie*, 3 (1), 11–28.

Freund, W. (2000): Familieninterne Unternehmensnachfolge: Erfolgs- und Risikofaktoren, Wiesbaden: Gabler.

Fritz, C.; Schauer, K. & Augustin, K. (2001): Unternehmensnachfolge – aber richtig! Ein Wegweiser zur gesamtheitlichen Gestaltung des Übergabeprozesses. Wirtschaftliche, rechtliche und psychologische Faktoren, Wien: Linde.

Fromm, E. (2009): Authentisch leben. Herausgegeben von Rainer Funk, 6. Aufl., Freiburg u. a.: Herder.

Fromm, E. (2005): Vom Haben zum Sein: Wege und Irrwege der Selbsterfahrung. Herausgegeben von Werner Funk, Berlin: Ullstein Taschenbuch.

Froschauer, U. (2012) [Ed.]: Organisationen in Bewegung. Beiträge zur interpretativen Organisationsanalyse. Mit einem Beitrag von Manfred Lueger, Wien: facultas.wuv.

Froschauer, U. & Lueger, M. (2012): Tradition eines Familienunternehmens: Nachfolge als generationsübergreifender Prozess, in: Lueger, M. & Frank, H. (Eds.): Wie erfolgreich Familienunternehmen handeln – Good Practice Fallanalysen. Eine Studie des Forschungsinstituts für Familienunternehmen an der WU, Wien: facultas.wuv, 94–131.

García-Álvarez, E. & López-Sintas, J. (2001): A Taxonomy of Founders Based on Values: The Root of Family Business Heterogeneity, in: *Family Business Review*, 14 (3), 209–230. https://doi.org/10.1111/j.1741-6248.2001.00209.x

García-Álvarez, E.; López-Sintas, J. & Saldana Gonzalvo, P. (2002): Socialization patterns of successors in first- to second generation family businesses, in: *Family Business Review*, 15 (3), 189–203. https://doi.org/10.1111/j.1741-6248.2002.00189.x

Garz, D. (2006): Sozialpsychologische Entwicklungstheorien: Von Mead, Piaget und Kohlberg bis zur Gegenwart, 3. erw. Aufl., Wiesbaden: VS Verlag für Sozialwissenschaften.

Gensicke, D. (2008): Luhmann, Stuttgart: Reclam.

Gersick, K. E.; Davis, J. A.; McCollom Hampton, M. & Lansberg, I. (1997): Generation to Generation. Life Cycles of the Familiy Business, Harvard: Harvard Business School Press.

Gerzer-Sass, A. (2003): Familienkompetenzen – ein Baustein für die berufliche Kompetenz, in: Knauth, P. & Wollert, A. (Eds.): Human Resource Management. Loseblattwerk, 48, Unterschleißheim: Deutscher Wirtschaftsdienst, 1–27.

Geulen, D. (1982a) [Ed.]: Perspektivenübernahme und soziales Handeln, Frankfurt a. M.: Suhrkamp.

Geulen, D. (1982b): Soziales Handeln und Perspektivenübernahme, in: Geulen, D. (Ed.): Perspektivenübernahme und soziales Handeln, Frankfurt a. M.: Suhrkamp, 24–72.

Gilgenmann, K. (1986): Sozialisation als Evolution psychischer Systeme. Ein Beitrag zur systemtheoretischen Rekonstruktion von Sozialisationstheorie, in: Unverferth, H.-J. (Ed.): System und Selbstproduktion. Zur Erschließung eines neuen Paradigmas in den Sozialwissenschaften, Reihe 22, Bd./Vol. 120, Frankfurt a. M. u. a.: Peterlang, 91–165.

Gillis-Donovan, J. & Moynihan-Bradt, C. (1990): The Power of Invisible Women in the Family Business, in: *Family Business Review*, 3 (2), 153–167. https://doi.org/10.1111/j.1741-6248.1990.00153.x

Goeke, M. (2008) [Ed.]: Praxishandbuch Mittelstandsfinanzierung. Mit Leasing, Factoring & Co. Unternehmerische Potenziale ausschöpfen, Wiesbaden: Gabler.

Goffman, E. (2007): Wir alle spielen Theater. Die Selbstdarstellung im Alltag. Aus dem Amerikanischen von Peter Weber-Schäfer. Vorwort von Lord Ralf Dahrendorf, 5. Aufl., München: Piper Verlag.

Goldthorpe, J. E. (1969): An introduction to sociology, London: Cambridge University Press.

Goode, W. J. (1967): Soziologie der Familie. Grundfragen der Soziologie. Herausgegeben von Dieter Claessens, Bd. 8, München: Juventa Verlag.

Gottschalk, S.; Höwer, D.; Licht, G.; Niefert, M.; Hauer, A.; Keese, D.; Woywode, M. & in Zusammenarbeit mit Verband der Vereine Creditreform e.V. (2010): Generationenwechsel im Mittelstand. Herausforderungen und Erfolgsfaktoren aus der Perspektive der Nachfolger, Baden-Württembergische Bank, Stuttgart.

Gross, N.; Mason, W. S. & McEachern, A. W. (1966): Explorations in Role Analysis: Studies of the school superintendency role, New York u. a.: John Wiley & Sons.

Grossmann, F.; Krainz, E. & Oswald, M. (1995) [Eds.]: Veränderungen in Organisationen: Management und Beratung, Wiesbaden: Gabler.

Groth, T. (2008): Gute Lösungen von Generation zu Generation: Langlebige Familienunternehmen, in: Schlippe, A. von; Nischak, A. & El Hachimi, M. (Eds.): Familienunternehmen verstehen. Gründer, Gesellschafter und Generationen, Göttingen: Vandenhoeck & Ruprecht, 30–41.

Groth, T. & Schlippe, A. von (2012): Die Form der Unternehmerfamilie – Paradoxiebewältigung zwischen Entscheidung und Bindung, in: *Familiendynamik*, 37 (4), 2–14.

Groth, T. & Slevogt, L. A. (2004): Success patterns of multigenerational family firms – theoretical reflections and empirical findings, in: *WIFU Working Paper Series Nr. 1*, Witten/Herdecke.

Haas, B. (2005): Der Patriarch, die Familie, die Firma und der Konflikt. Eine Falldarstellung, in: Simon, F. B. (Ed.): Die Familie des Familienunternehmers: Ein System zwischen Gefühl und Geschäft, 2. Aufl., Heidelberg: Carl-Auer Verlag, 75–114.

Habbershon, T. G. & Williams, M. L. (1999): A resource-based framework for assessing the strategic advantages of family firms, in: *Family Business Review*, 12 (1), 1–25. https://doi.org/10.1111/j.1741-6248.1999.00001.x

Habermas, J. (1968): Thesen zur Theorie der Sozialisation. Stichworte und Literatur zur Vorlesung im Sommer-Semester 1968.

Habermas, J. & Luhmann, N. (1976) [Eds.]: Theorie der Gesellschaft oder Sozialtechnologie – Was leistet die Systemforschung, Frankfurt a. M.: Suhrkamp.

Habig, H. & Berninghaus, J. (2004): Die Nachfolge im Familienunternehmen ganzheitlich regeln, 2. neu bearb. u. erw. Aufl., Berlin u. a.: Springer.

Halter, F. A. & Schröder, R. (2011): Unternehmensnachfolge in der Theorie und Praxis. Das St. Galler Nachfolge Modell, 2. Aufl., Bern u. a.: Haupt Verlag.

Hamer, E. (2001): Was ist ein Unternehmer? Was verdanken ihm Betrieb und Gesellschaft?, München: Olzog.

Handler, W. C. (1994): Succession in Family Business: A Review of the Research, in: *Family Business Research*, 7 (2), 133–157. https://doi.org/10.1111/j.1741-6248.1994.00133.x

Häring, B. (1954): Soziologie der Familie. Die Familie und ihre Umwelt, Salzburg: Otto Müller Verlag.

Hartmann, H. (1973) [Ed.]: Moderne amerikanische Soziologie. Neue Beiträge zur soziologischen Theorie, 2. umgearb. Aufl., Stuttgart: Ferdinand Enke Verlag.

Harveston, P. D.; Davis, P. S. & Lyden, J. A. (1997): Succession Planning in Family Business: The Impact of Owner Gender, in: *Family Business Review*, 10 (3), 373–396. https://doi.org/10.1111/j.1741-6248.1997.00373.x

Hasenzagl, R. & Stocker, F. (2006) [Eds.]: Unternehmensnachfolge: Herausforderungen, Chancen und Erfolgsfaktoren. Wiener Neustädter Managementgespräche, Wien und Graz: Neuer Wissenschaftlicher Verlag.

Haubl, R. & Daser, B. (2006): Familiendynamik in Familienunternehmen: Warum sollten Töchter nicht erste Wahl sein?, Frankfurt a. M.: Bundesministerium für Familie, Senioren, Frauen und Jugend, Abschlussbericht des ersten Projektabschnitts.

Haug, F. (1994): Kritik der Rollentheorie, 5. überarb. Aufl., Hamburg: Argument-Verlag.

Hecheltjen, G. (1998): Reflexion einer Nachfolge, in: Kappler, E. & Laske, S. (Eds.): Blickwechsel. Zur Dramatik und Dramaturgie von Nachfolgeprozessen im Familienbetrieb, Freiburg im Breisgau: Rombach Verlag KG, 36–50.

Hennerkes, B. H. (2004): Die Familie und ihr Unternehmen: Strategie, Liquidität, Kontrolle, Frankfurt a. M.: Campus.

Hennerkes, B. H. & Hund, T. (2008): „Familienunternehmen – quo vadis?", in: Goeke, M. (Ed.): Praxishandbuch Mittelstandsfinanzierung. Mit Leasing, Factoring & Co. Unternehmerische Potenziale ausschöpfen, Wiesbaden: Gabler, 255–267.

Hering, T. & Olbrich, M. (2003): Unternehmensnachfolge, München und Oldenbourg: Wissenschaftsverlag GmbH.

Herlth, A.; Brunner, E. J.; Tyrell, H. & Kriz, J. (1994) [Eds.]: Abschied von der Normalfamilie? Partnerschaft kontra Elternschaft, Berlin u. a.: Springer.

Heuring, M. & Petzold, H. G. (2005): Rollentheorien, Rollenkonflikte, Identität, Attributionen-Integrative und differentielle Perspektiven zur Bedeutung sozialpsychologischer Konzepte für die Praxis der Supervision, in: *SUPERVISION: Theorie – Praxis – Forschung,* 12. http://www.fpi-publikation.de/images/stories/downloads/supervision/HeuringPetzoldRollentheorieSupervision-12-2005.pdf Access: 17.10.2023

Higgins, C. A.; Duxbury, L. E. & Irving, R. H. (1992): Work-Family Conflict in the Dual-Career Family, in: *Organizational Behavior and Human Decision Processes*, 51 (1) 51–75. https://doi.org/10.1016/0749-5978(92)90004-Q

Hildenbrand, B. (2005): Familienbetriebe als „Familien eigener Art", in: Simon, F. B. (Ed.): Die Familie des Familienunternehmers: Ein System zwischen Gefühl und Geschäft, 2. Aufl., Heidelberg: Carl-Auer Verlag, 116–144.

Hilse, H. & Wimmer, R. (2002): Sind Unternehmer die besseren Manager? Besondere Chancen und Risiken von Führungsstrukturen in Familienunternehmen, in: Joka, H. J. (Ed.): Führungskräfte-Handbuch, Berlin: Springer, 343–360.

Hobi-Ragaz, G. (2008): Reproduktion sozialer Ungleichheit? Die Bedeutung von Eltern-, Kind- und Familienmerkmalen für den sozialen Status unter Gleichaltrigen der mittleren Kindheit, in: Eisner, M. & Ribeaud, D. (Eds.): Forschungsbericht aus der Reihe z-proso. Zürcher Projekt zu sozialen Entwicklung von Kindern, Bericht Nr. 06, Zürich.

Hofer, M. (2002): Familienbeziehungen in der Entwicklung, in: Hofer, M.; Wild, E. & Noack, P. (Eds.): Lehrbuch Familienbeziehungen. Eltern und Kinder in der Entwicklung, 2. vollst. überarb. u. erw. Aufl., Göttingen u. a.: Hogrefe-Verlag, 4–27.

Hofer, M.; Wild, E. & Noack, P. (2002) [Eds.]: Lehrbuch Familienbeziehungen. Eltern und Kinder in der Entwicklung, 2. vollst. überarb. u. erw. Aufl., Göttingen u. a.: Hogrefe-Verlag.

Hoff, E. H. & Grüneisen, V. (1978): Arbeitserfahrungen, Erziehungseinstellungen und Erziehungsverhalten von Eltern, in: Schneewind, K. A. & Lukesch, H. (Eds.): Familiäre Sozialisation: Probleme, Ergebnisse, Perspektiven, Stuttgart: Klett-Cotta, 65–89.

Hoffmeister, D. (2001): Mythos Familie. Zur soziologischen Theorie familialen Wandels, Opladen: Leske und Budrich.

Holleis, W. (1998): Die Leiden des jungen N.? Betrachtung aus dem Blickwinkel der jüngeren Generation, in: Kappler, E. & Laske, S. (Eds.): Blickwechsel. Zur Dramatik und Dramaturgie von Nachfolgeprozessen im Familienbetrieb, Freiburg im Breisgau: Rombach Verlag KG, 51–60.

Huber, C. & Leitner, R. (2011): Unternehmensnachfolge: Ein Leitfaden für die Praxis; Rechtzeitige Planung; Erb-, Gesellschafts-, Gewerbe-, Mietrecht, Haftung & Förderungen; Steuerliche Behandlung, 3. akt. u. erw. Aufl., Wien: LexisNexis.

Hubler, T. (1999): Ten Most Prevalent Obstacles to Family-Business Succession Planning, in: *Family Business Review,* 12 (2), 117–122. https://doi.org/10.1111/j.1741-6248.1999.00117.x

Hubler, T. & Ayres, G. (1996): Family Business Management Course, Graduate School of Business, University of St. Thomas, Minneapolis.

Hülsbeck, M.; Lehmann, E. E.; Weiß, D. & Wirsching, K. (2011): Innovationsverhalten in Familienunternehmen, UO-Working Paper Series 02–11.

Hurrelmann, K. (2002): Einführung in die Sozialisationstheorie, 8. Aufl., Weinheim und Basel: Beltz Verlag.

Hurrelmann, K. & Ulich, D. (1991) [Eds.]: Neues Handbuch der Sozialisationsforschung, 4. völlig neuüberarb. Aufl., Weinheim: Beltz Verlag.

Hurrelmann, K.; Grundmann, M. & Walper, S. (2008) [Eds.]: Handbuch Sozialisationsforschung, 7. vollst. überarb. Aufl., Weinheim und Basel: Beltz Verlag.

Iannarelli, C. L. (1992): The socialization of leaders in family business: An exploratory study of gender, Diss., University of Pittsburgh.

Ip, B. & Jacobs, G. (2006): Business succession planning: a review of the evidence, in: *Journal of Small Business and Enterprise Development*, 13 (3), 326–350. https://doi.org/10.1108/14626000610680235

Ischi, N. (1978): Die Erhebung interaktiven Eltern-Kind-Verhaltens durch systematische Beobachtung, in: Schneewind, K. A. & Lukesch, H. (Eds.): Familiäre Sozialisation: Probleme, Ergebnisse, Perspektiven, Stuttgart: Klett-Cotta, 44–64.

Jahraus, O.; Nassehi, A; Grizelj, M.; Saake, I; Kirchmeier, C. & Müller, J. (2012) [Eds.]: Luhmann Handbuch: Leben – Werk – Wirkung, Stuttgart u. a.: Verlag J. B. Metzler.

Joas, H. (1991): Rollen- und Interaktionstheorien in der Sozialforschung, in: Hurrelmann, K. & Ulich, D. (Eds.): Neues Handbuch der Sozialisationsforschung, 4. völl. neuüberarb. Aufl., Weinheim: Beltz Verlag, 137–152.

Joas, H. (1987a): George Herbert Mead. Gesammelte Aufsätze, Bd. 1, Frankfurt a. M.: Suhrkamp.

Joas, H. (1987b): George Herbert Mead. Gesammelte Aufsätze, Bd. 2, Frankfurt a. M.: Suhrkamp.

Joka, H. J. (2002) [Ed.]: Führungskräfte-Handbuch, Berlin: Springer.

Jünemann, E. & Schuster, N. (2004): Was ist ein kirchliches Krankenhaus? Theologische, ethnische und systemtheoretische Anmerkungen, in: *Renovatio*, 60 (1+2), 1–12.

Juritsch, E.; Nadvornik, W. & Gutschelhofer, A. (2007): Gern geschehen - Unternehmensnachfolge in Familienbetrieben, Wien: Linde.

Kaesler, D. (2006) [Ed.]: Klassiker der Soziologie, Bd. 1, Von August Comte bis Alfred Schütz, 5. überarb. u. akt. Aufl., München: Verlag C. H. Beck.

Kahn, R. L.; Wolfe, D. M.; Quinn, R. P.; Snoek, J. D. & Rosenthal, R. A. (1964): Organizational Stress: Studies in Role Conflict and Ambiguity, New York: John Wiley & Sons.

Kailer, N. & Weiß, G. (2005): Unternehmensnachfolge in kleinen und mittleren Familienunternehmen in Oberösterreich. Hemmende und fördernde Faktoren, Unterstützungsbedarfe und Gestaltungsmöglichkeiten, in: Schauer, R.; Kailer, N. & Feldbauer-Durstmüller, B. (Eds.): Mittelständische Unternehmen: Probleme der Unternehmensnachfolge, Linz: Trauner, 9–115.

Kaiser, P. (2005): Qualitative Methoden in der familienpsychologischen Forschung, in: Busch, F. W. & Nave-Herz, R. (Eds.): Familie und Gesellschaft: Beiträge zur Familienforschung, Oldenburg: BIS-Verlag, 257–289.

Kappler, E. & Laske, S. (1998) [Eds.]: Blickwechsel. Zur Dramatik und Dramaturgie von Nachfolgeprozessen im Familienbetrieb, Freiburg im Breisgau: Rombach Verlag KG.

Kasten, H. (2003): Geschwister: Vorbilder – Rivalen – Vertraute, 5. Aufl., München und Basel: Ernst Reinhardt Verlag.

Katz, R. & Kahn, R. L. (1978): The Social Psychology of Organizations, 2. Aufl., New York: Wiley.

Kaufmann, F. X. (1988): Familie und Modernität, in: Lüscher, K.; Schultheis, F. & Wehrspaun, M. (Eds.): Die 'postmoderne' Familie - Familiale Strategien und Familienpolitik in einer Übergangszeit, Konstanz: Universitätsverlag Konstanz, 391–415.

Keese, D.; Tänzler, J. K. & Hauer, A. (2010): Die Wahrnehmung gesellschaftlicher Verantwortung in Familien- und Nicht-Familienunternehmen, in: *Zeitschrift für KMU und Entrepreneurship*, 58 (3), 197–225. https://doi.org/10.3790/zfke.58.3.197

Keller, M. (1980): Soziale Kognition, Moralisches Urteil und Ich-Prozesse, in: Eckensberger, L. H. & Silbereisen, R. K. (Eds.): Entwicklung sozialer Kognition: Modelle, Theorien, Methoden, Anwendungen, Stuttgart: Klett-Cotta, 163–183.

Kempert, W. (2008): Praxishandbuch für die Nachfolge im Familienunternehmen: Leitfaden für Unternehmer und Nachfolger, Wiesbaden: Gabler.

Kepner, E. (1983): The Family and the Firm: A Coevolutionary Perspective, in: *Organizational Dynamics*, 12 (1), 57–70. https://doi.org/10.1016/0090-2616(83)90027-X

Kersting, A. & Kamper-Jasper, I. P. (2002): Die systemische Beratung interpersoneller Konflikte in Familienunternehmen, in: *Psychotherapeut*, 47 (2), 83–89. https://doi.org/10.1007/s00278-002-0209-x

Kidwell, R. E.; Eddleston, K. A.; Cater, J. J. & Kellermanns, F. W. (2013): How one bad family member can undermine a family firm: Preventing the Fredo effect, in: *Business Horizons*, 56 (1), 5–12. https://doi.org/10.1016/j.bushor.2012.08.004

Kidwell, R. E.; Kellermanns, F. W. & Eddleston, K. A. (2012): Harmony, Justice, Confusion, and Conflict in Family Firms: Implications for Ethical Climate and the "Fredo Effect", in: *Journal of Business Ethics*, 106 (4), 503–517. https://doi.org/10.1007/s10551-011-1014-7

Kieserling, A. (1999): Kommunikation unter Anwesenden: Studien über Interaktionssysteme, Frankfurt a. M.: Suhrkamp.

Kieserling, A. (1994): Familien in systemtheoretischer Perspektive, in: Herlth, A.; Brunner, E. J.; Tyrell, H. & Kriz, J. (Eds.): Abschied von der Normalfamilie? Partnerschaft kontra Elternschaft, Berlin u. a.: Springer, 16–30.

Klatetzki, T. (2008): Sozialisation in Gruppen und Organisationen, in: Hurrelmann, K.; Grundmann, M. & Walper, S. (Eds.): Handbuch Sozialisationsforschung, 7. vollst. überarb. Aufl., Weinheim und Basel: Beltz Verlag, 321–332.

Klatten, S. (2002): Werte im Wandel. Unternehmer in der vierten Generation, in: Schweickart, N. (Ed.): Unternehmertum am Beginn des 21. Jahrhundert, München und Zürich: Piper, 57–70.

Klein, S. B. (2010): Familienunternehmen - Theoretische und empirische Grundlagen, 3. Aufl., Lohmar: Josef Eul.

Klein, S. B. (2004): Familienunternehmen - Theoretische und empirische Grundlagen, 2. Aufl., Wiesbaden: Gabler.

Klett, M. (2002): Gründer, Eigner, Familienunternehmer. Ein Evolutionsgeschehen?, in: Schweickart, N. (Ed.): Unternehmertum am Beginn des 21. Jahrhundert, München und Zürich: Piper, 97–111.

Knauth, P. & Wollert, A. (2003) [Eds.]: Human Resource Management. Lose-blattwerk, 48, Unterschleißheim: Deutscher Wirtschaftsdienst.

Kneer, G. (2001): Organisation und Gesellschaft. Zum ungeklärten Verhältnis von Organisations- und Funktionssystemen in Luhmanns Theorie sozialer Systeme, in: *Zeitschrift für Soziologie*, 30 (6), 407–428. https://doi.org/10.1515/zfsoz-2001-0601

Kneer, G. & Nassehi, A. (2000): Niklas Luhmanns Theorie sozialer Systeme. Eine Einführung, 4. unver. Aufl., Paderborn: Wilhelm Fink.

Kollmer-von Oheimb-Loup, G. & Wischermann, C. (2008) [Eds.]: Unternehmensnachfolge in Geschichte und Gegenwart, Ostfildern: Jan Thorbecke Verlag.

Kommission (2003): Empfehlung der Kommission vom 6. Mai 2003 betreffend die Definition der Kleinstunternehmen sowie der kleinen und mittleren Unternehmen, in: *Amtsblatt der Europäischen Union*, L 124/36, 36–41. http://data.europa.eu/eli/reco/2003/361/oj

Kormann, H. (2011): Zusammenhalt der Unternehmerfamilie: Verträge, Vermögensmanagement, Kommunikation, Heidelberg u. a.: Springer.

Korunka, C. & Nosé, L. (2012): Zusammenarbeit auf engstem Raum: Familienunternehmen im Spannungsfeld zwischen Familie und Unternehmen, in: Lueger, M. & Frank, H. (Eds.): Wie erfolgreich Familienunternehmen handeln – Good Practice Fallanalysen. Eine Studie des Forschungsinstituts für Familienunternehmen an der WU, Wien: facultas.wuv, 150–179.

Korunka, C.; Frank, H. & Lueger, M. (2004): Die Bedeutung der Persönlichkeit für die Gründungsintention, die Gründungsrealisation und den Unternehmenserfolg, in: *Zeitschrift für Psychologie*, 212 (1), 25–39. https://doi.org/10.1026/0044-3409.212.1.25

Königswieser, R. & Hillebrand, M. (2009): Einführung in die systemische Organisationsberatung, 5. Aufl., Heidelberg: Carl Auer Systeme Verlag.

Kracke, B. & Hofer, M. (2002): Familie und Arbeit, in: Hofer, M.; Wild, E. & Noack, P. (Eds.): Lehrbuch Familienbeziehungen. Eltern und Kinder in der Entwicklung, 2. vollst. überarb. u. erw. Aufl., Göttingen u. a.: Hogrefe-Verlag, 94–123.

Krappe, A. & Schlippe, A. von (2010): Family Business as a brand on their own, in: *WIFU Working Paper Series Nr. 5,* Witten/Herdecke.

Krappmann, L. (1993): Soziologische Dimensionen der Identität. Strukturelle Bedingungen für die Teilnahme an Interaktionsprozessen, 8. Aufl., Stuttgart: Klett-Cotta.

Krappmann, L. (1977): Neuere Rollenkonzepte als Erklärungsmöglichkeit für Sozialisationsprozesse, in: Auwärter, M.; Kirsch, E. & Schröter, K. (Eds.): Seminar: Kommunikation, Interaktion, Identität, 2. Aufl., Frankfurt a. M.: Suhrkamp, 307–331.

Kreppner, K. (1991): Sozialisation in der Familie, in: Hurrelmann, K. & Ulich, D. (Eds.): Neues Handbuch der Sozialisationsforschung, 4. völlig neuüberarb. Aufl., Weinheim: Beltz Verlag, 321–334.

Krüger, W.; Klippstein, G.; Merk, R. & Wittberg, V. (2006) [Eds.]: Praxishandbuch des Mittelstands: Leitfaden für das Management mittelständischer Unternehmen, Wiesbaden: Gabler.

Kühl, S. (2011): Plädoyer für eine dritte Differenzierungsform. Organisationen, Gruppen, Familien, und Bewegungen als unterschiedliche soziale Systeme zwischen Interaktion und Gesellschaft, Working Paper 4/2011.

Lange, K. W. & Schiereck, D. (2003) [Eds.]: Nachfolgefragen bei Familienunternehmen: Unternehmenskauf und Private Equity als Alternative zur Börse, Heidelberg: Finanz Colloquium.

Lansberg, I. S. (1983): Managing Human Resources in Family Firms: The Problem of Institutional Overlap, in: *Organizational Dynamics*, 12 (1), 39–46. https://doi.org/10.1016/0090-2616(83)90025-6

Lee, Y. G.; Jasper, C. R. & Goebel, K. P. (2003): A Profile of Succession Planning among Family Business Owners, in: *Financial Counseling and Planning*, 14 (2), 31–41.

Leipold, B. & Greve, W. (2008): Sozialisation, Selbstbild und Identität, in: Hurrelmann, K.; Grundmann, M. & Walper, S. (Eds.): Handbuch Sozialisationsforschung, 7. vollst. überarb. Aufl., Weinheim und Basel: Beltz Verlag, 398–409.

Leman, K. (2012): Geschwisterkonstellationen: Die Familie bestimmt ihr Leben. Aus dem Amerikanischen übersetzt von Thomas Lardon, 9. Aufl., München: mvg Verlag.

LeMar, B. (2014): Generations- und Führungswechsel im Familienunternehmen. Mit Gefühl und Kalkül den Wandel gestalten, 2. vollst. überarb. u. erw. Aufl., Berlin und Heidelberg: Springer Gabler.

LeMar, B. (2001): Generations- und Führungswechsel im Familienunternehmen. Mit Gefühl und Kalkül den Wandel gestalten, Berlin u. a.: Springer.

Lenz, K. (2005): Familien als Ensemble persönlicher Beziehungen, in: Busch, F. W. & Nave-Herz, R. (Eds.): Familie und Gesellschaft: Beiträge zur Familienforschung, Oldenburg: BIS-Verlag, 9-32.

Levold, T.; Martens-Schmid, K. & Schuchardt-Hain, C. (2005): „Eigentlich müsste man dich klonen…". Familiendynamische Aspekte einer Nachfolgereglung, in: Simon, F. B. (Ed.): Die Familie des Familienunternehmers: Ein System zwischen Gefühl und Geschäft. 2. Aufl., Heidelberg: Carl-Auer Verlag, 210–263.

Lieckweg, T. (2001): Strukturelle Kopplung von Funktionssystemen „über" Organisation, in: *Soziale Systeme*, 7 (2), 267–289. https://doi.org/10.1515/sosys-2001-0206

Linton, R. (1965): The study of man, London: Peter Owen.

Löhr, D. (2001): Mittelständische Familienunternehmen im Generationenwechsel. Die Gestaltung des Übergangs als Aufgabe strategischen Risikomanagements, Aachen: Shaker Verlag.

Löhr-Heinemann, B. (2005): Erfolg hat eine Mutter. Chancen und Grenzen der Erfolgsprognose bei selbstständigen Frauen mit den Mitteln des Genogramms, Heidelberg: Verlag für Systemische Forschung im Carl-Auer-Systeme Verlag.

Loos, H. (2010): Wie werde ich meine Firma los? Ratgeber für KMU-Gesellschafter: Fallbeispiele, Tipps, Checklisten und Perspektiven, Hohenems und Wien: Bucher.

Ludwig, C. & Widinski, M. (2008) [Eds.]: Generationenwechsel: Steuerliche, unternehmensrechtliche und betriebswirtschaftliche Aspekte. Festschrift für Karl Bruckner, Wien: Linde.

Lueger, M. (2012): Routinisierte Irritationen. Zur dynamischen Stabilität von Organisationen, in: Froschauer, U. (Ed.): Organisationen in Bewegung. Beiträge zur interpretativen Organisationsanalyse. Mit einem Beitrag von Manfred Lueger, Wien: facultas.wuv, 99–121.

Lueger, M. & Frank, H. (2015) [Eds.]: Zukunftssicherung für Familienunternehmen. Good Practice Fallanalysen zur Family Governance. Eine Studie des Forschungsinstituts für Familienunternehmen an der WU, Wien: Facultas.

Lueger, M. & Frank, H. (2012) [Eds.]: Wie erfolgreich Familienunternehmen handeln – Good Practice Fallanalysen. Eine Studie des Forschungsinstituts für Familienunternehmen an der WU, Wien: facultas.wuv.

Lueger, M. & Suchy, D. (2012): Krisenentscheidungen: Die Transformation eines Familienunternehmens, in: Lueger, M. & Frank, H. (Eds.): Wie erfolgreich Familienunternehmen handeln – Good Practice Fallanalysen. Eine Studie des Forschungsinstituts für Familienunternehmen an der WU, Wien: facultas.wuv, 30–67.

Lueger, M. & Süss-Reyes, J. (2015): Family Governance als Strukturierung der Familie: Lehren aus den Fallanalysen, in: Lueger, M. & Frank, H. (Eds.): Zukunftssicherung für Familienunternehmen. Good Practice Fallanalysen zur Family Governance. Eine Studie des Forschungsinstituts für Familienunternehmen an der WU, Wien: Facultas, 199–236.

Lueger, M.; Frank, H. & Weismeier-Sammer, D. (2012a): Zur Dynamik von Familienunternehmen: Reflexionen zur Familiness auf Basis qualitativ-empirischer Fallanalysen, in: Lueger, M. & Frank, H. (Eds.): Wie erfolgreich Familienunternehmen handeln – Good Practice Fallanalysen. Eine Studie des Forschungsinstituts für Familienunternehmen an der WU, Wien: facultas.wuv, 210–235.

Lueger, M.; Froschauer, U.; Suchy, D.; Frank, H.; Nosé, L. & Korunka, C. (2012b): Entscheidungs- und Konfliktprozesse in Familienunternehmen: Empirisch-qualitative Analysen, in: Frank, H.; Korunka, C. & Lueger, M. (Eds.): Konfliktbewältigung in Familienunternehmen: Eine Studie des Forschungsinstituts für Familienunternehmen an der WU, Wien: facultas.wuv, 43–120.

Luhmann, N. (2006a): The Autopoiesis of Social Systems, in: Seidl, D. & Becker, K. H. (Eds.): Niklas Luhmann and Organization Studies, Frederiksberg: Liber & Copenhagen Business School Press, 64–82.

Luhmann, N. (2006b): Das Kind als Medium der Erziehung, Frankfurt a. M.: Suhrkamp.

Luhmann, N. (2006c): Organisation und Entscheidung, 2. Aufl., Wiesbaden: VS Verlag für Sozialwissenschaften.

Luhmann, N. (2000): Organisation und Entscheidung, Opladen u. a.: Westdeutscher Verlag.

Luhmann, N. (1998a): Die Gesellschaft der Gesellschaft, erster Teilband, Frankfurt a. M.: Suhrkamp.

Luhmann, N. (1998b): Die Gesellschaft der Gesellschaft, zweiter Teilband, Frankfurt a. M.: Suhrkamp.

Luhmann, N. (1995a) [Ed.]: Soziologische Aufklärung 6. Die Soziologie und der Mensch, Opladen: Westdeutscher Verlag.

Luhmann, N. (1995b): Funktionen und Folgen formaler Organisation, 4. Aufl., Berlin: Duncker & Humblot.

Luhmann, N. (1995c): Die Form „Person“, in: Luhmann, N. (Ed.): Soziologische Aufklärung 6. Die Soziologie und der Mensch, Opladen: Westdeutscher Verlag, 142–154.

Luhmann, N. (1994): Soziale Systeme. Grundriß einer allgemeinen Theorie, 5. Aufl., Frankfurt a. M.: Suhrkamp. [Luhmann, N. (2005). Social Systems. Stanford University Press.]

Luhmann, N. (1990): Soziologische Aufklärung 5. Konstruktivistische Perspektiven, Opladen: Westdeutscher Verlag.

Luhmann, N. (1989): Vertrauen. Ein Mechanismus der Reduktion sozialer Komplexität, 3. durchges. Aufl., Stuttgart: Ferdinand Enke Verlag.

Luhmann, N. (1988): Was ist Kommunikation?, in: Simon, F. B. (Ed.): Lebende Systeme: Wirklichkeitskonstruktion in der Systemischen Therapie, Berlin u. a.: Springer, 10–18.

Luhmann, N. (1987a): Soziologische Aufklärung 4. Beiträge zur funktionalen Differenzierung der Gesellschaft, Opladen: Westdeutscher Verlag.

Luhmann, N. (1987b): Soziale Systeme. Grundriß einer allgemeinen Theorie, Frankfurt a. M.: Suhrkamp. [Luhmann, N. (2005). Social Systems. Stanford University Press.]
Luhmann, N. (1986): Soziologische Aufklärung 2. Aufsätze zur Theorie der Gesellschaft, 3. Aufl., Opladen: Westdeutscher Verlag.
Luhmann, N. (1981): Soziologische Aufklärung 3. Soziales System, Gesellschaft, Organisation, Opladen: Westdeutscher Verlag.
Luhmann, N. (1976a): Sinn als Grundbegriff der Soziologie, in: Habermas, J. & Luhmann, N. (Eds.): Theorie der Gesellschaft oder Sozialtechnologie – Was leistet die Systemforschung, Frankfurt a. M.: Suhrkamp, 25–100.
Luhmann, N. (1976b): Funktionen und Folgen formaler Organisation, 3. Aufl., Berlin: Duncker & Humblot.
Luhmann, N. (1970): Soziologische Aufklärung 1. Aufsätze zur Theorie sozialer Systeme, Köln u. a.: Westdeutscher Verlag.
Lukesch, H. (1996): Leitbilder in der Familienerziehung, in: Vaskovics, L. A. & Lipinski, H. (Eds.): Familiale Lebenswelten und Bildungsarbeit. Interdisziplinäre Bestandsaufnahme 1, Opladen: Leske + Budrich, 153–184.
Lukesch, H. (1978): Sozioökologische Bedingungen im Schwangerschaftsleben und in der Erziehungseinstellung, in: Schneewind, K. A. & Lukesch, H. (Eds.): Familiäre Sozialisation: Probleme, Ergebnisse, Perspektiven, Stuttgart: Klett-Cotta, 90–113.
Lüschen, G. & Lupri, E. (1970) [Eds.]: Soziologie der Familie, Opladen: Westdeutscher Verlag.
Lüscher, K.; Schultheis, F. & Wehrspaun, M. (1988) [Eds.]: Die 'postmoderne' Familie – Familiale Strategien und Familienpolitik in einer Übergangszeit, Konstanz: Universitätsverlag Konstanz.
Maihofer, A.; Böhnisch, T. & Wolf, A. (2001): Wandel der Familie, Arbeitspapier 48, Hans-Böckler-Stiftung.
Matthias-Bleck, H. (2005): Die gesellschaftliche Etablierung der nichtelterlichen Lebensgemeinschaft, in: Busch, F. W. & Nave-Herz, R. (Eds.): Familie und Gesellschaft: Beiträge zur Familienforschung, Oldenburg: BIS-Verlag, 53–76.
Mätzener, M. & Schwarz, G. (2008): Erfolgreiche Betriebsübergabe in Familienunternehmen: Emotionen - Konflikte - Perspektiven, Wien: Linde.
Mayer, F. (2006): Unternehmensnachfolge aus der Sicht des Übernehmers – Übergabe der F.S. Mayer GmbH, in: Hasenzagl, R. & Stocker, F. (Eds.): Unternehmensnachfolge: Herausforderungen, Chancen und Erfolgsfaktoren, Wiener Neustädter Managementgespräche, Wien und Graz: Neuer Wissenschaftlicher Verlag, 133–138.
Mead, G. H. (1973): Geist, Identität und Gesellschaft. Aus Sicht des Sozialbehaviorismus. Aus dem Amerikanischen von Ulf Pacher. Mit einer Einleitung herausgegeben von Charles W. Morris, Frankfurt a. M.: Suhrkamp.
Mead, G. H. (1969): Philosophie der Sozialität. Aufsätze zur Erkenntnisanthropologie, Frankfurt a. M.: Suhrkamp.
Mead, G. H. (1936): The Problem of Society. How we become selves, in: Moore, M. H. (Ed.): Movements of Thought in the Nineteenth Century, Chicago: University of Chicago Press, 360-385.
Meierhofer, M. (1989): Frühe Prägung der Persönlichkeit. Psychohygiene im Kindesalter, 6. Aufl., Bern u. a.: Hans Huber.

Memili, A.; Chang, E. P. C.; Kellermanns, F. W. & Welsh, D. H. B. (2015): Role conflicts of family members in family firms, in: *European Journal of Work and Organizational Psychology*, 24 (1), 143–151. https://doi.org/10.1080/1359432X.2013.839549

Mendel, M. & Piper, N. (2005): Stabwechsel. Die schwierige Suche nach dem richtigen Nachfolger, München: Redline Wirtschaft.

Merton, R. K. (1995): Soziologische Theorie und soziale Struktur. Herausgegeben und eingeleitet von Volker Meja und Nico Stehr. Aus dem Amerikanischen von Hella Beister, Berlin u. a.: Walter de Gruyter.

Merton, R. K. (1973): Der Rollen-Set. Probleme der soziologischen Theorie, in: Hartmann, H. (Ed.): Moderne amerikanische Soziologie. Neue Beiträge zur soziologischen Theorie, 2. umgearb. Aufl., Stuttgart: Ferdinand Enke Verlag, 316–333.

Metzger, W. (1960): Der Auftrag des Elternhauses, in: Oeter, F. (Ed.): Familie im Umbruch, Gütersloh: Gütersloher Verlagshaus Gerd Mohn, 156–232.

Meyer, A. (2007): Unternehmerfamilie und Familienunternehmen erfolgreich führen: Unternehmertum fördern, Führungskultur entwickeln, Konflikte konstruktiv lösen, Wiesbaden: Gabler.

Meyer, A. & Oldenburg, D. (2008): Macht-Wert-Sinn(?): Werte- und Werteorientierung in Familienunternehmen, in: *Organisationsentwicklung-Zeitschrift für Unternehmensentwicklung und Change Management*, 27 (4), 17–22.

Mingers, J. (2003): Observing organizations: An evaluation of Luhmann's organization theory, in: Bakken, T. & Hernes, T. (Eds.): Autopoietic Organization Theory. Drawing on Niklas Luhmann's Social Systems Perspective, Frederiksberg: Copenhagen Business School Press, 103–122.

Mitscherlich, A. (1986): Auf dem Weg zur vaterlosen Gesellschaft. Ideen zur Sozialpsychologie, 16. Aufl., München und Zürich: R. Piper & Co. Verlag.

Moore, M. H. (1936) [Ed.]: Movements of Thought in the Nineteenth Century, Chicago: University of Chicago Press.

Moser, K.; Batinic, B. & Zempel, J. (1999) [Eds.]: Unternehmerisch erfolgreiches Handeln, Göttingen: Verlag für Angewandte Psychologie.

Müller, G. F. (1999): Dispositionelle und biographische Bedingungen beruflicher Selbständigkeit, in: Moser, K.; Batinic, B. & Zempel, J. (Eds.): Unternehmerisch erfolgreiches Handeln, Göttingen: Verlag für Angewandte Psychologie, 173–192.

Müller, V. (2008): Nachfolgetypen und Rollenkonflikte im Nachfolgeprozess von Familienunternehmen. Eine empirische Untersuchung, München und Mering: Rainer Hampp Verlag.

Müller Tiberini, F. (2008): Werte und Wertorientierung in Familienunternehmen: Fundament und Kompass zugleich, in: Schlippe, A. von; Nischak, A. & El Hachimi, M. (Eds.): Familienunternehmen verstehen. Gründer, Gesellschafter und Generationen, Göttingen: Vandenhoeck & Ruprecht, 181–191.

Müller Tiberini, F. (2001): Wenn die Familie den Laden schmeißt. Modelle zur Führung von Familienunternehmen, Zürich: Orell Füssli.

Nagel, R.; Oswald, M. & Wimmer, R. (2005): AROMA – Zwei Familien und ein Unternehmen suchen ihre Zukunft. Zur Zukunftssicherung in Familienunternehmen, in: Simon, F. B. (Ed.): Die Familie des Familienunternehmers: Ein System zwischen Gefühl und Geschäft, 2. Aufl., Heidelberg: Carl-Auer Verlag, 316–338.

Nassehi, A. (2012): George Herbert Mead (1863-1931), in: Jahraus, O.; Nassehi, A.; Grizelj, M.; Saake, I.; Kirchmeier, C. & Müller, J. (Eds.): Luhmann-Handbuch: Leben-Werk-Wirkung, Stuttgart und Weimar: Verlag J. B. Metzler, 269–271.

Nassehi, A. (1997): Kommunikation verstehen. Einige Überlegungen zur empirischen Anwendbarkeit einer systemtheoretisch informierten Hermeneutig, in: Sutter, T. (Ed.): Beobachtung verstehen, Verstehen beobachten: Perspektiven einer konstruktivistischen Hermeneutig, Opladen: Westdeutscher Verlag, 134–163.

Nave-Herz, R. (2007): Familie heute: Wandel der Familienstrukturen und Folgen für die Erziehung, 3. überarb. u. erw. Aufl., Darmstadt: Primus Verlag.

Nave-Herz, R. (2003): Familie zwischen Tradition und Moderne. Ausgewählte Beiträge zu Familiensoziologie, Oldenburg: BIS-Verlag.

Neidhardt, F. (1979): Frühkindliche Sozialisation, 2. neubearb. Aufl., Stuttgart: Enke.

Neidhardt, F. (1977): Schichtspezifische Elterneinflüsse im Sozialisationsprozeß, in: Wurzbacher, G. (Ed.): Die Familie als Sozialisationsfaktor, 2. neubearb. u. erw. Aufl., Stuttgart: Ferdinand Enke Verlag, 275–308.

Neuberger, O. (1976): Führungsverhalten und Führungserfolg, Berlin: Duncker & Humblot.

Nischak, A. (2008): »Leider nur ein Mädchen« – Genderaspekte bei der Nachfolge in Familienunternehmen, in: Schlippe, A. von; Nischak, A. & El Hachimi, M. (Eds.): Familienunternehmen verstehen. Gründer, Gesellschafter und Generationen, Göttingen: Vandenhoeck & Ruprecht, 84–92.

Oeter, F. (1960a) [Eds.]: Familie im Umbruch, Gütersloh: Gütersloher Verlagshaus Gerd Mohn.

Oeter, F. (1960b): Wandlungen der Familie, in: Oeter, F. (Ed.): Familie im Umbruch, Gütersloh: Gütersloher Verlagshaus Gerd Mohn, 9–80.

Olson, P. D.; Zuiker, V. S.; Danes, S. M.; Stafford, K.; Heck, R. K. Z. & Duncan, K. A. (2003): The impact of the family and the business on family business sustainability, in: *Journal of Business Venturing*, 18 (5), 639–666. https://doi.org/10.1016/S0883-9026(03)00014-4

Oswald, H. (2008): Sozialisation in Netzwerken Gleichaltriger, in: Hurrelmann, K.; Grundmann, M. & Walper, S. (Eds.): Handbuch Sozialisationsforschung, 7. vollst. überarb. Aufl., Weinheim und Basel: Beltz Verlag, 321–332.

Parsons, T. (1976) [Ed.]: Zur Theorie sozialer Systeme. Herausgegeben und eingeleitet von Stefan Jensen, Opladen: Westdeutscher Verlag.

Parsons, T. (1968): Beiträge zur soziologischen Theorie. Herausgegeben und eingeleitet von Dietrich Rüschemeyer, 2. Aufl., Darmstadt: Luchterhand.

Parsons, T. (1966a): Family Structure and the Socialization of the Child, in: Parsons, T. & Bales, R. F. (Eds.): Family, Socialization and Interaction Process, 6. Druck, New York: The Free Press, 35–132.

Parsons, T. (1966b): The Organization of Personality as a System of Action, in: Parsons, T. & Bales, R. F. (Eds.): Family, Socialization and Interaction Process, 6. Druck, New York: The Free Press, 133–186.

Parsons, T. & Bales, R. F. (1966) [Eds.]: Family, Socialization and Interaction Process, 6. Druck, New York: The Free Press.

Parsons, T. & Olds, J. (1966): The Mechanisms of Personality Functioning with Special Reference to Socialization, in: Parsons, T. & Bales, R. F. (Eds.): Family, Socialization and Interaction Process, 6. Druck, New York: The Free Press, 187–257.

Pearson, A. W.; Carr, J. C. & Shaw, J. C. (2008): Toward a Theory of Familiness: A Social Capital Perspective, in: *Entrepreneurship Theory and Practice*, 32 (6), 949–969. https://doi.org/10.1111/j.1540-6520.2008.00265.x

Petzold, M. (1999): Entwicklung und Erziehung in der Familie: Familienpsychologie im Überblick, Baltmannsweiler: Schneider-Verlag Hohengehren.

Peuckert, R. (2008): Familienformen im sozialen Wandel, 7. vollst. überarb. Aufl., Wiesbaden: VS Verlag für Sozialwissenschaften.

Pfannenschwarz, A. (2008): Qualifikationen von Unternehmensnachfolgern. Plädoyer für eine Ausbildungs- und Berufslaufbahn künftiger Unternehmer, in: Schlippe, A. von; Nischak, A. & El Hachimi, M. (Eds.): Familienunternehmen verstehen. Gründer, Gesellschafter und Generationen, Göttingen: Vandenhoeck & Ruprecht, 163–175.

Pfannenschwarz, A. (2006a): Nachfolge und Nicht-Nachfolge in Familienunternehmen. Bd. 1: Ambivalenzen und Lösungsstrategien beim familieninternen Generationenwechsel, Heidelberg: Carl-Auer Verlag.

Pfannenschwarz, A. (2006b): Nachfolge und Nicht-Nachfolge in Familienunternehmen. Bd. 2: Fallstudien zum familieninternen Generationswechsel, Heidelberg: Carl-Auer Verlag.

Plate, M. (2008): Geschwisterkonflikte in Familienunternehmen – Strukturelle Konfliktlinien, in: Schlippe, A. von; Nischak, A. & El Hachimi, M. (Eds.): Familienunternehmen verstehen. Gründer, Gesellschafter und Generationen, Göttingen: Vandenhoeck & Ruprecht, 65–83.

Plate, M. & Schlippe, A. von (2010): Organizational paradoxes and paradox management in family firms, in: *WIFU Working Paper Series Nr. 4*, Witten/Herdecke.

Plate, M.; Groth, T.; Ackermann, V. & Schlippe, A. von (2011) [Eds.]: Große deutsche Familienunternehmen, Göttingen: Vandenhoeck & Ruprecht.

Popitz, H. (1980): Die normative Konstruktion von Gesellschaft, Tübingen: Mohr.

Popitz, H. (1967): Der Begriff der sozialen Rolle als Element der soziologischen Theorie, Tübingen: Mohr.

Prisching, M. (1995): Soziologie: Themen – Theorien – Perspektiven. 3. erg. u. überarb. Aufl., Wien u. a.: Böhlau.

Rashad, R. (2013): The Power of Family Unity. How to Use it to Gain Economical Freedom for Generations, o. O.: XLIBRIS.

Rausch, K. (2007) [Ed.]: Organisationen gestalten, Lengerich: Pabst.

Reck, S. (1981): Identität, Rationalität und Verantwortung. Grundbegriffe und Grundzüge einer soziologischen Identitätstheorie, Frankfurt a. M.: Suhrkamp.

Reiger, H. (2007): Symbolischer Interaktionismus, in: Buber, R. & Holzmüller, H. H. (Eds.): Qualitative Marktforschung: Methoden – Konzepte – Analysen, Wiesbaden: Gabler, 137–155.

Reinhold, G.; Lamnek, S. & Recker, H. (2000): Soziologie-Lexikon, 4. Aufl., München und Wien: R. Oldenbourg Verlag.

Risak, J. & Nagy, R. (1999): Generationenfolge in Familienunternehmen: Übergaben erfolgreich gestalten, Wien: Service Fachverlag.

Risse, W. (1997): Die Unternehmernachfolge: Anleitung zur Geschäftsübergabe – für Unternehmer und Nachfolger, 2. Aufl., Renningen-Malmsheim und Wien: Expert, Linde.

Rizzo, J. R.; House, R. J. & Lirtzman, S. I. (1970): Role Conflict and Ambiguity in Complex Organizations, in: *Administrative Science Quarterly*, 15 (2), 150–163. https://doi.org/10.2307/2391486

Roberts, B. (1977): George Herbert Mead: the theory and practice of his social philosophy, in: *Ideology and Consciousness*, 2, 81–106. http://eprints.lse.ac.uk/id/eprint/683

Rose, A. M. (1973): Systematische Zusammenfassung der Theorie der symbolischen Interaktion, in: Hartmann, H. (Ed.): Moderne amerikanische Soziologie. Neue Beiträge zur soziologischen Theorie, 2. umgearb. Aufl., Stuttgart: Ferdinand Enke Verlag, 264–282.

Rossaro, F. (2007): Zu den Beständigkeitsmerkmalen von Familienunternehmen – Eine Analyse aus soziologischer und mikrotheoretischer Sicht, Diss., Berlin: Duncker & Humblot.

Rüegg-Stürm, J. & Bieger, T. (2012) [Eds.]: Unternehmerisches Management – Herausforderungen und Perspektiven: Festschrift für Prof. Dr. Peter Gomez, Bern: Haupt Verlag AG.

Runkel, G. & Burkart, G. (2005a) [Eds.]: Funktionssysteme der Gesellschaft: Beiträge zur Systemtheorie von Niklas Luhmann, Wiesbaden: VS Verlag für Sozialwissenschaften.

Runkel, G. & Burkart, G. (2005b): Einleitung: Luhmann und die Funktionssysteme, in: Runkel, G. & Burkart, G. (Eds.): Funktionssysteme der Gesellschaft: Beiträge zur Systemtheorie von Niklas Luhmann, Wiesbaden: VS Verlag für Sozialwissenschaften, 7–11.

Rüsen, T. A. (2009): Krisen und Krisenmanagement in Familienunternehmen: Schwachstellen erkennen, Lösungen erarbeiten, Existenzbedrohungen meistern, Wiesbaden: Gabler.

Rüsen, T. A. (2008): Parallele Krisenprozesse – paralleles Krisenmanagement: Das Familienunternehmen unter existentiellem Druck, in: Schlippe, A. von; Nischak, A. & El Hachimi, M. (Eds.): Familienunternehmen verstehen. Gründer, Gesellschafter und Generationen, Göttingen: Vandenhoeck & Ruprecht, 42–54.

Rüsen, T. A. & Schlippe, A. von (2007): Krisen in Familienunternehmen und Unternehmensfamilien. Über parallele, interdependente Dynamiken in Familie und Unternehmen, in: *Organisation Supervision Coaching*, 14 (4), 309–330. https://doi.org/10.1007/s11613-007-0043-7

Sambrook, S. (2005): Exploring succession planning in small, growing firms, in: *Journal of Small Business and Enterprise Development*, 12 (4), 579–594. https://doi.org/10.1108/14626000510628243

Schachner, M.; Speckbacher, G. & Wentges, P. (2005): Steuerung mittelständischer Unternehmen: Größeneffekte und Einfluss der Eigentums- und Führungsstruktur, in: *Zeitschrift für Betriebswirtschaft*, 76 (6), 589–614. https://doi.org/10.1007/s11573-006-0029-5

Schaller, A. (2001): Entrepreneurship oder wie man ein Unternehmen denken muss, in: Blum, U. & Leibbrand, F. (Eds.): Entrepreneurship und Unternehmertum: Denkstrukturen für eine neue Zeit, Wiesbaden: Gabler, 3–56.

Schaub, H. (2009): Nachfolgeplanung in KMU, Bern u. a.: Haupt Verlag.

Schauer, R.; Kailer, N. & Feldbauer-Durstmüller, B. (2005) [Eds.]: Mittelständische Unternehmen: Probleme der Unternehmensnachfolge, Linz: Trauner.

Schlippe, A. von (2012): Konflikte und Konfliktdynamiken in Familienunternehmen, in: *Zeitschrift für Familienunternehmen und Stiftungen*, 2, 43–48.

Schlippe, A. von (2011a): Paradoxien in Familienunternehmen, in: *Zeitschrift für Familienunternehmen und Stiftungen*, 1, 8–13.

Schlippe, A. von (2011b): Paradoxien in Familienunternehmen. Vortrag vor dem Verband deutscher Unternehmerinnen e.V., Witten.

Schlippe, A. von (2009): Zwischen Ökonomie und Psychologie: Konflikte in Familienunternehmen, in: *Zeitschrift für Konfliktmanagement*, 1, 17–21. https://doi.org/10.9785/ovs-zkm-2009-17
Schlippe, A. von (2007): Das Balancieren von Paradoxien in Familienunternehmen – Kultur mit Struktur versöhnen, in: Rausch, K. (Ed.): Organisationen gestalten, Lengerich: Pabst, 111–129.
Schlippe, A. von & Frank, H. (2013): The Theory of Social Systems as a Framework for Understanding Family Businesses, in: *Family Relations*, 62 (3), 384–398. https://doi.org/10.1111/fare.12010
Schlippe, A. von & Kellermanns, F. W. (2009): Emotionale Konflikte in Familienunternehmen, in: Schlippe, A. von; Rüsen, T. & Groth, T. (Eds.): Beiträge zur Theorie des Familienunternehmens, Bd. 1, Lohmar u. a.: Josef Eul Verlag, 173–202.
Schlippe, A. von & Schweitzer, J. (2009): Systemische Interventionen, Göttingen: Vandenhoeck & Ruprecht.
Schlippe, A. von; Groth, T. & Plate, M. (2011): Entscheidungsfähigkeit sicherstellen: Familienstrategie in Familienunternehmen, in: Plate, M.; Groth, T.; Ackermann, V. & Schlippe, A. von (Eds.): Große deutsche Familienunternehmen, Göttingen: Vandenhoeck & Ruprecht, 522–560.
Schlippe, A. von; Groth, T. & Rüsen, T. (2012): Paradoxien der Nachfolge in Familienunternehmen, in: *Konfliktdynamik*, 1 (4), 288–299. https://doi.org/10.5771/2193-0147-2012-4
Schlippe, A. von; Lösche, G. & Hawellek, C. (2001) [Eds.]: Frühkindliche Lebenswelten und Erziehungsberatung: Die Chancen des Anfangs, Münster: Votum.
Schlippe, A. von; Nischak, A. & El Hachimi, M. (2008) [Eds.]: Familienunternehmen verstehen. Gründer, Gesellschafter und Generationen, Göttingen: Vandenhoeck & Ruprecht.
Schlippe, A. von; Rüsen, T. & Groth, T. (2009) [Eds.]: Beiträge zur Theorie des Familienunternehmens, Bd. 1, Lohmar u. a.: Josef Eul Verlag.
Schmidt, M. & Schneewind, K. A. (1978): Elterliche Erziehungseinstellungen und -ziele als Bedingungen des Belohnungsaufschubs, in: Schneewind, K. A. & Lukesch, H. (Eds.): Familiäre Sozialisation: Probleme, Ergebnisse, Perspektiven, Stuttgart: Klett-Cotta, 164–175.
Schmitt-Rodermund, E. & Schröder, E. (2009): Innerfamiliäre Nachfolge in Unternehmen. Studie zur Förderung und Entwicklung des Nachwuchses in Familienunternehmen, Jena: Friedrich-Schiller-Universität Jena.
Schmitt-Rodermund, E. & Silbereisen, R. K. (1999): Erfolg von Unternehmern: Die Rolle von Persönlichkeit und familiärer Sozialisation, in: Moser, K.; Batinic, B. & Zempel, J. (Eds.): Unternehmerisch erfolgreiches Handeln, Göttingen: Verlag für Angewandte Psychologie, 115–143.
Schneewind, K. A. (2008): Sozialisation in der Familie, in: Hurrelmann, K.; Grundmann, M. & Walper, S. (Eds.): Handbuch Sozialisationsforschung, 7. vollst. überarb. Aufl., Weinheim und Basel: Beltz Verlag, 256–273.
Schneewind, K. A. (2001): Kleine Kinder in Deutschland: Was sie und ihre Eltern brauchen, in: Schlippe, A. von; Lösche, G. & Hawellek, C. (Eds.): Frühkindliche Lebenswelten und Erziehungsberatung: Die Chancen des Anfangs, Münster: Votum, 124–150.
Schneewind, K. A. (1982): Persönlichkeits-Theorien I. 1. Alltagspsychologie und mechanische Ansätze, Darmstadt: Wissenschaftliche Buchgesellschaft.

Schneewind, K. A. & Lukesch, H. (1978) [Eds.]: Familiäre Sozialisation: Probleme, Ergebnisse, Perspektiven, Stuttgart: Klett-Cotta.
Schneewind, K. A.; Beckmann, M. & Engfer, A. (1983): Eltern und Kinder. Umwelteinflüsse auf das familiäre Verhalten, Stuttgart: Verlag W. Kohlhammer.
Schneider, U. (1998): Das Nachfolgeproblem als Familiendrama. Zwei nicht gegebene Interviews, in: Kappler, E. & Laske, S. (Eds.): Blickwechsel. Zur Dramatik und Dramaturgie von Nachfolgeprozessen im Familienbetrieb, Freiburg im Breisgau: Rombach, 51–60.
Schreyögg, G. & Werder, A. von (2004) [Eds.]: Handwörterbuch Unternehmensführung und Organisation, 4. Aufl., Stuttgart: Schäffer-Poechel Verlag.
Schröder, E.; Schmitt-Rodermund, E. & Arnaud, N. (2011): Career choice intentions of adolescents with a family business background, in: *Family Business Review*, 24 (4), 305–321. https://doi.org/10.1177/0894486511416977
Schröder, E.; Schmitt-Rodermund, E. & Arnaud, N. (2010): Sensibilisierung für die unternehmerische Selbstständigkeit im Jugendalter, in: Berufsverband Deutscher Psychologinnen und Psychologen e. V. (Ed.): Psychologische Expertise für erfolgreiches Unternehmertum in Deutschland, Berlin: Deutscher Psychologen Verlag GmbH, 95–99.
Schulte, R. & Wille, C. (2006): Unternehmensnachfolgeprozesse in Klein- und Mikrounternehmen – Ergebnisse einer empirischen Untersuchung, in: Brost, H.; Faust, M. & Thedens, C. (Eds.): Unternehmensnachfolge im Mittelstand, 2. Aufl., München: Bankakademie Verlag GmbH, 393–416.
Schulze-Böing, M. & Unverferth, H.-J. (1986): Rationalität in komplexen Sozialsystemen. Zur Entwicklung des Rationalitätsbegriffs in der Systemtheorie Niklas Luhmann, in: Unverferth, H.-J. (Ed.): System und Selbstproduktion. Zur Erschließung eines neuen Paradigmas in den Sozialwissenschaften, Reihe 22, Bd./Vol. 120, Frankfurt a. M. u. a.: Perterlang, 14–90.
Schuman, A.; Stutz, S. & Ward, J. L. (2010): Family Business as Paradox, Basingstoke u. a.: Palgrave Macmillan.
Schütz, A. & Luckmann, T. (1994a): Strukturen der Lebenswelt, Bd. 1, 5. Aufl., Frankfurt a. M.: Suhrkamp.
Schütz, A. & Luckmann, T. (1994b): Strukturen der Lebenswelt, Bd. 2, 3. Aufl., Frankfurt a. M.: Suhrkamp.
Schweickart, N. (2002) [Ed.]: Unternehmertum am Beginn des 21. Jahrhundert, München und Zürich: Piper.
Segalen, M. (1990): Die Familie: Geschichte, Soziologie, Anthropologie, Frankfurt a. M. u. a.: Campus Verlag.
Seidl, D. (2006): The Basic Concepts of Luhmann's Theory of Social Systems, in: Seidl, D. & Becker, K. H. (Eds.): Niklas Luhmann and Organization Studies, Frederiksberg: Liber & Copenhagen Business School Press, 21–53.
Seidl, D. & Becker, K. H. (2006a) [Eds.]: Niklas Luhmann and Organization Studies, Frederiksberg: Liber & Copenhagen Business School Press.
Seidl, D. & Becker, K. H. (2006b): Introduction: Luhmann's Organization Theory, in: Seidl, D. & Becker, K. H. (Eds.): Niklas Luhmann and Organization Studies, Frederiksberg: Liber & Copenhagen Business School Press, 8–18.
Sharma, P.; Chrisman, J. J. & Chua, J. H. (2003): Succession Planning as Planned Behavior: Some Empirical Results, in: *Family Business Review*, 16 (1), 1–16. https://doi.org/10.1111/j.1741-6248.2003.00001.x

Sharma, P.; Chua, J. H. & Chrisman, J. J. (2000): Perceptions About the Extent of Succession Planning in Canadian Family Firms, in: *Canadian Journal of Administrative Science*, 17 (3), 233–244. https://doi.org/10.1111/j.1936-4490.2000.tb00223.x

Siefer, T. (1996): „Du kommst später einmal in die Firma!" Psychosoziale Dynamiken von Familienunternehmen, Heidelberg: Carl Auer Verlag.

Simon, F. B. (2012): Einführung in die Theorie des Familienunternehmens, Heidelberg: Carl-Auer Verlag.

Simon, F. B. (2011): Die Familie des Familienunternehmers: Ein System zwischen Gefühl und Geschäft, 3. Aufl., Heidelberg: Carl-Auer Verlag.

Simon, F. B. (2009): Organisationen und Familien als soziale Systeme unterschiedlichen Typs, in: Schlippe, A. von; Rüsen, T. & Groth, T. (Eds.): Beiträge zur Theorie des Familienunternehmens, Bd. 1, Lohmar u. a.: Josef Eul Verlag, 17–45.

Simon, F. B. (2008a): Familienunternehmen als Risikofaktor, in: Schlippe, A. von; Nischak, A. & El Hachimi, M. (Eds.): Familienunternehmen verstehen. Gründer, Gesellschafter und Generationen, Göttingen: Vandenhoeck & Ruprecht, 55–64.

Simon, F. B. (2008b): Von Generation zu Generation – Unterschiedliche Entwicklungsschritte von Mehrgenerationen-Familien-Unternehmen, in: Kollmer-von Oheimb-Loup, G. & Wischermann, C. (Eds.): Unternehmensnachfolge in Geschichte und Gegenwart, Ostfildern: Jan Thorbecke Verlag, 13–38.

Simon, F. B. (2007a): Einführung in die systemische Organisationstheorie, 3. Aufl., Heidelberg: Carl-Auer-Systeme Verlag.

Simon, F. B. (2007b): Einführung in die Systemtheorie und Konstruktivismus, 2. Aufl., Heidelberg: Carl-Auer-Systeme Verlag.

Simon, F. B. (2005) [Ed.]: Die Familie des Familienunternehmers: Ein System zwischen Gefühl und Geschäft, 2. Aufl., Heidelberg: Carl-Auer Verlag.

Simon, F. B. (2004): Gemeinsam sind wir blöd!? Die Intelligenz von Unternehmen, Managern und Märkten, Heidelberg: Carl-Auer-Systeme Verlag.

Simon, F. B. (2003): Gerechtigkeit, Richtigkeit und Rechtmäßigkeit. Entscheidungsfindung in Familienunternehmen, in: Lange, K. W. & Schiereck, D. (Eds.): Nachfolgefragen bei Familienunternehmen: Unternehmenskauf und Private Equity als Alternative zur Börse, Heidelberg: Finanz Colloquium, 35–48.

Simon, F. B. (2000): Grenzfunktionen der Familie, in: *System Familie*, 13, 140–148.

Simon, F. B. (1988) [Ed.]: Lebende Systeme: Wirklichkeitskonstruktion in der Systemischen Therapie, Berlin u. a.: Springer.

Simon, F. B. & Stierlin, H. (1994): Die Sprache der Familientherapie: Ein Vokabular; Überblick, Kritik und Integration systemtherapeutischer Begriffe, Konzepte und Methoden, 3. Aufl., Stuttgart: Klett-Cotta.

Simon, F. B.; Wimmer, R. & Groth, T. (2012): Mehr-Generationen-Familienunternehmen. Erfolgsgeheimnisse von Oetker, Merck, Haniel u. a., 2. unveränd. Aufl., Heidelberg: Carl-Auer Verlag.

Simon, F. B.; Wimmer, R. & Groth, T. (2005): Mehr-Generationen-Familienunternehmen. Erfolgsgeheimnisse von Oetker, Merck, Haniel u. a., Heidelberg: Carl-Auer Verlag.

Soeffner, H. G. (2010) [Ed.]: Unsichere Zeiten: Herausforderungen gesellschaftlicher Transformationen (Verhandlungen des 34. Kongresses der Deutschen Gesellschaft für Soziologie in Jena 2008), Wiesbaden: VS Verlag für Sozialwissenschaften.

Sohni, H. (2011): Geschwisterdynamik, Gießen: Psychosozial-Verlag.

Söllner, R. (2011): Unternehmen und Arbeitsstätten. Ausgewählte Ergebnisse für kleine und mittlere Unternehmen in Deutschland 2009, in: Statistisches Bundesamt (Ed.): Wirtschaft und Statistik, Wiesbaden: Statistisches Bundesamt, 1086–1096.

Stamm, I. (2013): Unternehmerfamilien. Über den Einfluss des Unternehmens auf Lebenslauf, Generationenbeziehungen und soziale Identität, Opladen u. a.: Verlag Barbara Budrich.

Stamm, I.; Schmiade, N. & Kohli, M. (2010): Familienunternehmer als Pioniere biografischer Selbstbestimmung?, in: Soeffner, H. G. (Ed.): Unsichere Zeiten: Herausforderungen gesellschaftlicher Transformationen (Verhandlungen des 34. Kongresses der Deutschen Gesellschaft für Soziologie in Jena 2008), Wiesbaden: VS Verlag für Sozialwissenschaften, 1–12.

Statistisches Bundesamt (2011) [Ed.]: Wirtschaft und Statistik, Wiesbaden: Statistisches Bundesamt.

Steiner, E. (2001): Die Rolle von familiärer Sozialisation für den Erfolg von Selbständigen, Working Paper 2/2001.

Stierlin, H. (1987): Ko-Evolution und Ko-Individuation, in: Stierlin, H.; Simon, F. B. & Schmidt, G. (Eds.): Familiäre Wirklichkeiten. Der Heidelberger Kongreß, Stuttgart: Klett-Cotta, 126–138.

Stierlin, H.; Simon, F. B. & Schmidt, G. (1987) [Eds.]: Familiäre Wirklichkeiten. Der Heidelberger Kongreß, Stuttgart: Klett-Cotta.

Stiftung Familienunternehmen (2011a): Deutschlands nächste Unternehmergeneration II: Eine empirische Untersuchung der Werthaltungen, Einstellungen und Pläne, München.

Stiftung Familienunternehmen (2011b): Die volkswirtschaftliche Bedeutung der Familienunternehmen, München.

Strauss, A. (1974): Spiegel und Masken. Die Suche nach der Identität, Frankfurt a. M.: Suhrkamp.

Stryker, S. (1977): Die Theorie des Symbolischen Interaktionismus, in: Auwärter, M.; Kirsch, E. & Schröter, K. (Eds.): Seminar: Kommunikation, Interaktion, Identität, 2. Aufl.; Frankfurt a. M.: Suhrkamp, 257–274.

Stryker, S. (1970): Die Theorie des symbolischen Interaktionismus: Eine Darstellung und einige Vorschläge für die vergleichende Familienforschung, in: Lüschen, G. & Lupri, E. (Eds.): Soziologie der Familie, Opladen: Westdeutscher Verlag, 49–67.

Suchy, D.; Nosé, L.; Frank, H.; Lueger, M. & Korunka, C. (2012): Konflikte in Familienunternehmen - Zum Stand der Forschung, in: Frank, H.; Korunka, C. & Lueger, M. (Eds.): Konfliktbewältigung in Familienunternehmen. Eine Studie des Forschungsinstituts für Familienunternehmen an der WU, Wien: facultas.wuv, 23–41.

Suess, G. J. (2001): Eltern-Kind-Bindung und kommunikative Kompetenzen kleiner Kinder – die Bindungstheorie als Grundlage für ein integratives Interventionskonzept, in: Schlippe, A. von; Lösche, G. & Hawellek, C. (Eds.): Frühkindliche Lebenswelten und Erziehungsberatung: Die Chancen des Anfangs, Münster: Votum, 39–66.

Sulloway, F. J. (1999): Der Rebell der Familie: Geschwisterrivalität, kreatives Denken und Geschichte, Berlin: Siedler.

Sundaramurthy, C. & Kreiner, G. E. (2008): Governing by Managing Identity Boundaries: The Case of Family Businesses, in: *Entrepreneurship Theory and Practice*, 32 (3), 415–436. https://doi.org/10.1111/j.1540-6520.2008.00234.x

Süss-Reyes, J. (2015a): Family Governance: Sicherung der Zukunftsfähigkeit von Familienunternehmen, in: Lueger, M. & Frank, H. (Eds.): Zukunftssicherung für Familienunternehmen. Good Practice Fallanalysen zur Family Governance. Eine Studie des Forschungsinstituts für Familienunternehmen an der WU, Wien: Facultas, 13–39.

Süss-Reyes, J. (2015b): Implementierung einer komplexen Family Governance Lösung: Kontext, Prozess und Wirkung, in: Lueger, M. & Frank, H. (Eds.): Zukunftssicherung für Familienunternehmen. Good Practice Fallanalysen zur Family Governance. Eine Studie des Forschungsinstituts für Familienunternehmen an der WU, Wien: Facultas, 141–174.

Süss, J. & Weismeier-Sammer, D. (2013): Familiness: Der Einfluss der Familie auf das Unternehmen. Wie die Familie Strukturen, Entscheidungen und die Unternehmensidentität beeinflussen kann, in: *Austrian Management Review*, 3, 60–66.

Sutter, T. (1997) [Ed.]: Beobachtung verstehen, Verstehen beobachten: Perspektiven einer konstruktivistischen Hermeneutig, Opladen: Westdeutscher Verlag.

Tagiuri, R. & Davis, J. A. (1996): Bivalent attributes of the family firm, in: *Family Business Review*, 9 (2), 199–208. https://doi.org/10.1111/j.1741-6248.1996.00199.x

Tazi-Preve, I. M. (2004): Vaterschaft im Wandel? Eine Bestandsaufnahme von Verhalten und Einstellung von Vätern, in: Cizek, B. (Ed.): Familienforschung in Österreich: Markierungen – Ergebnisse – Perspektiven, in: *Österreichisches Institut für Familienforschung*, 12, 109–129.

Tillmann, K. J. (2000): Sozialisationstheorien. Eine Einführung in den Zusammenhang von Gesellschaft, Institution und Subjektwerdung, 10. erw. u. überarb. Aufl., Hamburg: Rowohlt.

Toman, W. (1996): Familienkonstellationen: Ihr Einfluß auf den Menschen, 6. durchges. Aufl., München: Verlag C. H. Beck.

Tugendhat, E. (1979): Selbstbewußtsein und Selbstbestimmung: Sprachanalytische Interpretation, Frankfurt a. M.: Suhrkamp.

Turner, R. H. (1977): Rollenübernahme: Prozeß versus Konformität, in: Auwärter, M.; Kirsch, E. & Schröter, K. (Eds.): Seminar: Kommunikation, Interaktion, Identität, 2. Aufl., Frankfurt a. M.: Suhrkamp, 115–139.

Ulich, D. (1991) [Ed.]: Neues Handbuch der Sozialisationsforschung, 4. völl. neuüberarb. Aufl., Weinheim: Beltz Verlag, 137–152.

Ulrich, H. (1970): Die Unternehmung als produktives soziales System: Grundlagen der allgemeinen Unternehmungslehre, 2. überarb. Aufl., Bern und Stuttgart: Verlag Paul Haupt.

Unverferth, H.-J. (1986) [Ed.]: System und Selbstproduktion. Zur Erschließung eines neuen Paradigmas in den Sozialwissenschaften, Reihe 22, Bd./Vol. 120, Frankfurt a. M. u. a.: Perterlang.

Uphoff, N. (2000): Understanding social capital: learning from the analysis and experience of participation, in: Dasgupta, P. & Serageldin, I. (Eds.): Social Capital: A Multifaceted Perspective, Washington D. C.: The World Bank, 215–249.

Urnik, S. (2011) [Ed.]: Unternehmensnachfolge: Betriebswirtschaftliche, rechtliche und psychologische Erfolgsfaktoren, Wien: Linde.

Vaskovics, L. A. & Lipinski, H. (1996) [Eds.]: Familiale Lebenswelten und Bildungsarbeit. Interdisziplinäre Bestandsaufnahme 1, Opladen: Leske + Budrich.

Venter, W. P. & Kruger, S. (2004): The contribution of 'familiness' to the performance of family businesses, in: *Southern African Business Review*, 8 (3), 1–13.

Wallau, F. (2010): Die aktuelle Lage von Unternehmerinnen und Unternehmern in Deutschland, in: Berufsverband Deutscher Psychologinnen und Psychologen e. V. (Ed.): Psychologische Expertise für erfolgreiches Unternehmertum in Deutschland, Berlin: Deutscher Psychologen Verlag GmbH, 34–41.

Wandl, N. & Habenicht, U. (2011): Unternehmensübergabe nachhaltig gestalten. Den Generationenwechsel zeitgerecht einleiten und durchführen, Wiesbaden: Gabler.

Ward, J. L. (2003): The ultimate vision for continuity?, in: *Family in Business*, 78–79.

Weber, G. (2005): Familien- und Organisationsaufstellung als eine neue Beratungsmethode für Familienunternehmen – ein Fallbeispiel, in: Simon, F. B. (Ed.): Die Familie des Familienunternehmers: Ein System zwischen Gefühl und Geschäft, 2. Aufl., Heidelberg: Carl-Auer Verlag, 267–313.

Webster, J. & Watson, R. T. (2002): Analyzing the past to prepare for the future: writing a literature review, in: *MIS Quarterly*, 26 (2), xiii–xxiii. http://www.jstor.org/stable/4132319

Weick, K. E. (1995): Der Prozeß des Organisierens. Übersetzt von Gerhard Hauck, Frankfurt a. M.: Suhrkamp.

Weigelt, K. (1985) [Ed.]: Studien zur politischen Bildung: Werte, Leitbilder, Tugenden. Zur Erneuerung politischer Kultur, Bd. 8, Mainz: v. Hase und Koehler.

Weismeier-Sammer, D. (2014): The role of familiness for family business innovativeness, in: *International Journal of Entrepreneurial Venturing*, 6 (2), 101–117. https://doi.org/10.1504/IJEV.2014.062747

Weismeier-Sammer, D.; Frank, H.; Nosé, L. & Suchy, D. (2012): Ausgestaltung der Familiness in Familienunternehmen: Distanz als Mittel zur strukturellen Kopplung von Familie und Unternehmen, in: Lueger, M. & Frank, H. (Eds.): Wie erfolgreich Familienunternehmen handeln – Good Practice Fallanalysen. Eine Studie des Forschungsinstituts für Familienunternehmen an der WU, Wien: facultas.wuv, 180–209.

Weissman, A. & Schultheiss, B. (2006): Familienunternehmen – Auslaufmodelle oder Hoffnungsträger?, in: Krüger, W.; Klippstein, G.; Merk, R. & Wittberg, V. (Eds.): Praxishandbuch des Mittelstands: Leitfaden für das Management mittelständischer Unternehmen, Wiesbaden: Gabler, 71–87.

Weitzman, L. J.; Eifler, D.; Hokada, E. & Ross, C. (1972): Sex-Role, Socialization in Picture Books for Preschool Children, in: *The American Journal of Sociology*, 77 (6), 1125–1150. https://doi.org/10.1086/225261

Welter-Enderlin, R. (2005): Was steht auf Ihrer Bürotür, Frau Faust? Frauen in Geschäftsfamilien, in: Simon, F. B. (Ed.): Die Familie des Familienunternehmers: Ein System zwischen Gefühl und Geschäft, 2. Aufl., Heidelberg: Carl-Auer Verlag, 146–165.

Willke, H. (1996): Systemtheorie I: Grundlagen, 5. überarb. Aufl., Stuttgart: Lucius & Lucius.

Wilson, B. & Edington, G. (1987): First Child, Second Child. Your Birth Order Profile, New York: Zebra Books.

Wimberger, H. (2006): Unternehmensnachfolge aus der Sicht des Übergebers – WimTec 2006 ein zukunftsorientiertes Unternehmen mit Dynamik, in: Hasenzagl, R. & Stocker, F. (Eds.): Unternehmensnachfolge: Herausforderungen, Chancen und Erfolgsfaktoren. Wiener Neustädter Managementgespräche, Wien und Graz: Neuer Wissenschaftlicher Verlag, 139–146.

Wimmer, R. (2012): Die neue Systemtheorie und ihre Implikationen für das Verständnis von Organisationen, Führung und Management, in: Rüegg-Stürm, J. & Bieger, T. (Eds.): Unternehmerisches Management – Herausforderungen und Perspektiven: Festschrift für Prof. Dr. Peter Gomez, Bern: Haupt Verlag AG, 7–68.

Wimmer, R. (2009a): Wachstum in Familienunternehmen - Herausforderung und Bewältigungsstrategien, in: Wirtschaftsstandort Nordrhein-Westfalen 2008/2009: Europäischer Wirtschafts Verlag, 106–113.

Wimmer, R. (2009b): Familienunternehmen, in: Schlippe, A. von; Rüsen, T. & Groth, T. (Eds.): Beiträge zur Theorie des Familienunternehmens, Bd. 1, Lohmar u. a.: Josef Eul Verlag, 1–16.

Wimmer, R. (2008a): Familienunternehmen haben Zukunft, in: *Melitta Geschäftsbericht 2007*, 8-15.

Wimmer, R. (2008b): Das Selbst- und Fremdbild von Familienunternehmen – die besondere Produktivität dieser Differenz, in: Schlippe, A. von; Nischak, A. & El Hachimi, M. (Eds.): Familienunternehmen verstehen. Gründer, Gesellschafter und Generationen, Göttingen: Vandenhoeck & Ruprecht, 108–114.

Wimmer, R. (2007): Erfolgsstrategien in Familie und Unternehmen, in: Frasl, E. & Rieger, H. (Eds.): Family-Business-Handbuch. Zukunftssicherung von Familienunternehmen über Generationen, Wien: Linde Verlag, 30–46.

Wimmer, R. (2004): Familienunternehmen, in: Schreyögg, G. & Werder, A. von (Eds.): Handwörterbuch Unternehmensführung und Organisation, 4. Aufl., Stuttgart: Schäffer-Poechel Verlag, 267–275.

Wimmer, R. (1997): Allgemeine Thesen zu Familienunternehmen, in: Erfolgsfaktor Familienunternehmen, Schriftenreihe der Investkredit AG, Wien, 145–150.

Wimmer, R.; Domayer, E.; Oswald, M. & Vater, G. (2005): Familienunternehmen – Auslaufmodell oder Erfolgstyp, 2. Aufl., Wiesbaden: Gabler.

Wimmer, R. & Gebauer, A. (2004): Die Nachfolge in Familienunternehmen, in: *Zeitschrift Führung und Organisation*, 73 (5), 244–252.

Wimmer, R.; Simon, F. B. & Groth, T. (2004): Erfolgsmuster von Mehrgenerationen-Familienunternehmen, in: *Wittener Diskussionspapiere*, Sonderheft 2.

Winch, R. F. (1970): Theoretische Ansätze in der Untersuchung der Familie, in: Lüschen, G. & Lupri, E. (Eds.): Soziologie der Familie, Opladen: Westdeutscher Verlag, 20–31.

Wingen, M. (1985): Elternschaft, in: Weigelt, K. (Ed.): Studien zur politischen Bildung: Werte, Leitbilder, Tugenden. Zur Erneuerung politischer Kultur, Bd. 8, Mainz: v. Hase und Koehler, 391–416.

Wiswede, G. (1977): Rollentheorie, Stuttgart u. a.: Verlag W. Kohhammer.

Witte, E. H. (2005): Sozialisationstheorien, in: *Hamburger Forschungsberichte zur Sozialisationspsychologie*, Bandnummer 56. https://nbn-resolving.org/urn:nbn:de:0168-ssoar-374059

Wottawa, H. (2006): Psychologische Aspekte bei der Entscheidung für eine Unternehmensnachfolge, in: Brost, H.; Faust, M. & Thedens, C. (Eds.): Unternehmensnachfolge im Mittelstand, 2. Aufl., München: Bankakademie Verlag GmbH, 337–359.

Wurzbacher, G. (1977a) [Ed.]: Die Familie als Sozialisationsfaktor, 2. neu bearb. u. erw. Aufl., Stuttgart: Ferdinand Enke Verlag.

Wurzbacher, G. (1977b): Die Familie unter dem Aspekt eines lebenslangen Sozialisationsprozesses des Menschen. Hypothesen – Fragestellungen – Folgerungen, in: Wurzbacher, G. (Ed.): Die Familie als Sozialisationsfaktor, 2. neu bearb. u. erw. Aufl., Stuttgart: Ferdinand Enke Verlag, 1–32.

Wurzbacher, G. (1963a) [Ed.]: Der Mensch als soziales und personales Wesen. Beiträge zu Begriff und Theorie der Sozialisation aus der Sicht von Soziologie, Psychologie Arbeitswissenschaft, Medizin, Pädagogik, Sozialarbeit, Kriminologie, Politologie, Stuttgart: Ferdinand Enke Verlag.

Wurzbacher, G. (1963b): Sozialisation – Enkulturation – Personalisation, in: Wurzbacher, G. (Ed.): Der Mensch als soziales und personales Wesen. Beiträge zu Begriff und Theorie der Sozialisation aus der Sicht von Soziologie, Psychologie Arbeitswissenschaft, Medizin, Pädagogik, Sozialarbeit, Kriminologie, Politologie, Stuttgart: Ferdinand Enke Verlag, 1–34.

Youniss, J. (1980): Sozialisation und soziales Wissen, in: Eckensberger, L. H. & Silbereisen, R. K. (Eds.): Entwicklung sozialer Kognition: Modelle, Theorien, Methoden, Anwendungen, Stuttgart: Klett-Cotta, 49–63.

Zellweger, T. M.; Eddleston, K. A. & Kellermanns, F. W. (2010): Exploring the concept familiness: Introducing family firm identity, in: *Journal of Family Business Strategy*, 1 (1), 54–63. https://doi.org/10.1016/j.jfbs.2009.12.003

Zimmermann, P. (2006): Grundwissen Sozialisation: Einführung zur Sozialisation im Kindes- und Jugendalter, 3. überarb. u. erw. Aufl., Wiesbaden: VS Verlag für Sozialwissenschaften.

Zimmermann, P. (2000): Grundwissen Sozialisation: Einführung zur Sozialisation im Kindes- und Jugendalter, Opladen: Leske + Budrich.

Zwack, M. (2011): Die Macht der Geschichten: Erzählungen als Form der Wertevermittlung in Familienunternehmen, Heidelberg: Carl-Auer Verlag.